Economic Studies:
Contributions to the Critique
of Economic Theory

Economic Studies: Contributions to the Critique of Economic Theory

David P. Levine
Department of Economics, Yale University

Routledge & Kegan Paul
London, Henley and Boston

First published in 1977
by Routledge & Kegan Paul Ltd
39 Store Street,
London WC1E 7DD,
Broadway House,
Newtown Road,
Henley-on-Thames,
Oxon RG9 1EN and
9 Park Street,
Boston, Mass. 02108, USA
Set in Monotype Times New Roman
and printed and bound in Great Britain by
Morrison & Gibb Ltd, London and Edinburgh
Copyright David P. Levine 1977

Library of Congress Cataloging in Publication Data

Levine, David P   1948–

  Economic studies.
  Includes bibliographical references and index.
  1. Economics 2. Economics--History. I. Title.
HB71.L54   330.1   77–2710

ISBN 0–7100–8573–7

For Harry and Julie Levine

Contents

Preface

In economics there is nothing more elementary than the most complex of mathematical formulae, nor anything more complex than the most elementary of concepts. While the former is wholly without content, the latter contains, latent within it, the system of economic relations in its entirety. Only in an investigation of these simple relations – value, exchange, capital – are the real foundations of economic analysis to be found, and only the investigation of these simple relations, taken in their full simplicity, can make possible the distinguishing of economic science from among the differing conceptions of economic life.

The object of the present volume is the criticism of the manner in which the elementary relations of economic life are grasped in economic theory. In this sense, it is not incorrect to characterize the following as studies in elementary economics. Our premise is that the confusion and misdirection which baffles progress in all aspects of economic theory can be overcome only via the reconsideration of the whole of the conception of economic life upon which ongoing research is based, however consciously or unconsciously. To move beyond the *cul-de-sac* of contemporary economic analysis requires a return to its true starting point, and this in two interrelated senses. It is necessary to return to the historical starting point of economic science – classical political economy – and simultaneously to return to its conceptual starting point – the theory of value. Only from a true starting point is a real beginning possible.

The conception of economic life first presented in classical political economy and first raised to a systematic formulation by Marx has not since the publication of the first volume of *Capital* been the subject of a systematic and comprehensive theoretical treatise. Over the past hundred years this conception of economic relations has been subjected to vigorous criticism, to sympathetic commentary, and to further development in certain particulars. Yet, nowhere do we find a complete statement that could take the work of Smith, Ricardo, and Marx as the starting point for a comprehensive exposition of the science. Still, it is evident that the three volumes of Marx's most definitive work cannot be considered to constitute a finished and therefore conclusive argument. This holds especially for the unfinished last two volumes. However, even in the case of the first volume, the fact that the work as a whole remained incomplete left its mark on the treatment of value, capital, and production.

The present volume represents the first of a two-part work the second of which consists of a positive exposition of economic science based on the critique and further development of the work of Smith, Ricardo, and Marx. This work is projected to encompass two volumes under the title *Economic Theory*. In volume I capital in general and its circular movement are considered. Capital as self-moving value posits a process of its own production in the form of a labor process the product of which is the commodity and especially its value. In this volume we investigate the concepts of value and capital and the mode of their production. As will be already evident from the present volume, the secret of the whole of economic theory since Adam Smith has found itself locked away in the notion of a 'labor theory of value.' It is this notion which excludes a science of economic relations as much for its advocates as for those who attempt a coherent account for economic life in its absence. The concept of labor and its relation to value and to capital will necessarily be the central preoccupation of the discussion of volume I. From this discussion it will be seen that the connection of labor to value is indeed the necessary logical basis for the development of a systematic conception of economic life. In the final volume the system of capitalist production as a whole is considered. The process by which the latter sustains itself is the process of its self-expansion. It is within this total process that the system of particular producers, of prices, and of profit rates is determined, and it is this process the intrinsic laws of which account for the development of capital into a world system of production for a world market.

I first came to be occupied with the problems dealt with in this book while studying at the University of Wisconsin. The problems as posed, and the formulations as presented here, developed out of discussion begun there with Donald Harris, who as co-author of part II, chapter 6 shares equal responsibility for that analysis, and Nina Shapiro, who has made a special contribution to the development of the argument in chapter 8. I would like to thank both for their critical reading of early drafts of particular chapters and for continuous encouragement throughout the process of preparation of the manuscript.

The conception of economic theory which underlies the analysis presented here is not original. And yet, given the state of contemporary economics and social science more generally, its rediscovery has become a task which rivals its original formulation. Whatever progress I have made in this task has benefited from discussion with Lynn Levine. She is also, as co-author of chapter 9, equally responsible for the formulation of that argument.

The failure of current social theory results ultimately from the inability of the present-day intellect to exert itself in the pursuit of a truth whose existence it has repudiated and whose content argues against its most deeply felt prejudices. If these studies serve no other end it is sufficient that they point the way back to the real concerns of social theory. Beyond this it is only necessary that this task be pursued in a strictly scientific spirit without regard to any considerations not imposed by the requirements of the project itself:

Weltanschauungen can engage in controversy; only science can decide, and its decision bears the stamp of eternity. (*Edmund Husserl*)

Acknowledgments

I would like to thank the editors of *Economy and Society* for permission to reprint in chapters 3 and 9 material originally published in volume 3 (no. 3, August 1974) and volume 4 (no. 2, May 1975) of that journal and the editors of the *Australian Economic Papers* for permission to reprint in chapter 7 material originally published in volume 15 (December 1976) of that journal.

Part 1
Origins of Economic Science

Chapter 1
The science of wealth

I Wealth

1

Since the origins of economics as a science its definition has always been with reference to the manner of provision for the wants of the members of society. It is the circle of needs which defines concretely the livelihood of the family as of the state which provides for economic analysis its starting point both historically, as regards the development of the theory, and conceptually, as regards the theory itself. Indeed, it is the concept of need which, once subject to analysis, provides a first real insight into the character of economics and into the object of economic science. Yet, the notion of need taken with reference to the historical development of the science differs sharply from the concept of need which provides a fundamental component of the theory of economic life which emerges as the culmination of that historical development. The development of economic theory is no less the development of the concept of need which appears in its definition from the outset. Those wants of society and of its members which appear with the earliest writings in political economy exhibit an inadequacy of conception which requires and, indeed, gives rise to a definite development. It is only out of this development that political economy is able to establish itself as a science.

The conception of wants which provides the starting point for this development originates in the life of the family and is, then, extended to the society as a whole where the latter has the form of an aggregate of particular households and of the needs which they represent. In this sense, the definition of economic life proceeds first from the activity by which the family seeks to renew itself through the fulfillment of its needs. None the less, while the conception of need begins here, economic theory makes no further reference to the needs of the household, always preferring to take them as given. Thus, the needs of the household as such are posited outside of the theory so that the latter is itself unconcerned with needs so defined. The theory, far from occupying itself with the wants of the family, concerns itself from the outset with the type of need characteristic not of nature but of society, indeed with the kind of need which defines the specifically social life of the species.

The needs of the household which are bracketed in this way are determined for the family as an element of nature. The opposition out of which classical thinking seeks to derive a concept of society is that which opposes 'subsistence'

3

needs which are necessary to the individual so far as he engages in the renewal of himself and his family within nature, to those needs which are not determined by the necessities connected to the individual's biological existence. The fulfillment of needs which are given by the natural subsistence of the species does not, and cannot, form the subject-matter of the theory. To the extent that 'economics' has as its connotation the life process of the family, the manner in which it sustains itself simply as a limited unit, it does not provide the object for a systematic investigation by a distinct science.

The true social character of need is never fully grasped in classical thought since the social determination of need is never really separated from its determination in nature. It is the task of classical political economy to establish the specificity of economic theory as differentiated from and opposed to natural science. To accomplish this task classical thought proceeds by isolating the distinguishing feature of those needs characteristic of economic life. The needs distinguished in this way are substantially different from the needs of the family as defined by its subsistence within nature. But the reference point for this distinction is always nature so that the opposition also unites the two conceptions, distorting each and undermining the development of a real concept of society. There can only be a distinct concept of society where the type of need specific to the renewal of social life is established in its own right, as distinct from nature-given wants, by merit of its real determination not in opposition to nature but on the part of the life process of society. Classical political economy marks out this distinction but fails to establish it in a positive way, always falling back upon the natural system as the defining term for the conception of society.

To the extent that needs are determined by nature they must be presupposed by economic theory. Yet, since economics has as its object the investigation of needs and the means to their fulfillment this presupposition is tantamount to taking the whole of the theory as its own presupposition. It follows that the system of needs, were it defined exclusively in this way, would possess no social determination and could not provide the object for a specifically economic science. And, indeed, there exists no specifically social theory of the life process of the family as regards the provision of its needs where those needs are substantively and exclusively the needs of the family taken as determined within the species. For classical political economy there is an economic life within the family and there is as well an economic life of the state, but the theory concerns itself only with the latter. There is, then, a science of 'political economy' but no 'economic science.'

With the situation of wants and their provision within the household, economic life is considered as nothing more than an aspect of the life of the family. This reduction has also an historical origin in that prior to the emergence of modern bourgeois society economic activity remains to a greater or lesser degree within the family. Classical political economy removes economic life from the sphere of the family and in so doing makes possible for the first time a conception of the system of economic relations. This removal of economic activity from the family takes the form of its transfer from the household to the state. Conceptually, the equation of economic life with the family on one side and the state on the other precludes the development of a fully scientific conception of the system of economic relations. The economy is not made sufficiently distinct to allow for its conception to emerge. The project of classical political economy is to give birth to a new science precisely by marking out economic life and establishing its specificity. This requires a conception of the distinctiveness of economic interaction *vis-à-vis* the family and the state. For this to be achieved it is necessary to make clear the specificity of the system of economic relations, therefore to establish the peculiarly economic character of needs.

Need takes on its economic character first when it is displaced from the family to the state. This effectively emancipates need from the natural determination which results inevitably from the subordination of economic life to the family. Wherever the economy remains a subordinate part of the life of the family the system of needs and the production of the means to their fulfillment must continue to exist, to a greater or lesser degree, outside of social life. Only with the constitution of the economic system as a distinct sphere does it become possible to conceive of production as within society, therefore fully as an economic activity. While the identification of need with the activity of the household involves needs in a natural determination, the identification of need with the state makes of the former a political rather than economic reality, once again, it would seem, excluding the development of a conception of the economy as a distinct sphere. When political economy leaves behind the confusions bound up with the conflation of economic life with the family it does so only in order to grab onto a new confusion in its identification of the economy with the state (a confusion which is also, it might be added, connected to a real historical condition). But, whereas originally the conception of the economy is lost within the family so that the latter makes the former unnecessary, now it is the conception of the state which disappears into the economy so that the conception of a system of economic relations absorbs the concept of the state. The state becomes, in effect, an economic sphere. This means that the science which claims to treat the provision for the wants of the state deals, in reality, with the state as a system of economic relations, and therefore treats the economic character of wants. It is in this manner that the object of political economy first distinguishes itself.

Political economy considers economic activity so far as it involves relations of mutual dependence among members of a social division of labor which constitute the reference point for economic life not as the individual but as the collectivity, in particular the state. Relations within the collectivity defined in this way are, for classical thought, predominantly social relations which, as such, always transcend the presumed irreducible natural quality which is attributed to the system of economic interactions restricted to the particular household taken by itself. To this extent, once economics is replaced by political economy the provision of needs takes as its reference point a pre-eminently social reality which transcends directly the natural sphere. Still, the starting point is the notion of economic life defined with reference to the household and the retention of this definitional presupposition marks clearly the limits within which the economic life of the state can take on a social character. Indeed, political economy begins as that science which deals with the natural renewal of the state, therefore with the manner in which a series of natural activities preserve and maintain the system of social interactions. To this extent, political economy is predicated upon a contradiction: on one side, its object is a political, and therefore a preeminently social one which transcends the species existence of the household making of the latter a political unit; and on the other side, political economy retains for its object the nature-given requisites for the renewal of the household, the provision of its wants as defined within a natural sphere.

This last involves classical thought in a confusion of the nature of the wants whose provision provides the subject-matter of the theory of economic life. To the extent that the subsistence provided by economic activity is that of a social reality the needs which must be provided become themselves social in character rather than those needs connected to the nurture of the family as situated within a natural process. And yet, political economy considers these needs to be conceivable as extensions of the needs of the household still situated within the species and therefore as effecting its subsistence independently of the state. The science exists only so far as there is a subsistence of the individual which is specific to his membership in the state, therefore of the individual as a political entity, while political economy retains within its conception of subsistence the nurture of the individual or family as elements of a species, thereby reducing the political relations to relations of nature and eliminating any foundation for economic analysis as a science. Economics becomes a science only when the renewal of the species becomes a social act so that the species is itself constituted as a social reality, therefore when the original object of economic activity becomes a social object.

For the renewal of the species to constitute a social act the needs which must be fulfilled within that renewal must undergo an alteration so that the conception of the species is itself altered. The nurture of the family becomes the subsistence of a social relation. The conception shifts from the species to society, from the family as a part of the species to the individual as a determination of society. Political economy begins, therefore, with the transformation of need from that for the renewal of a natural relation to the renewal of social life. The crucial element in the conception of economic theory is not simply the notion of need taken in the abstract, but the conception of the kind of need which is characteristic in what classical political economy calls 'civilized society.' The necessity that the conception of need be made specific to modern society is the driving force behind the development of classical political economy to the standpoint of economic science. The contradictions which give rise to this development are concentrated within the classical conception of economics as the science of wealth.

The development of the concept of wealth is the other side of the development of the concept of need. Where needs are given by nature so also must the objects which fulfill those needs be provided in the same manner so that wealth is given as an element of nature, accountable to nature. Thus wealth is the produce of the soil, the resources of the earth, etc. By contrast, where the needs whose provision is the end of economic activity are social needs the objects which fulfill those needs and are the components of wealth must, perforce, be themselves social objects. Implicitly, the problem of wealth which confronts political economy is that of the constitution of wealth as a social substance. To be sure, there is no point at which this appears as explicitly problematic. Still, the concept of wealth undergoes, within classical thought, a definite development which, rather than altering its substance, serves to make explicit its hidden reality: that wealth is connected to the multiplication of need and that this multiplication of need and of the means to its satisfaction is the defining characteristic of civilized society, indeed of social life itself; and, further, that this multiplication of need is no more than an expression for the general principle of sociality in bourgeois society – value – and especially for the inner law of bourgeois economy – self-expanding value, capital.

2

What is 'luxury' or 'wealth'? The answer to this question provided by classical political economy takes as its reference point a form of human existence which is the antithesis of wealthy society, a hunting and gathering form of life which is prior to agriculture and industry and within which all needs are given and fulfilled by and within nature. This 'savage state of man' forms an antithesis for civilized (wealthy) society which allows for the conception of the latter.[1] The needs existing within the savage state are those needs bound up either with the renewal of the species, the economy of the household taken as a natural relation, or with the whims of the individual taken outside of any relation either natural or social.

It is only with the development of agriculture and especially with the introduction of 'industriousness' into economic life and into the method of provision of wants that the fulfillment of need is no longer restricted to the abundance of nature taken as existing independently and as making immediate provision for the needs of the family.

Out of agriculture there emerges a multiplication of needs and of the means for their satisfaction. This multiplication plays a fundamental role in the development of economic theory and is designated, by classical political economy, 'luxury' and later simply 'wealth.' The development of the connection between need, so far as it provides the subject-matter of economic thinking, and luxury obviates the link between need and the biological renewal of the species. It is no longer possible to take the determination of need as simply given so long as economic thinking retains its object of accounting for the emergence of civilized society, therefore for wealth and for the provision for the needs of society. The form which the recognition of this necessity takes in the development of economic theory is that of the division of production, and therefore of the division of needs into (1) that production and those needs connected to the subsistence of the members of society which is provided, in the first instance, immediately by nature (e.g. through hunting and gathering), and (2) an additional part of production connected to additional needs brought into existence with the growth of agriculture. The latter provides for the fulfillment of wants which exist over and above those which are provided directly by nature, while the former represent the subsistence of the members of society taken as outside of society, and provided for by nature. Where there exist no needs not given by nature and by the natural determination of the household, there exists no activity pointed towards the satisfaction of needs over and above those provided immediately by nature. In this case there is no sphere of economic relations subject to investigation by a specifically economic theory so that there can be no science of political economy. The science of wealth, therefore, does not study the subsistence and its renewal taken as provided by nature, but luxury and the process by which it is determined, its origins in society. So far as production is concerned, political economy begins where it is necessary to fulfill needs not posited by nature. Since, in the first instance, need was identified with subsistence and it only now begins to differentiate itself, political economy constitutes such needs which make up the object of its investigations as existing over and above, therefore to that degree apart from, nature.

This development is most forcefully expressed in physiocratic thought. The latter attempts, for the first time, to base economic thinking explicitly upon the distinction between subsistence and the 'net revenue.' The latter is understood simultaneously as solely the product of the soil (therefore of nature) and as the foundation of civilized life. Wealth, accordingly, is both the product of nature, since only the earth is productive of a net product, and the origin of society. The equation of the net product with wealth[2] reveals clearly the opposition between wealth and subsistence, therefore implicitly the opposition between wealth and the exclusive sphere of natural interaction. At the same time the net product is taken to exist only as the product of that same natural interaction from which it must be distinguished. Still, the identification of the net product with wealth marks the definitive break which makes possible the emergence of economic science. It becomes immediately apparent that the identification of wealth with the material requisites for the provision of wants has broken down. It is only to the provision of those wants over and above the subsistence that wealth is relevant. In this case the referent for economic life ceases to be the immediate relation of man to nature for which the household exists exclusively as an element of a naturally determined system, having become instead a relation within a process of renewal already displaced from the natural world.

For classical thought social needs, and the system of needs which emerges with their multiplication and is identified with wealth and luxury, exist always in a relation to nature. Here, however, this relation appears as also one of opposition, as additional to, as over and above, etc., therefore not simply as a part of the natural subsistence. To be additional to is, however, to remain in essence a part of so that the peculiar manner in which classical economics conceives of wealth as a surplus achieves an identification between wealth and subsistence which is implied by the manner in which they are distinguished. This identification leads simultaneously in two directions. Particularly in early classical thought the equation of wealth and subsistence, in which wealth exists solely as a multiplication of the subsistence, implied a reduction of the former to the latter. The implication of this reduction is, furthermore, that civilization, which emerges on the basis of wealth, is ultimately rooted in a natural sphere and reducible to a system of naturally determined relations. At the same time, the identification of wealth with subsistence as an increment to the subsistence tends towards the identification of subsistence and the natural process from which it originates with wealth, dislodging the presumed natural ground of both the subsistence and the net product. The analysis leaves behind any explicit consideration of the subsistence and its renewal and, by focusing exclusively upon the net product and its mode of utilization, leaves out of account the actual reduction of the wealth of nations to the provision for a natural subsistence.

The renewal of the subsistence comes to be relegated to a theoretical limbo: not legitimately to be included within the theory, which focuses exclusively upon the formation of wealth, and yet still retained as the implicit basis for the emergence of all wealth. The real problem for classical political economy is never that of the renewal of the subsistence, which is a problem for nature, but of the renewal of the surplus which, as we have seen, is not accounted for by nature. It is the investment of the surplus which brings about the increase of industry and wealth. To be sure, classical thought never consciously grasps this opposition between the natural process and the real subject-matter of the science of wealth. Still, that a departure from the standpoint of the naturally determined interaction is implicit in classical thought is clearly evidenced in the characteristic oppositions of classical analysis. The need which is the subject-matter of economic theory is not that need given by and fulfilled within the natural process but a new need outside of, over and above, that relevant to the household as an element of an animal species.

3

The form which this departure of need from its purely natural determination adopts in classical thought is in the first instance an exclusively quantitative one: the increase or multiplication of need. In the opposition of subsistence to wealth the latter appears as an increment to the former so that the opposition is one which connects the two categories as regards their substance, opposing them only quantitatively. This is apparent in the case of the Ricardian corn economy for which the substance of wealth is identical to the substance of which the wages fund is composed. Wealth consists, then, of that part of the corn produced which is not required for the renewal of the supply of corn at a given level. Wealth and subsistence are therefore identical as regards their composition. Furthermore, the equivalence established here is that of physical magnitudes defined not in terms of the intrinsic nature of wealth but in terms of the relation of subsistence to the requirements of a natural process.

It is, none the less, in the quantitative expansion of need as regards society as a whole that classical thought marks the specificity of need to a social relation. In this case the need satisfied by the production of corn is not that of the subsistence of the producers but that of the expansion of production itself so that the fulfillment of subsistence needs is no more than the means to the expansion of production and the increase of the net product, therefore of wealth. The element of subsistence is, in this case, definitely subordinated to the activity of wealth so that it is the wealth which determines the subsistence and gives to the latter an incipiently social character. At the same time that the opposition of subsistence to wealth equates the two, reducing the latter to an element of a natural process, that opposition also must be considered as incipiently one in which the natural principle (the subsistence) is forced to discover its ground within society (in the renewal and expansion of wealth). As a result the unnatural or extranatural character of wealth determines the subsistence as also outside of the natural process rather than as the basis for the incorporation of wealth into nature.

The needs which are satisfied by the wealth of nations are, by definition, given independently of the simple natural or biological renewal of the species. These needs derive from this opposition a social determination which makes them needs distinct in nature from those needs with which economic thinking originally defines its object. The implication of this displacement of need is that it is equally necessary to alter the conception of the objects which account for the fulfillment of needs (wealth). The substance of wealth comes, as a result, to be distinguished from that substance which provides for the subsistence needs of the species. It is precisely this result which, in the first instance, accounts for the emergence of a new science. The opposition of subsistence to wealth is, then, an opposition of substance between nature and society, between the natural substance which accounts for the renewal of the species within nature, and the social substance of which the wealth of nations is composed.

Such an opposition, however, is unable to sustain itself when confronted with the concrete analysis of the character of wealthy society towards which classical thought is driven. In a wealthy state the superfluities represent not simply the surplus over and above subsistence but come, more and more, to represent the specific character of the wants themselves. The needs which mark a civilized people are distinctive as civilized needs and the distinction between them and wants of an exclusively subsistence character is turned into a difference in kind. It is no longer simply a question of the satisfaction of need through economic activity but also a problem of the type of need characteristic of civilized society and the manner of its fulfillment.[3] The multiplication of need (luxury) brings with it a substantial alteration in the nature of, and therefore in the determination of, need. The concept of need appropriate to wealthy society and therefore the concept of need appropriate to the notion of wealth is distinguished from that of the need which is specific to the subsistence economy. The needs characterized as superfluous with reference to the subsistence economy are, by that fact, substantively unintelligible from the standpoint of the idea of a subsistence economy. The needs which appear originally as superfluous are not simply new needs in the sense of additional needs, but new needs in the sense of needs which emerge with a wholly distinct conception of need. Both need and wealth come to be predicated upon the determination of a social substance.

Wealth is the multiplicity of objects capable of fulfilling such social needs. Taken in this sense, wealth is an aggregate or collection of 'use-values.' Yet the use-value is not simply the object capable of fulfilling a need; it is also, so far as wealth is concerned, a component of wealth. It is not the particular needs whose fulfillment is made possible by wealth but precisely the multiplication of need which specifies wealth as the mode for its satisfaction. The multiplication of need is the type of need characteristic of civilized society and wealth is the multiplication of use-values, of objects capable of satisfying a multiplicity of need. What makes the use-value also a component of wealth is not the fact that it meets this or that particular need, but the fact that it exists as wealth only to the extent that it is situated within a system of use-values and thereby relates not only to the particular need but to the system of needs. Wealth is inherently multiple and, indeed, multiplied without limit. The provision for need involves use-value only where need is socially determined within a system of need, and where it is fulfilled not by nature but by the wealth of society. The particular need exists only within a system of needs and the particular use-value exists only within the multitude of use-values – wealth. A use-value is always an element of a totality composed of a system of use-values connected to a many-sided system of needs.

It is not the particular need taken by itself which corresponds to wealth but the multiplication of need and therefore the multiplication of relations capable of fulfilling need. Wealth is the multitude of use-values taken together and not the single use-value or even the whole taken as simply many single use-values. It is that aspect of the sum of use-values which makes of the whole something more than the sum of its parts, makes of many use-values wealth where no single use-value exists, by itself, as a component of wealth. Since wealth transcends the particularity of the use-value it therefore must as well transcend the particularity of the aggregate. Each use-value is, then, also a part of a whole which determines it not simply as use-value but as wealth. Once understood as intrinsically a component of wealth the use-value reveals its two-sided character as use-value and as wealth. With the multiplication of use-values and their development into wealth the latter ceases to be reducible to the collection of use-values so that wealth appears as made up of components which are simultaneously use-values and wealth where wealth comes to be, step by step, differentiated from use-value.

It is in this regard precisely the peculiarity of the need as a need which is produced by luxury which makes its particularity also subordinate to a totality. It is not the particularity but the contribution to the luxury of society as of its owner which makes it wealth. The status of the particular use-value as an element of wealth is its worth in making its owner wealthy, in giving him access to the wealth of society, to luxury, and thereby to civilization itself. The individual is wealthy (he is also civilized) precisely to the extent that he is able not to fulfill particular limited needs but to fulfill a multiplicity of needs so that his wealth is his access to the fulfillment of need in general. With the multiplication of need in wealthy society there proceeds a generalization of need which sets itself up in a relation of opposition to need. Wealth as the multitude of use-values is also wealth as the transcendence of particular use-values each taken as such, is wealth as the generalization of use-value, and finally as value.

The wealth represented in the use-value is its worth or its value so that the elements of wealth cease to be simple use-values, appearing instead as simultaneously particular use-values and as elements of wealth, use-values which have worth, therefore as values. Thus, the wealth of societies is 'an immense accumulation of commodities.'[4] It is not that wealth 'takes on the commodity form.' To do so it would be necessary to conceive of wealth independently of the commodity and therefore independently of the multiplicity of use-values. The commodity is nothing more than the use-value taken as a component part of wealth. Furthermore, since the concept of a use-value entails the relation to the type of need characteristic of civilized society rather than to the subsistence need, and since that type of need is determinate precisely in terms of the multiplication of need, the very notion of use-value already implies that it exists only within a totality, in this case of the wealth of the society. The determination of need, as regards its intrinsic character, involves the multiplication of need and the relation to a system of need no longer defined in terms of the fixed circle of natural subsistence. The use-value which is this relation of the object to need involves, thereby, a relation to the multiplication of need.

The generalization of need implied in the multiplication of need and in the situation of need in a relation to wealth brings with it the development of a relation to need in general. The unity implicit in the multiplicity of use-values and needs is expressed in a need for the system of use-values as a whole, a need which is substantially for wealth itself, not for this or that particular element of, or manifestation of, wealth but for wealth as such. The use-value which fulfills this need is money. Once money emerges as an object of need it is clear that the nature of need can no longer be considered in terms of the subsistence provided by nature for the individual or household. The need for money cannot be grasped in terms of any limited system of needs nor can it be connected to any limited sphere (limited either quantitatively or in terms of its composition) for the satisfaction of need. On the contrary, the need for money is the need for wealth itself which need attests to the separation of the existence of the commodity as wealth from its existence as the object of a particular need.

Need considered in relation to wealth has its social character first in its multiplicity and the social determination of the many-sided nature of need exists only in that this multiplication has no ground within a purely natural interaction. Yet, it still appears that the social determination of need, if not simply its extension beyond subsistence, differs from such a quantitative extension only in equally presuming a qualitative multiplication. Thus, the transformation of the intrinsic character of need remains, to this degree, an external feature which involves only its interrelation with a system of need and not the inner nature of the need itself. The specificity of need to society exists in the interrelation of the system of needs. This interrelation involves a substance which is distinguished from relation to particular need and multiplication of need, when it involves worth, or value. Thus, value emerges originally as the indifference to need which results from the multiplication of need in wealthy society.

Value, taken in this sense, remains a relation of need to need so that that relation which transcends the particularity of need and constitutes particular use-values as components of wealth is reducible to a relation of need. Value possesses, from this standpoint, a purely negative determination as that substance which goes beyond particularity of need by relating different particular needs. Political economy is restricted in its conception of value to this principle and, indeed, this is the sole manifestation of the value substance within the system of economic relations for which value exists always as a relation to particular use-value. This contradiction within the concept of wealth – that use-values as components of wealth must shed their character as use-values in order to exist as wealth but can only do so in relation to a system of commodities so that the universality of the value relation exists only as a multiplication of use-value – is the driving force behind the whole of the development of the system of economic relations. It is for this reason that, within economic science, value exists always as the indifference to particular need and as nothing more.

So far as the explicit conception of value is concerned classical political economy identifies value with price, therefore with exchange-value, and thereby reduces the value relation to a relation of particular use-values. From the standpoint of the identification of value with price any conception of a value substance which goes beyond the negative relation to use-value, that is any positive concept of value, is excluded. Classical thought only transcends this limitation of its conception of value when it first identifies value with labor time and then conceives of the laboring activity as intrinsically connected to the expansion of value. In Ricardian economics the contradictions of the treatment of value which lead to the *cul-de-sac* of the 'invariable measure of value' derive from the opposition between the labor theory of value, for which value is given a real determination of its own in the labor process, and the identification of value with price which excludes such a real positive determination. Similarly, in the *Wealth of Nations*, Smith grasps the interrelation of use-values as subordinate to the self-expansion of value when he considers the accumulation of capital as a precondition foɪ the development of civilized society. In this case the interrelation of use-values is the means to the end of the movement of value so that the interrelation of use-value rather than determining the value relation is itself determined by the self-movement of value. As a result the value relation, as capital, takes on a determination adequate to it which goes beyond the negative relation of use-values one to the other. It is precisely to the extent that classical political economy grasps the capital relation as the ground for the interaction of commodities that the value substance takes on a positive determination; at the same time it is only to the extent that value takes on a positive determination, at least implicitly, that classical thought is able to grasp the capital relation as that of the self-movement of value. It is with the concept of capital, as self-moving value, that value takes on a form within which it is emancipated from determination within a given system of needs and, instead, determines those needs as so many steps to its own unlimited increase. The equation of value and use-value implicit in the exchange relation is the starting point for the emancipation of value from determination in use-value. This emancipation is̃ only realized where the movement implicit in the notion of exchange-value is made explicit as the movement of value through use-value. This self-movement of value, capital, makes it possible to grasp within the economic sphere a substantive social relation existing as such, in a positive sense, therefore to grasp the system of economic relations as explicitly social relations. Without a concept of value which goes beyond the simple notion, intrinsic to the idea of wealth, of indifference to particularity of need, it is impossible to conceive of wealth as itself composed of a distinctive substance. It is not possible under such a restricted conception to grasp the indifference to particular need in a positive sense, to conceive of the indifference to need as also a real social relation, as more than accidental, and as grounded in the social process.

For political economy economic life as such is not fully constituted as a social reality so that its social determination remains implicit. The presence within the system of economic relations of a social substance is evidenced primarily in the multiplication of need and in the implied specificity of need to a process which cannot be internalized into the renewal of the natural world. The social determination of need, however, requires the development of a relation which, although operating through the interrelation of needs, none the less actively transcends the simple relation of need to need. The specifically social determination of need which is the object of economics as a science is manifest in the value relation, so that it is with the development of a theory of value that economics adopts for the first time its real object. It is the emergence of the value relation which makes explicit the operation of a social principle within the system of economic relations and thereby makes of the latter the proper subject-matter of social theory.

Economic analysis only becomes scientific when it is able to subordinate its particular principles to a total conception which is both systematic and concrete, which situates the entire system of economic relations within a single movement that determines each particular relation within a total process. Only in the form of a systematic whole can the real interconnections which unite the system of economic relations be made intelligible so that the driving force behind economic life be made explicit. Yet, the systematization of the diverse principles of economic interaction is not the result of the intention of the individual author, or of a school, to present existing knowledge in a consistent and connected form, therefore of the intention to impose systematic form upon a content which does not yet contain the unifying principle within it already in a well-developed form. Systematicity is not imposed upon the subject-matter but exists already implicit within it as its determining principle. Thus for economics to adopt a scientific standpoint it is necessary that it discover the central principle which unites the whole of economic relations in a systematic way. This requires that the analysis (1) attain the highest level of abstraction in order that the fundamental concepts may be grasped in a systematic way, and (2) determine the unifying concept which makes the systematic quality of the exposition an inner necessity rather than an arbitrary imposition.

In economic science that concept which makes the system of economic relations intelligible is the concept of value. It is for precisely this reason that the publication of the *Wealth of Nations* marks a real starting point since it is with this book that the analysis of value in general is explicitly pursued. Indeed, it is in the work of Smith that the value relation becomes a real subject for analysis and appears for the first time in direct connection with its determining principle – the consumption of labor-power by capital. Prior to the *Wealth of Nations* it is the multiplicity of use-values, wealth, or the net product as the basis for the expansion of wealth, that provide the central object of the science. Here this multiplication of use-value taken abstractly absorbs the whole of the conception. Before Smith the attempt to present the economic categories systematically, as with James Steuart, since it lacked its unifying principle, was ultimately a false systematicity. This is equally the case after Ricardo with the work of such of his followers as James Mill and John Stuart Mill. It is only in the line of advance which begins with Smith and proceeds from Ricardo to Marx that the analysis of value is constituted as the unifying principle of economic science so that a systematic conception, and therefore a really scientific conception, of the whole of economic life can be achieved.

II Value

1

Political economy begins to go beyond the identification of wealth with the quantitative expansion and qualitative multiplication of needs when it considers the mode by which needs are fulfilled to be internal to the system of economic relations. The multiplication of need becomes also a property intrinsic to particular need when the fulfillment of need takes place via exchange so that the system of need is constituted as a system of exchanges. Economic life is no longer simply the provision of needs but is now the provision of the system of needs through the system of exchanges. Indeed, the exchange system is that system of social interaction which is specific to the provision of needs. The economic character of need is necessarily connected to the mode of the fulfillment of needs so that commodity exchange and the multiplication of needs – wealth – are two aspects of a single reality.

In classical political economy the category which reveals this logic implicit in the notion of wealth is division of labor. The division of labor connects the multiplication of needs to the particularization intrinsic in their mode of fulfillment and thereby connects wealth to exchange. In this way the exchange system comes necessarily to stand for the manner of provision of needs in civilized society. The connection between the multiplication of need and the division of labor allows for the discernment of the social principle which underlies the specificity of the system of need to society. With the specification of the wealth of nations to the system of mutual interdependence implied in the division of labor the social character of wealth can no longer be restricted to its quantitative extension or to an external aggregation, but appears instead as a principle intrinsic to wealth, or to the commodity as the element of wealth. The social substance which makes of the use-value a component of the wealth of society is now more than the simple indifference of the commodity to particularity of need. This social substance has also a reality of its own so that the sense in which the aggregate of use-values taken as commodities is more than an external summation but the expression of a new principle intrinsic to the commodity can be made explicit. Thus value, as this social substance, can begin to emerge in a really determinate form, as more than the negation of use-value, only to the degree that it appears as endowed with a positive conception which is distinguished from its relation to use-value.

2

The property of the division of labor in which classical thinking identifies this social principle is not, in the first instance, the laboring activity itself. On the contrary, the actual division of labor is established by classical thinking in such a way as to defy any necessary expression of a social substance. For classical political economy the labor which is carried on within the division of labor remains always individual so that it is the interchange of labor and not the labor itself which expresses the activity of a social principle and, indeed, which is the sole manifestation of that social substance intrinsic in the concept of wealth. The only exception to this is the conception, considered at the outset of the *Wealth of Nations*, of division of labor within a given production process, in the production of pins. Here, classical thinking grasps the real social character of the labor itself. None the less this conception is little more than a prelude to the treatment of the division of labor as the opposition of independent commodity producers constituted in such a way as to establish the laboring activity as purely individual and as possessed of no intrinsic social character.

The significance of the division of labor for the concept of civilized society is not, then, predominantly in the social character of the labor which, on the contrary, is always identified with a purely natural interaction. This significance lies, rather, on a more abstract plane where classical thought attempts to grasp the division of labor not in terms of the labor itself but in terms of the system of mutual interdependence which is implied in the division of labor. This is not, so far as the conception of the social substance is concerned, directly a mutual interdependence of labors (which remain always independent) but a mutual dependence in the provision of wants. To be sure, this mutual dependence arises out of the character of the laboring activity of society as a whole and is in that sense tied to the interdependence of the labor. While this is not explicitly constituted as social labor in classical thought it remains always implicitly so, and this implication forms the real foundation of the so-called labor theory of value. None the less, the key to the comprehension of the connection between wealth and value is not in the immediate appeal to the character of the labor which is involved in division of labor but in the substance which accounts for the social character of that labor. And this substance is not in division of labor as such nor in the mutual dependence of labor but in the nature of the mutual dependence which defines the labor as social. The secret lies therefore not, at least in the first instance, in the conception of labor, but in the conception of mutuality, and it is to the latter that reference must be made in attempting to draw out a conception of that social substance which informs as well the concept of labor. In order to grasp the social principle which underlies the connection of division of labor to wealth it is necessary to consider the type of mutual dependence characteristic of society.

If we consider the division of labor as the manner in which a fixed system of needs is provided then, in effect, we are equating the division of labor with a natural symbiosis. From this standpoint the only issue is that of the interrelation of particular needs taken to be given and the concept of mutual dependence has a purely formal character implying no more than the reciprocal provision of naturally defined species needs. In this case the orientation is not to wealth and therefore to social needs but to the provision of a limited system of needs for which the determining characteristic is not the multiplicity of need but the specification of a particular composition of needs. Misunderstanding of the concept of division of labor always begins with its conception as a method for the provision of a fixed system of needs and therefore as a relation independent of the movement of and internal composition of wealth. This misconception takes the form in classical political economy of the notion of 'simple commodity economy,' an economy within which exchange is subordinate to the mutual provision of need and for which the distribution of needs is paralleled by a distribution of productive activities each specific to the particular product which corresponds to a particular need. Within such a production system the interrelations among the producers are not substantively value relations (although they are implicitly so and to that extent conflict with the conception of the system as that of the mutual provision of need). Within a simple commodity economy and within the division of labor as the means to the fulfillment of limited needs, value is incapable of adopting any independent existence and tends to be suppressed in the interrelation of particular need.

By contrast, that form of mutual dependence which marks the division of labor as informed by a social principle transcends the system of provision of needs precisely in that the needs which are provided within the system of social interaction have no longer a fixed and given character. The kind of mutual dependence which marks the system of social relations is a mutual dependence in the provision not only of the system of needs but of wealth implicit in that system, therefore a mutual dependence in the provision of needs already stamped with universality. The secret of this form of mutuality is that the reciprocal provision of wants, as such, is not its inner law. When we consider the provision of needs as a social relation embedded within a system of mutual dependence we consider such a provision of need as penetrated by universality in its emancipation from all natural fixity of need and all determination of its components in terms of such naturally fixed needs. Rather than a reciprocal provision whose substance is the given system of need we have a reciprocal provision whose substance is wealth, or value.

Where the provision of need is also the movement of wealth the social character of need and its specificity to the mode of its provision – exchange – become explicit. The concept of need already contains implicit within it the necessity that its provision involve the exchange system, therefore the movement of value. On one side, the fact that needs are provided through exchange implies that those needs have taken on an abstract quality so that their fulfillment cannot be identified with an immediately given and fixed material or natural principle. On the other side, exchange can only exist when need has this abstract quality since exchange presupposes that the particular need has also that universality which marks its economic character.

Need, so far as it is determined within a natural subsistence, is not only particular in its opposition to other particular needs, it is also fixed in its mode of provision. In this case the provision of need is connected irrevocably to a given material substance – the need for food is directly identified with a set of given natural substances, etc. In this way need and its fulfillment are externally fixed for the species within a natural system. Such needs cannot be fulfilled by use-values but only by naturally given, material substances, whose specificity appears, from the standpoint of the species, to be irreducible.

By contrast, the need which is fulfilled through exchange must have a universal quality such that its provision can take place through the system of economic relations. The multiplication of need which marks civilized society implies as well an abstraction of need from any identification with a material or natural substance, and requires that the object through which the need is fulfilled have also this abstract quality as a use-value and not a material substance. The fulfillment of need in civilized society is also an emancipation from the fixity of need which affects no less the concept of need, whose particularity in opposition to many particular needs by no means implies any material fixity with regard to the substance required for its fulfillment. The social substance which fulfills needs, use-value, is not determined by any material condition (food and clothing may adopt an endless variety of forms and may be formed out of an equally endless variety of materials) but only by its condition within society. Needs within society are themselves stamped with the universality built upon their multiplication so that the latter ceases to be their external summation becoming instead their intrinsic substance. Where need is irrevocably connected to a given material substance as the means to its satisfaction the multiplication of need, therefore wealth, is impossible.

In civilized society the provision of need through exchange presupposes and implies an abstraction of need which simultaneously frees the provision of need from any material determination and frees the needs of society from their natural fixity. This condition is both presupposition and result of the development of the exchange system. With the emergence of need in its economic conception men cease to look to nature for the provision of wants (whose substance is no longer provided by nature) and are forced to look, instead, to society.

It is in the acquisition of wealth that the owner of the wealth is marked as independent of particular need and as no longer determinate in terms of a fixed system of needs. By contrast, in a natural division of labor there is no wealth precisely because there is no emancipation of the individual from particular need and especially from his determination wholly in terms of need. However, once division of labor is identified with the principle of wealth it is tied not to particularity of need but to the multiplication of need. This is because wealth is not intrinsically the aggregate of use-values, therefore of relations to particular needs, but the universal substance independent of particular use-value. Wealth is the principle of universality implicit in the multiplication of the system of needs. As such it establishes the owner of wealth as free, free in particular of his determination within a system of fixed needs. Wealth, therefore, embodies a principle of freedom and universality.

The form of mutual dependence which marks the individual as socially determined and therefore marks the interaction as expressive of the social substance, is that which provides the individual not only with particular receptacles of need but also with an abstraction from all determination in terms of particular need. It is precisely in this system of mutual interaction which has been termed wealth that the needy individual in the pursuit of his needs achieves the transcendence from determination by fixed needs and thereby constitutes his full social determination. And in order for this emancipation to be accomplished it is essential that the individual call upon a system of interaction within which his dependence on the provision of need is matched by a dependence upon a provision whose substance is the abstract capacity to fulfill all need and therefore a relation to no particular need. The reciprocal provision of wealth, in and through the reciprocal provision of wants, involves the endowment of the individual, through a system of mutual interaction, with the property of independence of particular determination by need. Therefore, this system of dependence provides the individual with that universality and freedom which constitutes for him an abstract capacity for the fulfillment not only of particular needs but simultaneously for the fulfillment of his existence as free from determination in need.

If we consider the system of mutual dependence in terms of the provision of wealth then the substance of the interaction is in the recognition of each individual not solely in terms of his particularity but equally in terms of his universality, and it is this universality which makes possible his relation to wealth. This property not only particularizes the individual within a system of need but also equates all individuals as the potential owners of wealth, whose indifference to particularity of need takes on a positive quality when each is constituted as a free commodity owner recognized as such within a system of individuals characterized simultaneously in terms of their needs and in terms of their freedom from determination in need. The mode of existence of wealth is, then, the system of commodity owners equated one with the other as such, therefore as property owners who are able to provide for the needs of each other by merit not simply of their production of a particular use-value but by merit of their capacity to own and exchange property. Wealth is no longer the simple aggregate of use-values, but the system of needy persons determined in terms of need so far as their particular property is concerned and determined abstractly as persons in so far as their capacity to relate to the universality of wealth is concerned.

The commodity has been considered as a use-value to the extent that it relates to a particular need and participates in a system of needs. The abstract character of the need and of the substance by which it is satisfied stamps the commodity as the component of wealth and involves the commodity in an abstraction not only of need but from its relation to particular need. In the acquisition of a use-value the individual acquires the means to the fulfillment of a particular need. In the acquisition of wealth the individual constitutes himself, through his relation to particular need, as free from determination in his relation to any particular use-value. In contrast to use-value the value of the commodity is the relation of the commodity to its owner as such, as a concrete person recognized as capable of the proprietorship over commodities. And this property is intrinsically universal in that for the commodity owner the proprietorship over particular commodities is the emancipation from determination in the particularity of those commodities. In this way the commodity owner sheds as well the determination of his particular personality and property existing free from that determination as a commodity owner *per se*. The latter is that property which he shares in common with the system of individuals and which therefore equates them not in terms of their needs but in terms of their status as commodity owners. Qualitatively they are equal, to be distinguished only quantitatively by the amount, or value, of their property. Thus, while the use-value relates to the need which stamps the individual as particular, the value of the commodity relates it to its owner as simply a commodity owner whose abstraction from particularity simultaneously constitutes his universality as the freedom to determine himself through an act of will, which freedom is constituted in his equality with the system of commodity owners.

The economic character of need, which springs out of its multiplication and abstraction, involves the relation to the individual as a self-seeking, self-determining, commodity owner. The economic character of need is connected in this way to its private determination, private not in that it springs out of the autonomous self-determination of the isolated 'individual' of bourgeois economic thought, but in that the fulfillment of need is necessarily in and through the interaction of the system of individual commodity owners. Need has, therefore, a specifically economic character in that the abstraction and multiplication of needs is simultaneously the abstraction and multiplication of needy individuals. The universality of particular need is also its relation to the individual commodity owner. And even as this relation can never be grasped as a relation to *this* individual commodity owner taken in isolation, the relation of need can only be grasped as a relation to individuality, to the private, self-seeking, commodity owner.

The economic character of need can never, then, relate that need to society taken as an immediate collective entity, as a political unit, or as a family group. The social determination of need within the system of economic relations exists as the social determination of the private, self-seeking, individual and involves his privacy and self-determination as his social conditions. The needs through which he exists within the commodity system have their economic character precisely in that they also exist as private, individual needs.

3

The universality of the value substance derives, therefore, from its determination in the system of commodity exchange. The reciprocal provision of wants which emerges upon this basis, in which abstraction from the particularity of need is always present in the system of particular needs, takes place through commodity exchange. The sphere of exchange is the sphere of relations among concrete persons defined simultaneously by their particular needs and by the necessity that those needs be satisfied in a manner which effects a continuous and repeated abstraction from all such particularity. In this relation the particular poles establish their equality precisely in that act by which they express the necessity of acquisition of particular commodities. The exchange, then, is that relation in which the freedom of the individual is preserved and realized in a concrete and determinate social relation. More concretely the exchange involves the reciprocal recognition of freedom and independence through a relation of particularity and mutual dependence. Here, the sociality of the relation, which involves it in an interrelation of freedom and equality, is realized in a determinate interaction which constitutes the freedom and independence of the individual, his self-determination, by revealing the necessity that that freedom concretize itself in a particular determinate relation.

In the exchange the individual relates as commodity owner to another commodity owner where the only criterion which prevails, given the reciprocal provision of wants, is that of the confrontation of will on both sides. What is significant to the exchange is (1) the reciprocal provision of wants through the interchange of use-values, and therefore (2) the reciprocal recognition of the owners of the use-values as their proprietors from whom they can be acquired only in an exchange which constitutes both commodities and commodity owners as equals. Particularity exists here and is retained precisely due to the recognition on the part of each exchanger that the exchange is a relation of equality which overcomes the particularity of its determinate conditions. Here we have a relation of particular needs and particular persons within which their substantial equality and universality is effected and preserved.

Wealth exists, therefore, only as the term which mediates the interaction of the system of needy individuals whose particular needs are satisfied through an exchange which simultaneously realizes that universality which is characteristic of the needs of civilized society, but realizes that universality in a specific relation of reciprocal recognition of property-owning persons. Economic relations, or those relations through which the system of needs is preserved and maintained so as to realize its inner character, are relations among persons who interact one with another via exchange and whose interdependence takes on the form of mutual dependence built upon a basis of individual autonomy. Within the system of needy individuals the freely self-determining individual is strictly determined as such within relations of equality and reciprocal recognition. The freedom of specification in particular need constitutes each commodity owner as the same, as equally a commodity owner characterized only by the capacity for entering into commodity relations. This equality of commodity owners which forms the basis of their abstraction from determination in particular need is the real content of their freedom, and the determination connected to this equality is the origin of the determinate character of that freedom.

In civil society the concrete person discovers his self-determination not within his isolation, nor in an external sphere of arbitrarily posited laws, but within the system of individuals. The social determination of the person is here explicit in that his free self-determination exists in and through its sharing of a common substance with the freedom of the system of needy individuals. Individuality is here a social condition precisely in that for the concrete person his individuality is also situated outside, in another individual and in the system of individuals. Likewise freedom and self-determination find their way outside of this particular individual and his self-determination in order to constitute themselves as existing within the individual only because they exist within the system of individuals. Thus the particular individual finds his determination within himself, and is therefore free, precisely to the extent that he simultaneously finds that same determination and freedom outside of himself, recognizes it in another concrete person, and derives his freedom from its simultaneous existence within himself and within the system of needy persons. This reciprocity takes the form of, indeed exists concretely as, the system of mutual dependence which characterizes economic life. It is only in this respect that economic relations adopt an ethical quality[5] and are thereby capable of constituting the object of a distinct science.

Political economy begins with the multiplication of needs and of the means to their satisfaction – wealth. The science of wealth is peculiar in that the reference point for wealth is the system of mutual dependence among persons within which needs and the manner of their provision take on a social character.

The multiplication of needs and of wealth brings with it, indeed takes the form of, a multiplication of needy individuals. The system of needy persons determined by their particular needs and by the universality built upon their determination as free from specification in need, is synonymous with the system of social relations of civilized or 'civil' society. This system of relations provides for political economy a specific subject-matter. The specification of the object of economic theory to the relations of civil society is the primary achievement of classical political economy and makes it possible for the latter to pursue in a systematic way the analysis of those relations, laying bare their inner logic.

For classical political economy the needs which provide the object of economic activity are specific in their definition with reference not to the household as such but to the individual as determined within a system of individuals which together form a 'nation.' It is the connection between the multiplication of needs and the multiplication of persons which underlies the classical specification of economic life, in so far as it is the subject-matter of a new science, to the state. The state is, in classical thought, synonymous with civil society so that the analysis of economic relations is immediately identified not with the real treatment of political life as such but with the analysis of the social relations which determine the interaction specific to civil society. It is for this reason that economic science begins as an 'investigation into the nature and causes of the wealth of nations.'

III Capital

1

If the wealth of nations exists concretely as a vast accumulation of commodities, those commodities exist as the components of the wealth of nations only by merit of their subordination to wealth as a totality which goes beyond the mere summation of particular useful objects. The property of being also wealth is not imposed upon the commodity by an external interrelation with many other commodities but exists immanent within the commodity and alone allows the latter to constitute itself as an element of wealth. It is, then, not simply the aggregate of use-values which appears as wealth but the particular form which that collection takes, a substantive positive property of the totality which makes it more than a mere summation of independent elements. The elements of wealth, therefore, possess already an intrinsic interdependence as wealth. This inner dependence of commodities is traced, by classical political economy, to their emergence within a social division of labor. Societies are wealthy when they are possessed of a vast accumulation of commodities. But this accumulation of commodities is only really wealth when it is connected into the inner force of the society. Otherwise, where the wealth of society is an external quality, that wealth is only ephemeral, it is not truly characteristic and cannot distinguish the society as wealthy, civilized.

For classical thought wealth is a quality which derives from the inner nature of wealthy society and does not attach itself externally to a system of individual interactions which are themselves indifferent to wealth. Wealthy society, as civilized society, is a distinctive entity within which the quality of wealth is grounded in the activity of society itself. In classical political economy societies possess real wealth when those societies adopt the form of division of labor. It is the division of labor which produces wealth so that wealth can only be a real quality of society where that society takes the form of division of labor.

The division of labor is tied intrinsically to the concept of wealth in that it is only by and through the division of labor that the multiplication of commodities can be accomplished. Indeed, division of labor is synonymous with the division of needs and therefore with the multiplication of needs. Such a multiplication is both quantitative (the expansion of production and consumption made possible by the division of labor) and qualitative. Wealth is the multiplication of objects capable of fulfilling needs themselves the products of a process of multiplication and expansion. Division of labor implies also the opposition of particular productions and therefore of particular use-values and needs. Indeed, the division of labor is preeminently a principle of particularization of need and is in this sense inseparable from the notion of wealth.

The division of labor produces wealth; societies are wealthy and therefore civilized to the degree that they are marked by the development of a division of labor. Labor, as division of labor, is labor accountable to the development of a many-sided interdependence of the members of society, an interdependence which appears as peculiar to society and therefore both a social interdependence and an interdependence which constitutes the relations among the participants as social in character. For classical thought the division of labor is not simply one property of society, nor is it characteristic of one type of society, it is directly synonymous with the concept of society (of 'civilization'). Indeed, it is for this reason that the concept of wealth is intelligible only where the individual exists as a member of a totality, determining himself only in and through his interrelation with a system of individuals. The 'nation' which is the original reference point for the notion of wealth in classical political economy is synonymous with the system of individuals subordinated to a series of relations of mutual interdependence defined by a social division of labor. For classical thought the multiplication of needs is connected to a multiplication of individuals which together compose civilized society. The social character of economic life directed towards the provision of wants exists within the economic sphere first as wealth and luxury (the specification of needs to social life) and then as that activity which creates wealth and luxury: labor and division of labor.[6]

Economic theory begins with the notion of wealth and, more specifically, with the notion of division of labor which makes manifest the intrinsically social determination of wealth. The specificity of wealth as the object of social theory is first to the implied multiplication of need and therefore to the specification of needs to society, and second to the connection of need and its provision to the development of a many-sided interdependence of the members of society in the form of division of labor. The multiplication of need is no longer simply given but is now rooted in the process by which society renews itself. This conception of the wealth of society as determined by the life process of society is the basis for the attempt on the part of classical political economy to ground value in labor time and thereby to constitute the value substance which makes societies wealthy as produced by society.

2

For wealth to be determinate its presence must be considered as the result of a process. The science of wealth takes its object not only as it exists immediately (as the multiplication of commodities capable of fulfilling a system of needs) but also as it exists through a process and, particularly, as the result of a process. In this case wealth, and wealthy (or civilized) society, cease to be the arbitrary result of contingent circumstances and appear instead as the necessary result of the life process of society, generated within society and therefore accountable to society for their existence. The development of the concept of economic life is the development of a concept of the life process of wealth: the process by which it comes into existence and therefore the process by which its distinctive qualities are determined.

In classical political economy, however, the concept of economic life is never fully developed. Wealth is never fully constituted as an economic (rather than material or natural) substance so that the life process of wealth is never fully constituted as an economic process. The notion of wealth as a material substance which is typical of classical thought violates the necessary connection between wealth, the commodity, and value. Value, in this way, ceases to be the substance of wealth and becomes instead a material quality which has its origin, or production, within a purely material interaction. Classical political economy at one and the same time achieves the first real insight into the substance and mode of existence of wealth and violates that insight by depriving the concept of wealth of that social substance which alone makes its existence and process intelligible.

The distinctive quality of the classical concept of wealth lies precisely in the explicit connection of wealth to the exchange system and the grounding of the latter in the production of value which is the substance of all exchange. Once classical political economy has made of wealth a distinctively economic substance the production of wealth becomes necessarily the primary theoretical problem. If the presence of wealth is not simply given to society that can only be because wealth finds itself determined not by nature for society but within the economic life of society. This implies simultaneously that wealth is a social rather than natural substance and that its production is also a social rather than a natural process. In this regard the problem of the constitution of the substance of wealth as value becomes the problem of the origin of, therefore the production of, value. Yet, for classical economics the substance of wealth always remains ultimately a material substance so that the component parts of wealth are determined simultaneously by their value and by a principle which conflicts essentially with the concept of value, their materiality.

Once the substance of value, and therefore of the exchange system, is considered to be a material substance the production of value must equally be considered to be a material act. Production is the material interaction by which a social substance is produced. This condition marks the central contradiction of the classical concept of production and especially of labor. Within classical thought the substance of economic life emerges out of a process within which it has no existence and to the conception of which it is wholly indifferent. The idea that value can be provided by a material interaction violates the condition that the product must always exist as the immanent principle within its own process of production. Since the production of value is the process by which value comes into existence, value must already have an implicit existence as the determining principle of the production process. The latter cannot, then, be considered to have the character of a material interaction but must involve the activity of a social principle. In its conception of wealth and of the production of wealth, classical political economy is driven on one side to take the principle of social production – labor – as the inner law of the material production of wealth, and on the other side to consider wealth, the result of a material process, to be itself wholly material, therefore not wealth. This contradiction gives specific content to the classical conception of the process by which wealth comes into existence. Overtly, within classical thought, this is a process by which a material interaction gives rise to a new principle so that the opposition of the product – wealth – to its origin is a fundamental antipathy. This opposition of wealth to its origin is also an opposition within the classical concept of wealth as a material substance produced by nature and as a social substance the principle of the production of which is the distinguishing quality of economic life – wealth.

The original conception of the source of wealth in economic theory situates that source outside, especially within a 'natural' sphere. In the most systematic of the classical treatments of the movement of wealth, that of Quesnay, the starting point remains an irreducible natural condition. The real origin of wealth is the land. Land is the source from which all of the wealth of society springs and it is to the land that reference must be made in the account for the existence and development of wealth. On the land alone is there to be found a '*generation* or creation of wealth, which constitutes a renewal and *real* increase of renascent wealth.' Without the intervention of the land there can only be a 'combining' or 'adding together' of already existing wealth.[7] The material substance of wealth is nowhere made as irrevocably the result of the process of its generation. In this case the necessary cost which constitutes the

means to the production of wealth is the land, a principle whose fixity determines as well the movement of wealth.

The more acute and the more uncompromising is the establishment within
economic thinking of the natural sphere as the source of wealth the more
sharply are the contradictions in its conception of wealth revealed. This
paradox is also evident in physiocratic thought. At the same time that the
land is the only source of wealth, the land is considered, by Quesnay, as
incapable of the production of wealth. For physiocracy, nature alone produces all wealth, and at the same time nature, taken in its immediately given
state, as nature and nothing more, is incapable of the generation of wealth.
The life process of nature, taken without regard to the economic life of society,
generates no net product and stands not as a principle of wealth and civilization but of poverty and barbarism. Physiocracy finds itself trapped within the
classical notion of civilized society which inevitably connects wealth to
civilization and not to nature. For Quesnay it is not nature as such but the
mediation of nature by wealth which makes nature productive of wealth. 'It
must be noted that the most fertile land would be worth nothing without the
wealth necessary to provide for the expenses involved in cultivation.' And,
further on, 'the more wealth is employed in cultivation, the less men it
requires, the more it prospers, and the more revenue it yields.'[8] Since even
the most fertile land requires the mediation of wealth if it is to produce
wealth and, even more, is productive of wealth in proportion to the amount
of wealth invested, it follows that it is here the wealth which must itself be
accountable for its own production. It is no longer the case that wealth can
have its original source in the land which, taken outside of its movement has
nothing whatever to do with wealth. Agriculture produces wealth not as the
land but as wealth invested on the land so that it is not the land which produces wealth but wealth which produces wealth so that wealth is, with regard
to its production, prior to the land.

This is the embryo of a new concept of wealth. In the movement of wealth
classical thought discovers at each pole the identical principle. The starting
point is wealth and the end point is also wealth. Since wealth is brought into
existence by its own act the process within which wealth is determined is now
that of its self-movement, the endless cycle through which wealth preserves
and expands itself.

Wealth has ceased to exist merely as a collection of objects capable of fulfilling needs, or as a mass of commodities. Wealth exists now in and through
the circulation of wealth. Civilized society exists also, then, as this circular
movement or circulation of wealth. Wealth existing within this circular movement is wealth made determinate within a process of self-generation. The
circulation of wealth constitutes wealth not simply as commodities, nor
simply as value, but as capital, 'the indispensable basis of every remunerative
enterprise.'[9]

The great achievement of the physiocratic system is the constitution of wealth as 'renascent wealth,' therefore as capital. Yet, within the physiocratic conception the realization of the identity of wealth as capital must undermine fundamentally the first principle of physiocratic thought – the origin of all wealth in the land, and therefore the material production and substance of wealth. For the conception of wealth as capital it is essential that the substance of wealth lose its material character and be constituted definitively as value and that the generation of value be explicitly considered as an economic activity. This constitution is the project of post-physiocratic classical thought which takes the achievement of physiocracy, the conception of wealth as renascent wealth, as its starting point and only on this basis achieves a first real analysis of the nature and causes of wealth.

3

The determination of wealth within a material process determines the movement of wealth according to a principle of fixity, a given natural condition (the fertility of the earth). This is the condition which fixes the production of wealth, determining its magnitude. Originally such a condition existed abstractly, in the land. The land, as an irreducible starting point, generates the wealth of society. The development of economic theory from this point is the development of the idea that the condition which produces wealth is not given but is itself produced. This production of the objective conditions of production, which makes the latter capital, begins with the idea of the investment of wealth on the land and the implied constitution of the land as a field for the investment of capital. Since production originates with the investment of wealth the generation of wealth is set loose from any fixed condition given outside of the process of the total self-expansion of the wealth of society. In this case the production of wealth is freed from any identification with a given material substance (the production of corn on the land, or corn as wealth). Wealth is thereby freed within its production process of natural determination so that its production has also that universality intrinsic to its conception. Production becomes an unending process which, since it finds its requisites as its own internal conditions, moves outward in all directions and adopts any and all particular forms. As a result the production of commodities and the production of wealth are finally united since all commodities now contain within their process of production the principle of wealth, whereas previously only those commodities directly connected to production on land represented real wealth.

This development, it would seem, must explode the classical conception of wealth as a material substance fixed in its movement by a natural condition. And this is, indeed, ultimately the case. None the less, rather than leading immediately to the breakdown of that notion and its supersession by the conception of the production of a social substance, the emergence of the concept of capital must pass first through a further stage in its development. This stage marks also the highest development of classical political economy. In this phase of its development the science of wealth seizes upon the real principle of its production – labor – and constitutes that principle as a fixed condition which, rather than setting loose the self-development of capital, fixes that development in an arbitrary limiting condition – the costs of the production of labor as a material condition, or the 'subsistence' wage.

The concept of subsistence in economic theory, both classical and modern, signifies the production of the condition for the production of wealth as an activity outside of the movement of wealth, therefore the external determination of the circulation of wealth. The subsistence is a material condition whose fulfillment by wealth as the prelude to its cycle constitutes the substance of wealth as that material substance of which the subsistence is composed and constitutes the cycle of wealth as having a prior condition outside, in the subsistence of society. Since the subsistence of society is a prior condition the circulation of wealth ceases to be the life process of society and becomes instead an epiphenomenon of that life process. Civilized society is defined, however, as having its life process within the circular flow of wealth so that for civilized society the subsistence is itself wealth and cannot consistently be constituted as a true subsistence. Either the subsistence becomes a social substance (wealth) or wealth becomes a material substance. Once the wealth of society is produced by labor which regenerates itself through the consumption of a material substance provided out of wealth the latter becomes the increment to the subsistence, therefore a material superfluity.

In economic theory the subsistence fixes the movement of wealth, limiting the latter to the constraints of externally given conditions. Here, the costs of production determine the net product according, for example, to the given fertility of nature or according to the subsistence wage as a fixed material condition in the reproduction of labor (in the form of a given basket of wage goods determined by the 'costs of the reproduction of labor'). The self-movement of wealth becomes instead the circular flow of a natural, even physical, product and the dimensions of the circle remain fixed within the limits of purely physical constraints. In this respect the idea of a subsistence, which originally makes possible a concept of wealth in opposition to nature, simultaneously excludes the full development of wealth, and therefore the emancipation of economic life from the determination of externally fixed, contingent circumstance.

This is the case precisely to the degree that the costs of the production of wealth take the form of a subsistence and not the form of an advance of wealth itself and in so far as the magnitude of those costs are fixed not within the life process of wealth, therefore by the requirements of the self-expansion of capital, but by external conditions over which the process of wealth exerts no force. Where wealth is the 'surplus' or the 'net product' the process of wealth and movement through its cycle remain fixed arbitrarily by those factors accountable for the determination of the subsistence. So long as the cycle of

wealth cannot account for the costs of its production that cycle remains subject in its movement to the caprice of external circumstances. The self-
movement of wealth breaks down once the generative moment of its cycle
moves outside. To the extent that the subsistence is not itself determined
within the movement of wealth the latter cannot be assured so that the mode
of existence of wealth becomes unaccountable. Thus wealth ceases to find
any account for itself within the economic system and the object of political
economy is lost. Where wealth and its movement are not determined within
economic life, economic life ceases to be the process of their determination
and economic science loses its distinctive subject-matter.

The illimitability of wealth can only be realized within a process which is freed
from arbitrarily given fixed conditions and which, instead, provides within
itself the conditions requisite to its total motion. Wealth is, then, its own
process of renewal and expansion. It is the 'continual advance and return of
capitals.'[10]
In order to grasp wealth as capital, however, it is not sufficient simply to
consider wealth as produced; nor is it adequate to consider wealth as the
product of labor. What is essential is the conception of wealth as produced by
the investment of wealth and therefore to consider the labor which works in
the production of wealth to be labor working as capital. Labor appears here,
in the production of wealth, not as a material condition determined without
regard to capital, but as the unifying process of labor and capital, labor and
the objective means of labor both working as component parts of capital. On
one side the objective conditions of production exist as wealth, and on the
other the subjective condition exists as labor, which is determined not as a
natural condition existing for capital but in its relation with capital. The
conception of the labor process as the process within which wealth produces
itself is the objective of the classical theory of value, and it is this objective
which makes of the classical treatment of value a genuine theoretical project.

Chapter 2
Adam Smith: Division of labor, capital, and exchange

I Preface: The construction of the *Wealth of Nations*

1

Economic thinking in the classical period follows a line of development the logic of which is that of the emergence of a scientific conception of economic life. The systematic construction of a scientific idea of the system of economic relations presupposes the process by which the object of the science is displaced from the historically existing forms of wealth, taken in their immediacy as the material for observation and computation. This displacement is a process of abstraction by which the subject-matter of the science is grasped on a theoretical plane. The object of investigation becomes an abstract, therefore theoretical, object and the investigation becomes thereby a scientific investigation. This development involves a conception of the laws by which the wealth of society is governed and a conception of the intrinsic necessity of those laws.

The requirements implied in the abstraction of the object of investigation are of equal validity in all of the sciences. For the original emergence of cosmology as a science it is not sufficient that the observation of the heavenly bodies and their movements achieve a high level of sophistication. On the contrary, it is only by abstracting from the actually observed movements of empirically given and contingent astronomical objects that a scientific standpoint can be developed. The object of the latter is not the histories of particular planetary motions but the laws by which the movements of heavenly bodies are governed. The object of the theory is, then, an abstract object the abstraction of which is synonymous with its conception as governed by intrinsic laws. This means that the object of the theory is always conceptual and never immediately 'empirical.' It is never the phenomenon in its immediacy but always its conception with which the scientific treatment is concerned. In this regard the emergence of the science and the specification of its object are indistinguishable.

For classical political economy the contradictions intrinsic to its conception of economic life exclude the full consummation of that project which it has, for the first time, defined. The great achievement of classical thought lies in the determination of the system of economic relations as the object for a science. Yet that determination remains flawed in such a way as to exclude the full achievement of a scientific standpoint. This is nowhere more evident than in the greatest of classical texts, the *Wealth of Nations*. The *Wealth of Nations*, alone among the works of the classical period, attempts a systematic conception of economic life constituted by a theoretical construction of the concepts which make up the system of economic interaction. The logical determination of the concept of value and its self-development is the real object of the *Wealth of Nations* and while Smith is not always true to this object his text does provide, for those willing to search for it, the first real statement of the science.

2

The construction of the *Wealth of Nations* is sharply different from that of Ricardo's *Principles of Political Economy*. While the latter explicitly recognizes the priority of the theory of value (for reasons which are themselves only implicit), the former centers from the outset on the division of labor so that commodity exchange is seen as an expression of the division of labor and is to that extent grounded in a determinate economic process rather than simply posited. For Smith this procedure is clearly necessary and emerges as the predetermined product of the essential interrelations of the various categories under investigation. The starting point, therefore, depends upon the organization of the work as a whole, which organization is given explicit statement prior to the opening sections of what is the text of the *Wealth of Nations* properly considered. Once the organizing principles of the analysis are made explicit Smith considers them to be as compelling as they are self-evident.

Modern interpretations of the *Wealth of Nations* follow Smith in viewing the problematic of that work as self-evident. Nevertheless, a careful study of the analysis does not reveal the activity of a single unifying principle. Rather, what emerges out of such a study is the presence of contradictions within the text which reveal the simultaneous activity of alternative thematic structures connected to distinct conceptions of economic life. In spite of the fact that these co-existing alternatives have no place in Smith's comprehension of the composition of economic science they, none the less, will be found to determine the scientific claims of the work as a whole.

The evident subject-matter of the *Wealth of Nations* is the study of 'wealth.' Within the conceptual framework of modern economics this observation allows the theme of the work a clear formulation. For contemporary economic thinking the classical texts are the embodiment of the classical model of the growth of wealth. Their scope is determined by their preoccupation with economic expansion. In so far as this is the case it is possible to trace out a classical theory of economic growth in the light of which the specificity of classical thinking *vis-à-vis* modern economic analysis can be isolated.

On the other hand, while there can be no question but that Smith was concerned with the accumulation of capital and the progress of society, the *Wealth of Nations* cannot be made to reveal a theory of economic growth, in the sense of present-day economic analysis, as its critical focal point. An

investigation into the 'nature and causes of the wealth of nations' need not be
synonymous with a theory of economic growth. In particular, while the former
is predominantly a problem whose solution requires the dissection of the
internal mode of organization of a given economic system the latter precludes
the questioning of the inner logic of that system. As a theory of growth the
Wealth of Nations would be restricted to the quantitative description of the
changes in magnitude of a given economic system whose structure and
definition remain implicit in the analysis and theoretically undetermined. It
would consider the movement of capital and labor without considering the
necessary conceptual interrelation of capital and labor. Furthermore, the presupposition that Smith's investigation of nature and causes constitutes a
theory of growth assumes that the concept of wealth employed by Smith is
not only unambiguous in itself but is also the equivalent of its counterpart
within modern economic theory. Such an assumption may not be sustained
a priori while the concrete investigation of Smith's use of the term 'wealth'
will reveal its problematic character within classical political economy as a
whole.

The embedding of a theory of economic growth and of the progress of
wealth within an analysis of the nature and causes of wealth gives rise to acute
conceptual problems. These problems are not to be attributed to the inability,
in principle, of an analysis of the inner logic of the economic system to account
for its movement over time, but to the specific manner in which Smith
integrates a theory of capitalist economic relations and a theory of the growth
of the capitalist economy out of a non-capitalist origin. The methodology
which Smith employs excludes the satisfactory consummation either of the
treatment of capitalist economic relations or of the expansion of capital, the
'growth' of the economy as a whole. The result is the existence of a dual focus
within the *Wealth of Nations* which expresses itself in a differentiated thematic
structure. This differentiation expresses, however indirectly, the prevailing
multiplicity of conceptual structures characterizing the work as a whole. Thus,
what appears to be a problem of the growth of wealth is expressed by Smith
himself as a problem of isolating the *differentia specifica* of 'civilized society.'
By contrast with the 'savage nations of hunters and fishers' which are 'so
miserably poor, that from mere want, they are frequently reduced, or, at
least, think themselves reduced, to the necessity sometimes of directly destroy-
ing, and sometimes of abandoning, their infants, their old people, and those
afflicted with lingering diseases,' Smith considers 'civilized' nations in which,
although 'a great number of people do not labor . . . yet the produce of the
whole labor of society is so great, that all are often abundantly supplied, and
a workman, even of the lowest and poorest order, if he is frugal and industrious, may enjoy a greater share of the necessaries and conveniences of life
than it is possible for any savage to acquire.'[1] Similarly, when Smith considers
the introduction of the division of labor as the distinguishing feature of
civilized economy his first concern is not directly with the extent of that

division of labor but with its *presence*. The transition from barbarism to civilization is a once-over process of the introduction of division of labor and is, on the most general level, independent of the extent of the division of labor. In this connection Smith always speaks of society once the division of labor 'has been thoroughly introduced' (p. 259).

What appears to modern economics as simply a theory of economic growth is considered by Smith to be, in the first instance, an analysis of the transition from one form of economic organization to another. This, it must be emphasized, is reducible to a problem in the theory of economic growth only to the extent that the difference between civilization and barbarism is not a difference in kind but only a question of the differing forms of appearance of a given economic system. The idea of the transition between economic systems can itself be treated as a subsidiary problem within the theory of economic growth so long as the difference between such systems is considered to be an exclusively quantitative one. Primitive society from the conceptual standpoint of modern economic theory is characterized in terms such as the quantity of 'capital,' the productivity of 'labor,' and the amount of 'wealth.' These descriptive categories are precisely those employed in the analysis of modern economic systems so that the latter differentiate themselves only in terms of the quantitative state and level of development of relationships which are invariant to the transformation of primitive society into civilization. The fact that Smith himself viewed the problem in this way and that within the *Wealth of Nations* this conception of economic development forms a dominant theme has allowed all subsequent economic theory to absorb the entire argument of the *Wealth of Nations* into this single problematic. The investigation into the nature and causes of the wealth of nations is a theory of economic growth to the extent that the treatment of the relation of civilization to barbarism is an analysis of the transition from one to the other where the latter is nothing other than a more primitive form of an invariant structure of economic relations. The *contrast* which Smith presents in the 'Plan of the Work' between civilization and barbarism is, in this view, the prelude to a theory of the transition from one to the other and therefore of the growth of civilization out of barbarism.

However, once the problem is posed in this manner, which is consistent with Smith's own view, certain critical contradictions arise. The attempt to relate civilized society to savage society in terms of a *process* either of growth or of transition is baffled by the manner in which pre-civilized society is conceptualized within the *Wealth of Nations*. This is indicated immediately by the fact that there exists, within the text, no actual analysis of the transition from barbarism to civilization as a process but only an exclusively external opposition. This failure to sustain an analysis of a process of transition results in the conflating of civilization and barbarism along a number of dimensions while constituting the rise of civilization as a process of natural history, as a result of a propensity of human nature. This, as we will show, tends to obliterate the temporal distinction between the two states of man and reveal an altogether different basis of their integration.

For Smith, the contrast between civilization and the savage state of man does not reveal the latter as a primitive form of the former. In the confrontation of civilization and barbarism it is *society itself* that confronts the savage state of man not as a structurally distinct and prior economic system but as the *lack* of economic system. The entire existence of man in his primitive state is constituted as the negation of society. 'In the rude state of society . . . every man endeavors to supply by his own industry his occasional wants as they occur' (p. 259). Smith's characterization of this as a 'rude state of society' should not be allowed to obscure the explicitly non-social specification of the conditions posited. It is precisely the lack of that interdependence which defines life for Smith as social which characterizes the rude state of man. None the less, Smith characterizes the non-existence of society as a 'state of society' so that their difference becomes a difference in the development of an unchanging substance. This reduction would, of course, be the natural result of the reduction of the subject-matter of economic theory to the description of the quantitative movement of an economic system whose peculiar categories are only intelligible as specific forms of elements which are universal to human existence. The analysis of the difference between civilization and barbarism deals, then, with a change of form to which the content is indifferent.

The mutual interpenetration of civilization and barbarism and their reciprocal conceptual determination involves Smith in the comprehension of civilized society within the bounds of a *non*-civilized primordial existence of man while this latter is defined, as we will argue, by a series of eminently social facts such as exchange and the specific form of individuation and fragmentation implied by commodity production. The negation of civilized society is determinate in so far as it is defined as composed of the individual elements of capitalist economy, the individual personalities, without the relations which tie them together and give them their determinate character. Savage society, as the denial of civilization, finds itself defined precisely in terms of a specific form of production. On the other side, the conception of civilized society is distorted by its dependence on a non-social original constitution of man. But again, this is not an historically determined distortion but the product of the reconstitution of civilized society's own image as a logical construction. Indeed the positing of civilized society as a transformation of an external determination implies the domination of the conception of social life itself by a principle explicitly outside. This determination brings with it the exclusion from the system of economic relations of the inner force of its self-movement. To this extent civilized society ceases to form the object of a distinct science since the achievement of civilization is not marked by any qualitative rupture with the originally given, natural, conditions. The methodology intrinsic to this conception forsakes the scientific object immanent within classical thought.

However, a close investigation will reveal that such a methodology is not sufficient to characterize the construction of the *Wealth of Nations*. Not only does the savage state of man fail to define civilized economy but the conception of savage economy itself grows out of civilized society in such a way that the former has no existence except as the distorted reflection of the latter. The pseudo-historical method reveals itself, in this case, as a vicious circle in which the modern economic system is comprehended through its own distorted image, an image which it has itself projected and through which it obscures and obliterates its own internal character. This vicious circle is at the heart of the contradictions and complexities of the *Wealth of Nations*. Yet to argue that the pseudo-historical method expresses Smith's self-conscious reflection on the logic of his work cannot clearly establish the predominance of this principle in the structuring of the investigation as a whole. On the contrary, a close study of the text reveals the co-existence of differing conceptualizations of economic life and of differing perceptions of the object of the study itself.

It is the purpose of this section to expose the multiplicity of conceptions which make up the *Wealth of Nations*. It will be argued that the work is characterized by a compound infrastructure whose own complexity serves to hide the multiple thematic structure of the work as a whole. Organizing principles explicitly articulated by Smith are refracted through principles unknown to him or of which he is only partially aware. The result is that the construction of the work, in spite of its apparent systematic quality, is the product of the simultaneous action of differing and contradictory conceptualizations. To anticipate the results of this study, the fundamental duality of the *Wealth of Nations* is in its conception of 'civilized' society as *capitalist* society and therefore as determinate at the same time that civilization, and therefore bourgeois society, is built up of elements which are explicitly non-social in origin. The requirements of the first conception come into conflict with those of the second, giving rise to the primary contradictions and confusions of Smith's theoretical system.

The first moment of the determination of civilized society in the *Wealth of Nations* constitutes the latter as synonymous with the division of labor. Since civilized society is synonymous with the division of labor, non-civilized society is the *absence* of division of labor. In Section 2, below, we consider the conception of the division of labor in the *Wealth of Nations*. The focus of the discussion is on the manner in which the division of labor embraces social life, and the manner in which this connection is abridged within Smith's treatment of the division of labor. It is not simply that the division of labor has itself two sides – one social and one natural – but the specific manner in which the differing aspects of the division of labor are united in the analysis.

The social nature of the division of labor is challenged by Smith at two key points. First, Smith considers the social character of the mechanism by which the disparate elements of the overall production process are united (the exchange of commodities in the market) to be purely a matter of form; and, second, he considers the specifically social precondition of the division of labor (the accumulation of capital) to be a purely material condition: the presence of a 'stock.' Both of these reductions constitute the division of labor as simply a form of 'labor in general' not different, *in nature*, from the simple labor process of pre-civilized society, but only different in extension. This attempt to reduce social life to a natural condition is an attempt to place civilized and pre-civilized society on the same plane and in so doing to allow for their mutual determination by the simple category of 'labor.' Civilized society, social life, is the product of a *form of labor*, division of labor, where the simple labor process which underlies that form has a purely individual and natural determination.

In Section 3 this simple notion of labor is considered concretely and, in particular, in its relation to exchange. The grounding of exchange in labor has certain implications for the concept of labor. In the light of these implications the unity of the 'labor' of pre-civilized economy and the 'labor' of civilized economy breaks down. The specifically social character of the labor which grounds the exchange of commodities displaces that labor from its origin in pre-civilized society and denies to the latter the concept of labor itself. The exchange of commodities is conceived in the *Wealth of Nations* as first a process grounded in individual labor and subsequently as a process which denies the individuality of that labor. These two different conceptions merge to produce the central contradictions of the Smithian formulation of the labor theory of value. Smith simultaneously roots civilized society in the labor process which emerges out of the savage state of man and roots the labor process of the savage state within the conception of civilized society.

In Section 4 the manner in which these contradictions give specific form to Smith's version of the labor theory of value is considered. Within the latter the reduction of the differing forms of labor to a common substance (labor) is the theme of the theory of value and the specific function of the labor-commanded conception. At this point the real contrast which dominates the analysis emerges most clearly. The social determination of economic life is considered to be purely a matter of form, while the purpose of political economy is precisely to expose the social forms – social life itself – as no more than forms of appearance of the real relations – the material or natural process. This reduction appears as a central distinguishing theme of classical political economy.

II Division of labor and capital

1

The starting point of physiocratic thought is the *difference* of labor implied in the opposition of agriculture and manufacture. This construction deprives the concept of labor of that unity which makes of particular labors the particularizations of *labor*. The starting point of economic science, by contrast, is always the *division* of labor which rests upon a mutual dependence and therefore equality of labor. In the history of economic science the concept of division of labor marks out the system of interdependence of independent individual producers. It, therefore, is the concept by which the first treatments of the science grasp civilized society as a system of mutuality within which independent self-seeking discovers the ground for its autonomy and self-determination in a system of mutual dependence. Civil society appears to classical thought as synonymous with division of labor since division of labor always implies the interdependence of independent labors.

In this respect the starting point of physiocratic thought is antithetical to the conception of economic life. This opposition is most clearly marked in the work of Turgot who begins simultaneously with the opposition of different labors and with the division of labor. For Turgot the principle of inequality of labor, which is a principle of the irreducible particularity of labors, is posited in direct opposition to the principle of division of labor which always entails the universality of labor, therefore its social determination. The parochial quality of physiocracy is implied in its insistence on the unique productivity of the land. Smith and Ricardo appear in opposition to this conception as physiocracy without the elevation of land to a distinctive status. In the absence of the notion of agriculture as the origin of wealth, as determinant of the range and extent of production, etc., the principle of wealth must become a universal principle which accounts simultaneously for the origin of wealth and for its renewal. The universality implied in the concept of wealth can only be grasped consistently in terms of the division of labor where the divided labors are always penetrated by a universal social substance. The elevation of the concept of labor to this standpoint is the first achievement of the *Wealth of Nations*. But here, as throughout the *Wealth of Nations*, the discovery of a scientific concept finds itself overlaid with its false precursors.

Smith's own starting point is the division of labor which is the primary cause of the improvement in the wealth of nations. It is not the *extent* of the division of labor which is in the first instance critical, but the *presence* of the division of labor. Logically, for Smith, social life is grounded in the division of labor. In fact, a central theme of the *Wealth of Nations* is that the division of labor is synonymous with social existence, so that the conception of society comes to be identified with a particular form of the natural process of production, with a specific form of labor. The equation of the division of labor with 'society' and the logical priority attributed to the division of labor as the *origin* of society exclude any social determination of the division of labor. The latter is, rather, posited abstractly at the outset in the form of an outgrowth of nature. For this result it is critical that the division of labor not be seen to depend on any social relation, that it be possible to conceptualize the division of labor, in effect, independently of social life. In order to achieve this end it is sufficient to consider the division of labor as the breaking down of the work process into its naturally defined elements. That process is not itself altered in character but only in form of application. The work process is a common link between civilized society – social life – and the savage state of man – the non-social grounding of social life. The project of the first parts of the *Wealth of Nations* is to constitute the division of labor as such a simple determination.*

In this effort Smith attempts to consider the system of needs in terms of its origin in a mutual dependence of producers as a natural condition. Since the division of labor is outside of society the needs provided are also taken implicitly to be the fixed system of needs of the species within nature. More precisely, the absence of a social determination of the division of labor precludes the real social determination of the products of the division of labor – wealth. But, since the division of labor is the process within which Smith seeks to ground wealth and with it civilized society, it is necessary that the real social character of the division of labor assert itself even where that must contradict Smith's explicit conception.

The division of labor it turns out has certain pre-conditions: 'the accumulation of stock must, in the nature of things, be previous to the division of labor' (p. 260). This is not to be understood as essentially the description of an historical process but of a condition which springs from 'the nature of things,' in particular, from the nature of the division of labor. In other words not only is there a process in which the accumulation of stock *precedes* the division of labor but the very conception of the division of labor as it is to be understood in the *Wealth of Nations* presupposes the accumulation of stock. According to Smith (p. 259):

when the division of labor has once been thoroughly introduced, the produce of a man's own labor can supply but a very small part of his occasional wants. The far greater part of them are supplied by the produce of other men's labor, which he purchases with the produce, or what is the same thing, with the price of the produce of his own. But this purchase cannot be made until such time as the produce of his own labor has not only been completed, but sold. A stock of goods of different kinds, therefore, must be stored up somewhere sufficient to maintain him, and supply him with the materials and tools of his work, until such time as the produce of his own labor has not only been completed, but sold.

The specifically social character of civilized economy does not, therefore, emerge as the immediate expression of the division of labor but has presuppositions which are logically prior to the division of labor.

The accumulation of stock which serves as the condition for the division of labor appears in two forms: first, as the stock of the individual laborer, and second, as capital which is employed in the hiring of laborers. From the point of view of the individual worker the stock must be stored up '*either* in his own

* This reduction has also a certain historical basis which leads Marx to characterize Smith as the 'political economist par excellence of the period of manufacture,' *Capital* (New York: International Publishers, 1967), vol. I, p. 348.

possession or in that of some other person' (p. 259, emphasis added). Stock exists in two forms depending on whether it is owned by the worker himself or is owned by a capitalist who hires the worker. As stock it is, however, indifferent to its conditions of ownership so that in either case it is the stock, as such, which makes possible the division of labor. The simplicity of Smith's conception of stock as 'goods of different kinds' corresponds to the simplicity of Smith's conception of the division of labor as the division of 'work' into its various parts. For the theme of the *Wealth of Nations* as a whole to emerge it is essential that the capital which forms the pre-condition for the division of labor be considered as a form of the naturally defined stock of the individual. Only in so far as capital is reduced to stock is the production process of civilized society revealed to differ from that of the savage state of man only in form and in degree. However, when Smith follows through his conception of stock it is immediately revealed as a specific social relation: capital. The purely natural determination breaks down within the *Wealth of Nations* when stock is recognized as a form of capital and when capital is recognized to involve a specific social relation. But, the involvement of capital in a specific social relation is already implied, though not explicitly stated, by Smith in his discussion of the division of labor in production which has as its tacit precondition, the accumulation of capital and the social differentiation between capital and wage-labor.

At first, the accumulation of stock is considered as a pre-condition of the labor of the individual once the division of labor is introduced. However, the individual, who requires the accumulation of stock for his own maintenance, immediately divides his stock into two parts: 'he *naturally* endeavours to derive a revenue from the greater part of it; reserving only so much for his immediate consumption as may maintain him till this revenue begins to come in' (p. 262, emphasis added). It is not an accidental matter arising out of the whim of the individual that he divide his stock into capital and consumption but a naturally determined necessity. It is a necessity bound up with the idea of stock itself. Earlier in the work Smith argues that 'as soon as stock has accumulated in the hands of particular persons, some of them will naturally employ it in setting to work industrious persons, whom they will supply with materials and subsistence, in order to make a profit by the sale of their work, or by what their labor adds to the value of the materials' (p. 48). Stock cannot remain the stock of the individual (who is a particular person purely by merit of his ownership of stock) but is immediately transformed into 'capital.' Capital is stock owned by particular persons which returns to them a revenue. The revenue results from their hiring and setting to work 'industrious people' in order to make 'a profit by the sale of *their* work.'

It is essential to recognize at this point that not only has Smith explicitly defined capital as a part of stock but he has identified, in principle, the existence of stock with the existence of capital. It is in the nature of stock that it resolve itself, in major part, into capital. Furthermore, the resolution of stock into

capital involves Smith in the identification of stock in general with the existence of a determinate social system within which revenue is made off of the
sale of the results of the labor of others which others are hired out of capital.
'Whatever part of his stock a man employs as capital, he always expects it to
be replaced to him with a profit. He employs it, therefore, in maintaining
productive hands only' (p. 316). The accumulation of stock therefore means
the accumulation of capital and that form of economic organization which
exists where capital is accumulated is capitalist society.

Wealth, which now appears in the form of stock, appears simultaneously as
capital where the existence of wealth, and therefore of 'wealthy society,'
expresses itself not only in the distinction between saving and consumption
but in the bifurcation of society into those who own the stock and do the
hiring and those who own no stock but get hired. The fact that only 'particular
persons' accumulate stock signifies the existence of a social relation between
persons which is not evidently reducible to that which connects individuals
through the division of labor. Society involves not only the division of labor
but at the same time the concentration of labor in opposition to the means of
labor from which labor has been excluded. The expansion of capital and the
making of profit by the sale of the work of others becomes the pre-condition
of the uniting of labor with the objective conditions of labor.

There is, therefore, an opposition within the concept of stock (and therefore
wealth) as a pre-condition of the labor of the individual who owns the stock
and as a pre-condition of the labor of those who do not own the stock. This
latter is an opposition between stock as individual property and stock as
capital involving a social relation between capital and wage-labor.

The necessity of considering stock explicitly in its social existence, in terms
of the relationships (e.g. of property) which give it definite existence, subverts
the original conception of stock as simply means of labor, goods of different
kinds. The failure of Smith to retain the unity and simplicity of his original
conception in the case of stock has also implications for the concept of
division of labor. The labor exists in a definite relation to the accumulation of
stock and is not indifferent to the varying determinations of its conception.

2

The notion of the division of labor, as Smith employs it, hides two distinct
conceptual determinations.[2] The division of labor is, in the first instance, the
division of labor in production. The famous example of the first chapter of
the *Wealth of Nations* describes the division of the production of a given
commodity (pins) into a number of separate tasks each of which is allocated
to a separate individual (p. 4):

One man draws out the wire, another straightens it, a third cuts it, a fourth points
it, a fifth grinds it at the top for receiving the head; to make the head requires two

or three distinct operations; to put it on is a peculiar business; to whiten the pins is another. . . .

All of this is by way of contribution to the production of a single commodity (pins). The separate steps in the production process are connected directly without the mediation of exchange. The individual who straightens the wire does not purchase that wire from the person who draws it out so that the wire once having been drawn out is not itself (as yet) a commodity. This division of labor in production contrasts with the division of labor in society which is a relation mediated by exchange of commodities between commodity owners. Smith argues, on the immediately succeeding page, that the division of labor accounts for the 'separation of different trades and employments from one another' (p. 5). The division of labor is now the division of labor in society. The individual elements into which the labor is divided relate one to the other through the exchange of commodities. They are different 'trades and employments' not simply different tasks within a given trade or employment.

In principle, the division of labor takes a *given* work process and simply changes its form of application, separating off its constituent parts and allocating them to different individuals. The process, seen as a whole, is unaltered while the change in its application allows for a considerable increase in its scope. The lack of change in the work process as a whole is critical for the argument of the *Wealth of Nations*. It allows for an immediate comparison between the production process of non-civilized economy and the production process of civilized society which are, in substance, seen to be identical. Such a conception leaves the process of production in its purely natural state, a state independent of any introduction of illicit social form. The division of labor in society is, at first, such an illicit introduction of particular form as a defining characteristic of production itself. Smith, therefore, reduces the difference of form of the two aspects of the division of labor to a matter of appearance.

For Smith the division of labor in society is, in principle, identical to the division of labor in production but, due to the fact that in the case of the former the division of labor cannot be observed to operate within the confines of a given manufacture it is not readily visible as *the* division of labor. For this reason the division of labor in society as a whole has 'been much less observed' (p. 46).* Smith thereby takes the social form in which the division of labor 'appears' as purely illusory. This is a central characteristic of all of classical thinking for which social relations serve to distort and obscure the underlying 'real' process.

The fact that the products of the division of labor are exchanged is purely formal and has nothing to do with the nature of the division of labor itself.

* This statement leads Marx to argue that, for Smith, the difference between the division of labor in production (for Marx, in manufacture) and the division of labor in society as a whole 'is merely subjective,' *Capital, ed. cit.,* vol. I, p. 354; cf. Ronald Meek, *Studies in the Labor Theory of Value* (London: Lawrence & Wishart, 1973), p. 61.

Since there is no difference in nature between the two forms of the division of labor, when Smith directs his attention to either one separately there exists no compulsion for him to take the other into account. Where there is no difference neither can there be any relation.

The original standpoint of the *Wealth of Nations* is that of the reduction of the division of labor in society to the division of labor in production, therefore to the division of labor as such; implicitly this is the reduction of the social form to its natural substance. Yet, the text very rapidly reverses itself eliminating the division of labor in production from consideration and focusing exclusively on the division of labor among independent commodity producers, the conceptual basis of 'simple commodity economy.' The division of labor in society becomes the division of labor between independent producers, independent in that they own their own means of production, their own stock. The absorption of the division of labor in production into the division of labor in society leads to the general conclusion of the first chapter (p. 11):

It is the great multiplication of productions of all the different arts, in consequence of the division of labor, which occasions, in a well governed society, that universal opulance which extends itself to the lowest ranks of the people. Every workman has a great quantity of his own work to dispose of beyond what he himself has occasion for; and every other workman being in exactly the same situation, he is enabled to exchange a great quantity of his own goods for a great quantity, or, what comes to the same thing, for the price of a great quantity of theirs. He supplies them abundantly with what they have occasion for, and they accommodate him as amply with what he has occasion for, and a general plenty diffuses itself through all the different ranks of society.

Such a conception directly denies the social basis of the division of labor in production. The latter, as described in the example of the pin factory, presupposes the accumulation of stock in the form of capital. The notion of a division of labor in production therefore contradicts the idea that 'every workman has a great quantity of his own work to dispose of' and that 'every other workman' is 'in exactly the same situation.' The division of labor in production presupposes that 'particular persons' accumulate stock with which they put others to work in order to make a profit off of their labor. Thus, the division of labor in production is not simply the division of labor but the capitalistically developed and defined division of labor. It is the division of labor in capitalist production. What this means is that the transformed character of the production process which is the predominant concern of Smith's discussion of division of labor presupposes a determinate social form in which the expansion of the scale of production (which allows for the co-operation of large numbers of workers within the process of production) is made possible by the accumulation of capital.

On the other hand, the division of labor in society appears as a relation of independent commodity producers and therefore explicitly excludes the existence of stock in the form of capital. It is this latter which forms the basis of exchange. The division of labor in production presupposes the accumulation of capital which, in turn, presupposes the development of the division of labor in society. The division of labor in society implies mutual interdependence in production. The individual producer no longer provides for himself his basic necessities but comes to depend upon other producers. As a result of this development the individual producer must now store up a stock of means of subsistence to sustain him through the production period. The opposition between stock as wealth and stock as capital is revealed to be one side of the opposition between the two forms of the division of labor. Stock as wealth is a pre-condition of production for exchange on the part of the individual commodity producer. It is therefore a condition for the division of labor in society. Stock as capital involves the concentration of labor as wage-labor and therefore is a condition for the division of labor in production. Accumulation of stock as capital is a necessary condition for the division of labor in production but is not a necessary condition for the division of labor in society. The latter necessitates the accumulation of stock but not capital.

But now, what appeared at the outset as two aspects of one process, or, more correctly, as that process – division of labor – and its form – division of labor in society as a whole – has become two completely separate processes, two different and unconnected divisions of labor. What started out as the reduction of social form to natural substance now tears the form apart from its substance so that the division of labor among independent commodity producers is not division of labor in production at all, the former wholly excluding the specific existence of the latter. The contradictions of Smith's method result in two opposing constructions, one in which the different forms are reduced to a common substance and in which differences are attributed to appearance, and a second in which the different forms lose all of their intrinsic relation and constitute themselves in complete opposition one to the other, eventually to appear as distinct economic systems. The differing aspects of capitalist economy become different economies, different systems of production: simple commodity production and capitalist commodity production. The pseudo-historical method expresses the severing of the moments of the conception of capitalist production into opposing systems of production whose opposition leaves those distinct moments indifferent one to the other. In this sense, the two aspects of Smith's method merge since both have as their result the abolition of the intrinsic relations among the different elements of the conception of capitalist production, the breaking apart of the inner logic of capitalist economy.

At the beginning of Chapter I the exchange of commodities which serves as the social mediation for the division of labor has no substantial reality. Smith deals with division of labor and argues that the division of labor is given its real expression in the concentration of a group of workers within a given manufacture. In his discussion of capital, the implicit assumption of such a form of production, the accumulation of capital is made explicit as the pre-condition of production. By the beginning of Chapter IV, however, the whole of society, rather than characterized as one large manufacture, has become a large collection of merchants (p. 22):

When the division of labor has once been thoroughly established, it is but a very small part of a man's wants which the produce of his own labor can supply. He supplies the far greater part of them by exchanging that surplus part of the produce of his own labor, which is over and above his consumption, for such parts of the produce of other men's labor as he has occasion for. Every man thus lives by exchanging, or becomes in some measure a merchant, and the society itself grows to be what is properly a commercial society.

In this case society is made up not of co-operative workers engaged in one great production process but of independent merchants and therefore independent producers. The thrust of the original reduction of the division of labor in society to division of labor in production (or division of labor as such) is to obliterate the exchange relations which tie together the elements of the division of labor and therefore to constitute the different manufactures as simply parts of one great manufacture. The constitution of the division of labor as a division exclusively among independent producers, on the other hand, constitutes each individual not as a worker in a universal enterprise but as a merchant. To be sure, within the capitalist economy individuals may be both workers and 'merchants' in that they sell their labor-power in the market, their capacity to labor takes the form of a commodity. But what Smith has done is to sever the different determinations of the individual within capitalist economy and to constitute them as the sole defining characteristics of differing forms of production. Smith, however, always retains the differing elements within the overall unity of the category 'division of labor' which appears to be indifferent, so far as Smith is concerned, to its specific determinations. The concept of 'division of labor' undergoes no alteration but its use changes substantially and without explicit recognition. Such enforcement of unity of language where differentiation is indicated by the language itself characterizes classical thinking not only on the problems of capital and division of labor but equally on the theory of value and of the relation of value to labor. The opposition between society and the state of nature implies the indifference of the concepts of social thought to their specificity to social life. The distinctions which mark the social determination of those relations lose their force once society is reduced to its natural ground. The differentiation of concepts, the opposed aspects of division of labor, gives way to their reduction to a single, nature-given, relation.

3

It is necessary, at this point, to provide an account for the reversal of procedure in Chapter I of the *Wealth of Nations* in which the reduction of division of labor among independent producers to division of labor within a given manufacture becomes a reduction of division of labor within a given manufacture to division of labor among independent commodity producers. This reversal must be accounted for in terms of the differing manners in which Smith effects a theoretical account for economic life and in particular in terms of the presence or absence of such an account. The issue, then, is one of the presence or absence of adequate ground for the exchange system. Is that system to emerge as a moment of a self-generating process which accounts for exchange as an element on an ongoing cycle? Or is the exchange system to be simply posited as the expression of an underlying natural or individual force which must, from the point of view of analysis, be taken as given? Although the positing of the division of labor as such a force takes Smith at least one step beyond the standpoint of modern economics (for which the existence of division of labor would deny the central conception of exchange) it is none the less, for Smith, an abstract assertion of division of labor which remains unaccountable rather than systematically grounded.

This manner of treatment of the division of labor implies its exclusion from determination within economic theory. The division of labor appears as a natural or technical condition whose presence is arbitrary from the standpoint of economic life. This exclusion of the division of labor and refusal to give to it a social determination conflicts essentially with the classical notion of an identity of civilized society and division of labor. The latter not only asserts the social determination of division of labor but equates that determination with the conception of social life. So long as the division of labor is considered by Smith to be firmly established as the mode of production of wealth and therefore of wealthy society its connection to production tends to deprive it of its systematic connection to civilized society making of division of labor no more than a nature-given condition. On the other side, so long as division of labor is identified with civilized society it is the dependence established among independent labors and effected through exchange which is critical and this leads Smith to consider division of labor as a system of mutual dependence among independent consumers and producers – division of labor in society as synonymous with the concept of civil society.

The original reduction of division of labor among independent producers to division of labor within a given manufacture had as its rationale the constitution of a social form (the exchange of commodities) as an expression of an underlying material and natural process; the identification of division of labor among independent producers as a form of a materially determined working activity. The weakness of this reduction is that if it were made explicit then the determination of the origin of the division of labor becomes problematic. To be sure, as a purely natural process the division of labor has no economic origin. Yet, the very notion of division of labor serves to distinguish civilized from non-civilized society which distinction directly challenges the generality of the notion of division of labor. Closer investigation has revealed that the origin of the division of labor is in the accumulation of capital and that the latter is a specifically social process which is not directly reducible to a natural function of the individual. The concept of the 'stock of the individual' which roots the capital in an individual and natural property disappears almost as rapidly as it is asserted. This disappearance expresses the dominance of the capital relation and the inability of classical political economy to conceive of production independently of its capitalist form. So long as the division of labor is conceived in terms of the direct production process the accumulation of capital remains as its central pre-condition. The difference between civilization and barbarism cannot be grasped in terms of a difference in form of a naturally given labor process. In this case the relation between civilized and non-civilized society becomes problematic.

What Smith considers explicitly as the effect of accumulation of capital on the labor process is, in reality and implicitly within the text, the effect of the logical connection between capital and production. For Smith the existence of capital is confused with its process of emergence so that its self-movement is identically that process by which it comes originally into existence. This reduces the theoretical problem of civilized society once again to an historical problem, and the history appears as a deformation of nature (which, in a sense, it is). Once, however, the division of labor is tied to capital historically it is also tied to it logically. The implications of this connection are a central motive force in the argument of the *Wealth of Nations*.

Where the division of labor is conceived exclusively in terms of independent producers, 'merchants,' it no longer has the accumulation of capital as its pre-condition. A stock may be necessary but capital is not. With the division of labor in production, production itself has become a directly social process and not the immediate relation of the individual to nature. On the other hand, where the division of labor is exclusively a division among independent producers, production is a direct relation of the individual to nature, or, at least, appears that way. If this idea can be sustained then the division of labor, which is the *differentia specifica* of civilized society, can be rooted in a purely individual substance, without reference to the capital relation. Thus, that 'certain propensity in human nature . . . to truck, barter, and exchange one thing for another' (p. 13) becomes the basis of the division of labor. Now *the division of labor is the division of labor among independent commodity producers*. The conditions for this result are, first, the reduction of capital to stock and the denial of Smith's own assertion that stock is 'naturally' transformed into a fund for the hiring of 'industrious persons' in order to make a profit off of their labor, and second, the reduction of the division of labor to the division of labor among independent commodity producers.

The reduction of division of labor in society to division of labor in production establishes the natural character of the division of labor and therefore the relation of civilization to barbarism along a common dimension which is the given labor process. The reduction of division of labor to division of labor in society further establishes that the origin of the division of labor, therefore of society itself, is also natural and individual. In this way civilization is given a purely natural determination. Capitalist production is reduced to a natural function of the individual, has its real origin in the savage state of man.

The *Wealth of Nations* is two-sided in its treatment of production. It first obliterates any distinction in form of the production process taking the idea of production, in principle, to be independent of the social form in which it 'appears.' On the other side the peculiar social form of production serves as a pre-condition of production, as well as serving to define society itself. For Smith, the determinate social form is reduced to its natural definition as production as such while, by that very fact, production comes to be seen as socially determined. The distortions of the concept of social production which derive from Smith's conflation of the two aspects of the division of labor distort the conception of social life by attributing, on one side, the qualities of social production to man in general and to man's innate relation to nature and, on the other, attributing to nature the specific qualities of social production.

What remains problematic is the construction of the natural production process and the grounding of the division of labor in a natural propensity of the individual. Investigation of the relation of division of labor to exchange reveals the limitations of Smith's conception of nature and the rooting of nature so far as it exists for society in the peculiar conditions of capitalist production. The reduction of society to a natural condition has been considered in terms of the two forms of the division of labor and the relation of the division of labor both to the accumulation of capital and to the propensity of the individual to truck, barter, and exchange. The real status of nature as a distorted form of capitalist production emerges in the mutual determination of exchange and division of labor.

III Exchange and division of labor

1

The exchange of commodities is originally a relation which is rooted exclusively in the division of labor between independent commodity producers. On one level, Smith deals with simple commodity economy, a system in which each producer owns his own means of production and within which the labor embodied in a commodity is exclusively his own labor, i.e. the labor of the commodity producer himself. According to this interpretation (which is well-founded in Smith's exposition) the transition in the text which leads from 'real price' to the 'component parts of price' parallels, and is based upon, an historical transition in the development of the exchange economy. The two stages of the theoretical discussion reflect two stages of economic development: 'simple commodity economy' and 'capitalist commodity production.' The transition itself is characterized by the accumulation of capital and the emergence of a distinction between capital and wage-labor. In simple commodity production the only rule which governs the exchange of commodities is their 'real price' which is the amount of labor required in their production (i.e. the amount of labor of the individual producer himself) which is equal to the amount of labor which those commodities command in the market. With the accumulation of capital it becomes necessary for the producer to 'share' the product with the owner of the capital so that the return to that capital must equally be entered into the price of the commodity which is now determined as the sum of the distributive shares which are the component parts of the price.

The distinction between exchange based on labor time and exchange based on wages, profit, and rent does not originate in the existence of materially defined means of production but in the ownership of those means of production and in the social process through which they are united with labor in production. Within the *Wealth of Nations* this distinction, which is also a transition, bridges the 'historical' dividing line between exchange of equal commodity owners and exchange between labor and capital as well as the theoretical dividing line between the determination of exchange on the basis of real price and the determination of exchange on the basis of the component parts of price. The second transition is absorbed into the first so that the labor principle disappears within the realm of capitalist commodity production just as the capital-labor relation has disappeared within the definition of 'simple commodity economy.' The suspension of the labor principle within capitalist economy and its determination within the simple commodity economy hinges on the conception of simple commodity production. The labor theory of value originates with the grounding of exchange within simple commodity economy.

Within such an economy each worker is assumed to own his own means of production. It is precisely the *difference* in the nature of his labor which underlies the exchange of commodities. The laboring activity of the individual is wholly defined by his position in the social division of labor. The specificity of that labor is determined jointly with the specificity of the means of production employed by the laborer. The ownership of the means of production by the commodity producer may, therefore, be seen to imply the differentiation of labor as the foundation of exchange. This highlights the connection between the division of labor and the exchange of commodities. The difference of labor created by the division of labor is the origin of exchange. However, this difference of labor, in so far as it is also the qualitative basis of exchange, must also be seen to imply an equality of labor which is the quantitative basis of exchange. An exchange involves a comparison of qualitatively distinct types of labor and, therefore, an implicit reduction of those differences to a common denominator. It is in the exchange relation that this equality of labor first emerges.

If the entire social existence of the individual is defined by the exchange of commodities, so that his individuality as a commodity producer is not subject to the exchange relation as a social function, then the comparison of labor takes place exclusively within the act of exchange as such. The social character of the labor has nothing to do with the laboring act which takes place wholly outside of social life.* 'Labor' is a relationship between the individual and nature, therefore a purely 'natural' relationship (pp. 30–1):

Labor was the first price, the original purchase money that was paid for all things. It was not by gold or by silver but by labor, that all the wealth of the world was originally purchased; and its value, to those who possess it, and who want to exchange it for some new productions, is precisely equal to the quantity of labor which it can enable them to purchase or command.

Further on Smith adds that (p. 33, emphasis added):

equal quantities of labor, at all times and places, may be said to be of equal value *to the laborer*. In his ordinary state of health, strength, and spirits, in the ordinary degree of his skill and dexterity, he must always lay down the same portion of his ease, his liberty, and his happiness.

At this point the concept of labor is articulated by Smith independently of the division of labor so that labor is measured with regard not to its social relation but with respect to the individual and his 'ease, his liberty, and his happiness.'

On one side the labor principle which grounds the exchange of commodities arises directly and immediately out of the social division of labor which underlies the equality of disparate labors. On the other side the individuality of the labor is purely individual. The individualization implied by simple commodity economy obliterates the *social* basis of that economy, the division of labor. In this case the equality of labor is not simply expressed in the process of exchange, it is defined and determined in the exchange relation. The labor itself is purely individual and natural being defined wholly within the relation between the individual as a free subject (defining his happiness and expressing his freedom) and nature. It is at this point that Smith's analysis of the social process is seen to clearly emerge from and, therefore, depend upon the characteristics of pre-civilized economy. The individual in his pure relation to nature lacked the human qualities of the individual in his social existence. But, social life, which is at this point summed up in exchange, is defined with respect to a non-social, non-human substance and finds itself swallowed up by the conception of pre-human existence. The explicitly social aspect of the individual, his relation of exchange, has come to be defined as purely natural and individual, to have lost any legitimately social determination. Individuality stands here in opposition to society and not as the result of an individua-

---

* Cf. K. Marx, *Theories of Surplus-Value* (Moscow: n.d.), vol. I: 'The emphasis here lies on the equalization, brought about through the division of labor and exchange, of *my* labor with the labor of *others*, in other words with social labor (the fact that *my* labor too, or the labor contained in my commodities, is already *socially* determined, has fundamentally changed its character, escapes Adam)' (pp. 74–5).

tion brought about only on the part of and within society. Rather than a socially determined property of the individual, freedom comes to represent the individual's self-determination outside of society.

While this remains Smith's self-understanding and ultimate justification of the labor principle it is not to be presumed that such an analysis is capable of coherent expression. The contradictions intrinsic to this statement of the labor principle express themselves in a forced retreat within the text in the direction of a social grounding of the theory of value and of the idea of production.

2

Within the realm of simple commodity economy the labor of the individual as 'labor' continually strives for a social determination which it finds to be forced upon it by the connection between exchange and the division of labor. Labor, as purely subjective and therefore as purely individual, remains the same labor which *defines the individuality of the laborer*. The particularity of the labor is the product of the division of a social substance, the division of *labor*. Thus the very idea that individuality is expressed in labor seeks to give a specific content to that labor and therefore to the individuality as well. The labor involves, for the individual, precisely the laying down of a portion of his liberty; in other words the sacrifice of a part of his freedom as a self-defining individual. The individual now finds himself determined in the labor process which stands against him, opposes him. It is not pure, indeterminate existence that underlies exchange (as is the case, in principle, in the neo-classical theory of value) but an existence determined in the labor process. The individuality of that process emerges as the product of a specifically social fact: division of labor (p. 15):

The difference of natural talents in different men is, in reality, much less than we are aware of; and the very different genius which appears to distinguish men of different professions, when grown to maturity, is not so much the cause as the effect of the division of labor. The difference between the most dissimilar characters, between a philosopher and a common street porter, for example, seems to arise not so much from nature, as from habit, custom and education.

Equality of labor now becomes natural while the differentiation of labor and therefore its presumed origin in the individual personality becomes a purely social condition.

Labor is natural in that it springs from the common characteristics that define individuals as human. The principle which Smith establishes against pre-civilized economy overthrows the conception of the labor principle which is, in its original formulation, the direct expression of pre-civilized economic organization. For man, the only truly 'natural,' or adequately 'human,' form of existence is social. For Smith, the non-human now appears to be eminently unnatural while the social is natural in that it springs directly from the defining characteristics of human activity. As a result of this the natural equality of labor reflects a social condition of that labor.

The concept of 'nature' has undergone a shift from its origin in the relation of the individual to 'nature,' i.e. to that which is outside of the sphere of the human and the world of 'individuals.' Nature has come to signify social life and specifically the social relations of division of labor and exchange. This fluctuation of the natural condition between a social and a non-social connotation reappears throughout classical political economy. It reveals, in the use of language, that the original non-social state of man which was natural and now is unnatural derived its natural character from its conceptual dependence on the social production process. The latter, which is eventually identified with capitalist production, is natural so that the early and rude state of man is natural to the extent that it partakes of the characteristics of capitalist production: individual property, labor, and exchange. The early and rude state of man is, in this sense, very definitely a state of society.

Labor is natural in so far as it is quantitatively and qualitatively determined and judged through a relationship between socially determined individuals. But if the natural character of the equality of labor expresses a social condition then the quantitative measure of the laboring process, which is 'labor,' can no longer spring directly out of a relation between the individual and nature. If labor is defined individually then it cannot be 'labor' at all but only so and so's labor. There could be no objective principle for comparing one person's labor with another's. The status of the individual's work as labor could not come under consideration. Yet, Smith argues that 'there may be more *labor* in one hour's hard *work* than in two hours easy business, in an hour's application to a trade which cost ten years labor to learn, than in a month's industry at an ordinary and honest employment' (p. 31, emphasis added). The activity of the individual, his *work*, may or may not be *labor*; so that labor is distinguished from itself as 'work' and 'labor.' The principle devolves not on to the subjective evaluation of the work but on to the determination of whether the work of the individual is or is not labor and, further, the extent to which the specific type of work allotted to the individual by the division of labor incorporates more or less labor.

The transformation of work into labor takes place through the market. The adjustment of one type of work to another is accomplished 'not by any accurate measure, but by the higgling and bargaining of the market, and according to that sort of rough equality which, though not exact, is sufficient for carrying on the business of common life' (p. 31). On the next page Smith discovers that the difficulty which has stood in the way of his discovering this property of human activity is that labor is an 'abstract notion' rather than a 'plain, palpable object.' The social existence of the products of labor is, in practice, indiscernible when set beside their existence as 'plain, palpable objects.' For Smith, as for all of classical political economy, the social relations which form the real subject-matter of the science present themselves not as its object but as the central impediment of analysis. These social relations form a maze to which political economy holds the key. Political economy grounds the system social relations in naturally defined conditions of production without recognizing those natural conditions as the distorted expressions of social production.

The fact that work expresses itself as labor only through the market has already led Smith to conclude that the character of work as labor is an exclusively market phenomenon. But, at this point it becomes apparent that the work which appears as labor in the market is no longer independent of its incipient transformation into abstract human labor. It has already taken on a social character.

The 'abstract' existence of the commodities exchanged in the market is that they embody 'labor.' Labor is distinguished from work in the process of exchange in the course of which the work of the individual is compared with the work of other individuals and is measured by an abstract standard which emerges through the interplay of market exchange. It must be emphasized that it is no longer adequate to view abstract labor as the product of exchange *per se*. The market adjusts individual work to the standard of labor, it expresses the quantitative relation of work to labor, of the individual commodity producer to society. It does not, in itself, create the basis for equality of labor. For Smith the latter is a natural product (therefore a social product) the natural character of which is expressed in exchange. It exists to one degree or another within the laboring activity, it creates the individuality of that activity, and it measures simultaneously the natural and the social character of the individual's work.

The *Wealth of Nations* reproduces, within the concept of labor, the contradictions in the determination of the division of labor, capital, and exchange. The different perceptions of the individual, of nature, and of social life and the different principles which underlie their unity give to the work its complexity and its contradictory structure. At certain points the individual and the natural combine so that the relations are understood to be of a non-social character. Capital is nothing more than a mere form of appearance of stock. Labor is a relation of the individual to nature. But no sooner are such conceptions posited than they are forcibly broken apart. The individual character of the labor shows itself to be a product of the division of labor in society. In the process of defining the social relations of exchange as phenomenal expressions of a purely individual substance ('labor') that substance undergoes an internal restructuring and reappears in a radically different form. Equality of labor as the basis of exchange begins as labor determined by the individual, as purely individual labor. In viewing equality of labor as such a basis Smith notices the falling apart of labor into 'work' and 'labor.' But once this distinction is allowed both work and labor come to be transformed into explicitly social products. The individuality of labor, the work *qua* work is a product of the social division of labor. It is measured by an abstract social measure through which it is translated into labor. Whereas labor was originally individual and natural now it is natural because it is, or to the extent that it is, social. Within the division of labor the individual expresses his human existence through his external relations with other individuals and then through his existence as a socially defined individual. It is precisely the particular difference implied by the division of labor which also implies the identity of labor and the social mediation of the individual labors which transforms them into elements of the labor of society as a whole, or, more correctly, reveals them to be elements of that whole.

The differences implied by division of labor are differences not of the individual taken in isolation but of an individual whose very individuality is a product of a social process – division of labor – and, therefore, whose individuality is dependent on the location of the individual in the social whole. To consider a society in which differences of labor are not determined by the division of labor (are, in fact, purely individual) is to consider a condition within which the reconstitution of those differences into a social whole becomes impossible. Such a whole could be nothing more than the sum of its parts, possessing no substance not immediately contained in the individual elements. This is the real significance of the form of pre-civilized society which appears at the outset of Chapter VI (p. 47):

If among a nation of hunters, for example, it usually costs twice the labor to kill a beaver which it does to kill a deer, one beaver should naturally exchange for, or be worth two deer. It is natural that what is usually the produce of two days or two hours labor, should be worth double of what is usually the produce of one day's or one hour's labor.

In this case equality of labor is not grounded in a social process, either of the division of labor or of exchange of commodities. In the world of hunters of beaver and deer Smith presents a true savage society in that there exists a *difference* of labor without any division of labor. The very characterization of this as a difference of *labor* reflects the typical illicit introduction of specific social forms into savage society which, in fact, determine the savage state of man within the *Wealth of Nations*. The difference of labor in such a primitive society is important precisely because it is intended as an expression of division of labor which is not, however, predicated on anything other than the pure individuality of the activity of the individual hunter. There is no mutual dependence as exists within the division of labor in civilized society.

The *division* of labor, while it implies difference and opposition of labor, also requires a process of equalization by which the individual labors express themselves as elements of a whole, thereby revealing not simply their difference as specifically different applications of a common substance. The division of labor implies not only opposition but also dependence. The very category, 'division of labor,' implies at once the transparent and obvious *difference* of labor which forms the immediate subject-matter of the *Wealth of Nations* and simultaneously the 'abstract,' and therefore impenetrable, substance of that difference: labor.* For Smith the division of labor requires not only that individuals do different tasks (as is also true in the beaver and deer economy) but equally that these tasks be in fact different elements of a single production process. Smith goes so far as to intimate that all of the major tasks of production in civilized economy are parts of a single manufacture, and in so doing constitutes civilized society as one big work-place. 'In those great manufactures . . . which are destined to supply the great wants of the great body of the people, every different branch of work employs so great a number of workmen, that it is impossible to collect them all into one single branch' (p. 4). When the division of labor in society is considered as a form of the division of labor in production, then the production process which is subject to division is production directly by society as a whole. It is, therefore, a total production process, that original natural process which is divided into its constituent parts but must still assert itself as the underlying rationale of the individual processes into which it is divided. These latter processes are mutually dependent in so far as they are defined as parts of a whole and only in so far as they are so defined. In contrast to the beaver and deer economy no single process can exist in isolation so that the interconnections of the different processes are not purely external (as in the case of the exchange of beaver and deer which exchange is not necessary to production) but they are both external and internal. They are external in so far as the mediation of exchange becomes necessary to their unification. They are internal in the sense that the connections among the distinct processes are connections within a given overall production process. The unity of the production process as a whole, the mutual dependence of the different labors, therefore the *identity* of those labors, becomes the basis of the exchange of commodities. It is the exchange of commodities which links the individual parts of the whole to that whole.

Smith grounds the exchange of commodities in the difference of labor. First, it is grounded in the pure difference of individual labor (as in the hunting economy). In this case exchange is seen to have a purely individual and natural foundation, even when that exchange is rooted in division of labor. But this is adequate only so long as division of labor is identified with the simple individuation of labor, while Smith himself considers the difference of labor of primitive society as distinct from the division of labor which characterizes civilized society. It is division of labor which turns exchange into a process necessary for the sustenance of the individual which therefore constitutes that individual as fully a member of society. The division of labor constitutes the individual as determined in his individuality by a system of

* 'After different forms of concrete labor, such as agriculture, manufacture, navigation, trade, etc. had each in turn been declared the true source of wealth, Adam Smith, proclaimed labor in general, and namely in its general form of *division of labor*, to be the only source of material wealth of use-values,' K. Marx, *Contribution to the Critique of Political Economy* (Chicago: Charles Kerr, 1904), p. 67.

mutual dependence among individuals which is of a definitely social character. It is this form of mutuality implied in the division of labor which defines civilized society.

It is the peculiar division of labor of civilized society that not only serves as the foundation of exchange but also serves as the conceptual basis for the identity of labor, the equalization of labor, and therefore for the concept of general, abstract, labor. In so far as the concept of labor is itself dependent on the presence of civilized society the construction of primitive society as a society of exchange based on labor time involves Smith in the illicit intro-duction into the primitive state of man of relations peculiar to civilization. The notion of individuality based in the difference of labor which characterizes the hunting economy is a product of social production. Primitive economy no longer stands in opposition to civilized society as the natural form in relation to which civilized society is defined but as itself a distorted product of the conception of civilized society. The abstract labor which is the basis of exchange in the *Wealth of Nations* rather than forming a common element of savage and civilized society appears as the peculiar function of civilized society.

The division of labor entails a process which actively divides an original substance ('labor') but within which the divided poles retain that substance as an implicit unity. Labors do not simply exist as divided and separate but contain in their opposition also the unity of the common substance which defines each labor to be determinate only as a constituent element of the total social labor, as a part of labor. On one side, therefore, division of labor requires a process by which disparate labors reveal or express their equiva-lence; and on the other side, the common substance of labor must find implicit within it a force which drives it apart into its separate and opposing concrete forms. For Smith the exchange of commodities is that process which reveals the equation of labor within the division of labor. It is that process which, in effect, reunites distinct labors and forms them into a single whole. In the market, different products of different labors become equal and in so doing equate the labors employed in their production. The particular commod-ity, once brought into relation with another, different, particular commodity, reveals its intrinsic commonality with that apparently different commodity. Through the exchange of particular commodities the conditions for the renewal of the social production process are established, each particular labor reveals itself to be no more than a part of the total social labor. Particular labor now appears as general social labor.

But the exchange also effects a division of labors. Division of labor once posited in its form as opposition of labor requires a reunification via exchange. At the same time social labor posited as united requires division via exchange in order that it can re-establish the social labor process as a whole. Parti-cular labors must, then, exist as general labor subject to redistribution among particular production processes within the social division of labor. Yet this is only possible when particular labor exists not directly as such but only as incipient or implicitly particular labor in its existence prior to its particularization. This existence of incipiently divided labor is labor-power, the capacity of the laborer to engage in particular productions. Labor-power comes to be divided, to be distributed to particular production processes via its purchase and sale, via its exchange with capital. Indeed, for the division of labor to be effective the particular labors must lose their irreducibility so that the specialization of the labor is not within the particular activity but only in its location within a total process. With division of labor it is no longer the labor which particularizes itself through various tasks, it is the process as a whole which particularizes the labor. Since this particularity is not existent immediately within the labor, that labor appears outside of or prior to the labor process as wholly abstract and general, as labor-power.

In this sense it might be said that the purchase and sale of labor-power, the capital relation in general, exists implicitly within the notion of division of labor. How this implicit existence is expressed in the argument of the *Wealth of Nations* remains to be considered. The interpretation of Smith's theory of value must be reconsidered in order that it take into account this implied disappearance of the savage state of man along with the emerging dependence of the category of exchange upon the fully developed capital relation rather than upon the naturally given pre-social state of man.

With the division of labor constituted as a principle of mutual dependence of a specifically social character, the wealth of nations, which marks them as civilized, is required to exist in and through that system of mutual dependence. The existence of wealth once made specific to division of labor as its origin is also made specific to the mode of its provision: the system of commodity exchange. The explicit specification of wealth first to division of labor, then to capital, within the *Wealth of Nations* involves inevitably its specification to exchange.

IV The labor theory of value

1

The duality of Smith's theory of value has encouraged subsequent interpretation to treat the oppositions of that theory as contradictions between incompatible conceptions of the value problem: one in which the labor embodied in commodities is the determinant of their value and one in which the labor commanded by those commodities determines their value. Ricardo considers this to be the result of logical confusion while some later commentators appeal to the kind of pseudo-historical argument suggested by Smith himself at the outset of the chapter on the component parts of price. Neither of these positions is capable, however, of dealing adequately with the real relation of the different determinations of Smith's theory of value. The distinctive structure of that theory and the contradictions peculiar to it allow the differing determinations of the value theory to express different components of the value problem. The two theories of value while mutually exclusive on one logical plane also interpenetrate when considered on another. They emerge as different expressions of a single principle.

The contradictions within the statement of the labor-commanded principle allow that principle to both contain and deny the labor theory of value. When viewed in the abstract the labor commanded by a commodity may exist in two distinct forms. It may be labor already congealed in another commodity, previously expended in the production of that commodity. Alternatively the labor commanded by a commodity may be labor itself, the worker's laboring capacity as it is sold in the form of a commodity in the market.

For Smith the 'real worth' of a commodity is the labor expended in its production, the 'toil and trouble' of acquiring it. The value of a commodity to the person who owns it but does not wish himself to consume it is the labor for which it will exchange in the market. But this is the case even where it is not labor itself which is directly purchased by the commodity (p. 30):

What is bought with money or goods is purchased by labor, as much as what we acquire by the toil of our body. That money or those goods indeed save us this toil. They contain the value of a certain quantity of labor which we exchange for what is supposed at the time to contain the value of an equal quantity.

Even when we do not purchase directly 'labor' we none the less purchase 'labor' as it appears embodied in 'money and goods.' The purchase of labor embodied in a commodity is simply a special case of the exchange of labor for labor. The labor-commanded idea is not so much the direct denial of the labor-embodied principle as it is an attempt to incorporate that principle into a general statement of the foundation of exchange.

The conception of value as the labor which can replace through exchange the toil and trouble of the individual has two distinct implications. First, it ties value directly to labor, and second, it collapses the differing forms in which both value and labor actually appear into one form. In particular, it eliminates any distinction between labor as laboring activity and labor as a commodity in the market; between labor in process and labor as the past expenditure of human energy now fixed in a particular commodity. The analysis of value in the *Wealth of Nations* is an attempt to maintain this unity of meaning as regards value and labor in the course of working out the necessary differences between these forms.

The labor-commanded principle considers the purchase of goods by labor (the production process) and the purchase of labor by goods (the hiring of wage-labor) to be equivalently the purchase of labor by labor where the only difference is the form of existence of that labor. The immediate problem is to trace out the disintegration of this unity when it comes to confront concretely the exchange relation, the commodity form, and finally the commodity as a product of capital.

The labor-commanded principle is first viewed by Smith as expressing the direct exchange of the specific labor of a given individual for the labor of another individual, my toil and trouble for someone else's toil and trouble. That labor which is commanded by the commodity in exchange is labor which is embodied in the commodity purchased in that exchange. This is the notion, considered previously, of the exchange of commodities as the immediate expression of a social division of labor and as grounded in a division of labor among independent commodity producers. The labor which is purchased, indirectly, in this manner, is labor as it exists in the labor process, so much human activity expended in the past. This is the sense in which labor is the 'first price, the original purchase money that was paid for all things.' Labor in direct 'exchange' with nature is labor in its immediate concrete application, labor as it is defined in the division of labor and therefore as it is defined in opposition to other specific forms of labor. With the development of the division of labor the specific labor employed in the production of commodities can only be expressed as general labor through the mediation of exchange. In the statement of the labor-commanded principle the exchange of commodities connects directly individual labor (*my* labor) with another labor which is also directly individual.

However, according to Smith, once the division of labor is thoroughly established the individual comes to depend not upon the accidental and inessential exchange with another individual but on the world of exchange. 'Every man lives by exchanging or becomes in some measure a merchant, and society itself grows to be what is properly a commercial society' (p. 22). What is important from the standpoint of the individual is not the individual exchange in isolation but the individual exchange as one element or link in the continuous process of exchanging which encompasses all individuals and turns them into merchants. Each person's toil and trouble is not only comparable with the toil and trouble of another individual but with the toil and trouble of *any* other individual, therefore with toil and trouble as it exists apart from the individuality of its original definition. What is important is no longer the individuality of the labor and the exchange of individual labors but the exchange of my individual labor with general labor, with labor that is indifferent to the individual, with labor of a social character. In the exchange of individual commodities (and of the specific labor embodied in them) the peculiarity of the labor has become a matter of indifference as far as the principle of the exchange is concerned. With the division of labor in society this indifference becomes the basis of exchange.

None the less, in the labor-commanded principle the social nature of the labor which grounds the exchange of commodities, governs the proportionality of the exchange, is abridged at two points. First, the valuation process is a direct process and an immediate function of the individual and the specific labor of the individual. Where the labor commanded is the labor which has been embodied in another commodity it appears that it is specific labor of a determinate character rather than social, or abstract general, labor. Second, the measurement of the value of commodities does not confront the specificity of the commodity as the product of a given person's labor with a social measure, establishing the extent to which that labor is or is not a necessary constituent of the social division of labor. The exchange, rather than confronting the individual with a social measure confronts the individual with an individual principle where equality is not a socially enforced rule but the direct function of the confrontation of individuals who may define their own proportionality within the individual exchange and without regard to the social framework of that exchange as defined by the social division of labor. That social framework has no determinate existence within the individual exchange and cannot assert its necessity.

In the light of this result the labor-commanded theory is forced to effect a conceptual retreat and to reconstitute the exchange process in order that it not deny the social nature of production and the social mediation of exchange of commodities. It is necessary to make the quantitative principle of exchange qualitatively consistent with the nature of exchange as a process which asserts the indifference, therefore equality, of different objects and of different labors. For labor to ground exchange as a process of equalization of differences that labor must be socially equal labor. The measure and principle of exchange must be labor without regard to its specific form of application. Commodities, as the products of individual labor, must confront in the market a commodity which .represents the social character of labor, the embodiment of social labor and which can, therefore, measure the degree to which the labor of the individual is, in fact, an element of the labor of society as a whole. This, it needs to be emphasized, is not a requirement external to Smith's own framework. It is precisely the labor-commanded theory of value which, when viewed on one side, denies this social mediation, from the other, directly asserts its necessity and specific form.

2

In so far as the labor commanded by a commodity is not simply the labor embodied in other commodities, but also labor itself in the form of the laborer's capacity to labor (labor-power) what is purchased is not the specific labor required in the production of any given commodity but the capacity to do labor in general. The true value of a commodity is still the toil and trouble required for its production but it is possible to directly estimate and express that value in terms of the purchase of labor-power as a proxy and equivalent for the direct purchase of social labor itself. It appears, then, that in the purchase of labor-power by capital Smith has discovered a relation (the capital relation) which reveals the social nature of exchange and the mediation of exchange by abstract social labor.

This should not be interpreted to imply that Smith introduces, at this point, the concept of labor-power in its opposition to labor. On the contrary, the

specificity of labor-power (as the laborer's capacity to labor) in contradistinction to labor (the laborer's activity in the production of value) is given no
explicit recognition within classical thinking. The reasons for this absence of
distinction will be considered in detail throughout the subsequent discussion.
For classical thought the equivalence of labor and labor-power forms a central
theme which alone allows for the submergence of the capital relation into the
purely natural production of material objects and for the submergence of the
social determination of capital into a series of forms of nature. In order for
this effect to be realized it is necessary that the labor purchased as a commodity
and the labor itself, as so much abstract human laboring activity, be the same,
therefore that the notion 'labor-power' be absorbed into the notion 'labor'
and be allowed no independent existence. Just as the concept of labor-power
is about to emerge (and it is the implication of the labor-commanded theory
that this concept does emerge implicitly at a determinate stage in the classical
argument) it finds itself excluded from an explicit recognition and adequate
expression.

The exclusion of the distinction between labor and labor-power violates the
universality of each. The existence of labor-power as a commodity is synonymous with the abstraction of labor. With the purchase and sale of labor-power
the existence of labor as neither more nor less than so much labor is established. The commodity exchanged is the capacity to labor which once made
exchangeable implies the determination of labor without regard to a particular
object and particular personality. The commodity labor-power is separable
equally from the objective conditions of labor, which specify the activity to a
particular object, and from the personality of the laborer. Only in this way
can the activity within production be constituted as labor, indifferent to its
particular object, therefore objectless, purposeless, the simple idea of labor at
work in production.

The real value of a commodity, what it is really worth, is the time and
trouble expended in its production. The value of the commodity in exchange
is its value to the person who owns it but does not wish himself to consume it.
This is equal to the labor which it will command in the market. So far as the
commodity has value it stands for so much general labor and may be replaced
directly with the product of any other individual labor. To that extent, the
commodity represents labor taken without regard to its specific form. Value
in exchange is command over labor in general and not over the labor of a given
specific individual. Therefore while the worth of a commodity is its cost of
production its value in exchange is its command over 'labor' where, this time,
labor represents 'labor-power.'

The labor-commanded theory of value expresses directly the exchange of
commodities as the exchange of labor while the difference between the
individual nature of the labor and the social substance of that labor is concentrated in the exchange of commodities for labor itself. Not only is there no
quantitative difference between labor embodied in the commodity and the

amount of labor-power which it will purchase in the market but those different forms of labor are considered as directly equivalent and therefore commensurable. What is crucial is the unification of the differing forms of labor. This is, in effect, the true function of the labor-commanded principle; the true value of commodities becomes directly their exchange-value in the market and the difference of form is shown to be a mere difference of 'appearance' which can, upon investigation, be shown to disappear. It is the re-emergence of this difference which signals the demise of the labor-commanded theory and its replacement by a cost of production theory of value.

The inability of Smith to retain the equivalence of the differing forms of labor is closely connected to his inability to sustain the equivalence of differing forms of value. This inability is of considerable significance to the subsequent development of economic theory and, in particular, to Ricardo's development of the value concept and to the tendency within the Ricardian analysis for value to break apart into distinct forms.

For Smith it is already clear that value is, first, the toil and trouble expended in the production of the commodity where this represents the specific individual labor required in the work process. Value is, second, the toil and trouble of others which can replace that of any individual through exchange. It is command over the specific individual labor embodied in commodities by others. Even this second notion of value has two distinct determinations. It is the individual's subjective evaluation of the labor and has an exclusively individual basis and it is the individual element in the social division of labor whose individuality is an explicitly social product. Third, value is the average social labor required in the production of given commodities. This result is expressed when labor is made up in its opposition to 'work' so that the labor in the production process has itself a social character. In this case, the mediation of exchange transforms the individual expenditure of labor time into a general social average. Finally, value is the command of the commodity over other commodities and, in particular, over commodities in general. But where value is command over the world of commodities it is indifferent to the specificity of the commodity which it purchases in the market, and therefore to the specificity of the labor invested in that commodity. This appears as the command over the power of producing value, the command in the market over labor-power. The importance of these differences within the labor-commanded principle is that within that principle these differences do not exist. Value as labor and value as the command over commodities are one and the same. The individual labor within the labor process is directly comparable to, and therefore equivalent to, labor in general which appears in the form of command of the product of the individual labor over labor-power.

The labor embodied in the commodity is the substance and cause of the exchange while the labor commanded in the market measures that exchange and reveals directly the rooting of exchange in the general character of the labor employed in the production of the individual commodity. On one level this is the precise formulation of the labor-commanded theory of value. Labor commanded does not give value to commodities but it expresses that value, it measures the value of commodities. The importance of the existence of labor-power as a commodity is that it allows for the measurement of the exchange-value of commodities in terms of a measure which is, first, a commodity itself and is, second, directly labor and therefore measures not merely the exchange-value of commodities, their general command over the world of commodities, but simultaneously roots that power of commanding the world of commodities in general human labor.

Smith, by employing labor (implicitly labor-power) as the measure of exchange-value, appears to overcome the contradictions of his original statement of the theory of value. By ignoring the distinction between labor as a given quantity of labor time and labor-power Smith reunites the substance of value, human labor, with its existence in the market. Now the labor embodied in the commodity may be directly evaluated in the market. The link of exchange which mediates the individual commodity and the labor employed in its production with the social division of labor, revealing it to be an element of that social division of labor, serves to express immediately the real value of the commodity. In this way the fact that production is individual, tied to individually owned units of production which are not directly reconciled with the reproduction of society as a whole but are only determined in their social role through the fluctuations of exchange-value in the market, as a normal average of divergencies, in no way conflicts with the determination of value in social labor. The average about which the price fluctuates is directly the value of the commodity. But this is immediately the price itself. Therefore, there is, in principle, no fluctuation at all. The individual, specific labor which went to the production of the particular commodity is directly social and realizes itself as such in its exchange with the commodity labor-power. So long as the labor embodied in the commodity and the labor commanded by it are the same and so long as exchange-value is measured in terms of labor as a commodity there exists an immediate reconciliation of the individual and the social which requires no explicitly social mediation.[3] The labor-commanded theory of value reveals the non-existence of a difference between the isolated individual and the individual as an element of a social whole.

Where labor and labor-power are equated the existence of the laborer as a person, as the proprietor of his labor, is suppressed. The laborer is himself exchanged and becomes the property of his purchaser. His relationship to the purchaser of his labor-power is that of the commodity to its owner, as that of an animal to his owner. In the equation of labor and labor-power there is implicit the reduction of the laborer to the status of an animal and the exclusion of his existence within a social relationship. As an animal his activity has lost its social character and becomes purely natural and material. Laboring activity as the activity of the laborer is in this case purely natural. The equation of labor and labor-power, therefore, by reducing the laborer to the status of an animal, excludes any social determination of laboring activity so that the production process (1) ceases to be defined as a labor process and (2) the process of production loses any social character. As an animal the laborer is capable of 'producing' material objects (much as bees produce hives and birds nests) but he is incapable of producing any social substance, any value or any commodity.

Within the *Wealth of Nations* this view breaks apart at two points which emerge out of the conditions of the value problem as they are presented in Smith's own discussion. First, the measure of value, in its existence as a commodity, is itself subject to those fluctuations of price (in this case fluctuations in the wage) which reveal that the reconciliation of the individual with the social takes place through the averaging of incessant differences; and second, the labor commanded by a commodity and the labor costs of its production differ by the profit margin required when production is based explicitly on capital.

Since the individual is not immediately but only implicitly social he can become an element of the social whole only through a mediation. Individual production is directly determined by individual decisions on the part of the owners of the particular units of capital. The social character of production, the extent to which its products are appropriate in quality and quantity to the division of labor is only established *post festum*. It comes about after the production has taken place and when the product appears in the market as a commodity. Even were labor-power the measure of value it must be subject to fluctuations of its own value depending on the extent to which its supply is appropriate in quantity and quality to the needs of the social division of labor. A rupture appears in the relation of the value of the commodity to its expression. The value, the labor embodied in the commodity, remains constant while its expression alters with the fluctuations of supply and demand. Even with labor-power measuring directly the 'value' of commodities the necessity of a social mediation between individual units of production would emerge and, in fact, would be expressed directly in the fluctuations in exchange-value of labor-power itself (i.e. in fluctuations of the wage). The distinction which must exist between the individual and the system of individuals far from being abolished via the interjection of labor-power as the measure of exchange-value would now be internalized into the principle of value itself.

This result follows directly from the confusion of classical value theory over the measure of value and, in particular, the invariable measure of value. For Smith the problem of considering labor as the measure of value is that labor itself is not invariable in its value. The better part of the chapter on 'Real and Nominal Price' is taken up with an investigation of this deficiency of the labor measure and, in fact, of all candidates for the measure of value. This is a deficiency, of course, only to the extent that the mediation of price and labor via a social process (exchange) is itself a deficiency. That is, only in so far as it is necessary to the overall classical conception that the individual be directly

social so that the social exists immediately within the individual, does the
necessity of deviation of price from value challenge the analysis of the value
problem.

In the first place this deficiency is considered by Smith to be a weakness of
human nature (pp. 31–2):

Every commodity besides, is more frequently exchanged for, and thereby compared
with, other commodities than with labor. It is more natural therefore, to estimate
its exchangeable value by the quantity of some other commodity than by that of the
labor which it can purchase. The greater part of people too understand better what
is meant by a quantity of a particular commodity, than by a quantity of labor. The
one is a plain palpable object; the other an abstract notion, which, though it can be
made sufficiently intelligible, is not altogether so natural and obvious.

The lack of a direct determination of exchange-value in labor time originates
in a failure of perception. In this statement Smith explicitly confuses labor as
a commodity, which is no less plain and palpable than any other commodity,
with labor as social labor time, the social substance of the specific productive
activity whose product is the commodity. This social substance, far from being
an object of the exchange relation is an 'abstract notion.' What this confusion
implicitly recognizes is the central condition placed on the labor-commanded
principle: the identity of labor as it appears in the form of a commodity in the
market and labor as it exists within the labor process in the form of laboring
activity. Only if the labor purchased in the market is directly abstract social
labor time is the opposition between the social and the individual, intrinsic to
the exchange relation, eliminated.

Smith is forced to recognize that the labor which is purchased in the market
is, in fact, different from the labor of the immediate labor process:

Labor alone, therefore, never varying in its own value is alone the ultimate and real
standard by which the value of all commodities can at all times and places be estimated and compared. It is their real price; money is their nominal price only.

This statement expresses not only, as has been generally recognized, Smith's
rooting of labor in the subjective estimation of the laborer, but, also, and more
importantly, the idea that the labor invested in the production of commodities
is not itself a commodity since it is not subject to quantitative market variations. This conclusion is made explicit in the next paragraph where Smith
notes that (p. 33):

though equal quantities of labor are always of equal value to the laborer, yet to the
person who employs him they appear sometimes to be of greater and sometimes of
smaller value. He purchases them sometimes with a greater and sometimes with a
smaller quantity of goods, and to him the price of labor seems to vary like that of all
other things.

Again Smith writes off the difference between labor as a function of the
laborer, his practical activity, and labor as a commodity as a matter of

appearance. The fact that labor exists in distinct forms does not affect the essence of labor, its 'reality,' but only the appearance of labor in the 'popular sense' (p. 33). It is self-evident to Smith that labor is activity. Furthermore it is activity of an individual and natural character: it is the function of the individual in his relation to nature. The first task of political economy is to reveal the various forms in which this activity appears in modern society as just that, mere forms of appearance which must be reduced to their 'real' substance as pure natural activity, indifferent to such forms. To Smith any other conception panders to the confusions of the popular mind which is unable to penetrate the appearance, the form in which labor appears as a commodity.

Having established that the difference between 'labor' and 'labor-power' is a matter of appearance Smith is forced to admit that the 'distinction between the real (labor) and the nominal (money) price of commodities and labor, is not a matter of mere speculation, but may sometimes be of considerable use in practice' (p. 33). This is a critical transition in so far as it links the argument designed to expose the unreality of the difference between labor and labor-power with a detailed argument which gives emphatic expression to the very reality of that difference. The reality of the difference is, for Smith, to be found in variations of price. The remainder of this chapter concerns the inability of commodities in general, including the commodity labor, to measure and estimate the 'value' of commodities. In so far as labor in the form of a commodity is unable to measure the value of commodities which is itself nothing other than labor, the direct expression of labor-value in price breaks down. The variations of price express the mediation which connects, and also separates, the immediate labor process and the exchange which expresses, in fact determines, the extent to which that labor process has given value to commodities, the extent to which the labor expended in that labor process is socially necessary labor. If we link this connection up with Smith's earlier argument that the 'work' of the individual may or may not be 'labor' and interpret labor in that sense then the implication of the discussion of nominal price can only be that of a difference between the labor embodied in commodities, which is a social substance, and the market expression of that labor, the price of the commodity.

In principle the expression of work as labor involves the measure of that work according to the unit of general labor. But this measure is not direct for the reason that the product of labor is a commodity and must be measured in its existence as a commodity and therefore in price. That price – the commodity measured in some other commodity (money) – cannot be directly social labor since social labor is not itself a commodity. Labor measures work and expresses its generality. But where labor only exists embodied in the commodity the commodity measure could only be equally labor in so far as the commodity finds labor itself as a commodity in the market. It appears at first that labor-power serves this function so Smith asserts that the value of the commodity is the labor which it commands in the market. But it is immediately clear to Smith that this labor which is commanded is not, in fact, the same labor which he employed as the measure of work. The value of commodities, their real price, is not directly expressed in the market where all quantities are exchange rates which do not relate commodities to social labor as the substance of the work activity but relate commodities to other commodities. Exchange effects a social division of labor in which the mediation of the individual labors is not direct but is only effected as the average of variation. It is the attempt to measure exchange-value in labor that leads Smith into the conceptual *cul-de-sac* of the labor-commanded theory of value.

The labor-commanded principle breaks down not because it is impossible to measure commodities in labor (i.e. labor-power) but because of the difference between labor as the substance of work and labor as a commodity. Because of this difference the exchange-value of commodities in the commodity labor-power fails to reveal directly those commodities as simply so much average social labor time. The problem of the labor-commanded principle is the problem of measuring the commodity directly as the product of social labor so that the individual labor is immediately social labor and that social labor is directly the exchange-value of the commodity.

The underlying reason for this breakdown is that the labor commanded by a commodity in the form of the commodity labor-power is not, in fact, abstract human labor. The exchange-value of commodities in the commodity labor-power and the labor required in the production of those commodities are not equivalent. The commodity form intervenes so that even in the case of labor itself it becomes necessary to distinguish labor-power, the commodity, from labor, the substance of the value of that commodity.

This disjunction in the category of labor is, in the first instance, the result of the appearance of labor-power in the form of a commodity in the market. The purchase and sale of labor-power implies the capital–labor relation and production of profit. As a result a quantitative rupture occurs in the world of exchange relations. The labor embodied in commodities differs in magnitude from the labor which they command in the market where the latter is labor-power. The cost of production in the form of the wages bill is less than the value of the product estimated in labor hours. With the purchase and sale of labor-power the future labor commanded by a given quantity of past labor exceeds the latter by an amount equal to the surplus labor or profit. This rupture is the basis for the expansion of capital. Since labor-power produces value greater than the value given in its cost the purchase of labor-power is the purchase of future value, it is therefore the purchase of expanding value. To the extent that commodity production rests on the accumulation of capital and the buying and selling of labor-power the connection of value to labor always involves the capital relation.

3

The labor-commanded principle expresses, for Smith, the grounding of abstract human labor in the purchase of labor itself in the market. Implicitly Smith recognizes the dependence of the notion of socially equal labor on the commodity form and, in particular, on the commodity form of labor – labor-power. The language which Smith employs in this connection is significant. In each case the choice of formulation reveals the close connection within classical political economy between the concept of labor and the value form. For Smith value is 'labor commanded' in the market so that the connection between value and labor is immediately a value relation even within the definition of value itself. Labor, on the other hand, is the 'real price,' it is the 'cost' of production, it is 'purchase money.' Within the labor-commanded theory labor itself comes to serve, tacitly, the central functions of money, as expression and measure of exchange-value, of command over commodities. Smith notes this special use of labor when he indicates that it is, in practice, more often money which plays the role of measure of value. This specific use of language reveals that for classical political economy, the concept of labor in general is pre-eminently a market concept, a concept that emerges with the process of exchange and that can hardly be thought, let alone expressed, independently of the language of the market: price, money, cost, command over commodities, etc.

It is, therefore, in the value relation that the concept of labor emerges. Value expresses the indifference of the individual commodity to the particularity of its form of existence as a material object, to the concrete personality and needs of its owner, to the manner in which, as a use-value, it satisfies those needs, and to the specific, concrete labor which was expended in its production. In the exchange one commodity is replaced indifferently for another commodity or for commodities in general (i.e. for money).

A commodity has value, for classical political economy, in so far as it stands for so much 'labor.' But a commodity stands for a given quantity of labor only in that it can be replaced, through exchange, for other embodiments of 'labor'; therefore only in so far as that value is indifference to the specificity of that labor. Value is the quantum of social labor. Classical analysis only becomes aware of the social nature of labor when it comes to analyze the phenomenon of exchange because it is only in the exchange that the social nature of the labor is expressed. It is for this reason that prior to the discussion of exchange it is precisely the difference of labor, in the form of division of labor, which is crucial to the argument of the *Wealth of Nations*. The transcendence of the specific material character of the object within the exchange is the condition for the transcendence of the specificity of the labor required in the production of the object. But, we have already seen that the very specificity of that labor is dependent on the division of labor and therefore on the equality of labor (since division of labor also directly implies the equality of labor, the social nature of the individualized labor processes). It now appears that the difference of labor and the generality of labor are mutually conditioned. Thus the condition for the obliteration of the specificity of the labor embodied in a commodity is the condition for the existence of labor in general and the condition for the existence of specific labor is precisely that it be an element of general labor. Thus the process of exchange is not only necessary to the equalization of labor but it is also, by that fact, responsible for the difference of labor. While that difference is itself, implicitly founded on the equality of labor it is only with the explicit introduction of the social mediation of exchange that the social character of labor becomes explicit. Only in so far as it is necessary to view the product of labor as a commodity is it necessary to consider the product of labor as embodying abstract labor as its social substance, to consider the object as a product of *labor*.

In this case, what Smith is concerned to investigate is no longer the laws of the production of wealth *per se* but the law of the production of value. This result has the most profound implications for the classical system as a whole. We have seen how, in the *Wealth of Nations*, the concept of production comes from the very outset (in the treatment of the division of labor) to be tacitly displaced to the concept of the production of value, production based on capital. Capitalist production is precisely that production which is defined as the production of value. The aim and central goal of production is not specific objects of need but value itself, the continued production, reproduction, and expanded reproduction of value. The conclusion of the foregoing discussion is that production is 'labor' when it is the production of value. The intimate connection between abstract labor and the value form in Smith's analysis, the labor-commanded principle, the language in which Smith expresses the idea of labor, not only establish the interconnection between exchange, socially equal labor, and division of labor, but also the connection between the idea of production as a labor process and production whose aim is value, capitalist production.

The connecting thread in this conception is the unremitting equation of labor and value. This equation determines equally the specificity of the two concepts – value and labor – to economic theory. Value is no longer an accidental form but the necessary result of a process – the labor process. Labor is no longer the work activity of the species within nature but the process within which value is grounded. Value is specified to its production and that production, labor, is specific to the product as value. Labor, in this case, is not externally equated with a principle, value, which is foreign to it. Rather, labor is equated with value because labor is value (just as value is labor). Value is labor as result or product, and labor is value as the moving force in its production process. Labor is value at work, bringing itself into existence.

This constitution of production as a labor process in the specific sense of the process of the production of value and expanded value is the ultimate source of the ability of both Smith and Ricardo to grasp the social determination of wealth. By seeing production as the production of value, both Smith and Ricardo find themselves in every case concerned with the character of capitalist economy. The subject-matter of classical theory is displaced from the various alternate 'models' of distinct economies, from the conceptions of pre-civilized states of man and of simple commodity economy to capitalist production as such. The alternate models and systems of production are all constituted in terms of categories (exchange, labor, etc.) that come to be revealed as the categories of capitalist production. Those alternatives dissolve in their dependence and reappear as dependent and distorted expressions of capitalist production.

V Smith and Ricardo

Within the *Wealth of Nations* the reduction of society to nature takes place along two distinct planes: one in which they are opposed externally as alternative systems of economic organization and one in which they are opposed moments within the conceptions of civilized society itself.

First, the opposition of society to nature extracts the natural core from within social life. Pre-civilized society is defined as the absence of social determination (of the division of labor) and the central problem of political economy is defined as that of contrasting civilized society with the distorted image which it presents in the form of the savage state of man. When the opposition is viewed along this plane the reduction of society to nature takes the form of the relating of civilized society to its non-civilized predecessor. The key to the determination of the nature and causes of the wealth of nations is the discovery of a common dimension along which civilized society can be compared to the savage state of man and which reveals the former as the more highly developed form. For Smith the labor process serves this function and the difference between the two states of man is summarized in a difference of form of a labor process which is, in substance, unchanged. In this case the difference between civilized and non-civilized states relates to a common process – the labor process which is the conceptual basis of production in the savage state and of the division of labor of civilized society. The division of labor is a form of labor and only in so far as it is such a form can it serve as the immediate starting point of the *Wealth of Nations*. Only in so far as the division of labor can be conceptualized directly in terms of a process given naturally does it not require any prior conceptual determination within social theory. In effect, the division of labor, and with it the constitution of civilized society, falls outside of social theory.

The original problem of the *Wealth of Nations* requires that the contrast between nature and society be drawn along the dimension of opposing states of man. So long as political economy retains the category of wealth conceived as composed of materially defined objects independent of their appropriation within society, the problem of political economy can only be that of the determination of the *magnitude* of wealth. The fulcrum of analysis is always a non-social, material substance. Political economy can treat all of the characteristics of society only in their relation to the non-social substance of production and wealth. In the *Wealth of Nations* the determination of social life in the division of labor determines the social order solely as the means to the quantitative expansion of wealth where the latter is equally defined within the non-social savage state of man. Thus, Smith's conception of wealth directly reduces society to its antithesis.

At the same time Smith explicitly involves the production of wealth in the determination of the life process of civilized society. In light of this result society and nature come to be related along a somewhat different plane, as aspects of civilized society itself without reference to the non-civilized state of man. In this case the concept of wealth comes to be dependent upon that of capitalist production. This result emerges in the course of Smith's treatment of the measure of wealth. For Smith wealth is measured in value, in purchasing power in the market. Men's 'fortune is greater or less, precisely in proportion to the extent of this power; or, to the quantity of other men's labor, which it enables them to purchase or command. The exchangeable value of everything must always be precisely equal to the extent of this power' (pp. 30–1). In so far as Smith considers price to be the 'real measure' of wealth he has equated wealth not with the material substance of objects of human need but with the commodity form. Smith is no longer concerned simply with the analysis of the production of wealth but specifically with the production of commodities and of the value relation. The grounding of value in labor means for Smith that wealth itself is command over labor. 'Wealth, as Mr Hobbes says, is power. . . . The power which that possession immediately and directly conveys to him, is the power of purchasing; a certain command over all the labor which is then in the market' (p. 31). To argue that wealth is command over commodities and labor is to consider wealth not as a collection of naturally defined objects but directly as purchasing power. Wealth loses its natural determination and comes to require a social determination first as value, and then as labor. As can be seen from the above quotation the concept of wealth implies both value and labor so that wealth, value, and labor are jointly determined. If the difference between civilized society and the non-social state of man is to be one of quantity of wealth then the attributes of wealth (value and labor) must be common both to civilization and to its opposite. But since value and labor are products of division of labor they are peculiar to civilized society. As a result the notion of wealth is equated with that of commodities produced within a social division of labor. The equation of wealth with the commodity products of a labor process reveals the inner force of the science of wealth to be the determination of the system of economic relations through the self-movement of a social substance.

With the publication of the *Wealth of Nations* economic theory achieves its first real insight into the nature of its subject matter. The problem which stands before economic science is no longer that of the distinctiveness of its object but that of the difficulties intrinsic in the manner in which that object is constructed. After Smith the question of the distinctiveness of the system of economic relations is replaced by that of the investigation of the logic manifest within those relations. This is the task of Ricardian economics. With Ricardo economic theory begins to lose sight of the subject with which it is originally preoccupied. As a result the logic of economic analysis moves away from the concept of economic life and its specificity in the direction of the exclusive preoccupation with the question of magnitude. This brings with it the first truly rigorous statement of the problematic construction of the classical concept of value. Classical theory is forced to pay for this achievement, however, by giving up its own most compelling theoretical accomplishments. It is as a result of this that, in a well-known letter to Malthus, Ricardo explicitly eliminates the concept of wealth from political economy:[4]

Political economy you think is an inquiry into the nature and causes of wealth – I think it should rather be called an inquiry into the laws which determine the division of the produce of industry amongst the classes who concur in its formation. *No law can be laid down respecting quantity, but a tolerable correct one can be laid down respecting proportions.*

Ricardo does not transform political economy from a theory of wealth to a theory of distribution because of an arbitrary value judgment as to the relative significance of the two problems. It is, rather, because of this conviction that the phenomenon of 'wealth' cannot be made subject to law and that, therefore, there can be no science of wealth.

Chapter 3
David Ricardo: Value and capital

I Introduction

The priority of the theory of value and of the connection between value and labor are both results rather than starting points of the development of Ricardian economics. As the results of Ricardo's theoretical development they are implicitly accountable to that development. Within the *Principles of Political Economy and Taxation*, however, both the theory of value and the labor principle are simply posited in abstraction from any systematic deduction and argumentation. To that extent both positions take the form of arbitrary judgments. In other words there is no explicit argument for the labor principle, but at the same time the emergence of that principle within the development of Ricardian analysis reveals the existence of an implicit, unstated, argument for such a connection. This property of Ricardian thought is the source of the inability of the interpretations of the classical theory of value to uncover any systematic necessity that would lead Ricardo to the labor principle. Beginning, on the other hand, with the development of Ricardo's value theory the possibility of a necessary link between labor and value emerges in the form of a driving force behind the movement of Ricardo's thinking in the direction of the labor theory of value. This is a force which drives towards *the* theory of value in the sense that it is a movement in the direction of a consistent grounding of the exchange relation which will remove the latter from the external determination of nature and the individual. The notion of a theory of value taken in this more rigorous sense excludes necessarily both the treatment of exchange in modern economics and the peculiar form of the analysis of exchange presented in classical economics. Within the former the analysis of value seeks to account for exchange without establishing it to be a necessary element of an ongoing social process within which it is grounded by its systematic connection to the totality of social relations. The classical analysis, while on one side adopting the same procedure as that adopted by modern economics, at the same time articulates a conception of exchange which involves it in the implicit grounding of the latter in a social substance – labor. In this respect classical analysis emerges as the product of the simultaneous activity of the theoretically adequate conception within which exchange comes to be accounted for by a social process, and the activity of a methodology which derives exchange as the expression of given natural forces outside of any social determination. In the case of Ricardo, the absence of any systematic deduction of the relation of value to labor expresses the arbitrary element in his conception of the value relation. At the same time the existence of the labor theory, and the process by which it comes into existence, reveals the workings of a real theory of value which ties the latter into the self-determination of the system of social relations.

The objective to which Ricardo explicitly subordinates his theoretical work is, virtually in every case, a specific practical end. Ricardo's writing is dominated by immediate practical concerns and consists almost exclusively of essays taken up with current issues. Only in one published work (together with the unfinished papers on 'Absolute and Exchangeable Value') does Ricardo seem to transcend these limitations, but, even here, in his *Principles*, it is the principles of taxation which appropriate the bulk of attention and for which the theory of value appears as little more than a prelude.

To be sure, this practical orientation mirrors a quality not only of classical thought but of the whole of the history of economic analysis. It is a peculiarity of economic theory that the distinction between economic science and economics as a practical discipline is virtually never clearly drawn. The abstraction required to establish the scientific issues is always made imperfect by the subordination of theory to the requirements of external ends. This tendency has its origin in the failure of economics in particular, and social science more generally, to establish the abstract character, and therefore the theoretical determination, of its object. Social science, in the modern period is marked by a deeply embedded uncertainty regarding the theoretical intelligibility of its subject-matter. This uncertainty is sustained by the failure of the science to assure to itself a distinctive theoretical object.

The development of the Ricardian theory is an expression of this quality of economic thinking. The motive force which underlies the changing character of Ricardo's conception of value is simultaneously theoretical and practical. The practical ends to which Ricardo subordinates the theory lead both to the mystification of his scientific work and to the real development of his thought in the direction of a scientific standpoint.

II The development of Ricardo's theory of value

1 Ricardo's early writings

Ricardo's early works are dominated wholly by monetary questions. This is an important instance of the domination of Ricardo's thinking by specific practical issues. In this case it was the question of forced currency and the high price of bullion; later it was to be the more famous issue of the corn laws. But, whereas the latter issue forces Ricardo to deal with general theoretical questions the earlier problem does not.

It is most accurate to say that in this period Ricardo has no theory of value. This is true even though he had studied Smith's *Wealth of Nations* prior to his polemics on the price of bullion. It is clear that in this early period Ricardo does not subscribe to a labor theory of value in any definite sense. In his pamphlet on the *High Price of Bullion* (1810–11) Ricardo argues that gold and silver, 'like other commodities have an intrinsic value, which is not arbitrary, but is dependent on their scarcity, the quantity of labor bestowed in procuring them, and the value of capital employed in the mines which produce them' (vol. III, p. 52). Such a capricious assortment of factors is not intended as a theory of value but as a general summary of the kinds of phenomena which, in practice, may affect the prices of commodities. In other words, this is not a *theoretical* position which attempts, through abstraction, to isolate the characteristic and essential aspects of exchange, but a *practical* position concerned with the day to day determination of the actual level of prices. The crucial difference is the lack, in Ricardo's discussion of price, of any systematic organization of the differing elements of the value problem, the relegation of each to its appropriate level of abstraction, and the explication of the necessary conceptual links between the different elements.

During this period Ricardo holds to a position on the connection between wages and prices which he later will explicitly reject in light of his work on value. 'If a tax were laid on bread every commodity would rise, as there is no commodity to the production of which the labor of man is not necessary' (vol. III, p. 270). Such a position, as Ricardo soon comes to realize, is inconsistent with the labor theory of value since for the latter, in the form in which Ricardo adopts it, the price of a commodity is given independently of the distribution of income, by the amount of labor required for its reproduction. This latter conclusion is, on one level, precisely the distinguishing feature of the Ricardian theory of value so far as Ricardo himself was concerned.

Even though Ricardo had not, as yet, posed the problem of value or recognized the need for a theory of value, his analysis of the price of bullion places definite limits upon the way in which the value problem will later be posed and resolved. By arguing that labor is necessary to the production of all commodities Ricardo has limited the idea of the commodity to that of products of labor. This is a necessary limitation from the point of view of the construction of the classical theory of value. Tied in with this view is Ricardo's predisposition against the utility approach to the problem. Following Smith, Ricardo explicitly rejects utility as a foundation for a theory of exchange (vol. III, p. 284). In so doing Ricardo has implicitly rejected the grounding of the value relation in the immediate exchange of commodities between two socially undetermined individuals. Conversely Ricardo has taken the position that exchange must be grounded in a determinate process which is social in the sense that it is not the product of an accidental exchange which takes place within the context of the arbitrary whims of the parties concerned. According to Ricardo commodities have an '*intrinsic* value which is *not arbitrary.*' Value is intrinsic in the sense that it does not depend on the particularity of the specific individuals which happen to be engaged in the exchange.

According to Ricardo, the value relation is intrinsic to commodities which are the products of labor. There is implicit within this essentially practical position the whole of the Ricardian theory of value. This theory is implicit in the sense that the practical determination of commodities as the products of labor whose value is intrinsic immediately forecloses alternatives to the classical theory of value and provides the starting point for the articulation of a labor theory of value.

The specific elements which Ricardo emphasizes in the determination of value other than scarcity are the quantity of labor and the value of capital. This, along with the statement that value is intrinsic, suggests that the role of scarcity be interpreted in terms of the special problem of the influence of demand on price rather than in terms of a general theory of value. Furthermore, Ricardo's position on the effect of wages on value indicates that he has at the back of his mind a cost of production theory which may derive from certain strains of thinking in the *Wealth of Nations.*

The focal point is always, for Ricardo, the necessary connection between exchange and production and, indeed, between value and the production of capital. Ricardo nowhere considers production taken without regard to its determinateness within the circular movement of capital. For Ricardo there is neither production in general nor different forms of production, there is only the production by and for capital. Such production Ricardo considers directly equivalent to the expanded reproduction implied in the idea of capital as self-expanding value. Thus, implicitly, Ricardo considers production only in its determinateness as capitalist production. This specification always reveals itself in the equation of the production of capital with the accumulation of capital. On this issue Ricardo has already taken up the position of Smith and Quesnay, that 'a nation is only advancing whilst it accumulates capital' (vol. III, p. 274). Even though the currency controversy did not involve the problem of accumulation in any very deep sense (it, rather, had a tendency to eliminate that problem) the fact that Ricardo has expressed, at this time, the classical position on accumulation is not without significance. The typical focus of classical thinking prior to Ricardo is on economic growth. This orientation continues to infect Ricardo's thinking even in the light of his own critique of his predecessors. The question of growth necessarily requires a deeper concern with production and reproduction than does the problem of stability. By contrast, the construction of the neo-classical theory of value is predicated on an initial abstraction not only from growth but also from production in all its forms. This is the case in both the 'short run' of Marshallian supply and demand analysis and in the timeless equilibrium of certain versions of the Walrasian value theory. The currency question was an issue of short-run economic stability and as such obscured for Ricardo the specific connection between prices, production, and growth, which was later to provide the foundation of his work.

That Ricardo, in his treatment of the currency question was not forced immediately to confront the problem of value is connected to the specific character of the issue with which he was dealing. We have noted the importance of the production of commodities in the classical viewpoint. It is precisely this element which is missing from the conditions of the bullion controversy. This is due to the fact that money, especially at the time of the controversy, is not clearly produced either under competitive conditions or by means of commodities. The latter holds true of the forced currency of the time which was not convertible into gold or silver, and was therefore not produced at all in the economic sense of the word, but simply created by the printing press. The analysis of such a phenomenon, it must be emphasized, is not conducive to the development of a theory of value appropriate to the problem of an economy which reproduces itself over time.

Ricardo analyzes the price of money in terms of the level of economic activity on one side and the quantity of money on the other. Certain of his formulations are formally indistinguishable from a simple 'quantity theory of money.' We need not go into detail concerning Ricardo's position on the value of money, but it is important to bring out one element in his thinking which provides considerable insight into his approach to economic problems. The key to the understanding of Ricardo's theory of money is not a rigidly and arbitrarily fixed quantity of money but the notion of a given level of economic activity. So long as the price of money is held equal to that of the bullion for which it stands Ricardo's 'quantity' theory of money says no more than that the exchange-value of money is determined in precisely the same manner as is the exchange-value of any other commodity. The demand for money is governed by the level of production, but so too, for Ricardo, is the demand for any other commodity in equilibrium. In equilibrium it is the level of production that determines both the demand and supply for any given commodity. Ricardo's treatment of money is infected with the idea that money is a commodity like any other commodity whose value is determined in the same manner as that of commodities in general. For Ricardo, the quantity theory of money serves to root the discussion of money in the general framework of commodity production.

On the other hand, as soon as we drop the assumption that money is tied in price to bullion, the quantity theory takes on an altogether different significance. Now the level of production ceases to be the active side of the equation in terms of price determination; instead, it is the quantity of money which governs the exchange-value of money. The theory of value so far as it concerns money is thereby diverted from the question of production to that of supply and demand. What is important to recognize is that Ricardo's concern with value in this period is almost exclusively a concern with the determinants of the exchange-value of money under precisely these conditions (where money is not tied to bullion). Ricardo is not at all concerned with a general theory of value and in so far as he deals with the value problem his treatment cannot help but be colored by his preoccupation with money.

2 Ricardo's transition to the labor theory of value

When Ricardo turns to a discussion of the corn laws he takes up, for the first time, a practical issue which forces him to confront the central problems of political economy. The reason for this is that the issue of the corn laws is bound up with the problems of accumulation and distribution in a way that the currency questions are not. The currency controversy was mainly concerned with economic stability; with the corn-law debate the problem of economic growth and of the movement of distributive shares becomes the dominant theme. For Ricardo, the price of corn is directly the wages of labor which latter move with the former in so far as corn is taken to be the wages good. In this sense the theory of price is immediately the theory of distribution.

But there is also a deeper side to the distinction between the corn-law debate and the currency controversy. The former was concerned with a political issue in which the dominance of capital, of capitalist production, is implicitly at stake. The corn-law question is of special historical significance in that the conditions for the existence of capital are directly involved: the protection of profit and of the possibility for the continued expansion of capital. Since any barrier to the expansion of capital is also a barrier to the existence of capital and since the rate of profit is also the rate of expansion of capital, restriction of the rate of profit (the connection between the rising price of corn and the rising wage) and a fall in the rate of profit place the existence of capital in jeopardy. The typical concern of Ricardian thinking with the quantitative dimension of the capital–labor relation – the distribution of the net product between wages and profits – emerges as a concern over the conditions of capitalist production. What for Smith is a problem of the *differentia specifica* of capitalist production is, for Ricardo, a problem of the conditions for the preservation and full development of capital.

Ricardo's thinking at this time is in a process of transition and development. The key to understanding the significance of this transitional period is that it culminates not in the solution of the value problem but in the achievement of a clear formulation of that problem. Such an achievement requires, above all, the recognition of the *need* for a theory of value. Looked at from the other side, the transition represents a period of *evasion* of the value problem; a period during which Ricardo attempts to deal with the system of economic relations without dealing with value. Only when the analysis of these relations reaches the point where it can proceed no further without a theory of value does Ricardo finally come to pose the problem of the substance and measure of value.

The central relation of Ricardo's analysis in this period (and throughout the remainder of his life) is between wages, profits, and the costs of production of corn. The importance of corn derives from its dominant position in the subsistence wage. The price of corn, as we have indicated, enters into the problem of distribution in a way that the price of bullion does not. The connection between prices and distribution now becomes the pivot for Ricardo's treatment of value. Since value, for Ricardo, is always tied into distribution, and since the problem of value only arises originally as an element of the problem of the distribution of the net product, it is clear that, for Ricardo, the theory of value is a theory of exchange based on capitalist production for which exchange does not simply effect a social division of labor as in certain of Smith's arguments but also effects a continuation of the existence of the three main social classes, and, in particular, of the capital–labor relation. The connection between value and distribution reveals the complete absence in Ricardian economics of any conception either of simple commodity economy or of a non-civilized state of man which precedes the division of labor and the accumulation of capital. It is not possible for Ricardo to even attempt the articulation of a system of production other than that based on capital. To be sure, myths such as those which dominate an important dimension of the *Wealth of Nations* do appear at times in Ricardo's writing. None the less they do not possess the same presumed historical character and are explicitly tied to production within the limits defined by the capital–labor relation.

The elimination of simple commodity economy involves also the elimination of explicit consideration of the connection of exchange to the division of labor. Observe, in this regard, how Ricardo does not attempt to ground value in labor via an abstract treatment of the division of labor. Rather, for Ricardo, the connection of labor to value involves the explication of a property intrinsic to the commodity, as a commodity, and not requiring any explicit prior investigation of the division of labor. The labor theory emerges as the fulfillment of a general requirement of the conception of the commodity and of value. To the extent that commodity exchange is not to be treated as arbitrary within Ricardian theory but is to be shown to be necessary, a theoretical task has been established which drives Ricardo to formulate the general conditions of commodity exchange as those are required by the theoretical treatment of value itself. In this sense it is in Ricardian analysis that, for the first time, the truly general problem of the concept of value comes into existence. It might be said, then, that Ricardian analysis is distinguished by the generality with which the problem of value is treated. That problem comes to be more and more that of uncovering the substance of value as necessary to an adequate conception of exchange.

As a result of this new orientation, Ricardo, in his *Essay on the Influence of a High Price of Corn on the Profits of Stock* (1815) provides his clearest statement on the source of value up to that time. Ricardo begins to construct the problem in an abstract way, attempting thereby to isolate the essential forces. This involves, in particular, the assumption that competition be allowed to 'have its full effect' and that 'the production of the commodity be not limited by nature' (vol. IV, pp. 19–20). For Ricardo, this construction of the problem reveals the 'difficulty or facility' of production as the force which will 'ultimately regulate' the exchangeable value of commodities.

Yet while this position marks a notable advance over Ricardo's earliest views it falls short of fulfilling the requirements of a theory of value. It is clear from this statement that Ricardo has not solved the problem of price, nor has he clearly asserted a principle of value. There is, within this statement, no theory of value. While the number of labor hours provides a quantitative and objective principle upon which it is possible to base a theory of value, the 'difficulty or facility of production' does not. The conceptual ambiguity of this principle indicates that it contains implicit within it a number of alternate foundations for the treatment of value. Such a principle is unable to unify in a systematic manner the determinations of the value concept. In a letter to Say, of August 1815, Ricardo echoes the position of the *Essay on Profits* arguing that 'a commodity must be useful to have value but the difficulty of its production is the true measure of its value' (vol. VI, pp. 247–8). Ricardo makes the same point in a letter to Malthus (vol. VI, p. 241). When Malthus asks Ricardo what he means by facility of production, the reply, on October 7, 1815 is 'by facility of production I do not mean to consider the productiveness of the soil only, but the skill, machinery, and labor joined to the natural fertility of the earth' (vol. VI, p. 292). It is clear that Ricardo has not yet fully appreciated the implications of his original insight that the theory of value is concerned with commodities as the products of labor. The predominant element in the determination of value, at this stage of Ricardo's thinking, is a purely natural factor, 'the natural fertility of the earth.' There are two related reasons for this preoccupation: first Ricardo is not yet really concerned to articulate a theory of value, and second Ricardo, in emphasizing the natural conditions of production, is giving expression to a defining theme of the classical theory of value as a whole.

Ricardo focuses on the fertility of the earth, in the first instance, because his concern is not with a general principle of value but with the movement of price, the price of corn, and therefore with the forces which underly the direction of that movement. To be sure, such a concern must ultimately lead Ricardo to deal explicitly with the general problem of value. But Ricardo, at this stage of his thinking, is still preoccupied with a treatment of wages that is not clearly tied to the problem of exchange as such but with the problem of the price of a particular commodity, corn, the movement of which is peculiarly tied to the productivity of the earth. The solution of the problem of distribution does not as yet clearly hinge on a theory of value but appears to depend more on the sum of specific and distinct factors which in the case of the actual historical course of events influences the price of corn. It must be emphasized that the question of the movement of price over time and in the course of accumulation while dependent on a theory of value is not identical to the problem of value. The latter problem is predominantly posed, even within Ricardian economics itself (as in the *Principles*), in abstraction from the process of accumulation. On the other hand, during this period, Ricardo's specific concern is precisely the movement of price in the course of accumulation. Given that the latter is a much more concrete problem Ricardo is misled in its treatment away from the general theory of value and in the direction of the reduction of that general theory to the consideration of the specific forces which act upon the price of corn in the course of the accumulation process.

Ricardo's special concern with the fertility of the earth, as with the difficulty and facility of production in general, also has another background. So long as Ricardo continues to consider value to be governed by the difficulty of production it is possible for him to maintain that value is directly a product of a production process which is immediately a natural process, one governed by the characteristics of nature, the natural fertility of the earth. This conception of production is in implicit conflict with the idea that the value problem concerns products only in so far as those are the products of labor. This incipient two-sided character of Ricardo's view of production is a defining theme of Ricardian economics in its mature form. At that point it is necessary to incorporate the view of production as a natural process into a theory of value and distribution.

Ricardo's value theory is determined in its mode of formulation, particularly in this period, by the example of corn and the problems of the effects of production with inferior land on the price of corn and the wages of labor. Ricardo's treatment of value is inseparable from his treatment of production and distribution and, at this point, rent. The theory of rent and the theory of value form a logical unit. This is not to say that the logic is unexceptionable. It is not yet clear whether the higher costs, the greater difficulty of production, must be understood in terms of an intrinsic property of the land or in terms of the amount and skill of the labor required in production. Both factors are included while their logical connection with value is not spelled out. While Ricardo has not yet focused in on the value problem he has none the less come some distance from his earlier position. In particular, Ricardo has specified more clearly the conditions of the problem of value. He has achieved a level of abstraction which is quite distinct from that which characterized his previous position. By specifying the conditions of competition and reproduction, the 'production of the commodity be not limited by nature,' Ricardo is enabled to eliminate the influence of demand from consideration. This elimination, it needs to be emphasized, is in the nature of an active exclusion and not an oversight. For Ricardo, price is indifferent to demand not because of a failure to perceive the inner character of the interaction of supply and demand but because of the way in which Ricardo conceives of that market interaction (vol. VIII, pp. 276–7). Price determination in the market, while it appears to involve symmetrically the interaction of supply and demand, in reality provides little more than an arena for the expression of the conditions of production. Ricardo's treatment of value involves a conception of market interaction which requires abstraction from demand, and the treatment of the latter as a means to bring to realization the requirements of production. The solutions to the value problem implicit at this stage in his thinking point clearly in the direction of the labor principle. The step which he has not yet taken and which will eventually force him to try to adapt Smith's theory of value is that which forces him to confront the problem of value itself.

What emerges here, together with the particular view of the value question, is the necessity for its theoretical treatment. That necessity is not immediate but is the result of an extended thought process only at the end of which can the implicit issue be given direct expression. The value problem is not abstractly (and therefore arbitrarily) posed by Ricardo, but, rather, imposes itself upon Ricardo's thought processes. It is not the result of a value judgment but of a necessity which Ricardo comes to recognize step by step in the course of the working out of particular issues. To be sure, within the *Principles*, the connection of value to labor appears in a form which is both abstract and arbitrary. None the less, the emergence of the labor principle and the manner of Ricardo's adherence to it are by no means arbitrary, originating as they do within the logic of the development of Ricardo's conception of value.

In a letter to Trower of October 29, 1815 Ricardo expresses the intention to 'concentrate all the talent I possess' on those subjects on which his position differs from 'the great authority of Adam Smith, Malthus, etc.' (vol. VI, p. 316). The only subjects mentioned are rent, profits, and wages. The problem of value is not mentioned. The discussion in the letters to Malthus in this period is almost wholly taken up with the problem of distribution of income. In his reading of Smith the labor theory of value seems to go unnoticed even at those points where Ricardo is compelled to discuss the subject of price and value. This is also suggested by a letter to Ricardo from Mill at the beginning of November 1815 where Mill 'commands' Ricardo 'to begin to the first of the three heads of your proposed work, rent, profits, and wages – viz. rent.'[1]

The question of the distribution of the product thus appears in Ricardo's work as chronologically previous to the questions of value and price. In fact, the essentials of the Ricardian solution to the distribution problem were well in hand before he was to come to realize that a problem of value existed. The specific mechanism which accomplished this separation for Ricardo was the 'corn model' or 'one commodity model.'[2] In such a model the problem of distribution can be discussed in physical terms, and therefore independently of value. The corn model, in other words, allows Ricardo to evade the various issues bound up with exchange-value and its relation to distribution.

Formally, of course, the Ricardian 'corn model' is capable of extension to an indefinitely large number of commodities so long as production of corn is independent of production of the other commodities. The corn-model depicts a 'one commodity world' in so far as the world of commodities is decomposable in such a manner as to separate out one commodity which requires no other commodities for its own production but enters into the production of all other commodities. It is possible to consider this single critical commodity (the

E.S.—4

single 'basic' commodity in the sense of Sraffa's *Production of Commodities by Means of Commodities*) as itself constituting an entire economy since reproduction is conceivable in terms of that commodity in isolation. The critical economic magnitudes are determined without regard to the conditions of production of all of the remaining commodities. In this sense the corn model is the model of a one-commodity economy.

This conception has its origins going back to the earliest of writings within the classical tradition. The physiocratic notion, shared by Quesnay and Turgot, of the predominance of agricultural production and the special role of agriculture is given clear expression in this part of Ricardo's writing. Turgot's conception of the determination of the rate of profit begins with the return on land and then determines profit in other trades in terms of the possibility of investment of capital on land.[3] In fact, one of the critical characteristics of classical political economy as a whole is the peculiar role which agriculture was seen to play in the economic system. Even in Ricardo's later writing the movement of profit is governed by the movement of productivity on land. It is on land that production as a natural process, limited and determined by the natural conditions of the soil, seems to receive its clearest expression. Where production on land represents a comprehensive microcosm of the economy as a whole the social conditions of production are reducible to natural conditions. The relations between classes, the social division of labor, the exchange of commodities, the accumulation of capital, are all considered in terms of the natural conditions of production on land. The latter are prior to the determination of the social relations of production and distribution.

Smith and Ricardo take up a more advanced standpoint than that of Quesnay and Turgot precisely in making production fully capitalistic. This involves the constitution of production as universal in its indifference to the particular sphere of its operation. Social production is intrinsically many-sided production whose indifference to its particular application is manifest precisely in the multiplication and expansion of its sphere of activity. The advance to the standpoint of social production is to be found both in the development of political economy from Quesnay to Ricardo and in the development of Ricardo's own conception of production. At the end production is constituted as a labor process which produces capital only by producing a multiplication of commodities each of which stands equally as the embodiment of a common principle.

The effect of this is also felt in the concept of land. On one side the land stands for the irreducible sphere of natural interaction. Here production is defined in quality as the material product of the land (corn) and in quantity by the fertility of the land. Classical thought never fully succeeds in throwing off the limitations involved in this conception. The notion of land as the external natural sphere which opposes human action does not, however, exhaust the Ricardian conception. Within the Ricardian treatment of rent economic theory finds the first clear statement of the economic determination of land and of its specificity within the system of capitalist production. None the less, the treatment of land prior to the publication of the *Principles* is dominated by the pre-Ricardian, essentially physiocratic conception.

The manner in which Ricardo determines the rate of profit in his *Essay on Profits* is fundamentally dependent on this conception. In fact, that theory is only possible where production on land plays the special role considered here. Under these conditions a theory of value is extraneous to the determination of the distribution of income between wages, profit, and rent. However, as soon as this 'classical' view is dropped the theory of value comes to take on a critical role in the theory of distribution. Since no single industry or sector can stand for the economy as a whole it becomes necessary to determine profits on capital as they are determined in the market through the pricing of commodities.

The transitional period in Ricardo's thinking begins with the evasion of the value problem and ends with the confrontation with the theory of value. The critical moment is that in which Ricardo comes to recognize the need for a theory of value. This is a fact of some importance since it indicates the status of the theory of value in Ricardian economics. The attempted evasion of the issue reflects directly Ricardo's attitude according to which the problem of value is a complication to be gotten out of the way rather than a central problem of political economy. Ricardo's evasion of the value problem has its origin in the conception of economic life as determined within a natural interaction and by a natural principle: the land. The overthrow of the classical concept of production as always referring back to a natural factor brings with it the constitution of production as multiple and as involving a principle whose universality exists not in the immediate material unity of the product (corn) but in the force which drives towards ever more intensive multiplication and differentiation of productions.

Ricardo does not really stumble upon the value problem until he becomes convinced of the inadequacy of his earlier framework. As we have seen, the initial plans for the *Principles of Political Economy* do not include a section on value. When Ricardo confronts the impossibility of directly extending the analysis of the corn economy to one in which the different sectors of production are mutually dependent he is immediately forced to confront theoretical issues of a substantial character. But, as we have indicated, the mutual dependence is neither an arbitrary assumption nor an empirical generalization. The principle which underlies the mutual dependence of productions is also the principle which unites particular productions, revealing thereby their intrinsically social character. Between the one product system and the system of interdependent production of many products is the demarcation which separates the conception of production as natural interaction and the conception of social production.

What is fundamentally at stake in the extension of the corn model is not simply the realism of the construct but the manner in which classical economics first reduces the social relations of production and distribution to a natural substance (which emerges clearly in the case of the production of the products of land) and then confronts the implications of that reduction. In this sense there exists a close conceptual relation between Ricardo's corn model and Adam Smith's early and rude state of man. Both constructs extract the natural kernel which classical political economy discovers within capitalist economic organization and then constitute that essence of capitalist production (the pre-given natural production process) as a self-sufficient whole. The essence of capitalist production is production itself as a self-reproduction of nature which emerges as an alternative whole in opposition to its form of appearance (capitalist production). This discovery links not only Smith to Ricardo but also classical economics to the modern theory of production and exchange. The latter appears as a conception of economic relations which holds strictly to this element of classical thinking, driving it to its logical extreme, and giving to it its definitive form.

The conflict which eventually destroys Ricardo's corn-model conception of the economy is precisely the conflict between the corn economy as a 'model' of production in general and the corn-economy construct as a conception of capitalist production. The idea of production restricted to a single sphere conflicts directly with the conception of capitalist production. The latter is necessarily production without physical limit, production of 'value' which is indifferent to the specific embodiment of that value in a useful object of a definite kind. To that extent capitalist production must be conceived as the production of different commodities, as production of a social division of labor in which the identity of the production process as a whole does not emerge out of the identity of the object of production as a useful object but out of the independence within a general dependence implied by the social division of labor and exchange. As a result of this Ricardo is forced to eliminate the corn model from the theory of value and distribution. The classical framework has undergone a subtle yet profound alteration, the implications of which will serve to break it apart altogether. By following out, in a systematic fashion, the implications of the social determination of production Ricardo ends up eliminating the agricultural, and therefore natural, foundation of economic thinking. To be sure, these aspects of classical thinking continue to find expression within Ricardian economics. The opening sentence of the Preface to Ricardo's *Principles* constructs the problem of political economy in terms of the distribution of the products of the 'earth.' Yet this conception must now come into direct conflict with the theory of capitalist production so that throughout Ricardo's mature works there exists a tension between different conceptions of production and of capitalist production within which the consistent conception of capitalist production plays a critical role and within which the different conceptions are recognized not as the conceptions of different economic systems but as opposing conceptions of capitalist production only one of which can be sustained.

For Ricardo the immediate importance of the theory of value lies in the contradictions which the concept of value imposes upon the theory of distribution. The major effort in the *Principles*, from the point of view of Ricardian economics, can be seen as an attempt to demonstrate the validity of conclusions previously arrived at in the theory of distribution when that theory is extended to a world of many commodities, of economic interdependence. It is only at this point that Ricardo's evasion of the value problem comes to an end and he is, for the first time, forced to confront the need for a theory of value.

3 Ricardo's mature position on value and distribution

We have seen that in November 1815 Ricardo is still considering the writing of his *Principles* without a systematic treatment of the value problem. It is during the following month that Ricardo achieves his first definite insight into the need for a theory of value. In his letter to Mill of December 30, 1815, Ricardo first suggests the need to deal with price. But here he maintains the stability of the precious metals as the 'sheet anchor' for the remainder of his analysis where that stability of value is tied directly to causes connected specifically with gold and silver (vol. VI, pp. 348–9). The first mention of the need for a 'clear insight into the origin and law of exchangeable value' comes in a letter to Malthus of February 7, 1816 (vol. VII, p. 20). That Ricardo proceeded to grapple with the problem is indicated in a letter to Malthus dated April 24 of that year (vol. VII, p. 28). On October 14 Ricardo is still 'beyond measure puzzled to find out the law of price' (vol. VII, p. 83). Yet, judging by a letter from Mill of November 18 (vol. VII, p. 98) Ricardo has, at this point, adopted the labor principle and has occasion to deal with the effect of profits on prices. This should make clear the fact that the stumbling block in the development of Ricardo's theory of value was not the discovery of the law of value itself but the discovery of the need for a theory of value. Ricardo had written on economic problems for five years from 1810 to 1816 (and economic problems that were intimately connected with the question of price) before he came to recognize the need for a theory of value. Once he arrives at such a recognition in February 1816 it takes him eight months to reach what is effectively his mature position on value – a position from which he does not deviate substantially for the rest of his life.

In the year from November 1815 to November 1816 Ricardo has not only taken up the treatment of value in earnest but has also confronted the contradiction within the theory which will continue to disturb him through the remainder of his life. What Ricardo has discovered is that the rate of profit is tied into the determination of the exchange-value of commodities. If equal capitals invested for equal periods of time in different lines of production are to receive equal profits then the same total labor invested in production for different periods will result in different prices for the commodities produced.

On one level this can be viewed as a purely formal problem and there is little doubt that Ricardo wanted to view it in this way. As a formal problem the determination of prices loses any explicit relation to the concept of value. It is no longer the full determination of that concept which is at stake but only its quantitative expression. The exclusive consideration of the formal aspect of the problem (that is the problem of the *quantitative* connection between the equilibrium set of prices and the rate of profit)[4] makes impossible the explanation of Ricardo's continued preoccupation with this same problem as well as his refusal to accept his own criticism of the labor theory, his continuing determination to overcome the deviation of prices from labor-values. It is necessary, in particular, to explain Ricardo's position toward the end of his life, that 'it appears a contradiction to say a thing has increased in natural value while it continues to be produced under precisely the same circumstances as before' (vol. IV, p. 375). Ricardo fully grasps this aspect of the relation of profit to price (just as he understands the role of demand in price formation) yet he never fully accepts the fact that under competitive conditions commodities cannot exchange at their labor-values. He holds to the idea that, whatever the rates at which commodities exchange, they still possess an *intrinsic* value which Ricardo now specifies as labor.

The connection between value and labor which typifies classical political economy is not given any rational basis within Ricardo's writing. The entire discussion of this point within the *Principles* consists of references to the *Wealth of Nations* (vol. I, pp. 12–13). It is the concept of labor and of the relation of labor to exchange that is found in the latter which grounds the theory of value in the *Principles*. This presents the reader with an acute problem of interpretation given the ambiguities and contradictions of Smith's conception of labor. Ricardo, by appropriating, virtually without comment, Smith's concept of labor, equally appropriates all of the contradictions of that concept. To be sure, Ricardo eliminates the labor-commanded principle as inconsistent with production based on capital in order to clearly focus upon the immediate relation of value to labor. But, as regards that latter relation, its individual as opposed to its social basis, the role of means of production as 'capital,' the role of the division of labor in its various forms, Ricardo repudiates none of the paradoxes of the *Wealth of Nations*.

Smith himself is able to consider labor as the substance of value only because he starts out from the division of labor. Exchange is grounded in labor because it is grounded in division of labor while the latter is the given form of the natural production process. But once the specifically social preconditions for the social division of labor are recognized, in particular the dependence of division of labor on socially equal labor, the division of labor can no longer serve as a premise which grounds the theory of exchange but must itself be given explicit treatment within economic theory. In the absence of such an explicit analysis of the division of labor there can be no concept of social labor; or, at least, any concept of social labor must remain theoretically arbitrary. The idea of general labor and the connection between that labor and exchange has no explicit necessity within political economy. Any attempt to argue that the labor theory is grounded because of the explicit introduction of the division of labor, since it leaves the division of labor itself theoretically undetermined, indulges in the same confusions as the *Wealth of Nations* in regard to the idea of labor which underlies the social division of labor. From this standpoint the concept of labor and its relation to value remains an irreducible premise and is, therefore, arbitrary. This is no doubt the case in terms of the systematic articulations of the classical theory. On the other hand, the investigation of the Ricardian value theory has shown that so far as the development of that theory is concerned, the grounding of value in labor is not the starting point but the result of a thought process which culminates in the analysis of value of the first chapter of the *Principles*. In this sense, it needs to be argued that the connection between value and labor is not arbitrary but possesses a rational foundation within the structure of classical thinking. To be sure, this foundation remains always implicit, yet it has a definite expression in the labor theory of value of Smith and Ricardo.

The key to the development of Ricardian theory and to its eventual positing of labor as the substance of value is what we have termed the transitional stage of the development of Ricardo's theory of value, the period of the evasion of the value problem. In the corn economy labor serves exclusively in the function of mediating a purely natural process: the transformation of corn into corn. In this case there is no labor in the sense in which it is seen to emerge in Smith's analysis of socially equal labor or in Ricardo's own value analysis. The reduction of all production to the production of corn is simultaneously the reduction of all labor to that labor engaged in the production of corn. But this is, in effect, the reduction of labor in general, of socially equal labor, first to what Marx calls concrete use-value producing labor, and eventually to the purely physical category of 'work.' All reduction of labor to the application of human activity to a specifically determined task is simultaneously the reduction of labor in its social existence to labor in its purely natural presence. This is the case as regards Ricardo's specification of all production as the production of corn even so far as that specification is only implicit. The 'corn model' expresses with special clarity the central notion of difficulty of production tied to the natural fertility of the earth. Such a reduction also finds expression in the conflation within all of classical political economy of the different forms of labor, of Smith's confusion of labor and labor-power, as well as of the tendency of modern economics to consider labor as a 'factor of production physically defined.' In each case labor ceases to be an abstract notion and becomes instead a 'plain palpable object.' It ceases to have a social determination and becomes exclusively an element of a natural process.

In so far as the process of production is conceived as a purely natural process there can be no rational justification for the distinguishing of labor as the substance and measure of that process. Labor as work, as the purely physical relation of time to distance, is a relation of nature to nature. In this sense work is no more or less a necessary component of 'production' in its physical dimension than are raw materials, chemically defined. Further, as the source of work in this sense, the specifically human element is of no significance and is directly replaceable by other elements of nature, by animals, or even by inorganic sources of energy. In other words, it is precisely to the extent that the human element is taken to be exclusively an element of nature (that the concept of labor is predicated on a relation of 'man' to 'nature') that the relation of man to nature becomes a relation of nature to itself. 'Production' no longer has labor as its presupposition, so that the production of tools by man is production in the same sense that apple-trees 'produce' apples.

In this case production cannot be considered a category which is specific to economics but appears instead as a purely logical category – that of the transformation of inputs into outputs or, more generally, that of 'transformation' taken in general. Production as transformation has no specificity to economic life and is therefore incapable of determining economic interaction. Production 'in general' cannot ground economic relations since it is indifferent to the specificity of those relations. Labor, taken as synonymous with production in this sense can have no determinate relation to value and to the system of commodity exchange. Labor, taken in this sense, cannot account for the determinateness of its product as a commodity. The indeterminateness of production implies both the indeterminateness of labor as its active factor and the indeterminateness of the product of labor, so that the determination of the product as anything more than 'product' in the abstract must be extrinsic to its production. That determinateness is not, therefore, produced and is not, in reality, determinate. This is characteristic of the neo-classical concept of value and its relation to production. It is also the predominant standpoint of Ricardo's transitional period and can be seen to preclude any consistent labor theory of value.

In the *Essay on Profits* Ricardo begins his discussion of price by attributing to labor a special role in determining the value of commodities (vol. IV, p. 19):

The exchangeable value of all commodities, rises as the difficulties of their production increase. If the new difficulties occur in the production of corn, from more labor being necessary, whilst no more labor is required to produce gold, silver, cloth, linen, etc. the exchangeable value of corn will necessarily rise, as compared with those things. On the contrary, facilities in the production of corn, or of any other commodity of whatever kind, which shall afford the same produce with less labor, will lower its exchangeable value.

Yet, even here Ricardo hints that the rise in price which results from increasing difficulties of production of corn may or may not be the result of an increase in the application of labor. As remarked earlier, Ricardo attributes the difficulties of production not exclusively to labor but to the 'skill, machinery, and labor joined to the natural fertility of the soil.' Ricardo treats labor on the same footing as the natural factors of the production process (the natural fertility of the soil and the capital as means of production or 'stock') and thereby transforms labor into work.

On one side labor appears already as the key element since in the specific application of the doctrine it is only changes in labor which are relevant to movements and differences in value. On the other side, the explicit determination of value is not in labor *per se* but in labor as work, as an element of a process which also encompasses the natural fertility of the soil on the same footing with labor. Thus, the corn model of the transitional period (the 'difficulties of production' idea) contains two opposing conceptions of production; one in which Ricardo constitutes production as the self-reproduction of corn (nature communing with itself) and one in which Ricardo constitutes production as specifically a labor process. It must not be inferred from this that either the notion of the 'self-reproduction of nature' or the idea of a 'labor process' are given adequate formulation (strictly speaking there is neither a concept of nor any concrete analysis of the labor process in Ricardo's work). On the contrary, the notion of the self-reproduction of nature taken as the social labor process is intrinsically incapable of consistent formulation, while the labor process cannot emerge in an adequate form so long as it remains tied in this way to a 'natural' conception of production. Furthermore, these two conceptions of production are intrinsically inconsistent in their implications for the treatment of value since within the conception of production as the self-reproduction of nature it is not possible to isolate labor, or more correctly work, as the defining factor and thereby to constitute the natural process as a labor process. The attempt to interpret classical political economy and its theory of value as involving a choice of one 'factor' (labor) among a number of alternatives (e.g. 'land' and 'capital') is fundamentally fallacious in that the difference between the natural constitution of production and its constitution as a labor process does not involve labor as a common element. The concept of labor only becomes relevant in the case of the latter. Ricardo's transition from the corn model to the labor theory of value involves a transformation of the conception of production from that of the self-reproduction of nature to the social labor process. Only with the construction of a different view of production does it become possible to determine labor (as opposed to 'work') and to consider production as a labor process.

The peculiar character of production as a labor process is given expression by Ricardo in the first part of the *Principles*. In so far as the objects of desire are the products of labor (are 'procured by labor') 'they may be multiplied, not in one country alone, but in many, almost *without any assignable limit*, if we are disposed to bestow the labor necessary to obtain them.' Thus (vol. I, p. 12, emphasis added):

in speaking . . . of commodities, of their exchangeable value, and of the laws which regulate their relative prices, we mean always such commodities only as can be increased in quantity by the exertion of human industry, and on the production of which competition operates without restraint.

It appears that Ricardo has restricted 'production' to a limited sphere: the production of objects which is potentially unlimited in extent. But to consider this as a restriction on the concept of production is to confuse the 'production' of specific material objects with that production with which Ricardo is in fact (although not in explicit statement) concerned: the production of value and of capital. Production in the former sense has intrinsic limitations. That labor which produces a specific object of need, 'useful labor' is labor with an intrinsic limit, labor that is determined by the object, that is defined as finished by the production of a use-value. But Ricardo specifically excludes this as the subject-matter of political economy. Ricardo is concerned with that production which is *unlimited*. This latter is not a restricted component of production in general but differs *in kind* from the limited production of useful objects as well as from the self-reproduction of nature.

The value of the commodity is that property which stamps it as indifferent to particularity of need. The commodity as a value relates to its owner not as this particular individual with needs which specify and determine his particularity but simply as an individual capable of owning property and recognized as such within a system of commodity-owning persons made equal in their status as commodity owners. The equality of status of their owners before the market underlies the equality of commodities as repositories of value. This equality is not, however, simply posited in the abstract as the self-determined choice of individuals. It is, rather, imposed upon them, making them individuals only by merit of their socially defined equality. This determinateness of the value relation is grasped within classical political economy when the latter constitutes value as *produced*. However, given that value is a purely social substance it cannot be conceived to be produced within a process of a purely natural character. The labor which produces value is not, then, naturally defined, but the substance of a social process: commodity production. But for labor to be conceived as the principle of a social production process it must be distinguished from the simple activity of the laborer viewed as on a par with the activity of nature. The laborer, who supplies his labor, must be distinguished from the animal which provides work and this distinction cannot itself be of a purely physiological character. The capacity of the laborer to produce commodities is a social and not a physical capacity. By contrast where the capacity to labor is equated with the laborer himself who is exchanged *in toto* the laborer is reduced to the status of an animal, his autonomy as a person is abridged and the social character of his activity is denied.

For the production of commodities to take place the principle of commodity production – labor – must appear in the form of labor-power as a commodity in the market exchanged by the laborer as its sole proprietor. Yet, the existence of labor-power as a commodity in the market presupposes the existence of capital as self-expanding value. Since labor-power is the source of labor, therefore of value, it can only be purchased by capital since capital alone possesses the peculiar need for value and is defined by the need for value value and increased value. Labor-power, the capacity to produce commodities, only exists in the market as a commodity in its confrontation and opposition to capital, which as money advanced, is the form of existence of the world of particular commodities. In the purchase of labor-power, capital acquires the capacity for its own production and expansion.

Labor is the activity which takes place upon the hiring of the worker by capital. The consumption of labor-power is the labor process, the process of commodity production and therefore the process of the production of value and, ultimately, surplus-value. But the consumption of labor-power is only intelligible upon the basis of its finding a purchaser and therefore upon the premise that there exists a need which can be fulfilled by labor-power. Such a need is no particular need for a definite use-value since labor-power is, by definition, the capacity for the production of all, therefore any, use-value and is not limited in relation to particular need. The purchase of labor-power requires, therefore, a purchaser with no particular need, a commodity owner whose need is for the world of all particular commodities. This purchaser is capital and it posits labor-power as the fulfillment of its need only by first establishing value and the expansion of value as the need which is specific to it and which defines it as capital. Capital, as self-expanding value, posits labor-power as that commodity which fulfills this need of expansion. The consumption of labor-power is, therefore, already implicitly established not as production of particular objects of need but of value, and further, of surplus-value. The labor process is therefore no natural process of the production of 'things,' nor a simple process of the production of use-values; it is the process of the production of that universal social substance – value – and is therefore conceivable only as production on the part of capital. For labor-power to produce surplus-value it must become a part of, be united with, capital. The productivity of labor must become the productivity of capital just as the productivity of capital is recognized in classical political economy to be the productive activity of labor.

The Ricardo of the *Principles* takes as his subject the production of capital. Within the first chapter of the *Principles* the conditions of production are the conditions of the production of capital. Ricardo immediately presupposes a normal rate of profit (vol. I, pp. 33–4), so that production and exchange are predicated on the expansion of the unit of capital. The fact that the most elementary determinations of capital appear in Ricardo's work not as elementary determinations but as the totality of capitalist relations collapsed into their simplest elements excludes any notion of production which is untainted by the capital relation. Implicit within the simple conception of production put forward by Ricardo lurk the most complex and distinctive features of capitalist production as a whole. The production with which Ricardo is concerned is therefore the production of value and expanded value (profit). The aim of production is defined by the normal rate or profit. This, then, is production not of material objects but of value, and is the origin of the conception with which Ricardo begins the *Principles* of production 'without assignable limit.' Such production is not production for use but the production of value, production without limit in the specific object which always goes beyond any fixed limit.[5] The process which produces value and profit is not the process of production in the abstract but the 'labor process.' With this condition the specification of wealth to capital is rooted in the determination of the production of wealth. Thus, in commenting on Malthus's restriction of the concept of wealth to those products which are 'useful,' Ricardo agrees with the conception put forward and, without explicit notice, gives to that conception a radical interpretation. For Ricardo wealth only includes 'useful' products of land and labor, and 'useful' means 'those material objects which are capable of accumulation, and definite valuation' (vol. II, p. 14).

The labor process is intimately bound up with the value relation and connects the production of useful objects to the system of commodity exchange. The concept of a labor process is dependent on the concept of value. The subject of the theory of value, the value relation, has no existence outside of the system of commodity exchange. But the latter is directly a relation between commodities in which the exchange-value of one commodity (and therefore its value) is expressed in the particular embodiment of the value of the other (in the 'use-value' of the other commodity), specifically in the form of money. Value is, therefore, not expressible outside of the form of a particular useful object and therefore outside of the conditions which specify production to the use-value of the product. In this manner general labor is tied also to a particular production process and the 'labor process' is defined as the unity of the production of value and use-value.

In classical political economy the necessity of expressing value in the commodity and therefore the necessity of situating labor within the labor process, appears concretely in the treatment of the measure of value. In all cases classical economy measures value in a particular commodity and the central problem of the measure of value is that of finding the appropriate commodity, therefore the appropriate useful object, with which to estimate value. Smith employs the commodity labor-power and measures labor and value in the commodity 'labor.' Ricardo attempts to unearth an 'invariable measure of value' which is the peculiar commodity with the characteristic of measuring the value of all other commodities.

The necessity of discovering the correct useful object within which the value relation may be directly observed is founded in the fact that the commodity as a value only exists in relation to other commodities distinguished in form from the commodity. But since the value of the commodity can only be expressed in the use-value of another commodity the general labor embodied in a given commodity is only expressed through a relation which involves the specification of labor to its employment in the production of the commodity in which value is estimated. The expression of value in use-value drains labor of its universality and social determination. This violates the determinateness of the product as use-value to its constitution within society. The attitude of society toward the objects of need is not one of contemplation but the active process of forming the object. The commodity is not simply *there* as use-value, independently of its social condition. It does not become a use-value simply by entering, from outside, into a specific social relation, but is posited as a use-value only within that social relation, and in particular by the labor process.

The commodity as a value is not connected to any particular need, or to need in general, but to the production process considered without regard to fixed need. But, just as value is only expressed as exchange-value, and therefore as a relation of use-values, of objects of specific need, the substance of value, labor, is only expressed in the specific relation of use-values and therefore in a relation of specific needs. Labor must be embodied in a use-value, must be specified to its product in order for it to become abstract human labor. The production of the commodity as the unity of use-value and value is simultaneously indifferent to particular use-value and the origin of the particularity of use-value. It is the labor process in this sense which is the process of the production of commodities.

Ultimately, it is the concept of capital which destroys the original Ricardian constitution of the production process and that dissolves the conceptual basis of the corn model for which production is confined, in its conception, to a limited sphere, the production of corn. This is the case even within the *Essay on Profits* where Ricardo's primary concern is not with the conditions of production in the abstract but with the conditions of the production of profit. Only in so far as those conditions of production are considered to be the conditions of the production of capital does Ricardo recognize the limitations of the natural conception with which he attempts to grasp the problem of profit in this period of his thinking. In the *Principles* the implicit theme of the *Essay* emerges as the dominant theme. Ricardo's concern is with that production which has no limit, capitalist production. That which produces capital cannot itself be limited but must be equally indifferent to the specific useful object which has been produced. This principle of production without limit is abstract labor, that labor in terms of which it is possible for the first time to constitute production as the labor process, as the unity of the production of useful objects and of value. The production process is a labor process in so far as it has as its product not only a specific use-value but *value*. 'Labor' which produces value, abstract human labor, is labor without limit, indifferent to the specific useful form of its immediate object. The specificity of the labor to its product as a particular use-value originates not in the labor but in the means of production which, particularly as machinery, give to the labor and its product the particularity which defines the use-value. Illimitability is, therefore, intrinsic in the idea of labor and not the result of an external summation or generalization of 'particular labors.' When labor is made directly particular it appears that labor without limit is a special case of particular, limited labor, encompasses a sub-class of the latter, generalizes only a part of the conception of labor, while the latter also includes labor that cannot be repeated without limit (as, for example, the labor which produces works of art). But the labor which produces value is not a generalization of particular labors. Labor is tied to value not by an arbitrary restriction of the scope of the value problem but by the conception of value and by the conception of labor.

Labor is not working activity in the abstract, the moving principle of production in the sense of transformation without specification to its conditions and product. On the contrary, the specificity of production to economic life derives from the constitution of production as value in the process of coming into existence. Labor is value, not immediately, but as the active principle of a process. The specificity of the product to its production process is also the specificity of that process to its product–value. Thus value is not attached externally to production but exists immanent within production as its driving force and this mode of existence of value within its own process of production is what classical political economy calls labor. This conception of production is the classical 'labor theory of value.'

Ricardo's mature position on value is characterized by the consistent view of production as the production of value, as the labor process. The explicit determination of production as a natural process is eliminated. Ricardo no longer considers value to be the result of the difficulty of production but of labor. He considers the problem of value to be the problem of the production of capital and of profit. This is not to imply that the natural process has been purged from Ricardian economics. What has taken place is the elimination of any explicit presence of production as the self-reproduction of nature and the replacement of such conception by the labor process as both the natural production process and, simultaneously, the process of production of value, the labor process. Ricardo's mature position thus subsumes the natural world and the determination of the role of man as an element of nature into the process of capitalist production. This reduction has a logical basis in the fact that the labor process includes the process of production of use-values so that the production of value and the production of use-value are united in the product, the commodity, which is both an object of need and an object of exchange. Just as in the case of Smith, Ricardo considers labor as the universal social principle.

The transition from the second to the final stage of Ricardo's thinking on the value question contains, implicit within it, a resolution of the question: why does classical political economy consider labor to be the substance of value? This answer can be found in the transformation of labor from the status of one element within a natural process of production to labor within the labor process. This is simultaneously the transformation of the natural process into the capitalist process of production. In the transitional period the two views of production exist together but have distinct expressions. In the mature discussion of value all production is production based on capital. The emergence of production as exclusively the labor process is also the emergence of capitalist production as synonymous with production itself.

It is of the greatest significance that the emergence of the concept of labor and of the connection of labor to value is simultaneously the emergence of the *theory* of value. The necessity of passing beyond his earlier evasions of the value question is, for Ricardo, identically the necessity of connecting value to labor. There is, in Ricardian thinking, an identity between the emergence of the theory of value, of a systematic account for the value relation on the most general level, and the labor principle. But this cannot be adequately grasped as the *choice* of a value theory. Ricardo does not first come upon the necessity for a theory of value and then, subsequently, determine the labor principle as a principle of value. For classical political economy the necessity of a theory of value is the requirement that value and the exchange system be grounded in a social process, that the status of the object as a commodity be constituted as bestowed upon the object by its own process of production, that production be itself commodity production. A theory of value is synonymous with a grounding of the value relation in a social process from out of which it is seen to emerge. The requirement for a theory and the specific content of the theory are not, therefore, separable.

Ricardo's mature position on value can be defined in terms of the consistent link of value to labor and therefore the explicit introduction into economic analysis of the concept of labor. But the positing by Ricardo of production as the labor process, therefore as the process of production of value, comes into conflict with the requirement that the exchange of commodities conform to the conditions of capitalist production and to the formation of an average rate of profit. The clear comprehension of this paradox, which was of special import- ance to Ricardian economics, hinges on the understanding of the dual pre- supposition of capitalist production. It is essential, in particular, to recognize that the grounding of value in labor, and the exchange of commodities according to the principle of equal profit on equal capital advanced, are both conditions of capitalist production. Only in the light of this result is it possible to grasp the central dilemma of Ricardian thinking as a real contradiction.

In the foregoing discussion of Ricardo's concept of production we have indicated the sense in which the constitution of the production process as a labor process emerges out of the concept of production as the production of capital; production which is, in principle, without limit. Value is the category which grasps the indifference of the commodity to either the specificity of its owner or the specificity of the need which the commodity as a use-value is designed to meet. The labor process is the process of production of value in this sense and the labor which is the moving force of that process is itself possessed of this same indifference. It is that indifference which marks the production process as the employment of labor. This notion is the core of Ricardo's conception of exchange and originates with Ricardo's earliest thinking on the subject of price. The idea that commodities have an 'intrinsic value which is not arbitrary,' expresses the indifference of the commodity to the chance meeting of particular individuals and, therefore, its dependence on a substance which is indifferent to the particularity of those individuals, their particular needs and their particular personalities. This substance, which is 'intrinsic' to the commodity, is its value, and it is intrinsic not in the sense that it is to be found within the commodity as a material object but in the sense that it adheres to the commodity in its social existence, that it adheres in this sense to the commodity and not to the particularity of its owner.

It is possible to place this result into sharper focus by contrasting Ricardo's thinking on this point with that of the neo-classical theory of value. Within the latter the value of a commodity is wholly determined by the particularity of the individuals engaged in the exchange taken as a whole. It is their preferences, generated without regard to society, that interact to determine the exchange-values of commodities. In this case, a commodity has no value outside of the specific personalities present in the market at the moment during which it is exchanged. It has, therefore, only an exchange-value which is purely relative to the accidental meeting of individuals. Such an exchange-value is arbitrary and conflicts directly with the idea expressed by Ricardo that value is not arbitrary but intrinsic. The difference is that in the case of Ricardo the exchange of commodities is grounded in a determinate social reality and is, therefore, independent of the whims of the specific individuals in the market. Exchange has a social grounding which is expressed in the category of value. In classical political economy value is, therefore, both 'absolute' and relative. It is relative in that it is only expressed in a particular exchange and therefore in a relation of two specific commodities. But it is also absolute in that underlying that individual exchange is a social substance, value, which reveals the social nature of the exchange.

This notion of an 'intrinsic value' appears throughout Ricardo's mature writing and expresses the defining characteristic of Ricardo's mature position on the value problem. In this writing Ricardo's emphasis is on the contrast between 'absolute' and 'relative' or 'exchangeable' value (vol. IV, p. 396):

Anything having value is a good measure of the comparative value of all other commodities at the same time and place, but will be of no use in indicating the variations in their absolute value at distant times and in distant places.

So long as the meeting of individuals in the market place is accidental, that is, possesses no social determination but is purely individual, the exchange of commodities takes place at a rate wholly specific to time and place. Relative value has an existence with regard to a specific exchange. But absolute value is indifferent to time and place. In the case of the former there can only be the price of the commodity at a given time and place, there can be no 'intrinsic' or 'absolute' value which is independent not of exchange but of a specific exchange relation of two specific commodities at a given time and place. For Ricardo the notions of 'intrinsic,' 'absolute,' 'natural,' and 'positive' value all express the grounding of exchange in a social substance.

This implicit distinction of the *form* of value also has a presence in Smith's version of the labor theory of value. For Smith the exchange-value or relative value of a commodity may alter either with an alteration in the commodity with which it exchanges or with an alteration in the value of that commodity. On the other hand, the value of the commodity ought not to be subject to such fluctuation. The value of the commodity is fixed in the exchange relation between that commodity and labor. Absolute or real value is, therefore, expressed in the latter and when that exchange finds itself subject to those alterations peculiar to relative value Smith's entire conception of value and exchange is disoriented. The labor-commanded theory expresses the implicit, but as yet inadequate, distinction within Smith's theory of value between the exchange-value of the commodity, its relation to any particular commodity, and its value, which is its 'real price' and grounds the exchange relation.

The contrast between exchange-value and real or absolute value is the key to the refusal on Ricardo's part to exclude the connection between labor and value in the light of the implications of an average rate of profit for the relative rates of exchange of commodities. 'To me it appears a contradiction to say a thing has increased in natural value while it continues to be produced under precisely the same circumstances as before' (vol. IV, p. 375). The introduction of absolute value raises, for Ricardo, the problem of the constitution of that absolute value, the problem of its origin and substance. Within the Ricardian conception there exist two distinct resolutions of the problem of absolute value. First, Ricardo appeals to the previously established link between labor and value. This allows him to ground exchange in labor which is the origin of absolute value and grounds exchange-value. However, the inconsistency between this conception of value and the introduction of an average rate of profit forces Ricardo to seek an alternative basis for determining absolute value: the invariable measure of value.*

4 The invariable measure of value

Section VI of the *Principles* deals with the invariable measure of value. According to Ricardo the necessity for an invariable measure derives from the need to isolate the movement of 'real' value in the face of alterations in the 'relative' value of commodities. The distinction which lies behind the quest for

* The reason for the introduction of an average rate of profit at this stage in the analysis is connected to the method of construction of the argument of the *Principles* and, in particular, to the relation which emerges between capitalist production as a whole and the analysis of the labor process; cf. below, chapter 4.

an invariable measure is, then, that between value and the way in which it is expressed as a relation between two particular commodities. It appears, at first, that this invariable measure measures a real value which is ultimately labor. But, for Ricardo, the real value of commodities is not, strictly speaking, the labor embodied in them (vol. I, p. 44):

But if this cause of variation in the value medium could be restored – if it were possible that in the production of money for instance, the same quantity of labor should at all times be required, still it would not be a perfect standard or invariable measure of value, because as I have already endeavored to explain, it would be subject to relative variations from a rise or fall of wages, on account of the different proportions of fixed capital which might be necessary to produce it, and to produce these commodities whose alteration of value we wished to ascertain.

For Ricardo commodities possess a real value which is the origin of their value in exchange. Yet this real value is not accessible to economic science. It is not, in principle, capable of expression. All of the various circumstances which bring about variations in the relative rates of exchange of commodities relating to changes in labor requirements of production, in durability of fixed capital, in time periods of productions, etc. 'disqualify any commodity that can be thought of from being a perfectly accurate measure of value' (vol. I, p. 44). It is not, then, the difficulty of discovering such a commodity in the world of exchange but the impossibility of 'thinking' of such a commodity (vol. IV, pp. 395–6):

There are writers deeply impressed with the importance of possessing an absolute measure of value to which all things may be referred, and the question is not whether an accurate measure of this description can be obtained, but whether anything approximating it can be suggested.

The reason for this has nothing to do with the scarcity of appropriate objects but with the fact that the requirements of an invariable standard conflict with the concept of the commodity itself. The commodity, for Ricardo, is, first, a product of labor in the sense considered above, and second, the product of capital and as such required to be consistent with the conditions of capitalist production and, in particular, with equality of return on capital advanced. But, in so far as the commodity is a product of capital, by definition, its rate of exchange will not be invariant to changes in the wage and the rate of profit.

There are two problems involved here. First, the exchange-value of the commodity will alter independently of its real value and second the exchange-value of two commodities may alter without revealing in which the real alteration of absolute value has taken place. What remains problematic about the entire construction and forces Ricardo continually to revise and reconsider it down to the last months of his life is the determination of real value. That this is, in fact, problematic emerges when attention is directed to the manner in which Ricardo constructs the problem of the invariable measure and of the effect of changes in the wage on relative values of commodities. For Ricardo this is in every case posed as a problem of *alterations* in the wage or in the productivity of labor (vol. I, pp. 44–5):

If, for example, we were to fix on gold as a standard, it is evident that it is but a commodity obtained under the same contingencies as every other commodity and requiring labor and fixed capital to produce it. Like every other commodity, improvements in the saving of labor might be applied to its production, and consequently it might fall in relative value to other things merely on account of the greater facility of producing it. . . . I have already remarked, that the effect on the relative prices of things, from a variation in profits, is comparatively slight; that by far the most important effects are produced by the varying quantities of labor required for production; and therefore, if we suppose this important cause of variation removed from the production of gold, we shall probably possess as near an approximation to a standard measure of value as can be theoretically conceived.

While Ricardo indicates that the problem of measuring value would not be eliminated with the elimination of variations in value he still holds to the idea that it is such variations that underlie the value problem and if it were possible to eliminate them in the case of a particular commodity (such as gold) then a manageable, if not perfect, standard of value would be provided.

For Ricardo the value problem, by the last sections of the *Principles*, has become predominantly the problem of *variations* in value (which is a special concern of Ricardian thinking throughout the development of the Ricardian value analysis). The reason for this is that the entire notion of 'real value' disappears when changes in the wage are left out of account. When such changes are eliminated commodities may still possess a real value but it is not possible to give that real value any expression. The real value of the commodity is not the amount of the invariable standard (presuming the existence of such a standard) for which the commodity exchanges but the amount of the change in relative value in exchange for the invariable standard which comes about as a result of a change in the productivity of labor or in the wage. It is not possible, as in the case of Smith, to measure real value directly in labor-power and Ricardo explicitly denies Smith's resolution of the problem (vol. I, p. 46). In effect, where there are no changes there is no basis for making statements about the real value of commodities. Even in the face of such changes it is only possible to consider changes in real value and not the level of real value. It is precisely for this reason that the real value disappears in the absence of such changes. Ultimately, the failure of real value estimated in this manner to ground exchange is due to the fact that 'real value' has no, even relative, independent subsistence and ground. Once real value is severed from labor time it is no longer possible to distinguish it from relative value so that it becomes a special case of relative value (labor commanded in Smith and the invariable standard in Ricardo) which is still a relative value and, therefore, in principle incapable of grounding relative value.

The notion of real value considered in this sense, displays a tendency to dissolve directly into simple exchange-value and in so doing to fail to express any grounding of exchange-value outside of the immediate exchange relation. This dissolution of real value reveals the original inability of real value to distinguish itself from exchange-value. The invariable measure of value measures real value directly in the form of exchange-value. It therefore does not and cannot measure the absolute value itself, as distinguished from its form of appearance in the exchange. In classical political economy the necessity of expressing a distinction between value and the direct exchange relation in order to constitute value as a relation which is not arbitrary but 'intrinsic' is coupled with the necessity of collapsing value back into exchange-value. This typical trait of classical thinking also appears in Smith's version of the labor-commanded theory of value. Smith only speaks of the 'value' of a commodity to its owner who wishes not to consume but to exchange it. Yet this value which is expressed in exchange, is at the same time the 'real price' of the commodity, the 'cost' in labor. The submerging of real price into exchange-value and of the latter into value is precisely the role of the labor-commanded theory. Value only appears when an individual owns a commodity but does not wish himself to consume it. This expresses the fact that the commodity *as a value* is, in principle, indifferent to the specificity of its owner (though not, of course, to ownership in general). Value is only expressed in exchange-value for the same reason that, for Smith, work is only expressed as labor in the exchange relation. It is in the exchange that the equivalence of commodity owners *qua* owners of commodities is expressed. In the exchange the commodity directly asserts this indifference and generality, this purely social character.

The social character of the commodity, its existence as a product of labor, is only given expression in the exchange of commodities. This social character which is its value, therefore, is present to classical political economy only in the form of exchange-value. The labor-commanded theory of Smith and the invariable measure of value of Ricardo give immediate expression to the slipping of value into exchange-value and the resulting disappearance of the value concept. These conceptions freeze the value concept in the transition into exchange-value and attempt to express both value and its form in one category expressing and denying the distinction between them.

The labor-commanded theory forces the exchange-value of commodities to express itself in the commodity labor which is also the real price of commodities so that the exchange-value is directly the real price. The invariable measure of value is a commodity which therefore is capable of expressing exchange-value while at the same time possessing the property of revealing the alterations in real value. In the case of Smith the exchange-value in labor-power is directly the real value and in that of Ricardo the exchange-value in the invariable standard reveals directly the movement of real value. The labor-commanded theory serves a function comparable in this respect to that of the invariable standard.

The classical analysis of labor collapses the different categories of labor into a homogeneous whole, 'labor.' Similarly, the classical theory of value reduces the distinct determinations of value to the single notion of exchange-value. In the Ricardian invariable standard the phenomenon of absolute value is directly abolished within its mode of expression.

For Ricardo, the value of a commodity, its absolute value, is the incipient expression of the social character of the commodity form. In so far as the invariable standard serves to reduce the absolute value to exchange-value the social form merges with its individual expression: the individual exchange which has, as a result, lost any explicit social grounding. For Smith the labor-commanded theory of value collapses social labor into the application of particular labor, the social into its natural substance in the individual labor process. For Ricardo the invariable standard obliterates the social grounding of exchange. It claims to ground exchange while eliminating any necessary link between value, exchange, and labor. It is precisely the implicit recognition of this that leads Ricardo to argue that it 'appears a contradiction to say a thing has increased in natural value while it continues to be produced under precisely the same circumstances as before.' While it is a contradiction for Ricardo to argue at the outset of the *Principles* that the grounding of exchange in labor is a 'doctrine of the utmost importance in political economy' (vol. I, p. 13), and later to argue that commodities cannot in general exchange in proportion to labor-values, it is a contradiction with a rational foundation, a necessity within the classical system as a whole. Such a rational foundation is to be found in the emergence of a distinction between value and exchange-value as a requirement of the theory and at the same time of the reduction of the one to the other as equally a necessity of the theoretical movement as a whole. This simultaneous differentiation and reduction is the ultimate source of the fundamental contradiction of the classical theory of value.

III Value and capital

1

It is in the attempt to treat the capital relation as an exchange relation, therefore to treat it concretely rather than in abstraction from its systematic implications and conditions, that the breakdown of the classical theory takes on its most acute form. The dual existence of the wage as a price and as a share confounds the attempt to conceptualize value, price, and labor as equivalent. On one side, the interpretation of value as labor established the possibility of a scientific grounding of the exchange system and of the capital relation, while, on the other side, the confusion of the real content of that labor with a purely natural substance excluded any consistent interpretation of exchange in general and therefore of the exchange of capital for labor. The dissolution of the labor-commanded theory, which was designed to overcome these contradictions, was, as we have seen, intrinsic to it. Ricardo is unable to follow Smith and Malthus along this route as a result of his explicit recognition of the fact that the labor which is the substance of value is not itself a commodity. While Ricardo never actually distinguishes between labor and labor-power there can be no question but that the effect of that distinction was much more clearly recognized by Ricardo than by any other member of the classical school.

Ricardo's rejection of the labor-commanded theory drives him simultaneously in two directions. First, toward the articulation of the problem of an 'invariable measure of value,' and second, in the direction of the explicit recognition of the distinction between labor and labor-power and through that distinction in the direction of a concept of surplus-value. The former is the predominant path of classical thought since the invariable measure serves not to resolve the contradictions of the classical theory of value but to remove them to a higher level and reconstruct them in a definitive form. The second direction leads towards an incipient development of classical thought which opens up the possibility of a final resolution of these contradictions, but only at the cost of the abandonment of the classical conception of bourgeois economy as governed by 'natural' laws, therefore as a form of nature.

Ricardo, once directly confronted with the necessity of criticizing the labor-commanded principle as the latter is asserted by Malthus, states explicitly that there must be a difference between the quantity of labor which appears to the capitalist as his cost and that quantity which forms the substance and measure of the value of his product (vol. II, pp. 78–9):

But what is meant by a quantity of labor, being the cost of a commodity? – by cost, is always meant the expense of production estimated in some commodity, which has value, and it always includes the profit of stock. The cost of production of two commodities, as I before observed, may be in proportion to the quantity of labor employed on them, but it is essentially different from the labor itself.

Further on Ricardo states explicitly that 'the relative value of commodities is in proportion to the quantity of labor bestowed on them. That value may be double what the labor cost' (vol. II, p. 102). So long as Ricardo is forced to focus his attention upon the particular exchange relation between capital and labor he is also forced to recognize the distinction between the labor which forms the value of the commodity (including the commodity labor) and that labor which is itself a commodity. Labor is distinguished between that labor which is a commodity – labor-power – and that labor which is the cost of production of the commodity – abstract human labor, labor properly considered.

Yet Ricardo does not conclude from this implicit distinction between labor and labor-power that there is also a general distinction of value between the labor costs of production and the labor value of the product. Even though this distinction is practically made within the distinction between labor and labor-power it is never actually consummated and that for two interconnected reasons. First, as we have seen, Ricardo never actually conceives of labor-power and therefore of the specificity of the exchange between capital and labor. To this extent even though he repudiates the confusion of Adam Smith between labor as a commodity and labor as the substance of value he retains the conceptual basis of that confusion in the absence of a concept of labor-power (therefore, of course, equally the lack of a concept of labor). This absence is, as we have seen, the result of the reduction of labor to a purely natural substance and of the conception of production as a purely material interchange, a metabolism with nature. It is equally this natural conception of production which excludes a conception of surplus-value.

That this is the case becomes clear when it is pointed out that Ricardo does possess a concept of surplus *produce*. According to Ricardo 'profits come out of surplus-produce' (vol. II, p. 128), and this is by no means an isolated statement (cf. vol. II, pp. 134, 187, 211). The reason that surplus-value appears only as surplus produce is that Ricardo conceives of distribution as the material division of a physical product. This conception of distribution while predicated upon the specificity of the capital relation and essentially designed to account for that relation fails altogether to grasp that essential category which is alone capable of expressing the character of the exchange between capital and labor: surplus-value; fails, therefore, to express the capital–labor relation as an exchange and not as the simple redivision of a material product.

2

In the previous section the Ricardian theory was considered in terms of its development through distinct stages. The significance of these phases of the development of that theory is not, however, in their temporal interconnection *per se* but in the manner in which they reveal the different aspects of the Ricardian theory as a whole. The specific manner in which the conditions of social production and the conditions of the self-reproduction of nature are seen to interpenetrate gives Ricardian and classical theory their peculiar character. This interpenetration also holds the key to the correct compre-hension of the contradictions of the Ricardian theory of value. This is equally true with respect to the relationship which obtains between the theory of value and the theory of distribution.

The starting point, both conceptually and within the development of Ricardo's thinking, for the theory of distribution is the corn economy of the transitional stage of the Ricardian value theory. The corn economy serves to establish a radical disjunction between the determination of value and the analysis of distribution, between the exchange of commodities and the dis-tribution of the net product between the three great classes which contribute to its production.

In the corn economy the typical unit of production is the individual farm. The capitalist who runs the farm hires land from the landlord and workers to work the land. He has also a certain amount of 'capital' (seeds, etc.) remaining from the produce of the preceding year (as part of the output of that year).

Capital has the form of a 'wages fund,' the part of the product which is 'advanced' to labor at the beginning of the production period. It is the share of labor as a part of the product of the preceding production period. At the end of the production period the capitalist finds himself in possession of a certain amount of corn, certain obligations to turn over some part of that corn to the landlord as rent, and the necessity of advancing another part to the workers as wages. The capitalist retains a portion for his own consumption, for inputs into production in the following season, and possibly for the expansion of production. This process may, then, repeat itself in the following years.

In an economy such as this the distribution of the output is a wholly transparent process. It is the distribution of a physical product between the three great classes – workers, capitalists, and landlords. The output exists in the purely material form of a given amount of a homogeneous product, corn. The measurement of the net product is directly in terms of the natural units of corn. In this case the distribution of the product has nothing to do with the exchange of commodities. This result is the central core of Ricardian distribution theory. This is the standpoint from which Ricardo begins his thinking on the problem of distribution and this is the standpoint which underlies his thinking throughout his work on political economy.

The secret of the simplicity of the corn model rests on the total lack of exchange of commodities. More correctly, there is exchange of commodities – the chief focus of the model is the 'price' of corn – but there is no rationale for such an exchange; there is the commodity form (Ricardo always considers the products of labor to be commodities) without the substance of the exchange relation. Since only one product is produced and since it is only that product in combination with land and labor that is required for production there can be no exchange of the output of the individual farms. The only output is corn and this is the same in the case of each unit of production. Therefore the only inputs which are both required in production and are not the products of that same process of production are land and labor. Of course, it would be possible to consider the latter (especially labor) as equally output and in so doing to consider them as elements of the natural transformation process. On the other hand, for Ricardo, it needs to be emphasized that the process of production is not simply a natural process but the capitalist process seen as a natural process. In this respect corn distinguishes itself in that it is produced by a capitalist farm and for profit. Thus, for Ricardo, the only real product is corn and the reason for this is that the process which is explicitly a natural process is tacitly the labor process. Since land and labor are not considered products it would be possible, paradoxically, to constitute them as commodities. Indeed, this is precisely the procedure of neo-classical economics. The commodity derives its exchangeability from its scarcity, therefore from the absence of its full constitution as a product. In this case, corn itself becomes a commodity since it exchanges for land and labor. On the other hand, the introduction of the mediation of exchange is inessential to the distribution of the product. What takes place is not the exchange of capital for labor, of wages for labor-power, but the appropriation on the part of the workers of a part of the physical net product. This is direct appropriation rather than exchange since purchase of the corn outside of the unit of production has no rationale.

Ricardo considers the solution of the problem of distribution to resolve the distributive shares into the natural recompense of the three classes. The wage is the 'quantity of food that is . . . necessary for . . . subsistence,' and depends on the 'nature of man' (vol. IV, p. 14). Similarly, Ricardo writes that 'profits depend on wages, wages under common circumstances, on the price of food, and necessaries, and the price of food and necessaries on the fertility of the last land cultivated' (vol. VII, p. 78). The rent is 'that portion of the produce of the earth which is paid to the landlord for the use of the original and indestructible powers of the soil' (vol. I, p. 67). In other words the source of rent is the soil itself in its purely natural existence.

3

The critical link in constituting the shares of the product as natural is the severing of distribution from the value form (vol. VIII, pp. 194–5, emphasis added):

the great questions of Rent, Wages, and Profits must be explained by the proportions in which the whole produce is divided between landlords, capitalists, and laborers, and which *are not essentially connected with the doctrine of value.* By getting rid of rent, which we may do on the corn produced with the capital last employed, and on all commodities produced by labor in manufactures, the distribution between capitalist and laborer becomes a much more simple consideration. The greater the portion of the result of labor that is given to the laborer, the smaller must be the rate of profits, and vice versa. Now this portion must essentially depend on the facility of producing the necessaries of the laborer – if the facility be great, a small portion of any commodity, the result of capital and labor, will be sufficient to furnish the laborer with necessaries, and consequently profits will be high. The truth of this doctrine I deem to be absolutely demonstrable.

Ricardo's assertion that distribution is independent of value gives away the secret to Ricardo's theory of value. Value, for Ricardo, is purely formal, it is the social form of the underlying reality which is the physical distribution of a materially defined, natural product – corn. This is precisely the conception with which Ricardo begins the *Principles* (vol. I, p. 5, emphasis added):

The produce of the earth – all that is derived from its surface by the united application of labor, machinery, and capital, is divided among the three classes of the community; namely, the proprietor of the land, the owner of the stock or capital necessary for its cultivation, and the laborers by whose industry it is cultivated.

Here Ricardo accomplishes a two-fold reduction; all output is reduced to the output of agriculture, the sphere in which production emerges as founded on the qualities of nature, and the total product is identified with the net product. Distribution is seen at the level of the economy as a whole, precisely as it would appear within an isolated individual unit of production, as the distribution of a physical product. Ricardo's theory of production, viewed from this angle, takes as its subject precisely that conception which is typical of pre-Ricardian theory: wealth, in this case in the form of 'produce' (a somewhat advanced form it must be admitted since produce implies a connection between wealth and a labor process while wealth *per se* does not). The value form has been expunged and with it so also has the explicitly social character of production and distribution.

None the less, the social forms remain present in an implicit existence which has the force to eventually overthrow the entire construction. This force is expressed with special significance for Ricardo within the categories of wages and profits. It is the consideration of the natural process of distribution as a distribution between wages and profit that confounds the natural character of that process itself. In other words, the corn economy fails to stand up as a consistent framework (just as the savage state of man fails in the *Wealth of Nations*) in so far as it is constructed in terms of relations which require, in their very constitution, the full development of the social conditions.

While Ricardo starts out the *Principles* by considering the wage as a share in the 'produce of the earth,' in the chapter on wages he argues that 'labor, like all things which are purchased and sold . . . has its natural and market price' (vol. I, p. 93). It is not self-evidently equivalent to consider the wage as a basket of necessaries and to consider the wage as the price of a commodity. Ignoring rent, and following Ricardo's fixed capital, the question which underlies this contradiction is the following: to what extent, or in what sense, is it necessary to speak of the distribution of output between workers and capitalists (wages and profits) as also the exchange of commodities? That is, to what extent is the wage not simply a form of a natural bundle of goods but the quantitative determination of the relation of capital to labor? The answer to this can only be that it is necessary to speak of the 'wage' precisely in so far as it is the capital–labor relation which is under consideration, that is, precisely to the extent that the production process is the process of production of capital, the labor process, and not the natural process of the self-reproduction of nature. For the Ricardo of the *Principles* the wage is a price, it is the value of labor. The share of labor is determined by the value of labor where labor is a commodity whose value arises in the same manner as does that of any other commodity. To be sure, this constitution of labor as a commodity involves Ricardo in precisely those confusions which underlie Smith's theory of value. Labor as a commodity is a purely social entity with no necessary natural or physical grounding. Yet for classical political economy the labor which is a commodity, that specific social reality labor-power, is immediately

labor itself where the labor involved partakes of the contradictory determinations of the physical and the social which define it as the specifically
classical notion of labor. None the less, Ricardo here considers labor as the
labor which receives a share of the net product and therefore as labor-power
the commodity whose 'share' in the net product is determined by the system of
valuation. The 'one commodity model' denies the distinction between labor
and labor-power thereby denying the specificity of the latter, the commodity
character of labor-power, and the specific relation of the latter to capital.

In so far as the wage is a price it can only emerge on the basis of the system
of commodity production which presupposes the specific value relation which
we have already observed is only constituted as the production of capital.
Such production is intrinsically inconsistent with production as the production
of produce, of naturally defined objects. This is precisely the reason that such
production is inconsistent with any restriction to a limited sphere and
requires the simultaneous access to the world of commodity exchange and
production. To consider the wage on the basis of a corn economy is to consider a specific social relation without its rational foundation, a relation of
capital without the capital relation. Such a construction is analogous to the
beaver and deer economy of Adam Smith in which exchange based on labor
is treated in the absence of its rational foundation in capitalist production and
in the division of labor based on capital.

While the corn economy is ultimately incapable of dealing with the wage
relation it does attempt to construct a notion of the wage which is independent
of the production of value: the wage as a bundle of necessaries. In classical
political economy the wages-fund notion also has the following significance:
it collapses the exchange of labor-power with capital, the purchase of labor-
power with money, into the purchase of consumption goods by the worker,
and then collapses the latter into the direct appropriation of a part of the
physical net product by labor. In this way the wages-fund notion eliminates
the specific form of the capital relation as an exchange relation. The abolition
of the value form extends to the relation of capital to labor which, according
to this doctrine can be understood as a purely physical transfer or appropriation. The fact that the value relation mediates this transfer is purely formal
and needs to be penetrated by economic analysis in order to reveal the real
relation independent of exchange and the market.

In the case of profit, however, Ricardo is incapable of uncovering any
rational basis for its existence within the natural production process exempli-
fied by the corn economy. Profit, for Ricardo, is a residual, it is what is left
after the distribution of wages and rents. This residual character of profit
within the corn economy indicates the absence of any inner justification for the
profit share within that economy. In effect, profit can only subsist where there
is a gap within the constitution of the natural process. It might be said that
profit is the space which the social principle explicitly occupies within the
self-reproduction of nature, it is the point unoccupied by nature itself. The

social exists as a rupture within nature. Since profit is the social principle as it is present within nature, is a disjunction within nature, it is not possible for Ricardo to give any account for profit except by exclusion. Ricardo accounts for wages as the necessaries of the workers, for rent in terms of the fertility of the earth, and successfully removes the social form implied by the exchange relation by reducing all production to the production of corn. It is not, however, possible to account for profit, to ground it in nature for the reason that, so far as Ricardo is concerned, production of profit is inevitably capitalist production. Profit is produced, not given.* Land and labor appear as natural presuppositions of the production process neither of which is itself an output of that process so far as that process is conceived as social. The production of labor is not the subject of the profit-making calculus of the individual unit of capital. Both labor and land appear as that which produces rather than as the produced. But in the case of profit we are dealing with that which is at once pre-condition and product.

Wages and rents retain the character of natural shares, as opposed to profit, precisely because they are not produced, that is, in the capitalist sense and by the individual unit of capital. Capital, on the other hand, is the specific product of the labor process. Even in the corn economy the capital consists of corn which is distinguished from land and labor as a product of the capitalist production process and as the output of the unit of capital. Profit, therefore, as the return to capital, expresses immediately that the process of production is a process of the production of capital.

One recourse which Ricardo does in fact take is to attempt to reduce profit to a natural factor within the production process. Capital must, in this sense, be equated in form with labor and land as natural pre-conditions of 'production' where the latter is the production of material objects. For Ricardo this is made possible by the concept of capital itself. 'Capital is that part of the wealth of a country which is employed in production, and consists of food, clothing, tools, raw materials, machinery &c. necessary to give effect to labor.' Just as the wage is so much corn, capital is so much food, clothing, and so on. Capital becomes independent of value so that its quantity may increase 'without its value increasing, and even while its value is actually diminishing' (vol. I, p. 95). In this case capital has rediscovered its classical origins as stock and it becomes possible to consider the production of capital and value as natural processes. Within this same mode of conception Ricardo maintains (vol. VII, p. 377)

* Cf. K. Marx, *Grundrisse*, tr. M. Nicolaus (Harmondsworth: Penguin Books, 1973): 'Capital is now posited as the unity of production and circulation . . . Capital is now realized not only as value which reproduces itself and is hence perennial, but also as value which posits value. . . . Its movement consists of relating to itself, while it produces itself, at the same time as the foundation of what it has founded, as value presupposed to itself as surplus-value, or to the surplus-value as posited by it . . . capital thus posited as self-realizing value – is profit,' pp. 745–6.

that it is not because of this division into profits and wages, – it is not because capital accumulates, that exchangeable value varies, but it is in all stages of society, owing only to two causes: the one the more or less quantity of labor required, the other the greater or less durability of capital.

The constitution of capital as stock allows for the extension of the category of capital to all production both natural and social, both the reproduction of nature, individual production, and capitalist production. This brings Ricardo within grasp of the neo-classical conception, a conception which lurks throughout classical thinking. Profit is tied to the durability of capital (stock) so that the effect of profit on price is, in fact, the effect of the durability of capital joined to the movement of the wage. The extent to which the grounding of exchange in the natural process of 'labor' deviates from the natural measure of that exchange is measured by the durability of capital.

Once the category of capital and that of its quantitative expansion, profit, have been grasped as natural the only remaining question is that of the proportion which profit bears to wages. To give to profit a natural grounding is to take the conception of profit outside of social theory, leaving to the latter only the consideration of the specific quantitative expression of profit and the impact of the economic process on the pre-given capital relation. The predominant, almost exclusive, concern of the *Principles* is not with the theory of capital or the theory of distribution but with the proportion which profit bears to labor where the only theory of distribution is the theory of the movement of that proportion.* For Ricardo the production of value is given and it is its distribution that is the subject of economic science. Once capital has lost its character as the moving force of production, as both the pre-condition and product, there only remains the product itself. The process by which that product has arisen, which is the capital relation, has fallen outside of the domain of economic theory.

Thus classical political economy undergoes, in the hands of Ricardo, a two-sided development. On one side, the logic of the problem of value is considered for the first time in a manner sufficiently rigorous to lay bare the inner contradictions of the classical conception and necessitate that that conception suffer a fundamental reconstruction. In this way Ricardo lays the basis for establishing economic theory on a new and higher plane. At the same time the narrow, exclusively quantitative, logic with which Ricardo seeks to construct a conception of value precludes the definitive resolution of the contradictions built into the structure of classical thought. The latter, in its Ricardian form, ceases to be explicitly concerned with the concept of economic life and, instead, comes to focus exclusively upon the quantitative dimensions of its existence and movement. With Ricardo the problem of the determination of the object of economic science has effectively disappeared.

---

* Cf. Marx, *Grundrisse, ed. cit.*, p. 595: '(Ricardo) always speaks only of the division of an available, *ready* amount, not of the original positing of this difference.'

4

From one angle Ricardo considers a process of production which is natural. Similarly he faces a system of distribution which is also natural being governed by the productivity of the land and labor as well as the basic subsistence needs of the workers. Here production is the process of work and distribution the allocation of the physical product of the work process among the contributors to that process. From another angle Ricardo confronts these same phenomena of production and distribution, but as eminently social phenomena governed by laws that can no longer be interpreted as strictly natural. For Ricardo production is individual and natural but it is also social reproduction, the expression of the interdependence of individuals. Distribution is the distribution of the products of labor, but only as commodities. It is therefore governed by the market so that if distribution is natural it expresses its natural character in terms of exchange-value only to the extent that value is itself natural. Similarly while wages and profits are shares in the whole net product of labor, the worker actually receives his wage through individual exchange and the capitalist only receives his profit via the realization of the value of his output, i.e. through its sale in the market.

The explicit recognition that the process of production is also the process of the production of capital leads Ricardo, especially in his mature work, to reconstruct his theory of distribution in terms of value. Within Ricardian theory distribution conceived as distribution of a physical product is unconsciously transformed into the distribution of value. This latter also has two distinct determinations. First, Ricardo considers distribution as the distribution of labor, and second, he considers it as the distribution of real value.

The hidden transition between the distribution of produce and the distribution of value takes place in the first chapter of the *Principles*. First, Ricardo states that

it is according to the division of the whole produce of the land of any particular farm, between the three classes of landlord, capitalist, and laborer, that we are to judge the rise or fall of rent, profit and wages, and not according to the value at which that produce may be estimated in a medium which is confessedly variable.

This conception of distribution is precisely that which we have considered up to this point and it is remarkable that it is used by Ricardo as the immediate introduction to an argument for the treatment of the theory of distribution in terms of the distribution of labor. The beginning of the immediately succeeding paragraph reads: 'It is not by the absolute quantity of produce obtained by either class, that we can correctly judge the rate of profit, rent and wages, but by the quantity of labor required to obtain that produce' (vol. I, p. 49).

At this point the distribution of the net product is not to be estimated in physical terms (even assuming that that were possible). It is the relation of profits to wages which is critical and not their absolute level. But in this case it is not simply a matter of altering the theory of distribution from concern with absolute levels to concern with proportions but simultaneously of altering that theory from the constitution of wages and profits in terms of their natural existence to the constitution of wages and profit in terms of the relation between the two. In this case the distribution is in terms of labor. Yet, even this is not a resting point for the Ricardian theory of distribution. On the next page Ricardo takes the position that 'wages are to be estimated by their real value, viz. by the quantity of labor and capital employed in producing them, and not by their nominal value either in coats, hats, money, or corn' (vol. I, p. 50). Within the space of two paragraphs and one numerical example Ricardo has reproduced within his theory of distribution the distinct and opposing aspects of his theory of value.

From the original and transparent distribution of 'produce' Ricardo leads us through the labor-value determination of distribution to eventually end up with the distribution of 'real value' whose measure is the non-existent invariable measure of value. In effect, the distribution of the net product has become the distribution of value and of a value without any ground in a determinate social process. The development of the Ricardian theory is reproduced in the form of distinct and opposing conceptions of value and distribution.

For Ricardo distribution is a distribution of value. But this distribution of value is seen to simultaneously express the distribution of the product and the distribution of exchange-value. For Ricardo, value is exchange-value. This equation makes labor-time, which is the apparent substance of value, inadequate to its conception in so far as relative rates of exchange depend not simply on labor but also on distribution. Distribution as the distribution of value, becomes the distribution of a real value which is not simply the relative rate of exchange but an intrinsic value that is none the less exchange-value.

The distribution of value fails to grasp, even quantitatively, the distribution of the physical product since the latter is determined by forces other than those determining the former and since it is not even possible to possess a science of the magnitude of the latter which has no 'law.' At the same time distribution of value as distribution of real value leaves Ricardo without any clear ground for the theory of distribution. This emerges where changes in distribution are left out of account and the distribution of the real value emerges as a distribution of nothing. In the end, without a consistent conception of value Ricardo is left without a theory of distribution and without even the conception of the distribution relation. It is no longer clear what the distribution of income is a distribution of. This failure becomes a necessary one when the conditions of the problem are clearly set out. The distribution of the net product is constrained to conform to the natural conditions of production as the self-reproduction of nature, as a distribution 'not essentially connected with the doctrine of value' and at the same time to grasp the distribution of the net product as the distribution of the products of capital, of the process of the production of value and expanding value, which must conform with the conditions of the production of profit. Ricardo's resistance to the interposition of the value problem into the theory of distribution is explained by Ricardo's original conception of distribution; and the necessity of that interposition is equally explained by that conception of distribution. At the same time the failure of the labor principle together with Ricardo's resistance to abandoning that principle is explained first, by the necessity of grounding the exchange relation and second, by Ricardo's inability to constitute labor as the measure and substance of the exchange-value of commodities where those commodities are the products of capital.

The resistance to the concept of distribution as a distribution of value is a resistance to a conception of distribution as a social process. The separation of value from distribution reveals value as a social form ultimately irrelevant to the underlying natural reality. The abandoning of the concept of labor reflects Ricardo's inability to conceptualize the social grounding of the exchange of commodities and his ultimate retreat to the pure exchange relation. The invariable measure of value which is the end point of both Ricardo's theory of value and his theory of distribution finds a substance of exchange which possesses no social reality and yet seeks to root the individual exchange in a social process. This equally fails in that, as Ricardo himself argues, there can in principle be no invariable standard of value since such a standard would contradict the concept of exchange-value.

In the final analysis there is no such thing as the Ricardian theory of value and distribution. There exists, rather, a movement between contradictory conceptions held together by the inner necessity of the conception of the value relation on the one side and by the distorted mode of expression peculiar to that relation on the other.

Chapter 4
The world of capital

I Nature and capital

The object of classical political economy is to establish the 'natural' determination of the categories of bourgeois economy. This object is achieved, however, only in a contradictory and paradoxical sense. The immediate claim of classical thought is the grounding of the relations of capital in nature; but it finds that in so grounding those relations the category of nature, the fixed point with reference to which the capitalist world is conceptualized, comes loose from its moorings and, far from remaining fixed, shifts in meaning across the entire spectrum of bourgeois social theory. This fluctuation involves classical political economy in an attempt to reconcile within a single construction the most radically disparate conceptions of social life. On one side, the latter determined as an element of nature (the self-reproduction of nature in the Ricardian 'corn economy' or in the physiocratic conception of productive and unproductive labor) finds its origins both historically and conceptually outside of society. On the other side, nature, once brought into contact with the relations of bourgeois economy, loses its irreducible natural character and slips into a form indistinguishable from bourgeois economy. When classical political economy argues that the world of capital and its relations is natural it at once argues that the social world is rooted outside of itself and that the sphere outside of the social world in which bourgeois economy is rooted is the world of capital. The categories of bourgeois economy find their determination outside of capital, in nature. Yet when classical thought looks outside of capital for its natural ground it finds that that nature, once made concrete, is nothing other than capital itself. In order that classical thought be able to conceive the ground of capital as nature it must conceive nature as capital.

The category of nature possesses, in classical thought, this multiple and contradictory meaning. It appears as the non-human substance of human activity, and it appears as itself a determination of social life, as capital. On one side, nature absorbs social life into itself, naturalizes it, while, on the other, social life absorbs nature into its own process, making of nature a social product. On a different level, however, the absorption of social life into the natural process as its ground involves opposing conceptions of nature and of bourgeois economy. These conceptions both originate within classical thought, one as the truly and distinctively classical conception of nature, the

115

other as the peculiarly post-classical conception of nature. Nature as the external opponent of human activity, standing outside of society and opposing itself to society, is the nature of contemporary social science from which the individual and the system of interacting individuals has been excluded. The individual stands in isolation from nature as also from the origin of his own individual nature. By contrast, that nature which absorbs the individual into its own process, which turns the human element into a part of a natural process, stands not in opposition to the isolated individual but as the origin of the individual. Nature, in the truly classical sense, is a self-renewing process of which the subjective and objective elements are simply dependent, determinate moments. The total social process as the self-reproduction of nature finds the individual as an agent of nature and not as a self-subsistent, self-determining subject. It is this conception of nature which sharply distinguishes classical thought from all subsequent economic analysis. Within the process of the self-reproduction of nature there can be no conception of an abstract, purely individual, human need as the goal of economic activity. Human need is the need for the renewal of the natural process. It is also this element of the classical conception which allows it to grasp the economic process as the process of the self-realization of capital. The central property of nature as the self-subsistent unity of the economic process is also the central definition of capital as value which preserves itself through its own process. It is the concept of nature which on one side allows for a theory of bourgeois economic relations to emerge within classical thought, and it is the concept of nature which accounts for the peculiarly classical distortions of those relations.

For Ricardo the relations of capitalist production took on their natural form to the degree that they appeared to be necessary and not the result of 'temporary accident and cause.' The natural price, natural wage, natural rate of profit, were all natural to the extent that they were shown to be necessary. This necessity referred specifically to the conditions of the reproduction of the system of capital as a whole, implicitly to what Marx refers to as the 'reproduction of the total social capital.' In order for capital to posit its relations as necessary and determinate it must be constituted as a process which posits within itself its own pre-conditions. This self-sustaining process of capital is capital as a unity of production and exchange which, by production, posits the conditions of circulation and the realization of the value of the products, and which, by exchange and through exchange, posits the conditions for continued production. Out of this system of reproduction emerges a world of capital within which the conditions of reproduction appear on the market as the products of capital. Within the system of capitals the conditions of commodity production within each particular capital appear as the products of production within other particular capitals. The system of individual and interdependent reproduction contains the pre-conditions of capitalist production in the form of the products of individual capitals. Capital confronts its conditions of existence in the market now exclusively as its own product in the shape of the particular commodity products of a world of particular capitals.

Classical thought grasps the centrality of the opposition of individual units of capital as the adequate form for the total process of the self-realization of capital. Yet it also stops here, grasping the conditions of capitalist production as solely the products of individual, particular capitals. This enables classical thought to conceptualize the competitive process in abstraction from the reproduction of labor-power since labor-power, as that condition of capitalist production which is not the commodity product of a particular capital, is excluded. This exclusion plays a central role in determining the peculiarities of the classical conception of competition, social class, and the state. It is not that labor-power is determined without regard to the process of capital. On the contrary, the conditions of the reproduction of labor-power also include the breaking up of the total capital among independent firms whose particular commodity products and whose particular exchanges with labor make possible the reproduction of labor-power. The problem for classical thought is that these conditions, in particular of the production and realization of profit, are never conceptualized concretely and are, in fact, excluded at key points.

The construction of the reproduction and expansion of the total social capital and ultimately of the world of capitals poses essential problems for classical analysis. The entire project of classical political economy comes to hinge on this construction since it is upon the building up of a conception of the whole that the natural determination of capital must ultimately rest. The ability of capital to sustain itself through its own reproduction cycle is its ability to establish itself as the 'absolute' system of production, as synonymous with production. If capital is not capable of sustaining itself in this way then it cannot be the absolute mode of production and its categories cannot be natural. The issue is joined within classical analysis at precisely the point at which classical economy confronts the conditions for the expansion of capital. This posing of the problem of capital takes its explicit form within the theory of capital accumulation.

II The self-expansion of capital

1

The problem is posed in its most advanced form by Ricardo, who in the chapter on accumulation in the *Principles* establishes from the outset the key issue. Ricardo is unconcerned with the accumulation of capital as such. That is, the tracing out of the quantitative path of expansion of capital and its products in the manner of neo-classical growth theory is not in itself of any interest. Ricardo leaves aside altogether Smith's preoccupation with the expansion of wealth (at least at the initial point since he returns to it sub-sequently) in order to pose a different question: does the accumulation process

reproduce its own conditions or does it run up against barriers? Smith is concerned with the specific difference of capital and capitalist production, of the
origin of capital; Ricardo is concerned with the 'future of capital,' with the
potential intrinsic to capital, with the question of whether it does in fact have
a future. This question is, again, that of the universal, definitive, and absolute
character of capitalist production.

For Ricardo the existence of capital rests upon its expansion: for capital to
maintain itself is for capital to expand, and to do so without limit. This condition, while central to all classical thought, is neither explicitly deduced or
confronted by Ricardo but always assumed naïvely. Smith by posing the
problem of accumulation in terms of the origin of capital, confronts at various
times and in different connections the problem of capital as self-expanding
value. To that extent Smith is much more acutely aware of the specificity of
social production. Ricardo takes capital wholly for granted and asks only if
it is consistent with its own conditions. Thus there exists no chapter in the
Principles on accumulation but only a chapter dealing with the *effects* of
accumulation on profits and wages. This is the critical problem since the effect
of accumulation on the relation of profits to wages is the effect of accumulation
upon itself.

While this connection cannot be treated systematically at this stage of our
discussion it is possible to clarify the precise sense in which the relation of
profits to wages is the relation of capital to itself and to the conditions of its
expansion. The relation of the expansion of capital to the rate of profit is, for
Ricardo, a relation of capital to its conditions of existence, to its condition of
expansion, and to the distribution of the net product within that expansion.
The rate of profit is the foundation of accumulation and is, in fact, the rate of
accumulation. Allowing C to stand for total capital, a for the proportion of
profits invested in expansion, w for the wage rate, L for total employment, r
for the rate of profit and A for the rate of expansion of capital:

$$A = \frac{arC}{C}$$
$$= ar.$$

Since Ricardo takes the determination of the proportion of profits invested to
be a matter of the necessary consumption of the capitalist (operating on the
marginal land so that rent need not be paid out of profit), the rate of capital
expansion and the rate of profit become different expressions for the same
process: the self-expansion of capital. Furthermore, for Ricardo, the total
capital is made up exclusively of wage costs so that:

$$C = wL$$

and

$$r = \frac{R}{wL} \text{ where } R \text{ is total profit.}$$

Since wages and profits are estimated in 'value' (which is assumed to be the approximate equivalent of labor time) it follows, letting V stand for the Marxian category of variable capital, S for surplus-value, and e for the rate of surplus-value:

$$r = \frac{R}{wL} = \frac{S}{V} = e.$$

This last relationship is critical to the comprehension of the Ricardian theory of accumulation. At this stage in our argument it is only intended to establish the crucial connection within Ricardian thought between the distribution of the net product to capital and labor, the rate of profit, and the rate of expansion of capital. This relation, which underlies the entire Ricardian analysis of accumulation, also accounts for the peculiar manner in which Ricardo poses the problem of accumulation as the problem of the effect of expansion on wages and profits.

The question of the existence of limits to the expansion of capital presents itself to Ricardo in two forms and at two distinct points in his analysis. The first is the question of the fertility of the soil and the tendency of wages and rents to absorb the whole of profits as accumulation forces the producer of corn to retreat to less and less fertile units of production. The second is the problem of the 'general glut,' of the possibility that, independently of the costs of production of corn, the expansion of capital may run up against barriers in the conditions of the realization of the products of capital. In this case the question of the limits to growth is the question of the possibility that there could be too much capital.

Ricardo's treatment of the problem of the general glut reveals both the strengths and weaknesses of the Ricardian treatment of capitalist economy. It also reveals the origin of the Ricardian conception of a natural limitation to expansion in the form of the limited availability of fertile soil. Ricardo opposes the Malthusian position regarding the possibility of general overproduction on the ground that there cannot, in principle, be too much capital. The growth of capital far from being limited is self-sustaining so that the conditions for its expansion are given with that expansion so long as abstraction is made from the problem of the fertility of the soil. When capital is viewed on its own terms, taken within itself and without regard to the existence of external limiting conditions (as of the productivity of nature) it appears, for Ricardo, to be unlimited. The two aspects of the Ricardian theory of accumulation – that having to do with the effect of expansion on wages and profits, and that having to do with the possibility of general overproduction – express a duality within that theory of accumulation which sees capital expansion as intrinsically self-sustaining and then sees it as a natural process limited by the productivity of an externally given factor.

It is this dualism which defines the essentials of the Ricardian analysis of the accumulation of capital. If one makes abstraction from the externally given conditions of capital expansion, the fertility of the soil, then capitalist expansion must be conceived to be self-sufficient. Once the conditions external to capital upon which its expansion depends are made intrinsic to it capital no longer appears to be self-sustaining.

In the polemic with Malthus, Ricardo considers the world of capital to be the product of capital and therefore not as dependent but as limitless in its expansion, in its process of universalization. This conception of capital as self-sustaining is the foundation of the Ricardian analysis of expansion and of the whole of Ricardian economics in that it provides the ultimate foundation for the Ricardian conception of capital as natural. If capital is natural then expansion must also be natural, therefore necessary, and therefore possible. But at the same time that Ricardo conceives the natural world as the world of capital and as therefore implying the indefinite expansion of capital he conceives of capital as the self-reproduction of nature. In particular, he conceives of the production process of capital as directly equivalent to a natural process independent of the specific social 'forms' and relations within which it appears in modern bourgeois society. This supplies the basis for the other side of the Ricardian polemic with Malthus. From this standpoint, there can only be 'natural' impediments to the expansion of capital. The limits to growth are always seen by Ricardo as limits to the expansion of a production process which is immediate, individual, and in principle independent of a society of production, circulation, and reproduction. Since circulation, competition, exchange, now appear to be purely formal, limits to production cannot be found within them. Any limit to production is a limit to its direct natural process and not to the reproduction and expansion of a total capital as the unity of the process of the production of capital and of its circulation.

There is a profound dualism within this conception which needs to be made explicit. It is the social conditions of capital which allow for no internal barrier, and they disallow any such barrier precisely because of their social character which makes them (1) products, therefore social 'forms' as always produced and never irreducible, and (2) purely the appearance of a substance which grounds them, gives for them an account, and thereby determines their limits. It is the external grounding of social life within an irreducible nature which alone sets limits to, defines, and determines the scope of social production. But within classical economy this says at the same time that the social conditions taken in themselves are unlimited, self-sufficient, and capable of indefinite universalization. To the extent that Ricardo conceives, especially in the course of his polemic with Malthus, of the social conditions of capital without regard to their natural determination they appear to be unlimited, fully self-sufficient, and absolute. The poles of this duality are extreme poles on one side of which capital faces an absolute limit outside of itself, in nature, and on the other side of which capital, now set loose from nature (in relation with a nature which has become capital) is unlimited and also undetermined. Since nature alone can determine, ground, and therefore limit capital, capital taken outside of its relation to nature is undetermined, ungrounded, and unlimited.

This Ricardian view can be contrasted with that of Malthus for whom capital is not in principle self-sustaining and is under all circumstances incapable of producing the conditions for its continued existence. For Malthus the condition of all expansion of capital is the presence of an external sphere which can absorb the overproduction intrinsic to the idea of capitalist expansion. It is not, in this case, a matter of capital expressing an external dependence upon nature, but of capital as a social relation requiring a social world outside of capital for its maintenance and expansion. For Malthus expansion of capital requires the reproduction of unproductive labor as labor which is outside of the capital relation (e.g. feudal retainers, the clergy, etc.). By contrast for Ricardian economics, and for classical economy properly considered, accumulation of capital involves, in fact is synonymous with, the expansion of productive labor (labor which exchanges with capital) at the expense of unproductive labor. No argument could, therefore, be more alien to Ricardo than the argument that the expansion of capital rests upon the expansion of a world outside of capital – unproductive labor. 'A body of unproductive laborers are just as necessary and as useful with a view to future production, as a fire, which should consume in the manufacturers warehouse the goods which those unproductive laborers would otherwise consume' (vol. II, p. 421). Such a condition as that proposed by Malthus could only mean the existence of a contradiction *within* the expansion process of capital. This dependence of accumulation on its antithesis is for Ricardo a contradiction of the very idea of accumulation, a contradiction within the concept of capital, which must on that ground be eliminated. Malthus hints that the expansion of capital is inherently contradictory and that, therefore, the social conditions of capitalist production, may not, in fact be absolute. Ricardo purges the process of capitalist production and expansion of internal contradiction because he conceives it as, taken in itself, self-sustaining. This is the result both of his real insight into the concept of capital and of his reduction of that concept to its simplest determination: self-expanding value. The absence of contradiction within the category rests upon the simplicity of that category as it exists within Ricardian thinking. Capital is *simply* self-expanding value which rests exclusively on a basis of the immediate production process which equates self-expanding value with the expansion of a natural, purely material, process.

To the degree that, for Ricardo, all limitations to production are limitations of the material process of the transformation of nature by its own agents, the conception of that process is crucial. On one side, Ricardo sustains the conception that this process, while natural (or precisely because it is natural), is the direct production process of capital. Viewed in this way it is unlimited. On the other side, Ricardo conceives of this process as the self-reproduction of nature, therefore as limited by nature. At this point Ricardo closes in upon the conception of production as the 'allocation of scarce resources according to need' since nature appears in the form of an external limiting reality which confines human need. In neo-classical economics this conception is given its definitive form within which all of the conditions of capital accumulation appear as externally given and fixed resources ('factors') which restrain and limit need. Not only is the whole problem of accumulation one of deriving its external limiting conditions (of factor supply) but also the origin of, or 'motive' of accumulation is conceived as given and fixed rather than as posited by the social process itself. Accumulation becomes 'capital formation' with a fixed end or goal in future consumption and not the endless expansion of value. As such, accumulation is not only limited by nature (land, labor, etc.) but also originates outside of itself in the simple circulation of commodities extended over time, in the needs of individuals for particular commodities (their 'intertemporal preferences') which stand as the goal of capital formation.

2

The Ricardian conception of accumulation is, therefore, complex in that it incorporates two fundamentally different conceptions of expansion which are never clearly articulated or clearly separated. Within the concrete analysis of expansion the dualism of the Ricardian conception emerges as a duality in the 'motive' or 'reason' for accumulation, on one side the expansion of value, on the other side the fulfillment of particular need; on one side the conception of capital as the endless expansion of value, and on the other the conception of capital as goal.

These two conceptions also merge and interpenetrate so that it is never apparent which is predominant. Ricardo's actual statements on the motive to expansion simultaneously express both poles of this opposition, collapsing each into its opposite (vol. II, pp. 8–9):

But the argument is not about the motive to production, in that everybody is agreed – the accumulation of capital may go on so much faster, than laborers can be increased, that production must cease increasing in the same proportion as capital, from want of hands; and when they do increase, the laborers by their comparative scarcity to capital, can command so large a portion of the produce as to afford no adequate motive to continue to save. All men will allow that saving may be so rapid and profits so low in consequence as to diminish the motive to accumulation, and finally to destroy it altogether.

But what exactly is the 'motive to accumulation' upon which all are agreed? For Ricardo it is at once two things which are radically different but whose difference, while crucial, is missed entirely. The motive to accumulation is: (1) profits, in particular the *rate* of profit, the proportion of profit to capital, therefore the rate of surplus-value. Where the motive to accumulation is considered as a proportion, therefore as a relation of capital, the motive to accumulate is the process of expansion itself. If accumulation is rapid then the motive to accumulation is great since the rate of accumulation and rate of profit are jointly determined. The motive to accumulation as the rate of profit transforms accumulation into a self-moving force whose only motive or reason is accumulation itself. But, for Ricardo, the motive to accumulate is also (2) profits, as a portion of the produce, the total amount or share of profit in the net product. In this case the accumulation process has a real motive, a goal in the consumption and increased consumption of particular commodities. What emerges is not in fact opposing 'motives to accumulate' but one case in which accumulation is seen to require a motive or goal and one case in which accumulation is intrinsically opposed to any fixing of motive or goal.

The two-fold character of Ricardo's treatment of the motive to accumulate reveals the two opposing Ricardian conceptions of accumulation: accumulation of capital – value, and accumulation of material products – means of consumption. This duality is not, however, peculiar to Ricardian economics. The two sides of the Ricardian conception are also to be found in pre-Ricardian classical thought. The duality in the Ricardian treatment of expansion is characteristic of classical thought and expresses one of its defining qualities.

Within the *Wealth of Nations* the opposing conceptions of accumulation take the form of opposing notions of productive and unproductive labor. For Smith the problem of capital accumulation is directly equivalent to the problem of productive and unproductive labor; in his presentation it appears as the problem 'Of Accumulation of Capital, or of Productive and Unproductive Labor.' But within the analysis of accumulation the notion of productive labor breaks apart into two distinct and opposing notions. On one side productive labor appears as that labor which exchanges with capital. As such it depends upon a purely social condition: the relation of laborer to employer. Retainers and servants being hired out of 'revenue' bear no relation to the expansion of value and produce neither value nor surplus-value. They fail not only to increase capital but equally to sustain capital. It is for this reason that Ricardo took such vigorous exception to the Malthusian position on accumulation. That income from capital which is expended as revenue upon unproductive labor disappears forever from capital while that income of capital which goes to the hiring of productive labor not only maintains the capital expended but also increases it. When accumulation is seen in terms of the expansion of productive labor the accumulation of capital sustains itself and simply serves to establish the conditions for continued and accelerated accumulation.

Smith, however, shifts the conception of productive labor within the treatment of accumulation from that labor which increases capital to that labor which fixes itself in a 'durable' commodity which lasts. It is only possible to account for this reversal of meaning by recognizing the duality of the classical conception of accumulation considered above. Productive labor contributes to accumulation of capital, produces its own value, i.e. maintains itself as capital, and contributes to the expansion of value. This is true of both classical conceptions of accumulation and productive labor. The division occurs when the concrete meaning of accumulation is considered. Where the end of accumulation is accumulation itself it appears natural to consider productive labor in terms of the production and expansion of value. By contrast where the end of accumulation is seen as the realization of capital in consumption this conception of productive labor must undergo alteration. In the second case accumulation appears not as the self-expansion of capital but as the refraining from consumption of the immediate product of the production process. That which is invested is not consumed and this is the definitive characteristic of investment viewed in terms of the goal of consumption. Since investment is defined as the antithesis of consumption, therefore, in terms of consumption, the products of labor can only be invested where they can exist independently of direct consumption. The productive existence of the investment involves its standing opposed, in principle, and in time, to its consumption. By contrast, the production and consumption of services are directly equivalent acts. Since in the case of services (products which are not 'durable') production cannot be temporally distinguished from consumption, investment appears to be impossible (*Wealth of Nations*, p. 329).

The revenue of an individual may be spent, either in things which are consumed immediately, and in which one days expence can neither alleviate or support that of another; or it may be spent in things more durable, which can therefore be accumulated, and in which every day's expence may, as he chuses, either alleviate or support and heighten the effect of the following day.

This contradiction originates when Smith loses sight of the fact that accumulation of capital is not accumulation of objects of consumption but accumulation of value. To the extent that accumulation is the piling up of objects of use the money form is of no concern or interest. This is especially the case where, as implied by Smith, accumulation is an individual affair that concerns the particular objects possessed by the individual. Rather than conceive of accumulation in terms of money it is necessary, within this conception, to perceive the conditions of the process of expansion as they exist behind the money form, as a material process. It is that real, material, process of refraining from the consumption of particular, physically defined objects ('palpable objects') which stands behind the monetary form of expression of value. Here Smith's position is essentially that of neo-classical economics on the nature of the accumulation process. The durability notion is the neo-classical concept of capital. Capital is durable product. What it is important to bear in mind is the inner connection between this conception of capital and the conception of accumulation as finding a goal in consumption (*Wealth of Nations*, p. 625).

Consumption is the sole end and purpose of all production; and the interest of the producer ought to be attended to, only so far as it may be necessary for promoting that of the consumer. The maxim is so perfectly self-evident, that it would be absurd to attempt to prove it. But in the mercantile system, the interest of the consumer is almost constantly sacrificed to that of the producer; and it seems to consider production, and not consumption, as the ultimate end and object of all industry and commerce.

That which is so self-evident that it needs no proof is also that position whose falsity denies it proof, a result which Smith himself recognizes throughout the remaining sections of the *Wealth of Nations*.

The dichotomy within the conception of accumulation should not, however, be conceived to constitute itself in the form of an absolute bifurcation within the texts which would allow these texts to be neatly divided in two, one corresponding to the emerging neo-classical analysis and the other to an opposing conception of accumulation. To be sure, economic analysis does suffer such a polarizing development in the nineteenth century, which development is grounded in the contradictions of conception articulated here. On the other hand, the opposing conceptions never achieve independence of expression within classical thought but always exist in an uncertain unity. More precisely the distorted conception of accumulation as driving toward a fixed goal in individual consumption has a degenerative tendency which always serves to transform it, stage by stage, into its opposite.

Thus, for Ricardo and Smith, the conception of accumulation as the realization of needs in consumption is subtly altered within its expression when the characterization of need is made explicit. While it is the need for consumption which drives accumulation it is not particular material need but the limitless need of the individual. For Ricardo individual need is never exhausted. This means that while it is need which drives accumulation (as in neo-classical thinking) it is only need determined as limitless. To the extent that Ricardo conceptualizes need as unlimited it cannot be the neo-classical need for the consumption of utilities or for the satisfaction derived from that consumption. Need as demand for consumption is turned into its opposite and it is need in general, the need for the generality of wealth, the universality of need rather than its particularity, which is posited within classical thought. But such need is nothing other than the process of capital, the value process set loose and established as both means and end. The need for the world of commodities is the need for all commodities and therefore for no particular commodity. Such need can never be fulfilled by the consumption of any fixed bundle of useful objects since it is qualitatively opposed to that need which is so fulfilled. The fulfillment of the need as the need of capital can only be realized in the creation of a world of capital, therefore in the transformation of all products into the products of capital, into value. In this case production which can fulfill needs can only be production of and for value and not production for a limited and fixed end.

On one side, consumption is the goal of production. Malthus concludes from this that consumption limits production. Ricardo accepts consumption as the goal of production but specifies that consumption to capital – the consumption without limit, therefore, consumption by capital. The capitalist must consume but his consumption must always be directed toward productive ends, he must consume productive labor in whose consumption he realizes no particular end of satisfaction but only the end of expansion of his command over the world of satisfaction, over value. Thus, since (1) consumption is the goal of production, and (2) consumption has no limit, it follows that production also is unlimited. It is absurd to consider production as limited by consumption when consumption is simply the expansion of production. Malthus's position differs from that of Ricardo not in opposing Ricardo's view of consumption as the goal of the economic process but in opposing Ricardo's specification of consumption to capital. For Malthus, as for modern neo-classical economics, consumption stands apart from and opposed to production. For Ricardo consumption is no more than the means to continued production. This position becomes explicit when Ricardo eschews all pretense that consumption is the goal of production and states that 'the temptation to increase capital does not arise from the demand for its products, for that never fails; but from the profits arising from the sale of the products' (vol. II, p. 331). It is only where consumption is not the goal of production that production can find itself limited in the Ricardian analysis, i.e. by the fall of the rate of profit.

Ricardo eliminates the general glut, in principle, when he establishes consumption as a moment of accumulation rather than as its externally fixed goal. But the elimination of the possiblity of a glut requires more than the simple recognition that consumption and production form a unity. It is also necessary that that unity be conceived in a particular manner. For Ricardo the rejection of the abstract conception of consumption as outside of the process of capital is also the elimination of all difference between production and consumption. The relation of consumption to production becomes immediate. By contrast the possibility of a general glut rests upon the recognition that production is only a moment in the process of expansion of capital and, therefore, that its unity with the determinations of the process of capital as a whole is mediated by a series of relations which are required by the specification of the production process to capital. For Ricardo production ceases to be specifically production of value which requires realization in money and, therefore, the circulation of money, commodities, and capital. Ricardo conceives the production process to be absolute and not the complex of determinations of the process of production of capital. Since production possesses this absolute character its conception requires no mediating terms. As Marx points out, Ricardo's weakness is in viewing the 'bourgeois mode of production' as the 'absolute mode of production,' hence as 'a mode of production without any definite specific characteristics, its distinctive traits are merely formal.'*

* *Theories of Surplus-Value*, vol. II (Moscow: Progress Publishers, 1968), pp. 528–9. In his discussion of this central problem of the interpretation of classical thought Marx emphasizes

What needs to be emphasized is that this absence of 'definite specific character-istics' does not, for Marx, express the absence of an *ad hoc* historical specifica-tion, but the absence of a real determination of the concept of social pro-duction so that the missing specificity of the Ricardian conception is a failure to determine concretely the defining features of the production of capital.

III The direct production process and the process of capitalist production as a whole

1

Capitalist production does not determine itself concretely in the process of production of capital, the process of circulation of capital, and the repro-duction of the total social capital. It merely exists (i.e. all these processes exist) formally, that is abstractly, *vis-à-vis* the actual production process with regard to which they are purely external. This is the key to the understanding of the method applied by Ricardo to the object of his investigation, and to the con-tradictions of his analysis of all economic phenomena: value, surplus-value, capital, and accumulation. For Ricardo capital, or more correctly production, is indeterminate and is conceivable outside of and independently of its real conditions (e.g. circulation). Production is simply posited in the abstract and as given with regard to economic analysis. The real determinations of capital are then opposed externally to a conception of their production process which is foreign to them and which, therefore, contradicts them. This absolute opposition of the distinct relations of capital is typical of bourgeois social thought. The latter freezes the simplest relations of bourgeois society in order to formulate them as absolute conditions independent of and, therefore, implicitly opposed to the real system of bourgeois economic and social rela-tions taken as a whole.

The Ricardian rejection of the possibility of a general glut begins with the recognition of the implicit and necessary unity of production and con-

---

the equation of production and the self-realization of capital: 'Those economists who, like Ricardo, conceived production as directly identical with the self-realization of capital – and hence were heedless of the barriers to consumption or of the existing barriers of circulation itself, to the extent that it must represent counter-values at all points, having in view only the development of the forces of production and the growth of the industrial population – supply without regard to demand – have therefore grasped the positive side of capital more correctly and deeply than those who, like Sismondi, emphasized the barriers of consumption and of the available circle of counter-values, although the latter has better grasped the limited nature of production based on capital, its negative one-sidedness. The former more its universal tendency, the latter its particular restrictedness. The whole dispute as to whether *overproduction* is possible and necessary in capitalist production revolves around the point whether the process of the realization of capital within production directly posits its realization in circulation; whether its realization posited in the *production process* is its *real* realization,' *Grundrisse*, tr. M. Nicolaus (Harmondsworth: Penguin Books, 1973), pp. 410–11.

sumption and ends with their absolute unification and identification. This identification of consumption with production rests upon the absence of a concrete analysis of the production process as a process of production of capital. This involves Ricardo in a retreat back into the original Malthusian position that production is the production of objects of consumption and not of value. Thus while Ricardo rejects Malthus's position on grounds that it denies the limitlessness of need and the subordination of consumption to production, by collapsing consumption into production he eliminates the real basis for the appropriation of consumption into the process of capital as a dependent moment. This leads his argument back into the position from which he has just extracted it and forces him to conceive of consumption once again as the aim of production. The other side of his attack on Malthus, which exists in this unstable unity with the argument just articulated, is precisely an appeal to 'Say's law' which denies any mediation between production and consumption, constituting the aim of production as the immediate product of production.

Once Say's law is accepted the product must be conceived exclusively as material object[1] so that the determinations of the value form drop out and (1) the mediation of production by the total circulation disappears, and (2) the goal of production in the expansion of value also disappears so that production ceases to be capitalistic in character. The acceptance of Say's law is also the elimination of any concrete analysis of the immediate production process. Production stands outside of and ultimately opposed to the determinate social forms of capital. First, there is production which has no external conditions, and then there is the social form, the property relation which encases production, appropriates its products, allocates consumption and resources.

The absence of specification of production in classical thought appears as an absence of specification of labor. The determinateness of labor involves the distinction between labor and labor-power on one side and between past and current labor on the other. This lapse brings with it the failure to grasp the distinctiveness of 'constant capital' (past labor acting as means of production).

The absence of the category of constant capital in classical political economy can be traced back to the special view adopted by Smith and Ricardo of the production process and especially of the production of commodities. It has, therefore, an origin in a conceptual error which is necessary, given the fundamental characteristics of classical methodology. This is not to suggest that the historically given level of development of the productive forces did not play a role in the suppression of the category of constant capital. The level of development of capital, especially at the time of the writing of the *Wealth of Nations*, can certainly be considered primitive, and the absence of its explicit treatment may be considered understandable on general historical grounds. None the less, the implicit presence of the category of constant capital (as fixed capital in Smith) and of the organic composition of capital (for example in the Ricardian analysis of machinery) indicates very clearly that the suppression of constant capital within the analysis of value and accumulation originates not in the historical conditions of classical thought but in the manner in which that thought appropriates the categories of capitalist economy.

The suppression of constant capital becomes logical for Smith not as the result of observation of industrial practice (on the contrary, all practical discussion forces Smith to recognize the role of constant capital) but as a result of the peculiar classical conception of production adopted by Smith. Whenever production is viewed materially constant capital, in the guise of means of production, appears as a necessary element. But whenever production is production of commodities, therefore also of value, constant capital disappears and the total value – constant capital (c)+variable capital (v)+surplus-value (s) – becomes identical to the net product, the total current labor expenditure: $s+v$. This reduction is made necessary, for Smith, by his analysis of the relation of labor to value. Since all value is produced by labor, either paid or unpaid, all value must be reducible to labor so that we get: Total value$=v+s$. Constant capital, means of production, may be employed in the material process but it cannot produce value. Constant capital contributes value to the product only when it is viewed as the embodiment of past labor so that c, considered in terms of the production of value, is itself reduced to $v+s$. For Smith, it makes no difference, in principle, that this latter appears in the form of constant capital, 'dead' labor, rather than in the form of current labor expenditure, as the contribution of the commodity means of production rather than as the current contribution of labor-power. What is purchased with commodities is just as much purchased with labor as that which exchanges directly with labor itself.

It is precisely to the extent that Smith views labor as such to be equivalently the laboring act (the labor process) specified by the use-value of the product that the real distinctiveness of the concept of labor is suppressed. Thus the specification of the labor process to the particularity of the use-value of the product is made the act of labor rather than of the objective conditions of labor. Since labor is made accountable for the specification of the useful character of its product it loses its universality as value producing labor. With this conception the necessity of constant capital within the labor process is denied since the specification of labor to the particularity of its product is argued to exist immediately within the labor itself. This development requires that the existence within the total product of a value part which is the contribution of past labor already congealed into the form of means of production be explicitly taken into account. This specification of living labor to the production of a particular use-value is the work of past labor existing in a particular form–means of production. Were labor considered to act without the intermediation of past labor (constant capital) its ability to 'produce' value

$(v+s)$ would be excluded by its inability to produce commodities $(c+v+s)$. The unity of dead with living labor, of labor with its objective conditions is the labor process which produces particular commodities as the embodiment of so much labor time $(c+v+s)$ including new value equal to the expenditure of living labor $(v+s)$.

Smith ignores the difference of form between c and $v+s$ so that the relation of c to $v+s$, the organic composition of capital, $c/(v+s)$, is of no interest to him. The fact that one part of the total labor time embodied in commodities breaks off and opposes itself to the other becomes irrelevant. Smith ignores the difference of form between $v+s$ and c, treats it as inconsequential, and thereby loses the determinateness of the process of production as a capitalist process in which the expansion of surplus-value hinges on the opposition of c to $v+s$ – the organic composition of capital. That is, Smith thereby loses the determinateness of the process as a labor process, as a unity of two intrinsically connected but none the less different processes: the production of value and the production of use-value.

Smith's confusion also derives from the adoption on his part of the standpoint of the particular unit of capital as the absolute standpoint. For the particular unit the physical or material composition of the product, especially once the organic composition of capital is left out of account, is of purely secondary interest. Primary interest is necessarily devoted to the price of the product in relation to its cost of production. It is not only for Smith but equally for the individual capitalist that the difference between c and v can be ignored. The latter, far from being concerned with the relation of dead to living labor, is concerned with the relation of profit to the total cost (including the dead and part of the living labor together). Further, reproduction of constant capital is, from the standpoint of the particular unit of capital, the primary concern of another unit of capital (or of other units of capital) from whom the means of production and raw materials are purchased in the market. Aside from exceptional circumstances the individual firm is concerned with the value and not with the physical availability and nature of the means of production. However, from the viewpoint of the expansion of capital as a whole, the material production of means of production, the renewal of the constant capital as distinguished from the reproduction of labor-power, is essential. It, furthermore, becomes essential to even the individual firm at such times as the conditions of aggregate demand and supply bring home to it the uncertainty surrounding the reproduction and employment of constant capital. The distinction between dead and living labor, between constant and variable capital, forces itself into the consciousness of the individual capitalist when the explicit dependence of the conditions of his production upon the reproduction of the total capital is expressed, for example in the course of the cycle. It is in such cases clear that production has an intrinsically social character, not as production in the abstract but as the labor process.

2

In the classical conception the elimination of constant capital leaves as its residue not the 'circulating capital model' but the concept of production as the immediate relation of labor to nature with no intermediation either of means of production or of raw materials distinct from those that appear as identical to the product itself, as intermediate products (intermediate products are in this case no more than another form of variable capital). Abstraction from constant capital at this level effects a return to the one-commodity model, the corn model of Ricardo's early analysis of profit and growth.

Just as it is not production in general but production of a concretely social nature which requires the reproduction of constant capital and the opposition of dead to living labor, neither is it production in the abstract, taken without regard to its concrete properties, which requires the circulation of commodities. Thus when Ricardo focuses in upon the particular unit of capitalist production, the 'firm,' what he deals with is, in reality, only the immediate production process and not the unity of production and realization within a world of capitals. This view is consistent with the conception of the firm as a 'technical unit of production.' In effect, Ricardian economics collapses the conception of the world of particular capitals into the direct production process, inter-preting the categories of the expansion of capital as a whole (e.g. the 'indi-vidual unit of capital') as the categories of generalized production. This leads directly into the conception of the firm as a unit or locus of production independent of the concrete determinations of capital. But even here the direct production process is conceived as the totality of the relations of capital and, especially in neo-classical economics, it is within production as a technical process, presumed independent of capital, that all the determinate relations of capital take on the form of 'factors of production.' As a result the whole of the concept of capital, once collapsed into the immediate production process, comes to be independent of the unity of capitalist production as a whole, loses its concrete character and falls outside of economic theory.

For Ricardo the total elimination of the circulation of commodities elimin-ates all mediation between the individual firm and the direct production process of capital in general. In the absence of such a distinguishing of levels of analysis the level of capital as a whole falls into the more general level of the direct production process. The latter in turn must be conceived in such a manner as to emancipate it from any intrinsic necessity to realize itself outside of its immediate process, in circulation. This places a highly restrictive con-dition on the conception of the unit of production, of the direct production process *as* the particular unit of capital. Within this restricted conception the direct production process loses its determinateness to capital. Since, for Ricardo, production is not analyzed concretely as the production of capital, production in its natural existence is deemed directly adequate to account for capital. On the other hand, the exchange of commodities for money, the circulation of money and commodities, and the circulation of capital become external necessity, having nothing to do with, possessing no necessary origin in, the actual process of production and consumption.

Under these conditions the direct production process cannot be conceived as social in character. It must, on the contrary, become self-sufficient subsistence production outside of any determinate world of producers.Independence of the particular unit of production is the key to this constitution of production as non-social in character. This condition has long been recognized within neo-classical economics. The entire neo-classical theory of production has as its object the conceptualization of production as a purely material process independent of any social determination. In the course of the consummation of this project neo-classical analysis has generated a series of 'models' designed to capture the salient features of production taken in itself. Since the product of the isolated producer-consumer cannot be conceived to be directly a commodity and to possess any universal significance and value form it is a matter of indifference to the conditions of production as such whether that product happens to be 'exchanged' in a market. Such an exchange has nothing to do with production and must be conceived in such a way as to preserve the autonomy of production *vis-à-vis* exchange. This necessity accounts for the conception of exchange founded upon 'surplus production' favored within neo-classical economics.

Classical analysis, by collapsing the individual unit of capital into the immediate production process, generates a conceptual product very close to that of the neo-classical theory of exchange and production. The fundamental difference is based on nothing more than that for classical thought this conception of the direct individual producer is the result of the collapsing of two poles each of which retains a force within the final conception; whereas in the case of neo-classical economics only the identification of the direct production process and the unit of capital is retained, the movement is lost. Ricardo retains the notion of the 'labor process,' the general process of the production of commodities, even in his identification of the labor process with the activity of the individual firm. By contrast the neo-classical treatment of production includes no conception of the general production process, of the labor process as the production of value, therefore of value as a product. Neo-classical thought directly identifies 'production' with the immediate activity of the individual unit of capital. There is, in this case, no real existence within the analysis of the distinction (except in the form of an incipient contradiction within the concept of production). Classical economics conceptualizes the immediate production process as a labor process, then actively attempts to identify that conception with the individual unit of capital. Neo-classical thought, lacking this active moment, this process of collapsing one into the other, ignores altogether any distinctions. In Ricardo's thought, given the persistence of the two opposing moments, there is a collapsing movement between them, there is an explicitly recognized contradiction between the two levels (i.e. in particular between labor value and price). In neo-classical thought there is only direct identification. The result is, on one level, the same in both cases – the individual producer-consumer. But, on another level, the result is different since the Ricardian conception retains a residue of its origins in a contradiction explicitly recognized, in an actual process of conception. For this reason the contradiction is often explicit in Ricardo while it remains always hidden in modern economics.

Once production appears as self-sufficient the necessity of money as inter-mediary between individual production and the social conditions of produc-tion drops out. Money appears as a 'convenience' and not a necessity. This is the result of the fact that exchange has itself become convenient in particular cases but unnecessary in all cases. The necessity of money is the necessity that all production find a means of expressing its implicit social character, there-fore that production have such a character. Exchange is necessary only for that production which is not capable of sustaining itself without recourse to the products of other production processes, therefore without recourse to the purchase of the means of production in the market in the form of the products of other, intrinsically connected and mutually dependent, processes. The pro-duction of particular commodities on the part of a particular producer is not immediately a part of the reproduction of the system of producers as a whole. No overall law dictates the exact proportions of individual productive activity and ensures ahead of time the consistency of that activity with the general conditions of reproduction. Each individual producer must, therefore, measure his product against the requirements of the production system as a whole. He can do so, however, given the individual nature of production and of produc-tion decisions, only via exchange, that is, via the realization of the value of his product in a commodity which reveals to him the extent to which the produc-tion of his commodity is consistent in form and magnitude with the needs of society. Within such a system the necessity of exchange is expressed in the necessity of the realization of the value of the product of each producer in money, since money expresses directly the universal command of the product over other commodities. This universality requires for its expression independ-ence of particular useful form. Thus when commodities exchange for money they forsake their particular form and take on the general form of exchange-value. Money and the exchange of commodities becomes necessary to the extent that the individual producer is simply an element of the reproduction of the system of particular producers. He *must* realize the value of his products in money in order to sustain himself in production since only the money so acquired makes possible the repurchase of the means of continued production from other individual producers. The individual producer must go outside of the results of his own productive activity in order to purchase his various productive needs in the market with money. A barter economy, on the other hand, is essentially an economy of independent, self-sufficient producers for whom both money and exchange are a matter of convenience and not of necessity.

Once the necessity of exchange as an element of continued production is grasped the first element of that exchange which needs to be taken into account is that the individual producer must not only purchase the various particular commodities required for production in the market with money but he must also purchase in the market the general potential to produce commodities, labor-power, and he must purchase it not with his particular products but with money. What is relevant, then, for the problem of the accumulation of capital from the standpoint of the individual producer, is not the necessaries consumed by labor but the money costs of that labor, the money wage. Once, however, Ricardo reduces the production process to a self-sufficient individualized process the money form of the wage disappears, or at least becomes inessential. Ricardo, therefore, deals with the problem directly in terms of the necessities of labor and not in terms of the money wage so that the various conditions surrounding the relation of the money wage to the price of output (the profit margin) lose any influence upon the movement of the rate of profit. The individual producer shares out the products of his own production process with his workers so that again any purchase of labor-power with money or any realization of the value of output in money becomes inessential. The entire problem is reduced to the material exchange between the individual capitalist and his workers.

Under such conditions it is not so much a matter of the possibility of a general glut as of the meaning to be attached to 'generality' in the treatment of economic phenomena. The collapsing of the economic system as a whole into the immediate production process excludes any real conception of the total social capital and of capitalist production as a whole. The object of political economy can no longer be the progress of wealth in society; since society ceases to be a legitimate determination of analysis, there is no wealth of society. By collapsing capitalist production as a whole into the analysis of the direct production process Ricardo constructs a definitive response to Malthus, a response which abolishes any distinction between production as a direct individual process, as the production process of capital (the 'immediate production process') and as the process of capitalist production as a whole. Ricardo in order to respond to Malthus adopts not only Say's law but the central conception of the character of production and exchange of modern economics implicit in Say's law (vol. II, p. 306):

Whoever has commodities has the power to consume, and as it suits mankind to divide their employments, individuals will produce one commodity with the view to purchase another; – these exchanges are mutually beneficial, but they are not absolutely necessary, for every man might employ his funds, and the labor at his command, in producing the very commodities he and his workmen intended to consume; in which case, there would be no market, and consequently there could be no glut.

The abstractness of this conception of production originates in the absence of a connection between the production process and capital that would lead into an analysis of production as a concrete process involving co-operation, division of labor, formation of fixed capital, and development of the organic composition of capital. Production in the abstract does not involve the positing of the interdependence of production as internal to production. Only production of surplus-value is intrinsically interdependent production based not on particularity of need and particularity of activity but on its intrinsic universality, a drive within production toward its necessary condition of a world in its own image. Only the production process as the process of production of surplus-value drives to absorb the entire world into itself and to produce a dependence of all production on capital.[2] This dependence takes the specific forms, in the first instance, of the subordination of labor to capital and of the dependence of the worker on the purchase of his means of subsistence. This Ricardo directly denies when he states that the master and his employees may together produce the commodities directly required for their own maintenance (vol. II, p. 306). This condition of the exchange of labor with capital is the immediate basis of the determination of the production process itself in accordance with the needs of the production of surplus-value. This determination accounts for all advanced forms of interdependence which reveal directly the social character of production – ultimately in the form of fixed capital and expansion of the organic composition of capital. Where the replacement of living by dead labor has reached a developed stage the idea that any individual producer could directly produce the products required for his consumption must be excluded.

3

The starting point for the critique of the Ricardian theory of accumulation as a whole is precisely this recognition of the implications of the concrete analysis of the immediate production process:[3]

above all it is necessary to have a clear understanding of the *reproduction of constant capital*. The conception that accumulation of capital is identical with conversion of revenue into wages, in other words, that it is synonymous with accumulation of variable capital – is one-sided, that is, incorrect. This leads to a wrong approach to the whole question of accumulation.

The absence of constant capital reduces all dependence of the rate of profit to dependence upon the wage. Determination of the rate of profit is determination of the rate of surplus-value. As a result demand for products can only affect the rate of profit if the price of output relative to wages falls. Without the direct production process determined concretely there can be no reproduction of constant capital and without the circulation of commodities, an absence implied by the lack of a direct analysis of production, there can be no reproduction of the total social capital. The rate of profit is reduced to the rate of surplus-value and prices become directly equivalent to values.

In the actual process of capital, by contrast, the presence of constant capital, circulation, and competition, establishes a real basis for general crises. The presence of constant capital involves the determination of the rate of profit in the course of the cycle in terms of the utilization of fixed capital so that the rate of profit has a direct dependence upon the level of effective demand. Similarly, once the process of circulation is introduced it is apparent that the time which elapses between production and sale, realization of value, is relevant to the calculation of the profitability of production. Ricardo ignores general changes in price which may be associated with general fluctuations in demand as possible sources of a general crisis (or even as contributing factors since he ignores circulation and the time of circulation). In all of his discussion Ricardo continually reiterates the argument that profits depend only · upon wages, ignoring the temporal element involved in the calculation of the rate of profit. Ricardo calculates the latter directly in terms of the labor-value of commodities and wages, ignoring the fact that the calculation which is actually relevant to the problem is that of the relation of the cost price of capital invested at the time of purchase with the price of the commodity at the moment of its realization in the market. As Marx points out the essence of the circulation of commodities is to drive a wedge between the purchase of the means of production and the final sale of the product as well as between the purchase of the means of production and their actual entry into production. This wedge involves the lapse of time during which the configuration of market prices in accordance with which the original decisions were made can alter. That uncertainty exists in production means that production is not simply immediate but mediated, that we deal not with simple production but with the production of value and surplus-value, which must always be realized at some point in money.

With the introduction of fixed capital the intervention of the time of production becomes all the more acute since the realization of the value of a machine may occur over a period of many years during which time considerable fluctuations of value will normally be expected. The presence of fixed capital implies not only a contemporaneous interdependence of production but also a temporal interdependence. This latter has its expression in the movement of the rate of profit both over the long-run in the course of secular movements of the organic composition of capital and over the cycle within which the rate of utilization of capital will be the key to movement of the organic composition of capital and the rate of profit.

With this recognition of the general interdependence of production, of the application of fixed capital, of the requirement of the purchase of increasing amounts of labor-power, in other words of the eminently social nature of production the real link between overproduction in a particular sector and general overproduction emerges. Ricardo continually opposes the idea that overproduction and miscalculation in one sector can lead to the generalization of overproduction to the whole of industry. This argument, again, rests upon the elimination of the social character of production which would imply the existence of a production process of capital as a whole which is not the direct equivalent of the immediate production process so that individual production on the part of a particular firm is not immediately 'production in general' but requires a unification of the production, circulation, and reproduction of capital as a whole. This reveals once more the absence in Ricardo of any explicit conception of the total social capital and the necessary reduction, implied by that absence, of the capitalist firm to a purely natural production process which presupposes nothing other than the immediate presence of the elements of production in their purely material existence. Ricardo is unaware that the particular production process is a social process which, therefore, finds its pre-conditions outside of itself in a total system of production. The self-sufficiency of production which Ricardo deduces on the basis of production of capital, production without fixed end and goal, is transformed into the self-sufficiency of the direct production process which is reduced to a purely material interchange. The self-sustaining process of the expansion of capital, which requires that each particular capital find the pre-conditions for its individual production process in the market in the form of the products of the individual production processes of other particular capitals, is reduced to the direct activity of the individual producer-consumer.

This reduction also explains the possibility for a Ricardian critique of the Malthusian position on the level of effective demand given Ricardo's rejection of the possibility of laws of capital as a whole. At first it appears paradoxical that Ricardo can establish any position whatever on the issue of the general glut since the notion of 'generality' applied to economic phenomena has no real status within Ricardian thought. Keynes, in defense of the revolutionary nature of his own 'general' theory argues that the real break between his standpoint and that of 'classical' economics is the presence within his work of a treatment of the level of production which was taken as given and indeterminate for Ricardian and all pre-Keynesian thought. While it is both true and important that virtually the whole of orthodox economics between Ricardo and Keynes fails to give an account for the overall level of economic activity this fact should not be considered an oversight. The absence of a concept of capital as a whole rests on the collapsing of capitalist production as a whole into the direct production process of capital. Ricardo constructs a reply to Malthus which not only fails utterly to grasp the central problem of the determinateness of the world of capital (a problem of which Malthus himself hardly had an inkling) but actually deals explicitly with the notion of capital as a whole as if it were the immediate process of production of capital and, therefore, as if both levels of analysis could be equated.

In order to consider the unit of capital or firm as directly equivalent to the production process of capital in general it is first necessary to eliminate all distinguishing of units of capital and to reduce them to a common form. This is accomplished by abolishing all specificity of the production process, difference of organic composition of capital within production itself. Given this generalization of capital the only remaining difference between capital in general and the world of actual particular capitals is the intervention of the payment of rent on intramarginal land. Capital in general is capital employed in manufacture or on no-rent land. Capital as a whole, on the other hand, must also pay rent (in addition to profit) so that while in the case of capital in general:

$$R=S,$$

in case of the total capital (leaving interest aside):

$$R+N=S, \text{ where } N \text{ stands for rent.}$$

This condition, along with the elimination of differences in composition of capital and in turnover periods of capital, leaves profit and wages in a proportional relation (=the rate of surplus-value), therefore value (labor time) equal to price. The share of wages in the net product is

$$\frac{wL}{wL+P}=\frac{1}{1+e}.$$

The result is the key to the Ricardian treatment of capital as a whole as the generality of the direct production process. The marginal, no-rent producer becomes the 'representative firm' in the sense that it represents directly both the immediate production process and the process of capitalist production as a whole.

So long as Ricardo ignores the distinction between the total capital and the direct production process he is not required to draw any distinction between profit and surplus-value since they are, *ipso facto*, identical. This cannot, however, allow for a concept of rent. In order to deal with this problem Ricardo introduces the no-rent, marginal, producer who has the function of equating the two levels of analysis within a single production process: the production of corn on no-rent land. The latter is that production process which is simultaneously the direct production process of capital and the particular firm. On the other hand, whenever Ricardo speaks concretely of rent he is forced to consider profit and rent as constituent parts of a whole. Taking rent as a presupposition of analysis Ricardo introduces it at the very outset of his treatment of value, setting up an immediate opposition of value and price, of profit and surplus-value. By conceiving of rent exclusively as a relation of marginal productivity to productivity on the more productive units of land, Ricardo thereby constitutes the problem strictly within the confines of the self-reproduction of corn; thus, the whole which encompasses profit and rent has a purely natural character. This whole Ricardo invariably refers to as 'surplus-produce' since he deals only with the conditions introduced into capitalist production by the peculiarities of its natural basis. Thus only the surplus-value on land needs to be divided. And this division can be shown to have no effect upon the principles of exchange so long as the notion of the no-rent producer is allowed to stand for the total capital.

When rent is greater than zero the marginal producer is not, however, equivalent to the direct production process. When the direct production process (on the margin) is taken concretely as involving the production of surplus-value it necessarily involves the reproduction of constant capital and determination of the organic composition of capital so that the analysis of production as social production intervenes between the direct production process and the production and reproduction of a world of particular and opposing capitals. This intervention precludes the equation of the direct production process and the firm and therefore requires the transformation of values into prices, the transformation of surplus-value into profit, etc.

Once the individual unit of capital, the 'firm,' is conceived in the absence of its particularity as that emerges out of a concrete analysis of production and circulation, the real basis for the competition of capitals is lost. The idea that the growth of the total capital takes place via a process of competition of particular, opposing capitals, is also lost. To this extent the determinateness of the accumulation of capital and its laws and contradictions cannot be conceptualized. The accumulation of capital is the expansion of the unity of production and circulation and therefore involves the expansion and competition of capitals as particular, opposing units. Whether there can be a general glut when this is taken into account can only be determined in the course of the treatment of accumulation and competition. In the face of the determinate unity of production and consumption via circulation it is possible for capital to at the same time produce and reproduce its own conditions of existence, therefore to be self-sustaining, and to run up against limitations to its expansion. Such limitations, since the process as a whole is now constituted as self-contained, must be within that process itself, barriers to the expansion of capital which are also the products of the expansion of capital. The possibility of limitations and contradictions within a self-sustaining process eludes Ricardo since self-sustained for Ricardo also implies undifferentiated. The specific unity of the difference and the determinate requirements of that unity disappear within classical thought, leaving only the opposing poles of an undifferentiated unity, on one side, which is absolute and a difference without unity, on the other side, whose parts are independent of one another and therefore of the whole. These 'parts' as we have seen proceed directly to lose all particularity.

Since the particular capitals are no longer really particular and the analysis of their expansion is indifferent to their determinate relations with other particular capitals, accumulation is severed from competition and the process of competition loses its determinateness. By contrast, were the particularity of capitals to be taken seriously, the level of their analysis would distinguish itself in a series of critical features relevant to the problem of accumulation.

The realization of value and surplus-value in circulation would no longer be presupposed but would now be posited within the reproduction and expansion process itself. Realization would come to have its conditions in the accumulation of capital, therefore in the relations of particular capitals. In the face of this condition the rate of surplus-value (assumed by Ricardo to be equal to the rate of profit) could no longer express the key relation of capital which is now the relation of capital not directly to labor-power but to capital itself within which labor-power and its costs are posited as elements. This distinction is expressed in the difference between the rate of surplus-value and the rate of profit. In the former capital relates directly to labor-power as the source of its expansion. In the latter capital relates to itself as the sum of dead and living labor. The rate of self-expansion of capital is the rate of profit which must be distinguished from the rate of surplus-value. The rate of profit is also specifically different in that it is determined, in its movement, by the competition and accumulation of capitals. The absence of the distinction between the direct production process of capital and the self-realization of capital as a whole leaves classical thought without access to the essential categories for the analysis of accumulation: the rate of profit as opposed to the rate of surplus-value, price as opposed to value, fixed capital, constant capital, relative surplus-value, competition of capitals, circulation of capital, reproduction of the total social capital (and the category of the total social capital itself), and concentration of capital.

IV The competition of capitals

1

It may appear paradoxical that what has virtually without exception been deemed the central distinguishing feature of classical thought – advocacy of unlimited expression of the competitive process – is found to have no real existence within classical thought. To be sure, classical political economy is characterized by the most vigorous defense of *laissez-faire*. Further, all systematic analysis of economic phenomena within classical economy proceeds on the assumption of the fully unfettered operation of competition. None the less, free competition is wholly undetermined within classical thinking, in that it is posited abstractly without the real conditions required for its operation. This abstractness of the positing of competition is also essential to classical thought since the central theme of the classical treatment of bourgeois economy is that the freedom implied by the confrontation of individuals established as equal before the market is absolute. In other words the determination of the individual within the process of bourgeois economy is a self-determination which is synonymous with his freedom. Freedom of competition is the realization of this self-determination within a world of individuals. Thus the process of competition which appears within capitalist economy concretely as the confrontation of opposing particular capitals appears within economic analysis as the abstract opposition of self-determining individuals independent of the concrete determinations of capital.

It was shown in the previous section that this result has its origin in the reduction of the world of particular capitals to the immediate production process of capital and, therefore, in the reduction of that immediate production process to a directly material and natural process. Conceptually the latter also implies the reduction of the natural production process to a purely individual process. This conception has its realization within classical thought in the idea of 'simple commodity production' and more consistently within neo-classical thought in the closely related idea of subsistence production and surplus exchange. Competition as the process of the realization of the freedom of the individual in the abstract rests upon a basis of the construction of the unit of competition as the self-sufficient individual (the Robinson Crusoe) who determines himself and brings that determination to the market in order to realize it concretely in exchange. Within the neo-classical analysis this construction is made explicit when production is not only 'naturalized' but also eliminated from the entire market process. As a result the process of competition of particular units of capital becomes the opposition of individuals in the simple exchange of commodities. Competition comes to be determined within the most general and abstract conception of exchange.

This is the degenerative side of the classical conception of competition as the abstract confrontation of self-determining individuals. At the same time the assumption of freedom of competition is connected in classical thought to the determination of exchange and the world of exchange in nature. The competitive price is the natural price. In the connection of competition to nature classical political economy seeks to determine competition concretely, i.e. in nature, and thereby to show that while the formation of price is the realization of freedom it is a determination of a concrete form of freedom, freedom based on capital. The notion of nature has the significance for classical thought of being based on a world of capitals which is at the same time the product of capital. The price is natural to the degree that its determination takes place wholly within the confrontation of particular capitals and to the degree that the basis of the confrontation of those capitals recognizes equally the rights of each capital.

The duality of the classical conception of competition is typical and refers back to the dualism of the analysis of accumulation. Competition is the process by which the natural principle is realized and has as its condition the absence of external determination, therefore self-sufficiency. This means both that competition realizes the self-determination of capital and that it realizes the external determination of capital in nature. Both sides of this conception appear in classical thought within Smith's notion of the 'invisible hand' (*Wealth of Nations*, pp. 423, 508, 594, 597). The invisible hand creates society, as a whole, out of a world of individuals. The key to this creation is the absence of any determinateness of the social totality outside of the activities of the parts, the individual units and their products. This notion of competition resolves the problem of the conception of the whole as the world of capitals. Yet, as we have seen, it is critical to determine the extent to which the individual units which construct through their activities the system of capital as a whole are the simple determinations of the most abstract forms of the exchange system or the unity of a concrete process of production, circulation, and reproduction of capital. Within the latter unity competition appears as the confrontation of capital with itself, the 'relation of capital to itself as another capital, i.e. the real conduct of capital as capital.'[4] Within this relation the world of capitals is constituted as the product of capital. The determinations of that world (price, profit, accumulation, etc.) are self-determinations of capital and are therefore natural, capital in its natural, that is, adequate, existence. The individual unit of capital exists only as a particular unit of capital within this world of competition. The latter creates particularity in its continuing process of reproduction and expansion just as much as it is the product of particularity.

This is the dominant side of the classical conception of competition – the conduct of capital upon itself – which always grasps the process as a relation among particular units of capital. This must be clearly distinguished from that concept of competition, which is subordinate to this notion within classical thought and which comes to predominate within neo-classical economics. The conception of the particular unit of production as a unit of capital is critical. Were the unit of capital to be identified with the direct production process (a view toward which classical thought is always tending) competition would cease to involve the confrontation of particular units of capital and would be constituted as the reciprocal interaction of abstract, self-subsistent individuals. Competition would be the process within which the abstract freedom of the individual is realized in his relation to a system of particular individuals. This dual conception of competition relates to the twofold character of the classical conception of nature. On one side, where nature is identified with capital as the self-subsistent unity of the economic process, the natural or competitive price is the price which emerges within the concrete opposition of particular units of capital, specified not as individual producer-consumers but as firms. On the other side, where nature appears as the external, opposing force acted upon by the individual, the natural price is connected to the natural process of interaction of the individual with nature, the labor process as a work process. In Smith, natural price becomes the result of the immediate activity of the individual *vis-à-vis* the natural world. This natural price comes into conflict with that natural price which emerges out of the process of the competition of capitals and this contradiction is a contradiction within the concept of nature itself as at the same time both capital, the self-renewing economic process, and the external opponent of the abstract individual. These two poles are not, of course, wholly independent. The common intervention of the category nature involves also an interpenetration of the two conceptions at each level so that the natural relation of the direct production process is both the production of particular objects severed from relation to the ongoing social process and the production of value, while the competition of capitals is both the opposition of the determinate units of capitalist production and the opposition of individual capitals as abstract individual needs within a market. It is not only competition of capitals but also, as we shall see, the process of emergence of general interest out of the interaction of particular need.

2

In the confrontation of particular interest in the form of individual units of capital generality emerges not as the imposition of one particular interest upon the other, as the elevation of a given particularity to the general, but as the generalization of particular interest as a whole. For Smith any elevation of particular interest into general interest undermines liberty and that general interest upon which particularity rests. This is the core of Smith's opposition to physiocracy. Within the latter, while free competition is advocated, certain sections are more free than others. Production in agriculture is favored above all other investment of capital so that the investment in production on land as a particular sphere is favored directly and judged to be higher, more immediately congruent with the general interest, than capital investment in manufacture. To this degree there is, for Smith, associated within physiocracy the general principle of *laissez-faire* together with its opposite: the favoring of one particular interest over other particular interests, of agriculture over manufacture.

This universality of standpoint distinguishes classical thought as it appears in a fully developed form in Smith and Ricardo. They both also go further than neo-classical thought in that they always consider that the particular interests which need to be defended are not predominantly the interests of individuals *per se* but the interests of the individual units of capital, therefore the interest of capital itself. The defense of unfettered competition is in this context the defense of the real interest of capital. The general interest which needs to be preserved is the freedom of the expansion of capital. This is the main theme of all the classical strictures on taxation and on the activities of the government in the defense of the general good. For Smith the duty of the sovereign is precisely to turn aside all efforts of particular interest to become directly universal, that is, to become universal outside of the free play of competitive forces in the market.

Once competition is seen to realize the particularity of all interest the world of competition must be conceived to be adequate to all particular need. This adequacy of the world of capital is of profound importance within classical, and especially Ricardian, thinking. The special emphasis which this receives in Ricardo's writing attests to his peculiarly well-developed concern over the sufficiency of capital and its process, the absence of external dependency of capital. This notion of adequacy appears in the work of both Smith and Ricardo. In the former it emerges in the discussion of the colonization of North America and in the latter it appears in a critique of the Smithian position on the necessity of foreign trade.

Smith's analysis of the phenomenon of the growth of the North American colonies concerned two main points – first, the origin of the colonization, and second, the source of the rapid growth and increasing prosperity which distinguished this sector of the British Empire. According to Smith the colonization of North America was 'unnecessary' (*Wealth of Nations*, p. 525). This absence of necessity meant for Smith that there was an absence of reason for the colonization, that it was accidental and not grounded within the process of capital, not a necessary emergence from the process of expansion of the already constituted world of capitals. This lack of necessity describes a process of colonization which originates with the exclusion of certain groups and individuals from the existing economic system or with the decision on the part of certain groups or individuals that 'civilized society' was inadequate to their needs. This refers primarily to that group driven out of civilized society by intolerance and persecution on the part of particular individuals and groups acting through the state. Such persecution is unreasonable to classical thought since it contradicts directly the classical conception of society as intrinsically adequate to all need. It is contrary to the concept of bourgeois economy that particular interest should be excluded from the market system since the construction of that system is precisely the process of generalization of all particularity of need.

It is this same sense of the inner adequacy of bourgeois economy which leads Smith to an explanation of the prosperity of the American colonies. The keynote of all of Smith's writing on colonialism is the conditions of self-sufficiency and free internal self-development. There are fundamentally three such conditions: (1) Prosperity must be based on independence and the latter cannot exist without self-reliance. The condition for such independence is primarily the presence of fertile land in abundance. The emphasis which Smith places upon this condition reveals the natural ground of the self-sufficiency of the bourgeois individual. Freedom is driven to its most adequate expression where it finds the form of total self-sufficiency. Such a natural condition of freedom previews the predominant neo-classical conception of freedom as that of the self-sufficient producer-consumer who enters into social interrelation only when he freely chooses to do so, therefore at his personal whim. Abundant fertile land is not, however, a sufficient condition for prosperity. (2) The second necessary condition is the absence of external imposition of interest through coercion in the form of the use of an instrument (such as the state) for the domination of one or many particular interests by one or a group of particular interests. Prosperity and freedom, therefore, also require the reciprocal recognition of the right of each as a sovereign and self-

determining individual. (3) Finally, prosperity rests upon the prior achievement of a sufficient level of civilization on the part of the colonials who must,
in other words, be bourgeois individuals and not savages. The recognition
that the freedom of all encourages the prosperity of all is, implicitly at least,
not native to mankind but requires an historical process of development. This
is an interesting and important condition which cannot be considered in detail
here. The necessity of an historical process of development of bourgeois man
may be seen to possess two alternative foundations. First, it indicates the
recognition of the existence of the present-day bourgeois as a purely social
condition determinate not within the natural state of man but within his social
condition. In this argument Smith indicates that to be determined as a member
of civilized society is something quite distinct from being determined as a
member of the species.

On the other side, however, this same comment may reflect the intrinsically
anti-social character of the classical construction of the bourgeois individual
whose bourgeois character as a self-seeking, socially autarchic and dangerous,
animal finds its own first limitation within bourgeois society itself. In other
words, Smith reads the anti-social character of bourgeois man into the pre-
bourgeois epoch of 'savage society' whose conditions are then implicitly
recognized to be inadequate to the construction of bourgeois economy. In
this case it is not historical conditioning at all which is expressed but an
intrinsic contradiction within the conception of the construction of the economic system on the basis of self-seeking and autonomous individuals who
generate their own needs. The entire construction of the Smithian understanding of the prosperity of the American colonies rests upon the implicit
equation of growth and prosperity, first, with liberty and self-determination,
and then, with self-sufficiency and its conditions as the foundation of liberty.
The conditions of self-sufficiency are those of abundant land and independence.

Ricardo's position is more uncompromising still than that of Smith. While
at one stage of his argument Smith adopts the position of the intrinsic
adequacy of bourgeois economy, at another he accepts the possibility and the
necessity of interchange between bourgeois economy and the world 'outside,'
whether in the form of international trade or of general exchange with the
realm of non-bourgeois social relations. This is connected to the possibility
within Smith's thinking that the expansion of capital might outstrip the conditions for its realization (*Wealth of Nations*, p. 354):

When the capital stock of any country is increased to such a degree, that it cannot
be all employed in supplying the consumption, and supporting the productive labor
of that particular country, the surplus part of it naturally disgorges itself into the
carrying trade.

Similarly, further on, Smith argues that foreign trade

carries out that surplus part of the produce of their land and labor for which there
is no demand among them, and brings back in return for it something else for which

there is a demand. . . . By means of it the narrowness of the home market does not hinder the division of labor in any branch of art or manufacture from being carried to the highest perfection (*ibid.*, p. 415).

The discovery of America

. . . by opening a new and inexhaustable market for all the commodities of Europe . . . gave occasion to new divisions of labor and improvements of art, which, in the narrow circle of ancient commerce, could never have taken place for want of a market to take off the greater part of their produce (*ibid.*, p. 416).

For Smith, as for Malthus, the expansion of capital runs up against a barrier in the expansion of the demand for the products of capital. While Malthus meets this difficulty by positing a section of pre-capitalist and non-capitalist consumers who can absorb the surplus produce, Smith posits a world of capitalist economies each absorbing the surplus produce of the others (although what Smith actually has in mind is the world economy absorbing the surplus produce of British capital). Ricardo's answer to Smith is important since it is the direct extension of his reply to Malthus. In his debate with Malthus, Ricardo attempts to establish two points: first, the general adequacy of the capitalist economy to absorb its products, the unity of principle between production and consumption, and second, the immediate adequacy of the economic microcosm, the individual producer-consumer, to represent the whole of bourgeois economy. In answer to Smith, Ricardo falls back upon the same form of argument, this time asserting the adequacy of bourgeois economy as a whole to the productive use of its products (vol. I, pp. 295–6):

We manufacture commodities, and with them buy goods abroad, because we can obtain a greater quantity than we could make at home. Deprive us of this trade, and we immediately manufacture for ourselves. . . . It follows then from these admissions that there is no limit to demand – no limit to the employment of capital while it yields any profit.

For Ricardo the adequacy of capital is complete. Those commodities which are engaged in international trade may not be demanded at home but this does not imply that their production could not be transferred to production of commodities in demand in the home market. Ricardo argues for the possibility of collapsing production in upon itself. The world market can be reduced to the home market, the home market can be reduced to the individual unit of production and that can be established as the self-sufficient independent producer. Since Ricardo leaves aside all of the concrete characteristics of production he fails to recognize the special conditions of capitalist production – division of labor, concentration of capital, expansion of the world market, etc. Thus the primary implication of Ricardo's mode of argument is the collapsing of the system of capitals as a whole into the individual producer-consumer and thereby the equating of the former with the latter. At the same time it is important not to lose sight of the contradictory nature of this equation which, while identifying capitalist production with the activity of the individual producer-consumer and, therefore, with the production of a particular object of consumption, at the same time implicitly constitutes the activity of the individual producer-consumer as possessed of a universal character. The latter is latent in the founding of the original equation upon the mobility of capital, which alone in its indifference to particular commodity form can take on any particular commodity form. Ricardo's argument ignores the specificity of capitalist production, its determinate inner character, while at the same time connecting the concept of production to capital by endowing the former with a universal character.

For classical political economy the principle of capitalist production is a principle of freedom and of unfettered movement. This expresses directly the universality implied in the idea of capital. Capital exists only as a process of movement beyond all fixed limits. Capitalist production is the multiplication and expansion of production. The substance which is both the means of production and product is not a fixed material substance but the universal social substance value. When Ricardo grasps production as the production of value he grasps that production as intrinsically free of limitation in the particularity either of the material form or the use-value of the product.

And yet, at the same time, the free movement of capital is only possible in and through production of particular use-value so that the movement of capital also involves its fixity into particular form. Here it is the means of production, especially as fixed capital which make possible the movement and expansion of capital in the production of particular commodities by making possible the production of particular commodities. Investment of capital in particular means of production determines the useful character of production. For Ricardo this necessary condition for the determination of production, precisely since it makes production determinate, conflicts with the intrinsic freedom and universality of production as the production of capital. Ricardo, therefore, leaves aside the real determination of production in order to attempt to conceive of capitalist production as immediately universal, therefore as indeterminate.

The contrast with Smith is important. Even though Smith's own arguments for the necessity of world commerce fail to give to the latter any real justification they do rest on the limited but none the less important initial analysis of the production process with which Smith begins the *Wealth of Nations*. The argument within this discussion for a connection between the division of labor and the extent of the market is the explicit recognition that production and exchange are mutually conditioned, that production is not self-contained but requires a particular form of social mediation. To the extent that the concreteness of the production process is posited by Smith it becomes possible for him to think of the requirements of production not only on a national but also on a world scale. The analysis of capitalist production and the manner of its consummation carries with it the secret to the deduction of the world of capital including the world market, especially as it entails the positing of the conditions of production outside of the immediate production process of capital. For Smith, in contrast to Ricardo, the world economy is necessary to capitalist production. But at the same time that the universalization of capital begins to appear as the process of capital, Smith immediately denies this process by positing it as given. The world economy starts out as the economy of independent and sovereign states. There is no conception for Smith of that which might lie outside of the world of capital except capital itself. The discovery of America *immediately* opens a 'new and inexhaustable market for all the commodities of Europe.' Thus the full development of capital is posited as the immediate corollary of capital itself and not out of the process of development of capital, nor out of the accumulation of capital but as a given condition of that process of accumulation.

Once again classical thought collapses the concrete determination of a world of capital into the simplest forms of capitalist production and thereby excludes the deduction of that world as the concrete result of the real process of capital. It is not that Smith is incorrect in arguing that when capital looks outside of its boundaries it finds there only capital but he is incorrect in arguing that this discovery is immediate and not the end point of a process by which capital makes the world outside of it part of its own process, and then finds only capital within a world which is nothing other than the full realization of capital.

V The world of capital and the state

1

The world economy is conceived within classical political economy as identical in its morphology with the world of capitals. The notion of competition, with its dualisms and paradoxes, is the central category also of the world economy as that is conceived within classical thought. The problem of the world economy, for Smith and Ricardo, is the problem of the 'international' economy. Just as each particular capital realizes itself in opposition to a world of particular capitals, so also each separate group of capitals constitutes itself as a state in opposition to a world economy made up of individual national economies. In order for each bourgeois society to find outside of itself only the reflection of its own inner structure it is necessary that it find only capital in other particular forms. But just as in the case of the construction of the world of particular capitals the ground of the reflection of each capital in another capital and the competition of capitals is not consistently articulated in classical thought, so also in the construction of the world economy the opposition of capitalist states is without necessity and determination.

The general good arises out of the interaction of particular self-seeking through the unfettered competition of capitals. This reciprocal interaction involves the constitution of each unit of capital as the exclusion of the needs of every other unit and as, at the same time, the condition for the realization of the needs of all so that the general good emerges out of the free play of particular need. But it remains to be established in the case of the relations of particular countries, what constitutes the ground for the maintenance of freedom of each in the interests of the system as a whole. Smith and Ricardo effect an answer to this question which has the implication of recognizing the total lack of ground for the differentiation of capitals according to their national character. Competition in the world market, it is argued in classical thought, should be no different than competition within a national market, all barriers to competition should fall not only within states but between them as well. In effect Smith and Ricardo argue for the elimination of the state and they must argue for this elimination to the extent that within the analysis the state remains indeterminate and unnecessary.

For Smith the duties of the state are clearly limited (*Wealth of Nations*, p. 651):

According to the system of natural liberty, the sovereign has only three duties to attend to; three duties of great importance, indeed, but plain and intelligible to common understandings: first, the duty of protecting the society from the violence and invasion of other independent societies; secondly, the duty of protecting, as far as possible, every member of the society from the injustice or oppression of every other member of it, or the duty of establishing an exact administration of justice; and, thirdly, the duty of erecting and maintaining certain public works and certain public institutions, which it can never be for the interest of any individual, or small numbers of individuals, to erect and maintain.

The conception of the state which is embedded in the 'duties of the sovereign' as those are specified by Smith is distinctive in that it excludes any real determination of the state always reducing the latter to a dependent moment within civil society and even within the system of economic relations. Indeed, it is characteristic of classical political economy that the state be embedded within the interaction of particular self-seeking rather than distinguished from it as the sphere within which the implicit sociality brought to realization through the interaction of self-seeking be made the explicit and conscious basis of social life.

Thus Smith considers the state either simply as an instrument of economic activity involved in the establishment or preservation of 'public works' assuring to the system of economic relations the general economic conditions within which it is alone able to subsist, or Smith reduces the state to the 'administration of justice.' For the latter the conception of the state is precluded from going beyond the raising to explicit consciousness of the rights of individual self-seeking so that the ethical idea still exists only in and through the system of self-determination and individual 'self-interest.'[5] In this respect Smith constrains the state to a determination which remains confined to civil society and thereby excludes the possibility of moving beyond the system of self-seeking. The state is nothing more than that system made the explicit basis of economic action and the explicit law of individual interaction.

When classical political economy equates civil society with social life it, in effect, denies the full social determination of the individual whose existence is exhausted in his self-seeking and individual self-subsistence. Within the latter there exists no social principle in that there is no sphere within which the sociality realized in and through the interaction of private self-seeking could become the explicit basis of an ethical existence. Since the sociality of the individual is required to remain always implicit it appears to the individual not as the inner principle of his existence but as an external and arbitrary force. For classical political economy the state is just such an arbitrary force made external to the individual when his individuality is deprived of any real social substance capable of being brought to realization on a level higher than that of the interaction of private self-seeking. Thus the absence of a concept of the state is the absence of a full social determination of the individual and of civil society. Instead of a concept of the state classical thought takes the unification of the system of economic life in so far as that is not accomplished internally to be the result of an external instrument. The state has the form of an instrument through which the pursuit of *economic* interest can be raised to a higher level. While this does not constitute a real concept of the state it does grasp, in however one-sided a manner, the peculiarities of the self-conception of modern bourgeois economic and social life. For the latter, the conception of the state is that of a sphere of the interaction of private, even economic, interest. And, indeed, within capitalist economy the state tends always to be reduced in practice to an instrument of particular interest. Yet, even here, classical political economy fails to grasp that quality of capitalist economy which makes of the state little more than an instrument of particular interest. For classical thought the state does not go beyond the interaction of particular self-seeking except to make the necessity of that interaction explicit and, at the same time, the state is always considered to be above the interaction of particular interest and therefore implicitly to involve a principle which moves beyond the system of individual self-seeking, which, therefore, cannot be considered an instrument of particular interests and of the clash of interests.

2

Within classical political economy distinctions within the world of capital are, first, only distinctions among units of capital, and second, distinctions only of the most elementary and therefore abstract character. That is, the distinctions presuppose that, first, all units which are to be differentiated are units of capital, and second, that the units of capital are distinguished one from the other only in such ways as can be reconciled via processes internal to the economy itself.

The construction of the bourgeois economy as a whole rests solely upon the opposition of capitals. To this extent the only category of economic agents essential to the conception of the economic system as a whole is that of the individual capitals. This construction always tends to the elimination of the division of society into classes since all agents appear in the market as owners of capital.[6] To the extent that the world is composed only of capitals the interest of capital is also directly synonymous with the general social interest. On the other hand, once the purchase and sale of labor-power is explicitly recognized as a condition for the construction of the world of capitals then the latter is constructed not only out of the opposition of capitals but also out of the reproduction and expansion of the antithesis of capital. The necessity within the process of capital as a whole for the bifurcation of its world into capital and its negation imposes upon the world of capital an opposition of an intrinsically higher order than that of individual units of capital. The universality produced by the competition of capitals and the expansion of capital is, viewed from the standpoint of its own product, only a particular interest – the interest of capital. This idea of the general good must be realized in a concrete form to the extent that it needs to oppose itself to and defend itself against another idea which may also claim generality, so long as that claim is made on a basis different from that of capital.

It is for this reason that in bourgeois society the state is unable to exist as the realization of the ethical idea and must appear instead as the arena within which an opposition of ideas is sustained and as an arena within which the ethical idea opposes itself explicitly to its reduction into a realm of particular interest. In a period of transition the state can exist only in opposition to the idea of ethical life which idea must struggle to become the substance of the state.

In practice, classical political economy is forced to recognize the multiplicity of general interest. The two central themes of Ricardian economics are the explicitly recognized opposition between capital and landed property and the implicitly recognized opposition between capital and labor. The inverse relation between profits and wages together with the limited fertility of the soil links the expansion of capital with the impoverishment of both capital and labor to the benefit of landed property. At the same time the mechanism for the impoverishment of capital is the rising wage, so that the continued emphasis by Ricardo on the relation of profit to wages also reveals the central importance of the emerging struggle between capital and labor not simply in the form of wages and labor-power but also in the form of the capitalist class and the working class. For Ricardo the existence of capital is its expansion and the rate of that expansion is the rate of profit. The rate of profit is, in its turn, the ratio of profit to wages and is inversely proportional to the latter. The growth of capital implies the diminution of the share of labor in the product of its own activity.

As is apparent in a close investigation of the Ricardian theory of distribution social classes appear within that theory and play a central role. But at the same time the exact nature of that presence and that role is contradictory. The central contradiction emerges in the opposition between the conception of the class relation as the simple exchange of commodities and the conception of the class relation as the relation of classes taken as a whole, therefore as *classes* properly conceived. On one side, the working class appears in a form intrinsically inadequate to its conception, not as a class but as a commodity which is purchased by capital, not as the capitalist class but as its most elementary determination: self-expanding value. On the other side, Ricardo actually conceives of distribution according to the laws of capital as a whole, but in this case that distribution is independent of the commodity form and appears as the distribution of a physical product immediately transferred between classes presumed to be given, directly present, and irreducible. In the first exchange, the relation which underlies the formation of the classes appears as necessary from the standpoint of the process of capital but the actual emergence of classes does not. In the second, the class relation emerges as the corollary of distribution but the specificity of the relation as a relation of capitalist class to working class disappears. When Ricardo constructs the production process as the process of production of corn by means of corn and labor on the marginal land, the process of capital as a whole and the distribution of the product come to be wholly individualized so that while the class relation comes to be apparent it also appears to be wholly external and unnecessary. On one side, Ricardo considers the reproduction of the commodity labor-power but not in terms of the reproduction of the working class as a whole, and on the other, Ricardo considers the reproduction of the working class as a whole but not as determinate and necessary, as involving simply the sum total of the natural needs of the workers as individuals.

The abstract conception of production within which capital is forced to ground itself appears as production wholly independent of labor as the antithesis of capital. Labor and capital appear as simple unity in a production process for which labor is capital, given the absence of constant capital and the assumption that the reproduction of fixed capital is unnecessary. Within the simple unity of the production process as a natural process the determination of the intrinsically social character of that process disappears, with that disappearance the concrete determination of that labor which opposes itself to capital within production is replaced by the collapsing of labor, labor-power, and 'work' into an undifferentiated unity.

The social determination of capital and labor appear here (as in all subsequent economic analysis) as their external subordination to a category within which they are defined. Class, then, is a category which gives to capital and labor a social character, and yet, in its immediate presence, excludes from capital and labor any real social determination. For classical political economy social class and the state retain an unintelligible necessity for the conception of economic and social life, of 'civilized society.' It is this unintelligibility which gives away the secret of the failure of the classical conception to fully constitute the system of economic relations as a moment in the conception of social life.

Chapter 5
The specificity of classical political economy

I The social determination of production

1

More than one hundred and fifty years have passed since the decline of classical political economy. Yet the task of specifying its distinguishing features remains unfinished. At the same time, it becomes more and more evident that the weaknesses of neo-classical economics require, for their adequate comprehension, a coming to terms with classical thought. In spite of, or possibly because of, this fact the investigation of classical political economy has been removed from the agenda of contemporary analysis. Current economics is not only thinking which is blind to its origins, it is thinking which has blinded itself to those origins in order the better to remove from its sight the frailty of its own foundations.

The correct comprehension of the specificity of classical thought requires, from the outset, that the central contradictions of classical economics be taken beyond interpretation in terms of simple failure of analysis, limitation of technique, or apologetic (either conscious or unconscious) and be constituted instead as the logical results of compelling conditions explicitly and implicitly present within classical thought itself. The conceptual *cul-de-sac* of the classical theory of value – the invariable measure of value – is not simply a sign of weakness but equally a sign of strength, of that strength with which Ricardo in particular drives the conditions of classical political economy (and the contradictions intrinsic to those conditions) to their logical outcome. Each opposing, and apparently exclusive, pole of classical thought bears a necessity within the classical conception which serves to stamp that conception as definitely classical in character. The location of the peculiarly classical understanding of economic life is not in its consistent and systematic moments taken in isolation, nor in the presence of differing tendencies of conception taken as separate and independent, but in the unity (however unstable) of inconsistent and opposed ideas of bourgeois economy. It is, paradoxically, only in terms of the contradictions and inconsistencies of classical thought that its conception as a distinguishable theoretical standpoint can be determined.

The only economist to come any significant distance in conceptualizing the inner character of classical economics is Karl Marx. Marx seeks to sum up the nature of classical thought in terms of his notion of the 'social relations of capitalist production' and in terms of the manner in which these relations are grasped within classical theory. For Marx, the distinctiveness of classical political economy lies precisely in the fact that classical thought takes as its object the investigation of these social relations. As we have seen, even where classical thought attempts to grasp non-capitalist economic relations it finds that it has constituted nothing other than capital itself in a distorted form. For classical political economy the analysis of pre-capitalist economies – the savage state of man – and of explicitly non-commodity economies – the corn model – is implicitly the theory of bourgeois economy.

For classical economics all production is capitalist production and the analysis of production is directly the analysis of the social relations of capitalist production. But there is a sense in which this is also the case with respect to the neo-classical theory of production. That theory seeks to conceptualize production in general in terms of the notion of 'factors of production' which turn out, upon analysis, to be distorted expressions of the social relations of the capitalist economy – wage-labor and capital. It can be argued that each of the categories of the neo-classical theory of production ('land,' 'labor,' and 'capital') bears a special relation to what Marx calls the 'capitalist mode of production.' In this general sense the neo-classical theory of production also takes as its subject-matter the system of bourgeois social relations. To be sure, it does not view those relations as 'social relations' but, then, it is also the explicit object of classical analysis to penetrate the social character of capitalist production and thereby reveal its non-social and natural foundation.

Without denying the profound differences between classical and neo-classical theory it is necessary to emphasize that no simple formula is capable of grasping the specific difference which separates the classical and neo-classical schools of economic theory. The notion of 'social relations of production' has too often in the past been employed as an excuse for the systematic investigation of the specificity of classical thought. It appears that the sense in which classical political economy may be distinguished as the theory of the social relations of capitalist production remains uncertain. In particular, it is not established that the theoretical integration of classical analysis is adequate to the task of conceptualizing bourgeois economy. This does not imply that Marx's characterization is incorrect but only that it still requires clarification.

This clarification appears within Marx's own writing in the form of the determination of the limits of classical thinking:[1]

As regards value in general, it is the weak point of the classical school of Political Economy that it nowhere, expressly and with full consciousness, distinguishes between labor, as it appears in the value of a product, and the same labor, as it appears in the use-value of that product.

This failure is, of course, connected to the confusions of Smith's formulation of the labor theory of value and of the attempt to construct a labor-commanded theory in place of the labor theory. As we have seen the necessity of the dis-. tinction between past and current labor imposes itself upon the classical conception of value but always as an imposition from outside, as it were, rather than as a necessity revealed explicitly by the analysis and systematically integrated into the theory of exchange. The failure with regard to the distinctions within the category of labor is also reflected within the concept of value. According to Marx, 'it is one of the chief failings of classical economy that it has never succeeded, by means of its analysis of commodities, and, in particular, of their value, in discovering that form under which value becomes exchange-value.' Classical theory equates value and exchange-value, thereby denying to the latter as well as to all of its more concrete expressions (money, price, etc.) any adequate ground. Further, according to Marx, political economy 'has never once asked the question why labor is represented by the value of its product and labor time by the magnitude of that value.'[2] On one side, classical economy has succeeded in drawing out the connection between labor and value in making that connection the starting point of economic theory. On the other side, it has failed to investigate that relationship concretely, to work out the various determinations of the value form of the product of labor.

But the limitations of classical thinking in this sense have a two-fold character which has led to conflicting interpretations. Marx himself ties the inability of classical economy to investigate the commodity form to the fact that these forms 'bear it stamped upon them in unmistakable letters that they belong to a state of society, in which the process of production has the mastery over man, instead of being controlled by him.' As a result 'such formulae appear to the bourgeois intellect to be as much a self-evident necessity imposed by nature as productive labor itself.'[3] The central limitation of classical thinking taken in this sense is a limitation of vision, an inability to grasp the transitory nature of capitalist production, an inability to *see* the social relations of capitalist production as the social relations of one, historically limited system of production. This is, in one sense, a typically classical critique. We have seen Smith, time and again, ridicule the weakness of perception of the popular intellect which fails to grasp abstraction, holding fast to the 'palpable object,' or to the 'appearance.' For Smith, the difference between the popular conception of economic life and the scientific conception is a difference of vision, of ability to see beyond the immediately appearing forms to their ground in nature. Marx takes up this manner of criticism, turning it upon classical analysis itself. Where Smith criticizes the popular conception Marx criticizes Smith and upon the identical basis – the lack of ability to perceive anything beyond or beneath the surface forms of bourgeois economy, an inability to see those as *forms*.

This taking up of the classical manner of criticism is, on one level, the adoption on the part of Marx of the scientific aspiration of classical thought together with its full logical implications where classical thinking itself shies away from those implications. The necessity of going beyond the immediate forms to their ground in the ongoing social process is the necessity to see social relations not as either simply given, or as the product of unaccountable individual whim, but as *products*. Even to ground social life in nature is to ground it in a self-subsistent unity, a process which gives for it an account. But at the same time that Marx adopts this scientific side of classical analysis he also adopts the basic implications of the grounding of social phenomena in nature which denies to those phenomena any ground precisely due to the particular manner in which they are observed to be grounded. For Marx, just as for Smith and Ricardo, it appears at this point that the critique of vision, of *in*sight, tends toward the devaluation of social relations into forms which are *purely formal* and which are, therefore, reducible to their ground. When ground relates to its expression as natural to social there is an inevitable tendency for the social to disappear into nature, for the expression to disappear into its ground. This tendency is also apparent in the manner in which Marx attacks the classical conception.

If we interpret Marx to be arguing that the social relations of capitalist production can only be really comprehended as 'forms' of production, as one system of production, so that the value form of labor is what characterizes capitalist production, then in a deeper sense the Marxian critique of Smith and Ricardo becomes subject to absorption into the classical system itself. It is precisely the project of classical theory to demonstrate that the social relations of capitalist production exist only as forms of the real relations of man to nature. The reduction of socially equal labor to a form of labor in general is exactly the distinguishing feature of the classical concept of labor. Marx, in the course of criticizing such a reduction, virtually incorporates it into his own conception when he argues that it is the 'same labor' which, on the one hand, produces use-value and, on the other, produces value.

That Marx's position is, in fact, distinct from that which he criticizes is more clearly expressed at another point. In the *Theories of Surplus-Value* Marx returns to the question of the relation of the value *form* to the labor which is the substance of value, and argues that Ricardo's failure is that he 'does not examine the form – the peculiar characteristic of labor that creates exchange-value or manifests itself in exchange-values – the *nature* of this labor.' Ricardo is to be reproached because 'he does not even examine the form of value – the particular form which labor assumes as the substance of value.'[4]

In this case labor, in order to provide the basis for value, must itself undergo a transformation. The point is that it is not the category of labor independent of social form which underlies value but the specific labor which has as its object value. None the less, it still appears that this is a form of labor and the question may arise as to the constitution of the labor of which value-producing labor is one form and, further, what is meant by attributing to value-producing labor the status of a 'form.' Here again Marx, rather than definitively breaking with the classical conception, appropriates an essential element of that conception. For Marx, that[5]

the necessity of distributing social labor in definite proportions cannot be done away with by the *particular form* of social production, but can only change the *form it assumes*, is self-evident. No natural laws can be done away with. What can change, in changing historical circumstances, is the *form* in which these laws operate.

Just as in classical economy, the value of commodities is related to the labor which forms the substance of that value as the formal to the natural and as the social to the natural. In this case the relation of form to content is precisely that relation which typifies classical thinking and which Marx himself criticizes.

Marx's critique is important, however, in that it reveals the underlying difference in the manner in which Marx, at least implicitly, constructs the relation of form to substance. Thus, for Marx the deficiencies of perception of Smith and Ricardo are summed up in their treatment of the 'form of value as a thing of no importance, as having no connection with the inherent nature of commodities.'[6] It is not so much a question of whether value is the form of labor or whether the exchange-value is the form of value, but of the manner in which value serves to ground exchange-value. And this is, as we shall see in part II, precisely the same question which serves to reveal the central contradictions of the neo-classical conception of exchange.

2

In the first instance, classical political economy relates the form to its content as the accidental and inessential to the necessary. The implication of this is that the content is susceptible to conceptualization independently of its form, therefore of taking on different forms. Labor may or may not be division of labor, in either case it remains labor. Exchange-value is the form taken by the division of or the distribution of social labor in capitalist society which division may be effected through different formal arrangements in different forms of society. In capitalist society the distribution of the net product between the three classes takes place through the market, yet it is possible for such a distribution to be conceived independently of the market form and of the exchange of commodities, as a simple and immediate distribution of wealth. As a result the three classes and their relation do not involve the market mechanism as an essential distinguishing feature. Social classes are themselves determinate in natural terms and independently of exchange. In each case, by implication, what is real is the natural, physical substance of the relations of capitalist production.

The problem of political economy is defined as, first, the conceptualization of the real, the construction of a conception of the natural relations of production and distribution, and second, the reduction of the social form, the form of appearance, to its natural substance. It is this conception which Marx adopts when he argues that 'the science consists precisely in working out *how* the law of value operates.'[7] The primitive state of man in Adam Smith is the most explicit attempt within classical thinking to conceptualize the real as the natural. This along with the conception of the division of labor in the first chapter of the *Wealth of Nations* gives explicit form to the idea of a natural production process and, in particular, of labor as a natural substance. The division of labor is simply a form of labor and labor is the given, undetermined, natural substance of division of labor, of that labor which grounds exchange, of socially necessary labor, of labor congealed in commodities, and of labor as a commodity in the market. This is the conception of social production as the natural in itself. It is on the basis of this element within classical thought that the identification of production with the activity of the isolated individual producer-consumer is predicated. This aspect of classical economics which strives for a consistent conception of production and exchange in their purely natural existence is later taken up by neo-classical economics. The latter is the definitive form adopted by this idea within the history of social thought and as such reveals directly, in the most stark and uncompromising manner, the contradictions which any such conception must eventually display and under the force of which all such conceptions must eventually break down.

The contradictions implied in this equation of nature and society are the product of the fact that nature, as constituted by classical economics, is itself dependent on a determinate system of social relations. Our investigation of Smith's analysis of division of labor and of the construction of the early and rude state of society has revealed both to be expressions of capitalist production, ridden through and through with the results of the still implicit conception of capitalist economy. The division of labor presupposes the accumulation of stock and the stock which must be accumulated is necessarily to take the form of capital. Smith's argument that the transition of stock into capital is a natural one reveals the implicit necessity of the specific social form to the conception of its natural substance. Similarly, the dependence of the equality of labor on the value form, first, on the existence of labor-power as the commodity which measures value, and second, on the higgling and bargaining in the market which produces directly that general average, reveals the necessity of the value form to the labor which provides its substance and of the exchange relation to the abstraction of general labor.

For Ricardo the corn model reveals the distribution of income to be the natural process of the distribution of a physical product among the three classes which are necessary to its production. Ricardo separates value from distribution (that separation which is the necessary pre-condition for Ricardo's constituting distribution as superior to value) precisely in order to separate natural substance from its social form and to demonstrate the possibility of conceptualizing the substance without the form. The corn economy stands as the culmination, within classical political economy, of the drive for a consistent conception of production as the self-reproduction of nature. It is, therefore, not at all surprising that the conception of the corn economy should re-emerge subsequent to the breakdown of classical economy in a new and final form within neo-classical theory. The 'one commodity models' of the latter reproduce and intensify the contradictions upon which Ricardo's corn model was originally founded. The roots of the breakdown of the corn model are to be found within that model itself. Production within the corn economy is production on the basis of capital, production of value and expanded value, the labor process. The function of the corn economy is to reveal the law of the production of profit, expanded value, and therefore to expose the conditions of the production of capital, therefore of capitalist production. In the light of this result the full comprehension of capitalist production, emancipated from the restrictions implied by the corn economy, becomes necessary to the conception of production itself. In the *Principles* the categories of production are synonymous with the categories of capitalist production. Production comes to exist as the labor process, the process of production of value and expanded value. For Ricardo production has become 'directly identical with the self-realization of capital.' The form has not only become necessary to the content, it has directly replaced that content.

3

By considering production to be directly equivalent to the self-realization of capital Ricardo effects an abstraction from the concrete conditions of capitalist production as a whole within the conception of those conditions. That is, Ricardo effects an analysis of the direct production process of capital but only upon the basis of a contradiction. Ricardo focuses in directly upon the capital–labor relation in its real generality since he leaves out of account the system of particular exchanges among units of capital. He is left with the general relation of exchange between capital and labor which forms the basis of the analysis of the labor process. This abstraction drives Ricardo to conceive of the exchange of commodities upon the basis of the production of those commodities within a labor process, therefore to conceive of the exchange of commodities as grounded in the labor required in their production. The quantitative relation of capital to labor (the distribution of value between profit and wages) appears, as a result, to be independent of 'price' (of the determination of exchange among particular units of capital). Since the particular relations between individual capitals are left out of account commodities are seen to exchange at their labor-values and the only exchange which remains to be considered, that between capital and labor, is severed from the effects of the specification of differences between particular firms (as of time of turnover of capital and of organic composition of capital).

But since this abstraction is conceived to be immediately adequate to the conception of the self-realization of capital it must be immediately able to account for the 'firm,' for 'price,' etc. Abstraction does not distinguish two levels of analysis (that of the direct production process and that of the self-realization of capital) but equates those levels, collapsing one into the other and obliterating essential features of each. As a result, the concrete determinations of capital are not simply abstracted, they are almost wholly eliminated and only re-enter in order to come into conflict with the abstract conception. Production becomes not the labor process which contains within it the necessity of breaking apart into the domain of opposing particular capitals, but the direct relation of the individual to nature, the activity of the individual producer-consumer. Labor becomes the natural function of the individual while labor-power disappears and with it the determinateness of its relation to capital, in particular the character of that relation as an exchange. Just as the capital–labor relation is emancipated from the prices of commodities it becomes also emancipated from all value relation and turned into the distribution of a physical product among abstractly posited social entities – capitalists and workers. Thus when Ricardo makes abstraction from the self-realization of capital by equating it with the direct production process he at once sets the foundation for the analysis of the labor process and, therefore, of the relation of labor to value, and denies that basis by requiring that the direct production process and the abstract purchase and sale of labor-power account for the concrete determinations of capitalist production as a whole: profits, wages, prices, and the expansion of the total capital. The inability of labor to simultaneously account for exchange in general and for exchange among a system of particular capitals means for classical political economy that exchange has become unaccountable.

Once exchange has been refused its ground within production as a labor process the location of exchange as a subordinate element within a self-renewing process which is capable of giving for exchange an account disappears. Classical political economy constitutes the self-subsistent process within which the social relations are grounded as nature, and the production which grounds exchange as natural. When this grounding of exchange in labor, as that natural principle, is lost to classical thought the grounding of social life in nature is also lost and with it the central theoretical principle of classical thinking.

II Value and exchange-value

1

It is the elimination of the natural grounding of exchange that ultimately leads Ricardo to eliminate any determinate social grounding for exchange-value. For classical political economy the only grounding is in nature and the loss of natural ground is simultaneously the loss of the possibility of a content for economic relations. The ultimate expression of this tendency within

Ricardian thinking is in the positing of an invariable measure of value as necessary to the conception of the exchange relation. With the concept of 'real value' not only has labor ceased to relate to value as nature to its form but the form has come to express its necessity to the conception of exchange and in so doing has driven the substance of exchange – whether understood as the natural labor process or as socially equal labor – altogether outside of the realm of political economy. In real value (as in the labor-commanded principle) the form – exchange-value – and the substance – value – are united into one. As simultaneously form and content they cease to function as either form or content. This unity is precisely that commodity whose exchange-value is immediately the ground of exchange-value.

The original conception of value as a relation which requires a social grounding (which is intrinsic to the commodity and not arbitrary) yields to the conception of value as pure exchange-value which is grounded in exchange-value itself. The process, therefore, grounds itself and to that extent is not grounded at all. Within the neo-classical conception this result is effected by the equation of value with utility so that the opposition between 'use-value' and 'exchange-value' of classical economics is itself the opposition between value (equals use-value understood as utility) and exchange-value. The only substance of the commodity outside of its exchange is its use so that exchange-value is grounded in use. This result is necessary to the extent that the grounding of exchange-value in value is eliminated. Once the concept of value is lost and the theory focuses exclusively upon exchange-value, the relation of exchange of two particular commodities, a confusion of use-value and value becomes inevitable.

It is precisely this confusion which lies behind the construction of the Ricardian corn economy within which the common substance and the universal character of the product is its useful form. The one-commodity economy grasps the production of surplus-value as the production of a surplus product thereby directly equating surplus-value with a surplus of a particular useful form, therefore value with use-value.

Yet, for Ricardo, the concept of utility is not an acceptable alternative foundation for the theory of exchange and production. Ricardo distinguishes himself from neo-classical economics in that the equation of use-value and value is always an active process which is expressive of a contradiction and which results in a paradox. For neo-classical economics, on the other hand, the starting point is immediately utility so that the origin of this notion in the equation of use-value and value is suppressed and with that suppression the real contradictions implied by the equation are lost from sight (even if only to reappear in a different form). By contrast with the neo-classical theory, Ricardo always considers the usefulness of the product as an objective property independent of individual desire. Corn is useful by merit of its role in the reproduction of labor, and thereby of the economic system as a whole, and not by merit of the intensity of desire for corn felt by the individual worker. Thus Ricardo cannot grasp the equation of value and use-value as the category of utility and that equation always appears as imperfect and contradictory.

But Ricardo also finds himself unable to ground exchange-value in value, that is, in socially necessary labor time. Ricardo is unable, on one side, to turn in the direction of the category of utility due to his comprehension of the contradictions intrinsic to the origins of that concept; and on the other, he is unable to ground exchange in nature (labor) due to the contradictions attendant upon the manner in which he constructs the notion of the labor process. In the conception of the labor process as equivalently a natural interchange Ricardo conceives of the production of value as equivalently the production of use-value (ultimately of a purely material substance). Thus, while Ricardo rejects the concept of utility, which is the logical result of the equation of use-value and value, in his conception of production he tacitly accepts that equation as the basis of the concept of labor. Ricardo is left, therefore, standing in the middle. He is unwilling to ground exchange in utility since the former appears indifferent to the latter and at the same time he is unable to ground exchange in labor due to the fact that his notion of labor has tacitly incorporated the logical basis of the utility concept. Ricardo is, therefore, driven to the elimination of all ground for exchange. He loses the concept of value altogether and is forced to attempt to ground exchange in itself, to equate form with substance.

The problem of grounding exchange is the problem of finding that substance which, although not itself a commodity, determines the commodity character of the object. This substance is value. For neo-classical thought it is utility (the result of the equation of value and use-value), for classical thought it is labor. In this there appears to be an intractable opposition. On one level, such an opposition is clearly present. However once the category of labor, as that concept plays its part in classical economics, is considered concretely it turns out that it also contains within it the logical basis of the utility theory of value – the equation of use-value and value. This makes the classical concept of labor a contradictory one since it forms at once the logical basis of the unity of classical and neo-classical economics and the logical basis of their opposition. This contradiction emerges, as we have seen, in the disintegration of the category of labor within classical thought. For Adam Smith labor is the substance of value and is at the same time the measure of exchange-value. In the purchase of labor (i.e. labor-power) value and exchange-value are equated. The concept of labor identifies directly the exchange-value with value. Ricardo rejects this conception on the grounds that labor, taken itself as a commodity, cannot ground exchange, cannot serve as the substance of value. But with the rejection of the labor-commanded principle Ricardo is forced either to distinguish between labor and labor-power or to drop the notion that the substance of value is labor. He must, in other words, either constitute labor as a social substance tied intrinsically to the value form, or constitute labor as a natural process which, in its indifference to the value form, fails to provide an account for that form. Ricardo either equates labor and labor-power, constituting the labor process as natural and therefore value and use-value as the same; or he distinguishes between labor and labor-power, constituting the former as the social substance of value. In the former case Ricardo fails to ground exchange for reasons closely associated with those which underlie the failure of neo-classical economics. In the latter case Ricardo fails to constitute the capital relation as a natural one where nature is seen as the non-social ground of social life.

In effect, Ricardo refuses to take either road, or takes both at the same time. Refusing to distinguish between value and its form (exchange-value), Ricardo first equates value with labor and then denies that labor is the substance and measure of value. He, first, asserts the equivalence of value and labor, and then, questions the existence of any systematic quantitative relation between the two, or more correctly, between labor, value, and exchange. The ground of exchange stands in absolute opposition to the determination of the exchange and, in particular, to the determination of the magnitude of the exchange. The ground and its expression become disjoint. The expression of value in exchange, once set loose from its ground, seeks to establish for itself its own ground, itself as ground. This is accomplished through the intervention of the invariable measure of value: the commodity whose exchange-value is immediately the ground of exchange-value.

According to Ricardo the invariable measure, like any commodity (such as gold) which is suggested as a measure of value, can only be a 'perfect measure of value for all things produced under the same circumstances precisely as itself, but for no others' (vol. I, p. 45). The commodity is only capable of measuring its own value: 'This then seems to hold universally true that the commodity valued must be reduced to circumstances precisely similar (with respect to time of production) to those of the commodity in which the valuation is made' (vol. IV, pp. 386–7). Where each commodity has its own measure of value,[8] value is set loose altogether from exchange. The contradictions of a one-commodity economy are reintroduced as Ricardo eliminates the form of value, exchange, in order to establish the essential character of the exchange relation. Commodities do not exchange with themselves yet it is only within such an exchange that exchange-value is revealed to express real value and to possess a determinate ground. Exchange-value is only grounded where exchange-value does not exist, and where it cannot, in principle, be conceived.

Just as in the case of the corn model, Ricardo has eliminated the conditions for the existence of the economic relation in order to reveal the necessity of that relation. Ultimately, the notion of 'real value' reduces the exchange to the immediate exchange process where the necessity of a specific relation which was originally uncovered in the labor which is the substance of value gives way to a necessity whose expression denies that necessity. To ground exchange in labor is to ground it in a substance which is not itself conceivable in the absence of exchange. Labor is equated to value only because labor is value, value as it exists within the process of its own production. Value is not made equal to labor as something outside of itself which produces value as a result indifferent to the act which brings it into being. Value as the driving force in a process is labor. This connection is one of equality based on the opposition of the mode of existence of a single principle. Labor is value as a moving, generative process and value is labor as a result of that process. As a result, it is possible, by positing socially equal labor, to ground exchange, and in so doing to connect form to content in a manner in which they can express a mutual necessity. In this case the content, socially equal labor, can no more exist without the form than the form, exchange-value, can exist without the content.

The labor theory of value as it appears in classical thought results from the classical abstraction from the concrete conditions of capitalist production as a whole which is implied in the identification of the self-realization of capital with the direct production process of capital. But this equation is not in itself sufficient to establish the connection of labor to value. The latter also requires the, at least implicit, recognition that production so isolated in the production of value, is production of capital. Only production of value has labor as its principle and can be correctly characterized as a labor process. It is, therefore, equally essential to the classical theory of value that the mutual dependence of production and value be conceived so that the universality of each may be posited. It is necessary, in other words, to go beyond the equation of the production process and the self-realization of capital and to grasp, at least implicitly, the difference between the two. Where the direct production process is simply identified with the process of capitalist production as a whole the result is not the labor process but the conception of production as a natural interchange ultimately, as the 'one commodity economy.' The fact that classical economy sets out from the principle of labor-value reflects the incipient existence within classical thought of a distinction between production of value and the production of particular commodities on the part of individual units of production. The fact that this distinction, while present within the classical theory of value, is at the same time denied within the classical argument as a whole gives to the latter its peculiar character. The articulation of the labor principle within classical thought has the significance of demonstrating, for the first time, the manner in which the market system can be grounded. Adherence to the labor principle is adherence on the part of classical economy to a real theory of value and exchange. Retreat from the labor principle constitutes refusal to accept the implications of a theory of value and exchange, or more correctly, a rejection of the possibility of such a theory.

2

For Ricardo value ('absolute' value) is an expression for the labor embodied in the commodity. And yet, once Ricardo equates value with price, it appears that both cease to express the labor employed in the production of the commodity. The 'invariant measure of value' expresses this same contradiction in a definitive form. This expression takes the form of a mystification in the sense that a problem is posed whose terms exclude any solution. The concept of the invariable measure shares with the neo-classical concept of capital this property of conceptualizing, placing into a single term, a contradiction which taken concretely is incapable of consistent conceptualization. Here, the contradiction is reproduced on another level, the contradiction between labor and price reappears as a contradiction within the invariable measure: the latter is at once necessary to the adequate conception of value and yet cannot be 'found,' that is, the conditions for its definition exclude its existence. An invariable measure of value is a commodity whose price does not alter when the rate of profit alters. It is, therefore, a commodity whose price fails to express precisely that which it is the function of price to express – the equalization and differentiation of profit rates among distinct units of capital which differ. An invariable measure of value would express, could it be found, the immediate relation of labor-value to price since the effects of changing relative shares would be eliminated. It therefore would express the labor-value of a commodity in the form of the price of the commodity with no necessary special assumptions. This is the key. The invariable measure expresses value through price directly without the necessary intermediation of the analysis of value, surplus-value, and the labor process.

If this equation is excluded, however, we are left only with the commodity's price. The 'real value' measured by the invariable measure is not the labor embodied in the commodity but is simply its 'real value,' its rate of exchange with the invariable measure. Since the ground of exchange in labor is eliminated the invariable measure ceases to account for the exchange, to reveal the inner necessity of the commodity form. It, rather, takes that necessity as given and attempts solely to measure the given price relation. The problem becomes, in this case, no longer that of the theory of price, where the account for the exchange system is at stake, but the isolation of exchange from the remaining economic relations in order to neutralize the effect of the commodity form on the 'social relations of production' especially upon the distribution of income. Here not only is it no longer necessary to establish the necessity of exchange but the contrary becomes the case, it is necessary to indicate how it is possible to consider the economic system independently of the exchange relation, to conceptualize distribution independently of exchange thereby establishing the irrelevance rather than the necessity of exchange.

This same conception of economic theory has recently been resurrected by Piero Sraffa.[9] Sraffa's 'standard commodity,' which presents itself as a conceptually adequate expression for Ricardo's invariable measure, is 'embedded' in the 'physical non-human world of technology' and the exchange-values or 'prices' which emerge in this view of the economic process are 'embedded in the technology itself.'[10] The ground of exchange is specified as the 'non-human world of technology.' It is no longer 'labor' (either as socially equal labor or as 'work') that grounds exchange but the 'world of technology.' The invariable measure interpreted in this sense resolves the central Ricardian dilemma: the conception of distribution independently of value and exchange. An invariable measure measures value independently of the determinate social relations implied by the value form and therefore gives us a measure of commodities, products as commodities, which shears off their commodity character. If there were such an object as an invariable measure it would measure the world of technology directly, its construction relies exclusively upon the characteristics of the 'technology' and has nothing to do with the exchange of commodities. It is, therefore, indifferent to exchange and measures not the exchange relation but the technology in itself. In a sense it becomes possible to measure wealth in its commodity form without taking into account the determinate relations implied by that form, thus to abolish the commodity form within the commodity form.

The primary function of the 'standard system' is not, therefore, that of accounting theoretically for the exchange of commodities but of neutralizing the commodity form in order to pass behind that form to the substantive forces which determine the system of exchange. These are the 'non-human' world of 'technology' and the given distribution of income. The central theme of *The Production of Commodities by Means of Commodities* is that of the independent determination of technique and distribution, their independence of the value form. In the case of the distribution of income the 'standard ratio' or maximum rate of profit serves to express the link between the given technique and the distribution of income thereby severing the determination of profit from the sequence of price relations in much the way that Marx, and Marxian economists, have attempted to do through the use of the organic composition of capital.

Marx deals with the rate of profit in terms of its determination by the 'organic composition of capital' (the ratio of past to present labor time) and the 'rate of exploitation' (the ratio of paid to unpaid labor). It follows to the extent that this relation is employed, that the rate of profit is indifferent to the price system. Further, to the extent that labor is conceived in its classical form as purely natural, given by the natural productivity of labor independently of the value form, the rate of profit is jointly determined by the non-human technology and the given rate of exploitation. The latter, once conceived as the effect of the 'class struggle' is equally severed from any connection to commodity exchange. This conception of the rate of profit falls down (even upon its own assumptions) where there are differences in organic compositions of capital between sectors. In that case the ratio of surplus-value to capital invested (*R*) will differ from the rate of profit which, given the technique and the wage, equalizes return per unit of capital advanced (*r*). The equal rate of profit differs from Marx's average rate of profit (*r* differs from *R*) in precisely the same manner that 'prices' differ from 'labor values.' And this difference can be eliminated in precisely the Ricardian fashion, by introducing an invariable measure of value. It is only necessary to replace the value expressions measured in terms of the standard commodity to retain the basic conception of the autonomous determination of the rate of profit without abrogating the condition of equal profit on equal capital advanced. The average composition of capital of the economy as a whole is replaced by the composition of an average industry and becomes thereby independent of changes in the distribution of output between industries. This serves to achieve the end of severing distribution from the price system (since labor time is not considered to bear any necessary relation of dependence upon commodity exchange).

The external determination of price on the part of a given, and independently given, distribution of income and technique, leaves the latter in a wholly abstract and indeterminate form. The fact that the technique upon which the price system is founded displays an advanced division of labor and interdependence of production is not allowed to suggest any inner connection between the nature of the production system and the exchange of commodities or the expansion of capital. The distribution of income, to the extent that it is fixed quantitatively outside of the exchange system, appears itself to be determined without reference to exchange.

This abstraction of the conception of distribution and technology makes impossible any real conception of a price system. The rates of exchange or 'prices' bear no clear connection to an actual exchange system since they may be conceived directly in terms of the technology, the 'non-human world,' without regard to the specific intersubjective relation implied in exchange. Exchange as the realization within the social sphere of the freedom and equality of persons before the market gives way to exchange as a simple and subordinate quantitative property of a purely technical system. This conception fails to serve as a theory of price since it fails to reveal the exchange relation as necessary where such a necessity can only arise as the result of situating the concept of exchange-value within its relation to the economic system as a whole. As a result this conception fails to express its implicit incompatibility with a variety of distinct and opposing social 'forms.' The concept of 'reproduction' considered presents itself as the essential core not simply of the price system, but equally of the 'allocation of resources' within any economic system. This is, again, the conception of nature in itself and to the extent that the invariable measure expresses this principle it emerges as a conception of the self-reproduction of nature within which even the human only appears in the form of labor where that labor is nothing other than naturally defined 'work.' The introduction of a principle such as the equality of rates of 'profit' is incomprehensible to the extent that it is not revealed as necessary to the conception of the reproduction system. It is upon the intrinsic impossibility of such a conception as that which underlies this framework and seeks expression within it that each successive systematization of the concepts of economic science has broken apart.

The reproduction system carries within it the grounding of economic relations within a self-subsistent process. Where commodities are produced by means of commodities it is only the process as a whole which posits the conditions for its continuation. To the extent that the existence of the system is nothing more than the process of its continuation, the production of commodities by means of commodities is a process which posits the conditions of its own existence, which accounts for itself, and is in that sense self-determining. Within reproduction the pre-conditions and results are tied together. An account can now be given for the particular relation, as for example a particular price, in terms of the requirements of the process as a whole. Price becomes determinate in a way that is excluded in principle within the neo-classical conception. And yet, in the system of commodity production by means of commodities, the process within which prices appear as determinate is itself posited abstractly, indeterminately. The division of labor, the distribution of income, the categories of wages and profits appear totally arbitrary so that the mechanism of mediation between the disparate elements of the division of labor and of relating labor-power to capital – commodity exchange – is equally arbitrary. For there to be commodity exchange there must be a division of labor but the origin of division of labor is itself undetermined.

More importantly, it is implicitly asserted that the process of production and of the division of the product is conceivable outside of the system of commodity exchange. As a result the ground – production – and its expression – exchange – are related only as the essential to the inessential so that exchange appears itself to be arbitrary. So long as production is given abstractly, and its real dependence upon the commodity form and the value relation is suppressed, it loses any capacity to ground the exchange. The formal character of value is asserted and the account for the value relation disappears. Yet what has disappeared is precisely that accounting originally made possible by the introduction of the reproduction system and which is implicit in that reproduction system. In order to realize the theoretical power of the notion of production of commodities by means of commodities it is only necessary to recognize explicitly the dependence of production upon the value relation and the specificity of the labor process to the purchase and sale of labor-power as a commodity, the sole property of the laborer.

3

For classical political economy the impossibility of conceiving value directly as labor and of reducing the former to the latter leads to the provisional acceptance of a distinction between form and content. But the necessity within which this relation subsists refuses to acknowledge the independence of the content as natural substance *vis-à-vis* the form as a social relation. This mutual necessity of ground and its expression ties the natural principle (labor) to the social relation (value) in such a way as to absorb the former into the latter and thereby to deny to nature its natural determination so that nature becomes implicitly also social. Since within the classical conception as a whole, the only possible ground for a social process is in nature, the denial of the independence of the latter is immediately the denial of the possibility of a ground for the social relations under investigation. The ground disappears into its form of expression which latter, loses any substance, any determinate necessity. In order to recover the latter classical thinking constitutes the relations as their own ground so that nature re-emerges within the direct conception of the social relations themselves. These latter lose their explicitly social character.

It is none the less important to distinguish the two moments of the relation of social life to nature within classical theory. The forms which turn from their original status as the inessential to absorb both poles of the relation of form to substance are nothing other than the social existence and character intrinsic to what is originally constituted as the natural substance of the economic relation. But it is precisely within the *movement* of the conception from the first reduction of society to nature to the second revelation of society within nature that the grounding of the value relation within labor as a social substance emerges. It is this movement that denies to labor its natural determination and for an instant, as it were, constitutes social labor as the substance of value and value as the substance of the exchange relation. To be sure, the ultimate resting point of the analysis (which, on another level has no real resting point) is not in the consistent determination of the exchange in its explicitly social existence and in its necessary relation to capital and labor. It is, however, not the end point of the conception which is critical but precisely the movement of that conception, the vibration of the concept back and forth between the poles of the contradictions within which the problem is constructed. It is not the distinct themes in their isolation which are critical but their interpenetration and their mutual necessity, the manner in which each forces the other into a mold which it is unable to fit and which it is, in its original construction, designed to deny.

The scientific content of classical political economy is to be found in the necessity of the movement of its conception. This necessity is the product of the force exerted on that conception by the real relations in their self-determined and adequate form. As in the case of all false conception the denial of the true relation is also the statement of that relation and becomes explicitly so when the inner contradictions of the thought are revealed.

III Classical and modern economics

1

It is the object of classical political economy to account for the central relations of economic life by locating them within a self-subsistent process within which they are determined. This process is a contradictory one which is grasped, as a whole, by two closely related and yet opposing categories: nature and capital. Predominantly, all economic relations are grounded in the self-renewing process of nature. Society reproduces itself as nature reproduces itself so that society in its self-sustaining state is in a state which is natural. The prices which result from, and the distribution of income which is determined within, this process are all natural: the natural price, the natural wage, etc. Nature, taken in this sense, is that category within classical political economy, which makes possible a conception of bourgeois economic life which is truly theoretical since it locates each particular element, or relation, of economic life within a totality, and within a totality capable of accounting for its elements in terms of its own process.

But nature, within classical political economy, is not simply another term for capital which is, within its own process of self-development, capable of accounting theoretically for the central economic relations. Nature also opposes capital and in that opposition absorbs capital into nature, naturalizing it. This process of naturalization deprives capital of its own self-determination making of it a dependent moment in a natural process which, separated from capital, is itself unaccountable. Nature, as the self-subsistent *natural* process, cannot account theoretically for economic relations since it can only reduce them to a natural ground which, once taken outside of social life, can only be presupposed abstractly, as given, in the economic analysis. When the self-determination of capital is taken outside of capital and located in nature, nature is itself set loose from capital and determined in opposition to it. This is the beginning of modern, neo-classical economics. This beginning is, as we have seen, located within classical political economy and particularly in its category of nature. More specifically it is the opposition of nature to society which is the origin of the modern conception. Modern economics drives this opposition to its logical conclusion.

For modern economics the starting point of analysis is the individual which comes to oppose nature. Whereas within classical economics the individual is himself considered to be an element of the natural world and therefore to be determined by the process of nature and implicitly by the process of capital, in neo-classical economics the individual is excluded altogether from nature and also from any self-subsistent unity or process within which the individual may be accounted for. Just as the individual loses his relation to nature, as one element of a natural process, the individual loses his relation to capital as located within its self-determination. For modern social theory the individual stands outside. Since the individual stands outside he cannot be accounted for by a process either of nature or of capital since he is always determined independently. The individual is, therefore, self-determined; the abstract, isolated individual of the theory of the exchange economy.

But since this individual is self-determined in his relation to the ongoing social process he is, from the point of view of that process itself, undetermined. He is, therefore, not accountable to the social whole. It is, rather, the latter which is accountable to him. And since the social process is only accountable to the undetermined individual it is, ultimately unaccountable, undetermined. The theory of the exchange economy does not, then, give for social life an account, describe its self-determination as a process. In this respect the failure of modern economics is a failure to establish itself as a *theory*. Since it does not account for and determine economic relations it can in no way be said to grasp those relations, to theorize them. This is the origin of the central contradiction of modern economics.

2

In the neo-classical conception the interaction of independent self-seeking can realize nothing of a higher order since the determination of that interaction is exclusively egoistic in nature and excludes the existence of any social substance. Thus while the 'invisible hand' of Adam Smith remains the acknowledged law of economic life the universality which is seen to arise out of individual self-seeking has lost its substance to be replaced by the summation of irreducibly independent principles. Here there can be no general good which arises out of individual self-seeking because it is already present as the real substance of that self-seeking, a general good that lives in and through the interaction of particular individuals. Instead the interaction of egoistic interest is only able to consummate the general good as the many particular self-interests taken together where the egoistic principle allows for no real social determination. What is lost in this conception is precisely the constitution of the individual within a system of individuals. Instead, individuality is severed from its real foundation in the reciprocal recognition of autonomy and freedom, so that the latter lose all determinateness, adopting instead the form of pure indeterminateness, of 'negative freedom.' This indeterminateness is the substance of economic life in the neo-classical conception.

Rather than coming to life within a system of mutual interdependence and reciprocal recognition the individual lives within a shell of his own making the rule of which is the exclusion of all necessity of social and economic interaction. The relations which are constituted by and among individuals are all grounded in their egoistic self-determination. The medium within which these relations subsist is that made up of the objects of individual desire so that all relations between individuals can exist only as the mode of expression of the relation of individuals to objects. In this way the pure self-determination of the individual will not be violated by his economic existence.

The irreducible particularity of the relation of individual to object expressed in the notions of 'desire' and 'preference' excludes equally the social life of the individual and of the object. The individuality of the former is not a condition built upon a complex system of social interaction and social determination but a uniquely particular state which can be grasped conceptually, if para-doxically, only as 'individual.' On the other side the irreducibility of the individual is reflected in the object which appears not as a social substance but as an impenetrable material reality. The relation of individual to object is made up, then, of a uniquely particular psychic state on one side and an immediate physical presence on the other. The individual loses, thereby, the complexity of his real physical and social determination as member of the species, as commodity owner, as citizen, member of a family etc. and exists as nothing more than the undifferentiated and indeterminate unity of his social and biological constitution – as one 'individual.' Likewise the object loses the complexity of its physical and social reality as physical object, property, use-value, and as commodity, existing instead as the undifferentiated unity of a social and a physical determination which are excluded in the abstraction which leaves aside their determination in favor of an empty unity. The relation of individual to object constructed on this basis and the interaction of individuals which arises out of it provide the object of economic analysis for modern social thought. On this basis the attempt is made to consummate a conception of economic life.

This construction involves the equation of the distinct concepts by which the system of economic relations is determined. This equation dispels the real determinacy of the individual and the object, leaving as its residue only the empty unity on one side of 'individual preference' and on the other of 'resources' or 'utilities.' This suppression of determination has as its result, with regard to the commodity owner, the notion of individual preference or desire, as regards the commodity itself, the notion of utility, and as regards the production of the commodity, the notion of capital as a scarce factor of production.

Part 2
The Character of Contemporary Economic Thought

Chapter 6
The allocation of resources

I Exchange

1 The commodity and the exchange relation

Economic thinking, in so far as it has been of a systematic character, has always taken as its point of departure the analysis of the value of commodities. The treatment of exchange, capital, and distribution, is considered to hinge upon the correct comprehension of the value relation. Yet, it is this very primacy with regard to the proper order of economic analysis which, while on one level allowing for a certain unity within the history of economic thought, on another level hides the fundamental distinguishing features of the different conceptions which make up that history. It is, therefore, necessary from the outset to draw the sharpest distinctions of subject and method where those distinctions are the least apparent.

In the case of the modern, or 'neo-classical,' school the treatment of value is the basis of a deduction of the individual exchange which reveals directly the central unifying principle of all economic thought: the efficient allocation of scarce resources among competing ends. This unifying function is, as we shall see, not simply of a heuristic nature but goes to the heart of neo-classical economics. For the latter exchange reveals directly the operation of 'economic behavior.' The exchange of commodities stands as the most elementary of economic relations due to the fact that exchange is the active existence of the inner and hidden force within the otherwise isolated individual. The force which is expressed in exchange is, taken in itself, inaccessible to the investigator. The individual as the locus of needs is a container in which those needs are enclosed and to which only the individual has direct access. Within the exchange need takes on a definite and observable existence. It emerges from its container to reveal itself in a social act. This social act, exchange, is not directly equivalent to need *per se* but is only the expression of need (and, so far as neo-classical economics is concerned, the only expression of need). For neo-classical economics individual need is not simply an active force, it is *the* active force whose expression is commodity exchange and the price system.

To the extent that economics takes the individual (therefore a specific locus of need) as given, economic behavior becomes the adjustment of the social world in the form of exchange and the market to the individual data. For this conception to be sustained it is necessary that exchange in all of its manifestations exist as the expression of the individual and not itself deny the givenness of the needy individual. The categories of value and exchange must be demonstrated to arise in a consistent manner from the original positing of the individual where the latter is not itself the product of exchange and the world of exchange. Were need a product of the exchange system the individual as a repository of his own passions and desires would disappear and re-emerge as the socially determined individual, i.e. the individual isolated by society and therefore produced in his individuality by society.

The requirements of the consistent deduction of exchange on this basis are, first, the establishment of exchange as an intersubjective relation which presupposes the givenness of individual need, and second, the location of the exchange within the system of economic relations (as of production in particular). It is the manner in which the neo-classical analysis attempts to meet these requirements that will be the subject of the following discussion.

The specificity of the neo-classical conception emerges within the apparent 'fact' of a common point of departure of the different types of economic analysis. Neo-classical analysis posits from the outset the individual commodity owner as the basis of exchange; always dealing with exchange as, first, a relation of individuals to objects (or 'utilities'), and then, of individuals through those objects. The definitive feature of this conception is that the commodity, as economic good, does not itself possess a social determination. For neo-classical exchange analysis the commodity must be *brought to* the market by the individual who is its owner. Taken in one sense, this is an evident necessity of any theory of exchange. On the other hand, that it should form the starting point of the conception reveals not a general requirement of economic theory but a specific requirement of the neo-classical analysis. The necessity of subsuming the 'good' into its owner in so far as it enters into an economic relation (actually exists as a commodity) seems less compelling when opposed, for example, to the procedure of classical economics, and especially of Ricardo who had little concern for the commodity owner as distinct from or opposed to the commodity. The notion of the commodity owner is, within Ricardian analysis, absorbed into that of the commodity itself so that the owner retains no independent existence as opposed to, and therefore in relation to, the commodity. The owner in his specificity is wholly extraneous to consideration of the properties of commodity exchange. The commodity viewed in terms of its value is indifferent to the individuality of its owner so that the exchange of commodities is conceived as precisely that, the exchange of commodities.

Implicit in this 'classical' conception is the commodity not as a thing which enters, as it were, from outside, into a social relation or a social existence, but the commodity as directly a social entity with a determinate social existence implicitly involving the exchange relation. There is, therefore, a sense in which the necessary condition of exchange is found not within the owner taken in the abstract but within the commodity. For Ricardo the particularity of the owner plays virtually no role and Ricardo fails altogether to explicitly recognize the specification of the exchange relation by the individual commodity owner.

Ricardo's failure to grasp the relation of the commodity to its owner involves an implicit restriction of the social character of the commodity which is typical of classical political economy and to a lesser extent of Marx. To the extent that the value intrinsic in the commodity is conceived as a natural property of the commodity and by that fact independent of its relation to the individual – that is, is conceived as labor in the sense of classical theory – the intrinsic value of the commodity is not distinguished from an individual relation as a social property but only as a natural property. The commodity relation as a value relation does not, in this case, involve the recognition of the freedom and equality of persons. Value, rather than a relation to the individual recognized as such by other individuals, appears as a purely natural property of the commodity. Thus to exclude altogether the systematic relation of the commodity to the individual (now recognized as such only within society) in the treatment of value relegates the latter to a natural condition while the isolation of the relation of the commodity to the individual in the absence of the social determination of individuality excludes any substantive determination of exchange and of a value substance.

This failure of Ricardian economics emerges at the same time as the result of Ricardo's implicit conviction that the commodity itself contains the conditions of the exchange relation, it contains value. As a result it is possible for Ricardo to speak of the 'intrinsic,' 'absolute,' 'real,' or 'positive' value of the commodity, conceptions which are wholly antithetical to neo-classical thinking for which value can only be relative to the specific individual or system of individuals who happen to present themselves to the market at a particular point of time. Within neo-classical thinking value is given to the commodity by its owner and by the specific individuality of that owner. By contrast, for classical political economy implicitly and for Marx explicitly, the commodity itself does not exist in a world constructed outside of society but the commodity, as a commodity, is already appropriated by society and therefore possesses a social determination. To speak of the commodity is not to speak of a 'thing' given to society, or to the world of 'individuals,' from outside, but of something which is an element of a social whole and, therefore, a determinate system of social relations. Thus the commodity, in order for it to exist as a commodity, is not brought into society by its owner as is the case in the neo-classical conception of exchange.

With the direct relation of the individual to given objects of his desire taken as the primary data of analysis the treatment of that relation becomes the first step toward a conception of economic life. This treatment takes the form of the so-called 'theory of consumer behavior.' It needs to be emphasized, in this connection, that the whole of the subject-matter of the elaborate apparatus of the 'theory of consumer behavior' is the isolated individual subjectively contemplating the objects of his need. It is in this manner that the foundations of the conception of demand come to be located in individual psychology so that those foundations are removed from economic analysis. To the extent that these foundations of economic analysis cease to be aspects of an ongoing social process the theory of demand is denied any real ground within economic theory.

This is in sharp contrast with the classical and Marxian procedures which contain no theory of consumer behavior (either implicit or explicit) in the sense in which that is interpreted by modern economics. The treatment of exchange in terms of a prior theory of consumer behavior is connected to a specific conceptual deduction of the exchange relation and to a specific formulation of the relation of commodity to commodity owner. For neo-classical economics the consumption of utilities is the point of departure of the analysis due to the fact that the act of consumption is the immediate relation of the individual to the objects of his desire. Consumption is the *sine qua non* of the economic process since it is that wholly individual act which is the over-riding goal of the system of economic relations. As such, consumption is the rational foundation of all truly economic behavior. The theory of consumer behavior seeks to grasp the immediate relation of the individual to the objects of need and of consumption. The needs of the individual must be formulated within a theory of consumer behavior precisely because taken outside of a relation to those needs the commodity remains wholly inert. The specification of need becomes, in this way, the basis of the entire deduction of the exchange system.

By contrast, within classical theory consumption is not viewed as an individual act which directly connects the undetermined individual with the object of his need where both individual and object are taken to be given. Nothing is of greater importance to the critique of the neo-classical analysis of value than to grasp the difference between consumption taken as individual act and consumption as an aspect, or moment, of a social process. It is significant in this regard that Ricardo never considers consumption within the analysis of value. Consumption is only a proper subject of investigation for Ricardo when he takes up the conditions of the reproduction and expansion of capital as a whole, in particular in the course of his polemic with Malthus on the question of crises. Implicitly, consumption becomes a discernible economic function only when it opposes itself to production *within* an ongoing process of reproduction. Similarly, Marx considers consumption in opposition to production only in the course of his investigation of the conditions of the reproduction of the total social capital. Here the distinction between 'means of consumption' and 'means of production' is important to the concrete determination of the conditions of reproduction but only as two mutually determined elements of a single process. To be sure, Marx also considers need in relation to value where the latter is only capable of existence within its relation to 'use-value.' Use-value is the relation of the commodity to need and is a condition for the possession on the part of the commodity of value. None the less use-value is not the relation of the commodity to the subjective desire of the abstract individual but to the need of the individual as determined within society, therefore to a socially defined need.

The result of the relegation of the category of consumption to the level of the analysis of reproduction is that consumption does not simply oppose itself to production, for example as end to means, but it equally and necessarily imposes itself as part of production. Consumption of 'means of consumption' is also production of 'labor' while the production of commodities is also consumption of 'means of production.' This latter result presupposes a condition which will become critical in the treatment of the relation of production to exchange and scarcity. Production as consumption of means of production implies, within a system of reproduction, that production must also create the requisites for continued production since the conditions of the given act of production are used up within that act. Production as consumption therefore implies production of commodities by means of commodities. In this case there exists no purely physical distinction between consumption and production since means of consumption in their use (i.e. in their consumption) are means to the reproduction of the economic system. This unity of production and consumption exists only for the process taken as a whole while the fragmentation of the individual elements of that process serves to obliterate its unity and to leave consumption in a purely external relation to production, as the relation of a given goal to the means for its attainment. In the construction of the process as a whole, on the other hand, the end dissolves into the means just as the means disappear into the end, leaving only the process itself split into distinct but intrinsically connected moments.

This constitution of the unity of consumption and production is given a clear formal expression in Piero Sraffa's notion of the 'production of commodities by means of commodities.'[1] Within this framework a formal system of exchange is constructed for which there exists no discernible goal which can be taken to be the motive of the economic process and which can be taken to be given to that process from outside. On the contrary, the production and exchange of commodities is, implicitly, a self-sustaining process which itself posits the necessary conditions for its own continuation. Consumption, rather than the goal or end of the process is itself determined by the movement as a whole. Consumption is not the individual act which stands apart from production and reproduction but a necessary condition intrinsic to the ongoing process where the process of reproduction includes the use of materials themselves created by that process. Consumption is the production of commodities taken as the destruction of the very products which appeared, for a moment, as the goal or end of that production. It is only in the freezing of that limited moment and its hypostatization into a self-contained act that it becomes possible to constitute individual consumption as the aim of production.

When society is constructed in terms of the ongoing and self-sustaining process of the reproduction of capital and of the 'production of commodities by means of commodities' it absorbs the individual in a specific manner. And that manner of absorption does not simply determine the motivations and goals of individuals, it determines the sense in which the separate units of the economic system are 'individual.' Individual consumption as the moment of a process of reproduction is altogether a different matter from the individual act of consumption of the neo-classical conception. For the latter it remains important, and necessary, to speak in terms of goals and motivations as the starting point of the science; for the former it does not. From the point of view of the positing of a group of isolated individuals, the social process, the market system, appears as the determination of their actions and, therefore, of their motivations; that is, their specification in terms of needs. By contrast, from the point of view of a social process which posits its own conditions and which is, therefore, self-sustaining, the individuals become determinations of the system as a whole. The system is indifferent to their particularity except in so far as that particularity has itself been posited by the movement of the total process. Individual need as a moment of the social process is not given by the individual but produced within that process. Furthermore, those needs become intelligible (and therefore capable of theoretical treatment) only in terms of their appropriation within the social process.

The distinction between consumption and production, their separation into opposing acts, exists only for the individual unit of production and for the individual unit of consumption taken in isolation. Further, the separation of consumption is more marked the more the economic process is individualized and thereby isolated into a direct relation of individual to given objects of his need. In this case what is essential is the isolation of production from consumption and their independent determination. In the following discussion the manner in which this isolation is accomplished is considered along with its critical implications for the theory of exchange. This isolation involves more than the simple articulation of a self-evident aspect of social life; i.e. its economic aspect. The full implications of the procedure become clear once the construction of the whole is attempted upon the basis of isolated individual units particularized in the manner of modern economic theory. Once production and consumption come to oppose one another in this manner their unity emerges as a purely external composition of distinct and conflicting parts. On the side of the theory of exchange the interpretation of consumption as a definitive act, as a singular event, stands in the way of a construction of a whole within which consumption and production must relate as composing elements.

2 Scarcity and exchange

For neo-classical economics it is not the commodity itself which possesses a subjective character but the commodity as it relates to the preferences of its owner and, in particular, as it allows for the expression of his desires. The content of the exchange relation as established on this basis is that of the givenness of the world of 'utilities' with regard to the preferences of the individuals who appropriate those utilities. First, objects are brought into a relation with individuals, then those individuals bring the objects into a world of exchange. The preferences of the owners of the commodities and the intrinsic properties of the objects are not determined within the exchange process but stand as conditions external to it. Not only is the unconditioned character of needs and of the objects of their fulfillment given but those needs and those objects are given independently one of the other so that the commodity, *qua* economic 'good,' is indifferent to the world of human need, having the status of a fact given to that world. That need is given in this sense is by no means an accidental feature of the theory of exchange. On the contrary it is a necessary implication of the conception of the economic sphere upon which the deduction of exchange is based. The economy is defined as the realm of the allocation of scarce resources among competing but given ends. It is intrinsically contradictory for such a conception to determine, in any way whatsoever, the nature of needs within the exchange system itself.

Within the neo-classical conception the idea of a system of needs and of needy individuals made determinate within the system of economic interaction as a whole gives way to the notion of individual preference. The conception of the type of need and of the means to its fulfillment characteristic of civilized society which defined the original object of economic science is replaced by the conception of individual desire existing without regard to the type of mutual dependence characteristic of social life. It is for this reason that the transition from classical political economy to neo-classical economic analysis is marked by the replacement of the concept of 'need' with that of 'preference.' The term 'need' already contains within it the element of determination while the specificity of the notion of 'preference' is to be found precisely in the absence of determination. The fulfillment of need is a requirement of existence so that the needs of the individual are also the specific requirements implied in his existence as an individual. Need is, then, a relation of mutual dependence among individuals. By contrast, an individual retains his individuality regardless of the satisfaction of his desires. Individual preference is connected to particular individuals and to the actual fulfillment of desire only by accident. Individual preference is by its nature indeterminate, a matter of caprice, while individual need is intrinsically determinate, marked by its inner necessity.

Concretely, exchange, on these premises, emerges in the following manner: The original relation of individual preferences to existing 'goods' is one of scarcity where scarcity is defined as the relation of given individual desires to the available world of objects which are capable of fulfilling those desires. Such objects are 'scarce' when the available supply is inadequate to completely satisfy the desires of individuals.[2] It is from this quality that the properties of ownership and exchange are derived, and it is this property which can only be revealed in ownership and exchange. The presence of scarcity as the foundation of economic activity is traced to preferences of individuals which are the data of the analysis. They cannot in principle be investigated as to their specific properties. With respect to the theory as a whole, needs are stationary and indeterminate.

For neo-classical analysis the exchange rate or price of a commodity is understood as a 'scarcity index.' This involves a substantial judgment about the nature of the market system. Price measures the scarcity of objects and it is that scarcity which makes those the objects of economic activity. Economizing behavior is founded on the premise of scarcity which premise rests on a specific construction of the relation of the individual to the objects of his desires. The specificity of the neo-classical notion of scarcity (for example, *vis-à-vis* that of everyday economic practice) is embedded in the individuation of personality within neo-classical thought and in the construction of the relation of subjective need to the objects which meet that need. That is to say, the specific notion of the commodity as scarce is tied to the notion of the commodity as an object introduced into society by its owner and therefore as devoid of any intrinsic social character. Thus the specification of exchange as immediately requiring the relation of the individual to the commodity specifies the commodity as devoid of social determination and thereby necessitates the construction of a relation between objects and desires which introduces the object into the exchange relation. This construction involves the specification of the neo-classical concept of scarcity.

Given that objects are scarce they become subject to appropriation. According to the neo-classical construction appropriation arises as a result of the condition of scarcity rather than scarcity as the result of appropriation. This is an essential link in the argument. In so far as the condition of scarcity presupposes appropriation, as that condition which makes things scarce the scarcity of objects becomes a social fact, one bound up with the recognition of private property. On the other hand, if scarcity is tied directly to the relation of objects to individuals then appropriation derives its basis from scarcity rather than vice versa. This is precisely the deduction which is favored by neo-classical thinking:[3]

useful things which exist only in limited quantity are capable of being appropriated and actually are appropriated. In the first place, these things are amenable to seizure and control, in view of the fact that it is physically possible for a certain number of individuals to gather the entire existing quantity of such a thing for themselves, with none of it left in the public domain.

Thus, in the first place, property exists as a result of those physical attributes of commodities which allow them to be 'gathered' or 'seized.' Taken in this manner there is no way in which 'property' is distinguishable as a relation from 'consumption;' both are the immediate relation of the individual to the object.

Appropriation is a presupposition of all neo-classical analysis but within that analysis, appropriation is considered to be deducible from the concept of scarcity. Within this conception the individual outside of society may as readily be a proprietor of objects as the individual who is directly a part of a social whole. This result rests on the divorce of appropriation from social life and its construction within the will of the individual given outside of society. Thus, according to Menger:[4]

economic character is by no means restricted to goods that are the objects of human economy in a social context. If an isolated individual's requirements for a good are greater than the quantity of the good available to him, we will observe him retaining possession of every unit at his command. . . . Hence economic and noneconomic goods also exist for the isolated individual.

Not only do scarcity and economic behavior exist for the isolated individual but so also does appropriation (the 'retaining possession') so that it is possible to consider appropriation without the recognition of individual property on the part of other property-owning individuals.

For modern social science the relation of individuals to the objects of their desire is independent of their systematic determination within a system of mutual dependence. The relation of individual to object is therefore irreducible and unitary. All relation of individual to object is the purely egoistic relation of immediate contact. As a result the concept of the individual in his relation to an objective reality loses all specification to a determinate social reality. The immediacy of this relation is expressed in the concept of desire. The relation of the individual to the object, since immediate, is also singular so that all determinate relations of individuality (of will and of need) are the single relation of desire. On the side of the individual this requires the equation of his existence as a property-owner with his existence as a needy individual (the equation of will and need). On the side of the object this requires the equation of its existence as property, its value, with its relation to need, use-value: on one side, the individual as locus of personal desires; on the other side, the object as a utility.

The neo-classical conception is that of a given world of objects upon which individuals are set loose. These individuals are 'needy' but the specific character of those needs is not determined. The individuals then gather to themselves as much of the world of goods as they are physically able until the entire supply is appropriated. More generally, the 'active' element of the process is suppressed and the objects of individual desire are conceived to be delivered or given to each individual in arbitrarily fixed bundles. The individual emerges as the passive receptacle of both his needs and his possessions, receiving endowments and absorbing utilities in consumption. Finding that they possess more of certain objects than they 'need' individuals hit upon the idea of exchanging those objects for those possessed but not needed by others. Thus scarcity leads through appropriation to exchange, and the market system emerges as the product of the activity of property-owning individuals *vis-à-vis* scarce objects.

On the other hand, implicit in the definition of appropriation is the idea of an action taken with regard to a world of individuals, the excluding of others from consumption of the object appropriated. In this case property has a purely social character and presupposes a determinate social framework within which ownership and appropriation are recognized. The recognition of the individual as a property owner requires that he be defined in relation to other individuals as their equal who as such is intrinsically possessed of the right to claim ownership. The existence of property involves the recognition of that right and the exclusion of 'appropriation' by force which would directly deny the equality of the wielder of force and his victim. The exchange of objects of need requires, and in fact realizes, the equality and freedom of the exchangers, their status as commodity owners. But this equality, without which there could be no exchange, is an eminently social property of individuals (precisely their property of being individual persons) and cannot be conceived outside of the reciprocal recognition on the part of a system of exchangers.

The notions of the individual and his property are intimately bound up, therefore, with that of exchange. This connection is also recognized, if in a somewhat distinct form, within neo-classical economics. Within the latter it turns out that property does, in fact, presuppose more of the 'social' than simple recognition of ownership. It also requires the realization of freedom and equality (of the status of the individual as a property-owning person) in the exchange:[5]

In the second place, those who do this (appropriate objects) reap a double advantage: not only do they assure themselves a supply which can be reserved for their own use and satisfaction; but, if they are unwilling or unable to consume all of their supply themselves, they are also in a position to exchange the unwanted remainder for other scarce utilities which they do care to consume.

The 'gathering' of scarce objects by needy individuals now appears 'rational' only in light of the existence of a market. It is precisely the logic of exchange which is expressed in the activities of individuals toward objects. Not only does it appear that the transformation of the world of objects into 'scarce resources' is predicated on the appropriation of those objects, therefore, that scarcity is a determination of the social condition of property; but the very composition of the needs of the individual which lead him to appropriate objects and thereby make them scarce appears as the result of the location of that individual within the market system. The individual appropriates even those objects for which he has no need in order that he may exchange them for objects which he does need. In this case the aim of appropriation is exchange and appropriation takes place on the presupposition of the existence of the exchange system. The conditions under which the abstract individual will, through action based on his personal desires, participate in the construction of an exchange relation are not given with the mere existence of the individual as such but presuppose an individual whose desires are determined, at least implicitly, by his existence within a market economy. The derivation of exchange presupposes, furthermore, the existence of other individuals who, recognized in their individuality as the equals of the exchanger (whose equality and individuality is therefore a social condition), are assumed to bring to the exchange objects which the original exchanger lacks, from the ownership of which, therefore, he has been excluded. In other words, the original argument for a connection between scarcity and appropriation reverses itself and becomes an argument for appropriation based on exchange and therefore on the existence of the market. Deduction of the exchange is itself predicated on the presence of the market and is to that extent not the deduction of exchange at all. Scarce objects are appropriated but it is only in their appropriation that they reveal or express their scarcity. The reason for this is that it is appropriation based in an exchange system that *makes* objects scarce. The basis of exchange in property and scarcity is, in reality, the basis of scarcity in the specific social facts of exchange and property.

This series of contradictions points to a critical juncture within the neo-classical conception of the market mechanism. The neo-classical construction of the market is designed to comprehend the operation of the price system in terms of the undetermined individual and his given preferences. Neo-classical economics takes as its presupposition the individual *tout court*. The simplifying assumptions of the theory are designed, first, to construct the relation of the isolated individual to the world of objects, and subsequently, to build up a conception of the whole on this basis. Given that the relation of individual to object is a purely individual one which connects a socially undetermined individual to a given, physically defined, object, the exchange relationship emerges as the whole of the social existence of individual and object. With this hypostatization of the individual the exchange becomes directly a relation of undetermined individuals to utilities (which are also undetermined in so far as they are not themselves the products of an ongoing process). The entire social world consists of the exchange relation so that the construction of the exchange without regard, for example, to conditions of production, far from distorting the price mechanism, reveals directly its real character. But under-lying the requirement of the isolation of economic actor and economic function is the further requirement that within the function so isolated the economic principle be allowed clear expression. The construction of the abstract individual is assumed to leave him free to enter into or remain outside of all economic and social intercourse. The system of economic relations becomes the expression of the *choice* made on the part of the individual. The economic principle is, therefore, that of the choice both of the fact of the entry into economic interrelation and of the specific form of that entry. Having isolated the individual exchange, the method applied in the deduction of the model of economic activity must deal with the necessity of attributing a specific content to the relation of individual desire in order that that relation may lead to the deduction of exchange based on scarcity; that is, that the individual will be driven to choose exchange. For objects to exist as scarce it is not sufficient that the individuals and the objects of their desires be isolated. It is also necessary to demonstrate that the 'individuals' so isolated possess the attributes necessary to set in motion a world of exchange.

There is an immanent danger involved in the conceptual reversal which transforms scarcity as ground of exchange and appropriation into appropriation and exchange as ground of scarcity. To the extent that the individual is truly isolated and considered to generate his own personal definition of the composition and intensity of his desires, it becomes impossible to make the transition from the individual to society and still have any consistent notion of an exchange system. With a true individual foundation of exchange each 'exchange' becomes an individual, empirically given, event. Each market occurrence is equally an isolated event with no intrinsic connection to a series of interconnected and mutually conditioned market places. The fact of the occurrence of an exchange or of a group of exchanges hinges upon the whims of the individual participants and upon the given endowments which they bring with them. These whims cannot, in principle, be assumed or expected to recur in the appropriate relation one to the other to allow for the recurrence of exchange. The continuity of the exchange system is therefore outside of the strict domain of this conception. In order to account for not only the possibility of an exchange but for the existence of exchange and of a system of continuous and recurrent exchanges it is necessary to specify the endowments of individuals, their preferences, and the temporal manner of alteration of those preferences and endowments in such a way as to, first, bring the individuals to the market, and then, to periodically draw them back to the market. Such specification is tantamount, however, to the imposition of the requirements of the exchange system upon the individual, to the determination of preferences and endowments outside of accidents of nature and individual, self-generated, whim. The consistent construction of a social world of exchange relations, of an exchange system, denies the purity of the individuality of its parts and transforms them, at least implicitly, into social products. As such products it becomes necessary at once to give a theoretical account within the analysis for the underlying conditions of exchange, to account for individual preferences and endowments as themselves social products. Society, or the exchange system, cannot, then, simply be composed out of the sum of its individual elements, therefore reduced to the individual components, since those components are themselves determined by society.

3 On the abstract character of neo-classical economics

The original articulation of the neo-classical theory of exchange was predicated on the principle that the connection between exchange and scarcity could be established as valid through argument which appeals to the innate structure of human psychology and, therefore, forms a premise of economic action rather than a hypothesis capable of vertification within action. Human activity is considered directly synonymous with economizing behavior so that the notion of scarcity which underlies the whole concept of economic practice possesses an irreducible validity with regard to which any suggestion of a necessity for emprical verification would only serve to reveal ignorance of the basic principles of economic knowledge. The fact that the subject-matter of economics is itself 'subjective' and 'individual' (i.e. innate to the individual) allows for exact knowledge within economics as a result of the direct access on the part of the investigator to the human attributes which underlie economic behavior.

What this form of argumentation serves to accomplish is the attribution of a specific content to human desire which enables the deduction of exchange and scarcity in terms of that desire. The simple and abstract notion of desire, taken in itself, is not capable of bearing the weight of the deduction of scarcity and exchange. It is, therefore, necessary not only that exchange be based on purely individual desire but also that that individual desire have a specific content which is not arbitrary and which implies the expression of desire in a particular economic activity. Individual preference, taken in the abstract, is not clearly and necessarily a force which drives individuals to appropriate objects to the point where the world of 'utilities' has been transformed into the world of private property. Appropriation of objects to the extent of their availability is not a result of human desire *per se* but of the specific assumptions which must be built into that desire and which must be given some conceptual justification within neo-classical thinking.

The appeal to the 'self-evidence' of the postulational basis of economic reasoning was essentially an appeal to an intuitive rather than systematic foundation for the concept of exchange. This appeal to intuition served, and still serves, as a line of defense against criticism of the logical structure of the theory which latter is allowed a degree of autonomy. Where a specific line of reasoning comes into question the intuitive argument may still be protected by its degree of independence of any specific mode of formulation within the theory. In this case the conceptual edifice, together with the basic premises as formulated concretely within the theory of exchange (the concepts of value, exchange, need, scarcity, etc.) need not be given rigorous formulation but, rather, are allowed to enter the analysis on an intuitive basis, without benefit of systematic investigation and formulation. As a result the interpretation of the central relations of economic life becomes elusive to a degree. Economic affairs are understood to involve the allocation of 'scarce resources' regardless of the status of the specific construction of the concept of scarcity which we have considered above. Even were that to be found wanting this would not disturb the general idea of the economy as a machine for the allocation of scarce resources. The latter may be expressed in distinct formulations but exists independently of any particular formulation. This involves a separation between the implicit 'underlying' conception of the economic process as a whole (as involving 'scarcity') and the systematic articulation of a theory of exchange on explicitly stated premises. This separation comes to be accepted within modern economics when the latter appears in the form of a 'model' of exchange; an axiomatic construct logically independent of any conceptual basis, a construct from which the 'interpretations' of its elements are 'detachable.'[6] The idea that exchange is based upon scarcity becomes separated from the actual statement of the manner in which exchange is based upon scarcity. Weaknesses and contradictions of the 'theory' of exchange are prevented from infecting the 'underlying' perception of economic life.

Yet, while the abstract statement of the postulates of economic science might appear to possess the necessary self-evidence, once those postulates are questioned as to their meaning, what they, in the practical construction of the science both imply and require, their status as an unambiguous and satisfactory foundation for economic reasoning breaks down. There emerges instead a lack of clear and definite meaning which is itself attributable to the method which lies at the core of the construction of the neo-classical theory of exchange. Koopmans illustrates the dangers of the traditional approach with the example of the economic assumption that 'each consumer has a complete preference ordering of all commodity bundles the consumption of which is possible to him.' As clear and distinct as this assumption may appear it falls short of adequacy for the purposes of modern economics in that it 'denies the consumer such privileges as the joy in random variability in consumption, as well as its opposite, the comfort of consumption habits somewhat rigidly maintained under varying circumstances.' It further denies to the consumer 'the noble urge to respond with sacrifices to the distress of others, as well as the less highly regarded gratification in levels of conspicuous forms of consumption outoing those of others.'[7] One could, of course, go on indefinitely cataloguing the forms of behavior which the postulates of economic science deny to the individual. It follows that the self-evident postulates, if allowed to exhaust the significance of modern economic analysis, would relegate the latter to a narrow range of activities properly considered 'economic.' In other words, there appears in this case to be a rupture between the 'proper' meaning of economic activity and the range of activities actually considered within the theory. It appears that the narrow postulational basis of the original neo-classical analysis is not self-evident. Once the foundations of the theory become purely intuitive they can hardly remain compelling; that which is self-evident to one need not be so to another.

Current economic thinking takes the position that this deficiency can be remedied by replacing the monolithic structure of reasoning identified with 'economics' by the original adherents of the neo-classical analysis by a series of alternative reasonings, by a 'model of models' (Koopmans). In this case there is no single conception which adequately describes the essentials of the economic realm of social life but different conceptions dependent upon the different, empirically given, conditions. It is clear that the shift in approach is mainly important in that it ceases to be possible to argue that the conditions necessary for the deduction of the exchange system in neo-classical analysis have any necessary justification, that price phenomena express 'scarcity' in any rigorous sense of the term, or that the conception of resource allocation has any special importance, any more than an accidental relation, to the actual economic forms found to prevail in the modern world.

The neo-classical theory of exchange is unable to account for the prevailing market system as a necessary result of evidently compelling conditions. The isolation of the exchange and utility relations, their construction in a state of suspension *vis-à-vis* the social whole, laid the foundation for the deduction of exchange as a function of scarcity. But at the same time that it established the conditions for the deduction of price as a scarcity index it eliminated the condition for a deduction of exchange as a necessary relation of otherwise isolated individuals. Since the construction of the individual involves precisely his extraction from the social whole and, therefore, his isolation *vis-à-vis* the actual system of economic relations there no longer exists any source for the concrete determination of the individual. The consistent interpretation of the 'individual' isolated in the manner of neo-classical thinking severs that individual not only from production (as the positing by society of the objects of need, the denial of their giveness) but also from the subjective motivational requirements of an exchange economy as those are recognized within neo-classical economics itself.

Since it is not possible, in principle, to attribute the necessary content to individual desire required for the grounding of exchange and scarcity the latter cannot be interpreted as logically deducible from desire. Only the specification of preferences to the market system allows for the deduction of exchange, but in this case the deduction becomes circular and it is no longer possible to interpret need as an independent force underlying exchange. Desire comes to be identified with exchange behavior so that the latter is set loose from its determination in desire. As a result, the notions of utility and of preference are drained of theoretical content. Originally, the market system was the expression of the activity of individual preference, it was the method of indirect access to the force which underlies market behavior. At this point, however, any necessary link between individual desire and market exchange has been severed. Market behavior is no longer the expression of desire since the statement of a connection of behavior to desire has no definite theoretical significance, appears to add nothing to the conception of the behavior taken in itself.

The indeterminancy which modern economics itself perceives within the logic of its reasoning has driven economists to abandon altogether the task of accounting for the system of economic relations as a systematic and internally coherent whole, of accounting for the logical structure of the price system and of connecting that system to an underlying foundation. It is, in fact, logical, given the weaknesses of the modern theory of value, that it should lead into a purely 'behaviorist' interpretation of economic affairs which eschews any pretense of grounding behavior outside of itself; holding fast to the identity between the expression of need in behavior and that behavior itself so that the latter loses all ground. This conception attests to the intrinsic difficulties involved in the original project of neo-classical economics – that of accounting for exchange as the expression of scarcity and individual preference – and to the resulting impossibility of consummating that project in a consistent and conceptually satisfactory manner. The contradictions of the theory of individual preference and exchange also account for the retreat into the notion of 'revealed preference' which, as a purely formal system, hardly makes or is capable of sustaining any theoretical claims whatever as regards the nature of economic relations.

The relation of exchange to need within neo-classical economics may be characterized in terms of the relation of a force (individual preference) to its form of expression (exchange). The exchange is therefore understood in terms of the underlying force which it expresses. This is precisely the method by which sense is made of the exchange phenomenon, by which it is grasped 'theoretically.' Yet, at this point, it becomes clear that the force in terms of which exchange is to be understood is incapable of grounding that exchange, it has disappeared altogether into the exchange. For neo-classical economics there is no longer force and its expression but only that expression 'understood' in terms of itself. With this result the force may clearly be left out of the analysis altogether and with it any aspiration to the providing of a theoretical account for exchange phenomena. None the less, while systematically the theory is left with a 'nothing' in the place of the content of the exchange relation, it still proceeds, and in fact finds itself forced to proceed, to the construction of a comprehensive theory of the economic 'system' built upon this empty foundation. It is necessary, then, to go further and consider the necessity which underlies the peculiar line of development of the argument of neo-classical analysis.

In the following sections the specific manner in which modern economics constructs the exchange economy is considered. The nodal point in this entire construction is the conception of production in the exchange economy. It is in the manner of treatment of production that the specificity of the neo-classical conception of the economy is given its definitive expression. The notion of production is intrinsically bound up with the coherence of the economic process as a whole and, in particular, with its ability to sustain itself; i.e. with the extent to which the conditions of its existence are adequately formulated. Only with the explicit introduction of an ongoing process of production and reproduction can the relations of economic life emerge as determined by their location within a systematic whole. In the absence of production all such relations – of need and of resource supply – must remain fixed, immobilized by the absence of the explicit consideration of their source as *products* of a process within which they are defined and determined. Production establishes the basis for the exchange system to emerge as a continuous and recurring form by accounting for the conditions of that emergence. On the other hand the actual manner of construction of the exchange economy is explicitly designed to deny the only source of its own coherence: production as an ongoing process. Since exchange is to emerge as the result of caprice it must not be accountable to an ongoing social process which serves to fix it and impose a particular course upon it. The exposition of production becomes, therefore, problematic since, while such an exposition is necessary in order to account for, and ultimately ground, exchange it must also conflict directly with the conception of exchange as the expression of the whim of the unconstrained individual. Without necessity and limitation there can be no theoretical account and yet the primary condition placed upon the neo-classical theory of exchange is that of deducing exchange in the absence of all necessity and determination.

4 The construction of the exchange economy

The archetype of the exchange 'system' is the two-sided exchange which is presented in the Walrasian analysis prior both to the introduction of many-sided exchange and of the various forms of 'production.' In the original simple model the whole of the economy is composed of two otherwise isolated individuals who 'meet' solely in order to exchange. These two individuals possess neither social ties outside of the particular exchange nor the attributes of members of a determinate social order, such as an exchange-based economy. The individuality of the exchange is absolute both as regards the individuals involved and as regards the conditions of its existence. Every exchange is one of a kind (hardly even an individual instance of 'exchange'), independent of every other exchange.

This construction of the particular exchange suggests a further isolation of the exchange process which involves exchange in the absence altogether of intersubjective relation. The famous isolated individual of economic thought (who has already made an appearance in the treatment of property) is sufficient condition for the elementary conception of the entirety of economic life including the 'price system.' From the point of view of neo-classical economics it is not a question of[8]

whether a single person who operates simultaneously as supplier and consumer should ever want to resort to implicit prices for decentralized decision making. The principle point . . . is that if a line of separation exists it defines a price system that makes such decentralization possible.

In this case the entire economic world is composed of a single 'individual' so that the individual and the social are directly merged in such a way as to dissolve society into the system of irreducible individuals, abolishing even the specifically individual character of the latter. Individuality can only be made intelligible on the basis of the recognition of the individual as such within a system of individuals. Thus individuality implies not only opposition but also equality such that the particularity of the individual can be sustained only on the basis of his universality, the discovery within the particular of the activity of a universal substance. Denial of this condition is at the core of the neo-classical conception of the economy and is expressed in a method which constructs the economy *as a whole* in isolation so that a limited, one-sided, aspect of the economic process (a single moment of its conception) emerges as the economic system *in toto*.

On one level such constructs, or 'models,' are intentionally simplistic. They are not intended to exhibit in a comprehensive manner the whole of economic relations but to isolate, through abstraction, the central distinguishing features of the exchange economy in such a way as to allow the analysis to extract the essential characteristic of all exchange and of all exchange-based phenomena. Methodologically, however, the results of the elementary constructs are of wide significance. It is in the manner of construction of the simple models that the conditions for their consistent extension can be determined and, therefore, the possibility of their extension to the complex of economic relations. Clearly, if such an extension takes place via the 'addition' of economic relations which, in their implications, contradict the conclusions derived from the simple constructs the latter lose not only their theoretical function but equally their status as 'simple' models.

Such a result would be of the greatest importance since it is precisely the construction of the simple models which allows for the isolation of the central theme of all neo-classical economic thought. It is precisely the role of the simple model to express directly the salient features of the economy which are still *present* within the complex 'real' structure but are not readily visible. The simple model expresses the truth of the actual economic process. Thus according to Walras:

the exchange of two commodities for each other in a perfectly competitive market is an operation by which all holders of either one, or of both, of the two commodities can obtain the greatest possible satisfaction of their wants consistent with the condition that the two commodities are bought and sold at one and the same rate of exchange throughout the market.

This is the theme of the entire exchange analysis. The problem of economic theory is that of, first, constructing a model in which this principle is directly revealed, and then, of extending that model in such a way as to reveal the complex relations which overlay the simple exchange in the actual economic system as expressions of the original principle:[9]

The main object of the theory of social wealth is to generalize this proposition by showing, first, that it applies to exchange of several commodities for one another as well as to the exchange of two commodities for each other, and secondly that, under perfect competition, it applies to production as well as to exchange. The main object of the theory of production of social wealth is to show how the principle of organization of agriculture, industry, and commerce can be deduced as a logical consequence of the above proposition. We may say, therefore, that this proposition embraces the whole of pure and applied economics.

The simple model plays not only the role of introduction and of 'parable' but of mechanism of direct access on the part of analysis to the inner core of all economic phenomena. It sets the stage for the articulation of a comprehensive model of the economic whole by isolating the key relationships and categories in terms of which the social world is grasped in its economic aspect. In particular the simple model allows for the articulation of the concept of scarcity and of exchange based on scarcity which is, in one sense, the concept of a purely economic activity.

The simple model of the two-sided exchange considered in the previous section has the critical property of altogether severing exchange from the production of commodities. As we have argued, it is essential to the original neo-classical conception of scarcity that the utilities or objects of need be given to the individuals who appropriate them. Scarcity rests on the givenness of objects. Scarcity of given commodities is hardly reconcilable, on the other hand, with the existence of objects as *products* unless their character as products is constructed in a specific manner. The extension of scarcity to the realm of production involves a specific argumentation which gives to the neo-classical theory of exchange and production its specific character and its peculiar categories.

No clearer statement of, nor firmer evidence for, the peculiarity of the relation of production to exchange in neo-classical thinking could be required than that presented, again as a simple model, in Karl Menger's *Principles of Economics*. 'To begin with the simplest case, suppose that two farmers, A and B, have both previously been carrying on isolated household economies.' The condition of the problem is the isolation of self-sufficient producer-consumers. They exist, at the outset, in total isolation from each other and from any market system. They are precisely the individuals considered in Koopmans's treatment of the decentralization of decision making:

But now, after an unusually good harvest, farmer A has so much grain that he is unable, however profusely he may provide for the satisfaction of his needs, to utilize a portion of it for himself and his household. Farmer B, on the other hand, a neighbor of farmer A, is assumed to have had an excellent vintage in the same year. But his cellar is filled from previous years, and because he lacks additional containers he is considering pouring out a part of the older wines in storage which dates from an inferior vintage year.

To this extent production has already been introduced as the basis of exchange. Yet, on closer examination it is clear that it is not production in a systematic sense but the purely accidental and conceptually arbitrary *over*production which makes possible an exchange relation. Production has taken place wholly without consideration of exchange so that the existence of a surplus for exchange is not a necessary result built into the production process but an historical accident. Even here, however, it is difficult for Menger to withhold the systematic necessity which production imposes on the market system and which that system imposes on production. 'Each farmer has a surplus of one good and a serious deficiency of the other.' Again, by a peculiar theoretical reversal production of a surplus as condition of exchange becomes production of a definite need for exchange, the production of a lack, the lack of commodities needed but not produced:

The farmer with the surplus of grain must completely forgo consumption of wine since he has no vineyards at all, and the farmer with a surplus of wine has no foodstuffs. Farmer A can permit bushels of grain to spoil on his fields when a keg of wine would afford him considerable pleasure. Farmer B is about to destroy not merely one but several kegs of wine when he could very well use a few bushels of grain in his household.

Menger introduces an illicit and striking condition into what originated as self-subsistent household economies: the division of labor. That the wine producer should find himself at the end of the year in possession only of wine and, therefore, faced with the prospect of starvation is wholly inconceivable in the absence of a market as a condition of the problem. That exchange should emerge in this manner presupposes that the individual farmer is already a part of a social division of labor and produces, for example, wine when he knows that he must have grain (and cloth, etc.) because he knows at the outset that he can exchange wine for grain (and for cloth and his other necessities) and has, in fact, produced only wine precisely in order to exchange a part or all of it for his other necessities. He has produced for exchange. It is not because of accident or because of the peculiarities of individual farmers *qua* isolated producer-consumers but because of the social division of labor and exchange that the 'first farmer thirsts and the second starves when both could be relieved by the grain A is permitting to spoil on his fields and by the wine B has resolved to pour out.'[10]

In this case the overproduction, for example, of wine, appears as a 'surplus' only to the extent that exchange is *not* possible. When production has taken place for exchange the product, from the standpoint of the producer, takes the form of a surplus only to the extent that he fails to transform that wine into the various products which he requires. When, on the other hand, the wine is seen to stand for so much of the various commodities required for consumption and production in the future it is the wine as *value* which has become the object of production. In this case its status as a 'surplus' no longer hinges on the immediate need of its producer for wine but upon the value of the wine in the market relative to its cost of production. Menger has 'slipped' into a conception of exchange as based on a division of labor. To this extent the exchange is not a self-contained act which relates two otherwise isolated individuals but a dependent aspect of a social process. The notion of individual exchange, far from being self-sufficient, goes beyond itself in the very articulation of its pre-conditions.

The phenomenon which this 'slip' on Menger's part obscures but which Menger wishes to express is the pure exchange for which the notion of a surplus signifies that part of production which is not itself necessary to continued production within the individual household. This surplus consists of utilities which are consumed but do not in the act of consumption enter into a process of production. Such articles are intended solely for consumption in the strict neo-classical sense of the term. In this way the notion of exchange of a produced surplus continues the consumption–production dichotomy within a system of continued production. The condition for this result is precisely that production be conceived as a purely individual act (just as consumption was conceived as an individual act).

The inner connection between production and exchange is abrogated within the neo-classical analysis of exchange, first, through the elimination of production from the conception of exchange and then by the construction of exchange as the exchange of a produced surplus. These two conditions are, in fact, equivalent, for in the second, the fact that the surplus-products exchanged are 'products' does not bear on the exchange itself. This same condition is written into the modern theory of the exchange economy of Arrow and Debreu. As Koopmans points out 'the hardest part of the specification of the model is to make sure that each consumer can both survive and participate in the market, without anticipating in the postulates what specific prices will prevail in an equilibrium.' To write exchange as a moment of an ongoing economic process which embraces reproduction and division of labor is to establish conditions outside of the exchange strictly conceived which serve to determine its form and dimension. Exchange which mediates a social process does not move with the degree of freedom required in the deduction of exchange as the product of the relation of individual preferences to scarce resources. Only in its isolation from the movement of the social process as a whole can exchange be considered exclusively in terms of the relation of preferences to utilities given outside of the conditions which produce those preferences. The necessity that consumers exist into the next period is one aspect of the requirement that the exchange of commodities not lead into consumption as a definitive act but into consumption as an element of an ongoing process. Consumption is necessary to the continued existence of consumers and in so far as exchange is a condition for consumption exchange is necessary to the continuation of those consumers.

By contrast, the specification of commodities as connected to individual owners and deriving their value from that connection is tied to the necessity of determining rates of exchange exclusively within the pure exchange economy, the market taken as an isolated event. Koopmans goes on to point out that Arrow and Debreu succeed in constituting exchange rates as wholly market determined by assuming[11]

first of all that the aggregate supply set contains a point which supplies just a little more of every commodity than is necessary, as indicated by some point in the aggregate consumption set, for every consumer to survive. Second, they assume that each consumer can, if necessary survive on the basis of the resources he holds and the direct use of his own labor, without engaging in exchange, and still have something to spare of some type of labor which is sure to meet with a positive price in equilibrium.

The rates at which commodities exchange come to be determined exclusively within the act of exchange and without regard to the requirements of the totality of economic relations. Exchange is relegated to that sphere within which the autonomous individual is given expression and within which the determination of exchange-value as an element of production and the complex of interdependent economic relations is excluded. Production is wholly individual and considered as a process which can, in principle, take place as subsistence production on the part of the isolated individual outside of society. Society becomes, as a result, the exchange relationship *tout court*. Exchange, far from one determination of the theory of social life, has come, even in the presence of production, to exhaust the content of social life. Society becomes the sum total of relations of individuals one to the other within which the absolute autonomy of each is preserved. Such relationships are all exchange relationships since it is within the exchange that it is alone possible for the autonomy of each to be preserved within their relation to others.

This construction leads directly into the indifference of exchange *vis-à-vis* production. It is this construction, furthermore, which allows neo-classical economics to set out the analysis of exchange wholly without regard to any notion of production. The conditions of production are constructed in such a manner as not to impinge upon the exchange process. To be sure, production provides the material objects exchanged, but it neither grounds that exchange by providing it with a necessity and rationale nor does it govern the quantitative dimensions of that exchange (the relative prices). On the other side, while consumption is the aim and goal of production and consumption is mediated by exchange it is only surplus consumption which is so mediated, so that both the consumption and exchange are not conditions of production, and so that consumption is explicitly precluded from the status of one aspect of the ongoing production process. Production is the self-contained generation of products which as products are indifferent to their direct consumption or to whatever exchange may mediate that consumption.

Neo-classical thinking is compelled to introduce production into the pure exchange economy precisely in order to establish the coherence of the exchange economy. This fact expresses the role of production as, implicitly, that process which accounts for the continuation of the economic system, which *is* that continuation. The economic system, including the exchange relation, viewed as *product*, is grounded, exists as result and can therefore be accounted for conceptually. Without production the very existence of the exchange relation is inexplicable. Yet the original exposition of exchange is based on a principle which directly denies the coherence of the exchange system. Koopmans asserts that it is essential that the analysis not anticipate in its construction of the conditions of exchange the existence and dimension of that exchange, therefore that the exchange must be an arbitrary act which is the product of individual whim. Exchange as exchange of produced surplus retains the indeterminacy of exchange while giving an account for the subsistence of the individuals who are potential participants in the exchange. As a result of this conception of production the exchange remains arbitrary. Yet it is this very characteristic which, while necessary to the neo-classical conception, denies to it any determination and necessity, Even with subsistence production there is no accounting for the exchange relation. And without this giving of an account, without this determination and necessity, there is no *theory* of exchange. The individual remains undetermined (free and independent). In order to derive a theory of the exchange system it is necessary to introduce the social conditions that alone make the theoretical conception possible. Without these social conditions the original positing of the individual is simply the assertion of an individuality which can lead nowhere other than back into that individuality. It is the individual relation conceived as product that allows for the determination of that individual relation, which, in fact, allows for its conception. The manner in which production is conceived is, therefore, critical, since it reveals directly the opposition between a conceptually adequate determination of the economic process and a conception which strives to elicit a concrete theory of exchange in the absence of all determination. Neo-classical thinking is forced to introduce, step by step, production as an ongoing and self-sustaining process, precisely in order to ground and account for the simple exchange relation, because it is only within that ongoing process that exchange can reveal a determinate content. Yet, the exchange, once definitely rooted within that ongoing process, loses the qualities of the neo-classical conception of exchange as the allocation of scarce resources according to individual need.

5 Production in the exchange economy

So long as the objects exchanged are products only in the limited sense of surplus products considered in the previous section, the deduction of exchange based on production differs in no essential respect from exchange as it emerges within the pure exchange economy in which all forms of production are excluded. Viewed in terms of their origin it is true that objects of exchange are produced, but viewed in terms of that exchange itself the status of those objects as products is wholly inconsequential, so that those objects viewed in terms of the exchange relation are not, in fact, products. This construction of the exchange economy, therefore, preserves the separation of exchange from production. On the other hand, it fails to demonstrate the operation of the economic principle (scarcity) for exchange based on production when that is exchange of products properly considered. This failure has two sides. First, it is necessary to show how the economic principle still governs exchange where the objects exchanged are truly products and therefore where their status as products imposes itself on the exchange. Second, and this is simply the reverse of the first point, it is necessary to demonstrate that production is also governed by the economic principle so that the existence of commodities as products does not contradict their scarcity. This second requirement is essential because if the objects present in the market are not taken as given but as products then one of the original conditions for the deduction of the category of scarcity is directly threatened. There must be some sense in which objects are scarce even though they are not given. From what has been said thus far it appears clear that this general requirement of the neo-classical theory of exchange is not internally consistent. On one side, there must be exchange based on production, therefore exchange as constrained by an external condition not synonymous with individual preference, not therefore evidently the direct expression of such preference. On the other side, there is the condition of exchange as expressive of free choice which presupposes the absence of constraint and therefore indifference *vis-à-vis* production.

The danger involved here is implicitly recognized by Walras in the manner in which he constructs the argument of the *Elements*. The argument begins, as we have seen, with the pure exchange economy for which production is altogether excluded. Walras then makes the claim, considered above, that the results of the treatment of the simple model are extensible to the world of economic relations and, in particular, to production. This does not, however, involve the immediate introduction of production as a self-sustaining and ongoing process but only in the attenuated form of production on the part of given factors of production. Only after considering production within which the factors which enter production are not themselves products does Walras attempt to constitute production by objects which are themselves products. This two-stage character of the argument is critical since it reveals the hesitation on the part of neo-classical thinking to consider production as a self-sustaining process where products are produced by commodities which are themselves products.

Clearly, where utilities become products through the transformation of objects which are not themselves products it is possible to sustain the idea of scarcity if only by shifting that scarcity back one stage in the economic process. Products, as the transformations of scarce factors, are themselves scarce since they represent, and in a sense embody, those original scarce factors. Furthermore since the products are distinct in nature from the factors which produce them there is a clear distinction both physically and in terms of function between production and consumption. The confusion introduced into the neo-classical construction of the idea of consumption as the goal of production by the identity of consumption and production within the ongoing process is eliminated since the character of production as an ongoing process is abrogated. It is because products re-enter production as inputs, and re-enter in the course of their consumption, that it becomes impossible to consider consumption as an end but only as a mediating term in a circular process which is without discernible end. On the other hand, where production is a 'one-way street' leading from factors of production to products, there emerges a definite end point to the process, the products which do not themselves become factors of production. The act of consumption can be clearly distinguished and separated from the production process even though the means of consumption are the products of that process. This is not the *result* of the scarcity of resources but the *meaning* of scarcity within the framework of production in the exchange economy. Speaking strictly the use of the term scarcity is only relevant to the analysis of exchange where either (1) production is absent altogether and exchange exists independently of the origin of the objects exchanged, or (2) where production takes on the special form considered here. Otherwise the concept of scarcity loses any rigorously determinate sense.

The fact that commodities are products in this limited sense does not impinge on their givenness with regard to their consumption. What is given in this case is not so much the commodity *per se* but the commodity as the embodiment of scarce factors. Through the law of cost of production scarcity of factors imposes itself on the exchange of commodities and the consumption decisions of individuals impose themselves on the direction and magnitude of the individual production processes. As a result both production and exchange are constituted, even in their unity, as expressions of the economic principle.

This conclusion hinges on the construction of production as a process rooted in given factors of production, therefore as a process which is self-contained and capable of isolation. To be sure, the goal of production is given to production from outside, from the preferences of individuals; yet, given that goal, the actual production process has no intrinsically social character, becomes a purely technical problem. In fact, production in this sense is *the* technical problem where that problem is defined as the determination of efficient means for the achievement of a given end. The idea of production based in scarce factors of production is the rational foundation of all ideas of modern social theory concerning efficiency, rationality, and adjustment of means to ends. Modern social thought signifies by the term 'technique' the method of transformation of scarce, but not directly needed, resources into objects of direct need. A technique is therefore a means for the allocation of resources. Given the articulation of ends and the supply of resources it stipulates the possible adjustments between ends and resources.

But just as the original notion of scarcity (which contains in germ this peculiar conception of technology) is predicated on the givenness of objects of desire and on the exclusion of any intrinsic social determination of those objects outside of their direct relation to individual preference, so also does this more advanced conception of exchange based on scarcity depend essentially on the presence of factors of production as given with regard to the process as a whole. This positing of the conditions of the economic process from outside is still the critical condition in the conception of exchange.

For production to relate to consumption solely as means to its end two conditions are necessary. First, production impinges on consumption and exchange only in creating the objects of consumption, strictly, therefore, in the presentation of objects to the world of consumption and not in creating the character and status of the act of consumption itself. For this condition to be sustained it is necessary that the process of production be separated from that of consumption and that each be allowed its independent subsistence. Second, consumption must be a final act which forms the end point of a determinate economic process. Only in this case does consumption not turn back into production, and give to the latter not only its goal but also the means to that goal.

The separation of consumption from production is the theme of a group of key theorems within the construction of the neo-classical theory of exchange, those concerning the separation of convex sets. Typically the focus is on the efficiency of decentralized decision making, on the conditions within which such decentralization is both possible and efficient. Such decentralization is, as we have seen, possible even in the case of a single individual for whom the economic problem exists in the form of the question of the existence of a 'price system' with the 'help of which Robinson the producer can separate his decisions from those of Robinson the consumer and laborer.'[12] The theme of the entire construction is that of the separation of economic functions. Without this separation the notion of efficiency disappears. The separation and isolation of individual producer-consumers and of individuals acting as consumers and as producers is essential to the construction of the economic system as a whole in such a manner as not to impinge upon the autonomy of the individual constituent elements of that whole. The intrinsic connection between the peculiar treatment of production in terms of the transformation of scarce factors and the construction of the economic system as a whole in terms of the sum of the parts is critical to the comprehension of the theory of production and of the firm articulated within the neo-classical framework. The notion of the system as a whole as the *sum* of its individual parts is equivalent to the notion of those individual parts as intrinsically isolated and separable one from the other and each from the conditions of the social whole. For the sum the individual parts lose all qualitative character except that of dimension, of pure quantity. Here all that remains of the elements is an irreducible unity, each a single unit within the total. As a result sums are always comparable without regard to the qualitative properties which differentiate their component units.

The conception of the economic system as an elementary totality (a sum total) brings with it the full isolation, the irreducible singularity, of the component parts. Consumption by the individual consumer must take the objects of consumption as given and relate to those objects in terms of needs which are private and specific to the particular individual. The scarcity or givenness of objects must be a property of the presupposed relation of individual need to a world of things and not the result of the appropriation, as a social act, of the objects and of the market mechanism.

The condition for the evaluation of the efficiency of the economic system is that that economic system be constructed as the sum of its individual parts so that the efficiency of the parts is the efficiency of the whole. Production by factors of production sustains, in general, the conception of, first, the separation of production from consumption, and second, on another level, the separation of different production processes. Each process is, in effect, defined not only by the product which it produces but by the particular factor or factors of production for whose scarcity the product stands. Where such conditions are met total independence of productive units is assured. Each product is the transformation of a separate factor and simply stands for the scarcity of that factor. In this case, production as a whole is the simple summation of individual productions. Since inputs are not themselves products and do not themselves have any significance outside of the individual unit of production and particular industry, the distinction between production and consumption which appears for the individual producer is directly extensible to the system of production and exchange as a whole and with it so also is the idea of efficient allocation of scarce resources.

This is the origin of the peculiar construction of production in terms of factors of production which construction, as we have seen, sharply restricts, in fact excludes, the introduction of the objects of consumption as products. Such a degenerate form of production explicitly excludes the positing of the conditions of production within the movement of the economic process itself and relegates those conditions to the status of presupposed givens. The other side of the construction of production in such an attenuated form is the elimination of the interdependence of economic activities which is a primary condition for the construction of the neo-classical conception of the exchange economy. The two, apparently separate, threads of the argument merge at this point. The isolation of economic actor and economic function on one side is the exclusion of production as a self-sustaining process on the other. The 'production of commodities' as the production of the conditions for continued production necessarily implies the interdependence of economic function, the interdependence of consumption and production and of the individual units of production and of consumption; therefore, the specification of each individual element of the economic process as only conceivable in terms of its determinate location within the movement as a whole.

For exchange of 'products' to be exchange based on scarcity it is necessary that those products be the products of factors of production not themselves produced. But this is also the condition for the independent determination of the individual production process. The latter must be determined without regard to the reproduction of the economic system as a whole. On the other hand, where the 'factors' of production are the products of separate production processes each process becomes a dependent link in a social division of labor and in a process of reproduction of capital as a whole. Each unit of production is a dependent moment whose very definition, whose goal, and whose requirements, derive from the movement as a whole.

The explicit treatment of production is found to be necessary within the neo-classical conception in order to establish a basis for the existence and continuation of the exchange system. Yet the movement from the premises of consumer behavior and the exchange relation to the production of commodities requires explicit treatment in order to assure that the production of commodities is consistent with exchange and in order that production itself be characterized as the effect of the operation of economic forces and, in particular, of individual preference. The argument which leads into this result and which establishes production as a legitimate process within the exchange economy is contained within the theory of capital. It is the emergence of capital which accounts for production as a logical extension of the exchange system.

II Capital

1 The concept of capital

The neo-classical theory in its simplest form entails only the direct exchange of utilities one against the other. The basis for the deduction of this exchange is in the attribution of preferences of a specific character to the individuals engaged in the exchange system. This specification of preference is at once essential to the derivation of a consistent price system and at the same time incapable of any legitimate theoretical derivation – it is in the nature of an arbitrary assumption. Characteristically, the deduction of the capital relation rests upon a connected further specification of preference rather than upon a deduction based upon the immediately given conditions of the exchange economy. This specification has to do with the intertemporal nature of preferences. To argue that time, taken in the abstract, alters the previously specified character of individual preference requires an additional assumption which further specifies that preference. Why this particular specification is the one invoked will become apparent in the course of the construction of the neo-classical concept of capital.

It may be mentioned in this connection that the introduction of time is not, in itself, the basis of the transformation of the theory of exchange into the theory of capital and production. The conditions of the original theory of exchange in no way exclude the passage of time and the temporal dimensions of the exchange process, since unspecified, may be of any magnitude. The introduction of time into this process would necessarily be redundant were it not that preference is presumed to be specific to time. It is, therefore, not at all a question of time as such, but a question of the presumed relation of preference to time.

Within neo-classical thought the problem of capital concerns the allocation of scarce resources over time. The fundamental idea is that of the *choice* of an intertemporal consumption stream, of the maximization of intertemporal utility. In the choice of the desired stream the rate of interest appears as the proportion of gain in the future to current sacrifice. The amount of 'capital' is the amount of consumption forgone in the present (therefore 'invested'). Where the commodities consumed in the future are the same as the commodities given up in the present, or where there is only one object of need which is given up in the present in order to be consumed with interest in the future, the calculation of the amount of capital and its rate of return is straightforward. The actual physical quantity of the good invested can be directly opposed to the magnitude of the return and a direct calculation of the profitability of the changeover to the alternate stream is possible by comparing the net return on capital to the rate of time preference. On the other hand, where there exists more than one consumption good involved in the exchange over time, or where the consumption forgone is consumption of a good different from that received in the future, the calculation must be in value. In this case a measure of the value of capital must be derived which leads to consistent conclusions regarding the relation of consumption forgone to the return on investment.

In the absence of production, the determination of the value of consumption forgone need only be consistent with the formation of price in the exchange economy as a whole via the interaction of a system of needy individuals. A complication is immediately introduced when production is allowed since the relation of value invested to value returned must now also be consistent with the externally given conditions of productivity. With the introduction of production the concept of capital undergoes an expansion of meaning so that it also becomes necessary to establish that capital as so much consumption forgone is synonymous with capital as 'produced means of production' and as 'intermediate product.'

In the absence of production each individual receives an income stream of a given shape (from nature). This is analogous to the initial endowment of the theory of exchange. Such an endowment is presumed to be adequate to sustain the individual throughout his lifetime as an isolated consumer. In this state the individual either combines his direct effort with nature (as in picking berries) or he simply receives, from nature, an income which is consumed. The theory of capital and interest considers the optimal rearrangement of that stream. Such a rearrangement, in order that it be made to yield a return on capital, must involve a change in the total value received and not simply in the form of that value; that is, not simply in the particular utilities consumed. In the absence of a difference in total value the rearrangement of the consumption stream over time involves only an alteration in the particular useful objects consumed and not in total utility. In that case the phenomena of intertemporal consumption and exchange would reduce to the simple exchange of commodities of the exchange economy without capital and interest. The distinguishing feature of exchange with capital formation and a rate of return is that the total value received depends upon the time shape of the receipt of consumption. Individuals, then, must be sufficiently eager to change their time shape of consumption that the time pattern becomes itself a source of utility over and above direct consumption. The date of consumption becomes a characteristic which affects the utility gained in consumption. This is the first and most general condition which is introduced for the deduction of capital and interest.

The second condition placed upon the theory is that the choice of an income stream express a preference for present over future consumption. Only if such a preference exists will a premium be paid for present goods, therefore will future goods be discounted. With the presence of such a premium and state of preferences, any shift in the lifetime stream of income cannot be a simple rearrangement of consumption from one period to another. Any shift of consumption from one period to another, from present to future, must involve the receipt of a greater amount of consumption in the future than is foregone in the present.

The questionable theoretical basis for this condition is well recognized within neo-classical economics. On one side, the neo-classical treatment of capital seems clearly to require time preference which favors present over future consumption. Without this specification a positive rate of return would not arise. On the other side, the simple positing of individual preference hardly allows for any systematic deduction of a positive preference for present over future consumption, or, indeed, for any preference whatever as related specifically to time. In order to shore up this difficulty the theory of capital provides a long list of *ad hoc* justifications for positive time preference (in the form of Bohm-Bawerk's 'reasons' for interest, or in the more modern form of 'life-cycle hypotheses' regarding the propensity to save).

If it is simply assumed that time preference is positive, then, on the further assumption that the production of commodities allows for the expansion of consumption, that is, that the amount of the inputs into production is exceeded by the amount of output, it is possible to deduce production and to incorporate the latter into the exchange economy. Production becomes one mechanism for rearranging the intertemporal stream of consumption, a means for storing up utilities to be consumed at a later date, and is therefore subordinate to final consumption. Production thus becomes subordinate to the process of the exchange economy and conceivable within that process. Assuming that an individual possesses objects having utility u and a time preference of 100 per cent then he would be willing to exchange u in period one for any bundle of utilities having utility greater than $2u$ in period 2. If, therefore, by entering commodities of value u into production he could receive in period 2, say, $2.3u$ as productive output then such an individual, if he were to act rationally, would engage in production.

Production fits logically into the conception of exchange only in this manner because production is, before anything else, the 'refraining from' direct consumption of objects of desire. So far as neo-classical thought is concerned, to employ utilities in production is to give up the possibility of realizing their value in the present, that is in immediate consumption. Production is, then, the antithesis of consumption and in that respect would appear to conflict directly with the underlying rationale of the exchange economy. *Prima facie*, production contradicts the theory of exchange. This result can only be denied by the subordination of production itself to individual preference which requires, first, that the direct refraining from consumption be made reasonable in the light of individual preference. Without this, production would remain irrational when opposed to the possibility of consuming the commodities which go into production.

But the subordination of production to the conditions of the exchange economy requires yet another condition. While the elimination of immediate consumption is directly implied by the idea of production this elimination must be only a temporary displacement or postponement. To refrain from present consumption, therefore to engage in production, can only be rational if the act of refraining from consumption is motivated by consumption, in this case future consumption. This means, in particular, that production must end in consumption.

It is important to emphasize that production in the exchange economy is not simply assumed to take place but is explicitly made rational according to the conditions of the exchange system. To that extent it is deduced within a definite line of argument employing a methodology which in one important respect is identical to that employed in the initial deduction of the system of exchange. In particular, the specification of preferences is made such as to lead individuals, on the basis of their desires, to enter into production. Up to this point no greater harm has come to the conditions of the analysis of exchange than that originally inflicted by the necessity of specifying need so as to deduce exchange itself. By this reasoning, the rate of return is easily grasped within the methodology of neo-classical economics, and consistently so, as long as the arbitrary specification of preference is allowed.

However, the deduction of production requires an additional assumption, different in kind from that which specifies preferences in such a way as to generate the system of exchange and to extend that system to include exchange over time. It is further necessary to assume that the 'productivity of round-about methods of production' is given and diminishes with the intensity of application. On one side, it must be assumed that production itself is 'productive,' that is, yields a surplus according to its own mode of organization, that it is productive viewed in a wholly material, or technical, manner. On the other side, this productivity must diminish with the increased intensity of application of the production process (or with 'the degree of roundaboutness'). These conditions while unnecessary to the simple deduction of a rate of return on capital (as consumption foregone) are necessary to the treatment of production. It is of considerable importance to note that these conditions do not involve assumptions of the character employed in the construction of the exchange economy. The specification of need has nothing to do with the specification of the nature of production. It is, therefore, necessary to investigate more closely the nature of the special assumptions required in forming production into a process internally consistent with the exchange economy.

2 Capital and production

Within neo-classical economics, the derivation of production logically presupposes the prior specification of time preference if it is to contribute to a theory of interest. Further, this specification must be independent of the conditions of the productivity of 'round-about' methods of production. In other words it is illicit to argue that positive time preference emerges *because* of the possibility of engaging in round-about methods of production. Time preference is the logical basis of the deduction, within neo-classical economics, both of the rate of interest and of production. While the latter is made possible by the conditions of technology, assumed given, it is made rational only by the conditions of time preference.

This limitation of production in its relation to the discounting of future consumption was pointed out very early by Bortkiewicz. It can be readily grasped through the use of a simple example. Assume that production is a possibility but that the future consumption made possible by production is not discounted so that x units of a good consumed today have a value to the consumer equal to that of x units consumed at some future time. If it takes a time period p to transform x into $x+x'$ the person in possession of x at time zero is, in effect, in possession of $x+x'$ in period p (if he so chooses). It would appear that the person possessing x at period zero has an advantage over the person possessing x at period p since the former, in effect, possesses $x+x'$ in period p. Since $x+x'$ is greater than x consumption of $x+x'$ should yield greater utility than consumption of x. The result would seem to be that out of the difference in period of receipt of the consumption, of the original x, emerges a difference in utility consumed. Further, $x+x'$ in period p is also $x+x'+x^*$ in period $2p$. As a result even if the person endowed with x in period p were to invest it he would only receive $x+x'$ in period $2p$ and would remain behind now by the amount of x^*. However, once it is assumed that the individual with the greater initial endowment will eventually, after some finite time interval, consume the results of his investment, the individual who has received an initial endowment at a later period is immediately enabled to catch up with and equal the consumption of the individual with the earlier endowment. If we assume the simplest case, for example, that investment is only productive for one period (because the productivity of round-about methods disappears for lengths of time greater than p), then both individuals are enabled to consume the same alternative consumption bundles (x or $x+x'$), the only difference being in the periods in which such consumption is possible. Since this difference has been assumed to be, from the point of view of the calculation of utility, no difference at all, it follows that even with the possibility of production there will be no preference for present consumption unless such a preference is already posited outside of the conditions of and possibility of production.

It also follows, from this example, that x units in period zero are, in the absence of time preference, equal *in value* to $x+x'$ units *in period zero* since, by waiting, the owner of x can transform them into $x+x'$ in period p, the only difference in consumption being the time in which it takes place. This result is of special importance since it reveals concretely the manner in which the production of commodities denies to those commodities the character of scarce resources and thereby removes them from the category of objects of economic action, from the category of commodities.

If we assume more generally that any given bundle of consumption goods X may be transformed, given sufficient time, into any other conceivable bundle Y via production, then X and Y must be conceived, from the point of view of the neo-classical conception, as equal in value. More precisely, all rational basis for exchange between commodities at fixed rates disappears. No meaning can be attached to the exchange of commodity x for commodity y where x can be transformed into $2x$, or into y, or into $3y$, or into some combination of x and y. Since x can be so transformed over time it is, from the point of view of utility equal to $2x$ and to y and to $3y$, so that the owner of x is indifferent (so long as he remains indifferent to time of consumption) to possession of x, of $2x$, of y, of $3y$, etc. Clearly, under such conditions it would be absurd to conceive of x, y, or any combination thereof, as either scarce or as having a rate of exchange determined by their scarcity. This is to be expected when it is borne in mind that the foundation of the neo-classical conception of scarcity is in the givenness of the objects of need. This givenness is directly denied by the phenomenon of production which makes the objects of need also products. Since there is no scarcity (in the absence of discounting of future consumption) there can be no rational basis either for possession or for exchange. Furthermore, to the extent that inputs into production differ physically from the products, the round-about methods cease to be 'more productive' in any clearly intelligible sense. The absence of the value relation means the absence of any unity among the diverse objects of consumption ('utilities') so that the product ceases to be quantitatively comparable to the means of production; any concept of surplus product drops away.

At this point the conditions of positive time preference, diminishing productivity of round-about methods of production, and termination of the circuit of capital, reveal their true significance. It is on the basis of these conditions taken together that the circuit of capital becomes the simple circulation of commodities extended over time and that production may be incorporated into the theory of exchange without contradicting that theory. The latter is possible so long as time is scarce and so long as there is diminishing marginal productivity to cut off the expansion of value via production.

On the presupposition that present consumption is preferred to future consumption it becomes possible to incorporate production into the exchange economy without immediately denying the conditions of exchange. None the less the introduction of production into such a framework requires that production adopt a particular form. Production must be intrinsically 'productive.' That is, regardless of the system of value and exchange the act of production must yield a surplus product. Production exists only as a means to the end of the expansion of future consumption and not as a process which sustains itself. In other words, production has an irreducible existence which is independent of the market system and which can be taken up at the whim of that system. In this respect production possesses a character analogous to that of the original objects of desire of the simple exchange economy: it is given, available for incorporation into exchange, but does not require within its own constitution the conditions of exchange.

However, not only must production be present in this sense, as 'surplus-production,' but the productivity of available round-about methods must diminish with the intensity of their application. The greater productivity of round-about methods of production must diminish in order that production maintain future consumption as its goal. If the rate of return on investment were greater than the preference for present consumption and continued to be greater (or even increased) with capital deepening then there would be no limit to such capital deepening and, therefore, to investment. Investment in the present could only be for consumption in the indefinite future, investment for the purpose of future investment. In this case, the notion of scarcity would disappear altogether from both the spheres of exchange and production. The termination of the circuit of capital is the result of the condition of diminishing marginal productivity. This termination is synonymous with the circuit of capital finding itself subordinate to external conditions, subordinate to ends of consumption instead of being either *self*-sustaining or *self*-limiting.

On one side, the original derivation of the circuit of capital and its construction as the simple circulation of commodities extended over time, as a relation of consumption (present to future), is predicated upon the condition of positive time preference. All conception of interest, capital, and production as determined by and limited in consumption begins with this notion of the discount of future consumption. The scarcity of products is the result of the time required in their production and of the relation of preference to time posited within the neo-classical analysis. On the other side, the termination of the process of capital formation depends upon the condition of diminishing marginal productivity. Capital expands towards the goal of future consumption because the expansion of capital is made into the means of adjustment of present to future consumption. With production, this expansion is terminated, and therefore realized as adjustment to future consumption by the condition of diminishing marginal productivity. While time preference makes possible capital formation within the determination of the system of individuals oriented towards consumption of utilities, diminishing productivity realizes, within the conditions of production, this end point of capital expansion in consumption.

In sum, four conditions are necessary to the consistent integration of capital and production into the theory of the exchange economy. The simple deduction of capital and interest, where capital is nothing more than deferred consumption, rests upon two conditions:

1 The specification of preference in relation to time.
2 Preference for present over future consumption.

The conditions for the deduction of production within the exchange economy include the further requirements that:

3 Round-about methods of production be 'productive.'
4 Diminishing marginal productivity of capital or diminishing return to extensions of the 'degree of roundaboutness.'

These four conditions make possible the treatment of capital and production within the theory of the exchange economy.

So far as the critique of the theory is concerned this must vary in form according to which of the conditions, or pairs of conditions, are being considered. Those conditions dealing with the intertemporal specification of preference can only be criticized in connection with their total lack of systematic foundation, with the fact that they are arbitrarily posited and can be as easily and correctly rejected as accepted. As regards this aspect of the theory of capital the neo-classical argument can claim no theoretical force. Beyond this, it can be shown that the specific assumptions, while arbitrary from the systematic standpoint, appear eminently plausible when viewed in terms of their real origin in the process of capital and in the specificity of capitalist production. Such an origin, of course, denies directly any possibility that they may serve to ground the production of capital.

Leaving aside the conditions of intertemporal specification of preference, the treatment of production needs separate analysis and criticism since the positing of production goes beyond the methodology employed in the derivation of the exchange system. It is necessary to consider somewhat more concretely the nature of production as it is conceived within neo-classical thought and to deduce the precise character of that production which alone is consistent with the treatment of exchange. With the introduction of commodity production the elementary notion of capital as future consumption loses its transparency. Future consumption no longer is required to take the form of the refraining from the current use of objects of desire. Capital appears in the form of produced means of production which may differ in nature from the objects of direct consumption. In the light of this result (that consumption forgone is no longer of objects which are materially identical to those to be consumed in the future) the identification of produced means of production with 'intermediate products' and with 'consumption forgone' is no longer direct and must be established via argument. It is necessary, in particular, to show that produced means of production, even though not themselves consumable, still represent consumption foregone and that the relation of this foregone consumption, of 'capital,' to the return of future consumption is consistent with the original rationale for investment, that of preference for present consumption. In the light of this analysis the special and arbitrary conditions placed upon the character of production in order that it may be made consistent with the idea of scarcity of capital as the origin of interest may be clearly exposed.

Within the neo-classical conception of exchange the value of a commodity is grounded in and expressive of the manner in which that commodity relates to the consumption preferences of individuals. On this basis the derivation of capital begins with the notion of consumption as the goal of economic life. Where the circulation of commodities involves the circuit of capital it must be shown that the realization of the value of commodities in consumption is still the rationale of the peculiar circuit through which they run as elements of capital. What is crucial here is the difference between the 'simple circulation of commodities' and the circulation of capital. In the former, commodities exchange for money in the market only in order that they may, via money, be transformed into other commodities more immediately fitting into the needs of the commodity owner. By contrast, in the circuit of capital the value advanced as capital passes through the commodity form only in order to expand into an increased fund of value. This is the most general conception of capital and is common in form to all theories of capital. The problem which is specific to the neo-classical conception is that, in the case of the circuit of capital, the expansion of value as such cannot itself be the goal. Rather, it is the realization of the expanded value in consumption which can alone serve as rationale for the capital process. There can be no independent movement of value, no self-development, no value process *qua* value process. All value relations are expressions of the external relation of commodities in consumption, their falling out of (and permanent exclusion from) the circuit and movement in order to realize themselves as objects of direct consumption.

Capital is precisely that circuit of commodities which does not, at least directly, have consumption as its end, which, furthermore, rather than terminating at a given point in order to re-establish its conditions outside of its own process, finds its conditions within its process of expansion. This characteristic of the circuit of capital appears to deny directly the concept of purposive activity upon which all modern social science is founded. For neo-classical thinking, all economic behavior is the adjustment of scarce means among competing but given ends. The end of all economic activity, the goal of the entire economic process, is consumption. This goal must, therefore, be revealed within the circulation of commodities which is a mediating process between means and ends. Furthermore, this goal must be revealed in such a way as not to deny the means–end relation conceived as a condition of *scarcity* of means in relations to ends.

The problem of capital appears in neo-classical theory in the form of the need for the derivation of the capital relation in a way which denies the self-expansion of value as the basis of that relation and re-establishes that basis in the consumption of utilities. The problem is then one of the deduction of the capital relation within the theory of exchange in such a form as not to contradict the essential character of that theory. The concept of capital is required to spring out of the subjective value analysis. Within such a theory capital will only *appear* to be self-expanding. Instead, it is made to be, *in actuality*, the simple circuit of commodities *extended over time*. This construction then serves a dual role. First, it serves to establish a concept of capital consistent with the theory of exchange. Second, it serves to ground the introduction of production into the exchange economy in such a form as not only to fail to contradict the conditions of the exchange system but to be itself dependent upon those conditions. This is the task which the modern theory of capital has set for itself.

3 The neo-classical parable

The particular construction that has been developed for the purpose of conveying the neo-classical conception of profits reflecting the relative scarcity and technical productivity of the factor 'capital,' is that of an 'aggregate production function.'

The aggregate production function provides the basis for a 'model' of production and distribution designed to leave aside the implications for the theory of capital of the system of price relations. The abstractions required in order to effect such a construction are not considered defensible in themselves but only in terms of the intuitive appeal of the conclusions which are derived from that construction. As a result the treatment of capital ceases to be constituted as a theory of capital and is drawn instead as a 'simple parable.'

Since the simple construct cannot be conceived to possess any scientific status it is considered to be a parable. The whole point of such terminological sleight of hand is to prevent the untruth of the simple models from reflecting upon the status of 'neo-classical economics' itself. This intentionally ignores the fact that the contradictions intrinsic to the neo-classical conception not only discredit the simple 'model' but at the same time establish the necessity of formulating the central propositions of neo-classical thought in terms of simple models, therefore in terms of precisely the parables whose validity is not considered defensible. In so far as it is even possible to conceptualize the neo-classical notion in a systematic manner it must be possible to do so within the simple models – this is precisely from whence their simple character derives. It is, therefore, incorrect from the outset to characterize the simple models as mere 'parables.' They are synonymous with neo-classical economics to the extent that the latter is expressible (i.e. in words).

It is appropriate to examine here the internal structure of the parable in order to demonstrate precisely how the parable embodies the central features and propositions of neo-classical theory and reveals thereby the limitations of that theory.

The neo-classical parable is set out in terms of an economy which produces a single good, say, corn, using labor and stocks of corn as means of production. At the center of the parable is the production function for corn:

(1) $Y = F(K, L)$

which relates output of corn Y to inputs of corn-as-capital-good K and labor L. Production is assumed to be subject to constant returns to scale (F is linear homogeneous). Because of this we can rewrite (1) per unit of labor as

(2) $y = f(k); \; y = \dfrac{Y}{L}, \; k = \dfrac{K}{L}.$

The function $f(\cdot)$ is continuously differentiable with positive and diminishing marginal products of the factors. In particular, a 'well-behaved' production function satisfies the 'Inada conditions'[13]

$$f(0) = 0; \; f(\infty) = \infty$$
$$f'(k) > 0; \; f''(k) < 0$$
(3) $\lim_{k \to 0} f'(k) = \infty; \; \lim_{k \to \infty} f'(k) = 0.$

The full significance of these conditions will appear later. For the moment their meaning should be clear: it is always possible to find techniques for producing more (or less) output of corn per man by adding to (or reducing) the stock of corn relative to labor (the corn–labor ratio) no matter what the size of that stock is, short of infinity.

In a one good production system 'capital' is that part of output which is not directly 'consumed.' It is piled up and enters into production to be realized in consumption in the future. The advantage of the assumption of only one good produced rests first upon the fact that capital appears within such a system in its pristine form as pure deferred consumption. It is at once deferred consumption, produced means of production, and intermediate product. All the senses of capital are directly merged. With more than one product capital may still appear as intermediate product (in so far as consumption is still the end of the process as a whole) but the extent to which it is 'deferred consumption' does not emerge directly from the production system itself, from the act of production as intrinsically deferred consumption. Since capital is a good which is not directly consumable it is not directly deferred consumption. If its physical character precludes its immediate consumption then its use in production is not physical evidence that its owner has forsaken consumption. It becomes necessary to provide a further demonstration that the capital good represents or embodies future consumption, which demonstration will not spring directly from the material process of production itself. Formally it would be equally legitimate to view the consumption good as future production and investment. Directly, the production of capital is the result of the existence of a rate of return on its value since consumption of the means of production is excluded. The idea that consumption is future production and investment makes sense to the extent that capital is seen as 'self-expanding value' and subordinates consumption to its process of expansion. Capital accumulation as consumption on the part of productive labor in Smith's treatment of capital accumulation is a revealing instance of this opposition between classical (and to a greater extent Marxian) modes of thought and neo-classical thinking.

The preceding describes the available 'technology.' Given this technology and facing competitive markets with given price of output, wage rate of labor w, and rental rate of the capital good r (which, in this context, is the same as the rate of profit), the individual producer chooses that technique of production (a corn–labor ratio corresponding to a point on the production function) which maximizes his return (minimizes costs). This requires that in equilibrium that technique is chosen at which the marginal product of each input equals its price. We therefore have the equilibrium conditions

$$(4) \qquad r = \frac{\partial Y}{\partial K} = f'(k)$$

and

$$(5) \qquad w = \frac{\partial Y}{\partial L} = f(k) - f'(k)k.$$

By combining (2), (4), and (5), we get

$$(6) \qquad y = f(k) = w + rk.$$

Thus, payment to the factors according to their marginal products automatically exhausts the total product, which is in keeping with Euler's theorem.

The marginal product conditions (4) and (5) express in this context the profit-maximizing (or cost-minimizing) criterion for choice of technique that would be observed by each and every producer operating in competitive markets. Of course, under competitive conditions, the prices w and r are given to the producers. But, from the point of view of the economy as a whole, there is still a question of how these variables are determined. Equations (4) and (5) by themselves are sufficient to determine only two of the three variables, w, r, k. One of these variables (or a ratio of two of them, say, the 'wage-rental ratio' w/r) must be given independently in terms of additional equation(s).

It is at this point that certain analytical complications are suppressed due to the assumption that there is only one good which serves simultaneously as means of production and output. In a model of production with many 'capital goods,' the neo-classical assumption of a well-behaved production function is maintained with the different capital goods as inputs, then there is a marginal product for each of the capital goods taken separately in each line of production. The competitive equilibrium condition expressing the profit-maximizing choice of technique is that the money value of the marginal product (which is the marginal product times the price of output) of each type of capital good is equal to the money rental of the capital good (which is the price of the capital good times the rate of profit) and is the same in all lines. Thus the connection between the marginal product of the individual capital goods and the rate of profit is indirect: it goes by way of the prices which themselves depend on the rate of profit. When there is only one produced good which serves as capital good the situation becomes quite different. For then the relative price of this commodity is unity (it exchanges one to one against itself). Prices therefore drop out of the marginal product condition and, there being only one capital good, there is correspondingly only one such condition. A direct relation is thereby established between the marginal product of the capital good, which is a purely technological datum, and the rate of profit. The marginal product of the capital good is in turn uniquely related to the stock of the capital good per man due to the assumptions concerning the production function. It follows that there is a one-to-one correspondence between the stock of the capital good and the rate of profit.

At a given rate of profit, one technique is chosen. At a different rate of profit, corresponding to a different equilibrium position for the economy as a whole, the technique chosen, and hence the corn–labor ratio, would be different. It is possible to derive from the production function and the marginal-product conditions the exact relations that would prevail among the wage rate, profit rate and quantity of the capital good per man in different equilibria. Specifically, differentiating (4) and (5)

(7) $$\frac{\partial r}{\partial k} = f''(k) < 0$$

and

(8) $\quad \dfrac{\partial w}{\partial k} = -f''(k)k > 0$

which give the slopes of the equilibrium relations, the signs of which reflect the assumptions governing the production function. Associated with any corn–labor ratio is a unique set of factor prices and vice versa. An increase (decrease) in the quantity of one factor relative to the other is associated with a lower (higher) relative price of that factor.

It is possible to combine the two relations (4) and (5) to get a relation between the wage and profit rates that would prevail in different equilibria. By virtue of the Inada conditions, $r = f'(k)$ is a single valued function and therefore has an inverse such that

(9) $\quad k = k(r); \ k' < 0.$

Substituting (9) and (4) into (5) gives

(10) $\quad w = f[k(r)] - rk(r).$

This is the wage–profit frontier corresponding to the given technical conditions. A frontier such as this, giving the wage and profit rates consistent with the given technology under competitive conditions, could be computed from any technology in which any number of goods (not just one) are produced by themselves and labor.[14] Because of the special conditions underlying this particular frontier, however, certain special results follow. Specifically, from differentiation of (10) (or from dividing (8) by (7)) it follows that

(11) $\quad -\dfrac{\partial w}{\partial r} = k$

so that the absolute value of the slope of the frontier at any point on that frontier is equal to the quantity of the capital good per man. Furthermore, after multiplying (11) by r/w we get

(12) $\quad -\dfrac{r}{w}\dfrac{\partial w}{\partial r} = \dfrac{rk}{w} = \pi$

which says that the elasticity of the frontier at any point is equal to the ratio of total profits per man and wages per man or the relative share π of profits and wages in the net product.

Thus the parable tells us that, knowing only the quantity of the capital good per man and the technology, we can find from the frontier the corresponding wage and profit rates that would rule under competitive conditions. The elasticity of the frontier at that point gives the relative share of profits and wages. The distribution of income is therefore completely determined by technology and relative factor 'endowments.' An increase (decrease) in the quantity of one factor relative to the other lowers (raises) its price. The distribution of income varies accordingly, depending on the particular form of the technology, that is, depending on the 'elasticity of substitution.' In this way, the analysis incorporates the argument that relative factor prices reflect relative 'scarcity' of the different factors, and the amount which each factor gets from the aggregate product is determined by technology and relative factor endowments.

4 Capital formation and economic growth

Capital appears, within the model of production, as a product, therefore as 'produced.' To account for its existence requires, at this stage, introduction of the act (or acts) of 'capital formation.' It is this consideration which ties the problem of capital to that of economic growth.

In the essential neo-classical conception saving has nothing to do with capital accumulation and economic growth properly considered (although capital is 'accumulated' and the economy may 'grow'). Saving governs the 'endowment' of capital relative to labor, and, in particular, the relative capital intensity. This conception is most sharply distinguished where it is assumed that the population is stationary (and without a special argument there is no reason to assume otherwise). In this case there will be an approach to the stationary state which involves capital formation up to the desired capital stock but there is no accumulation of capital properly considered. This conception does not include any necessary process of sustained growth but only of growth which terminates when it runs up against the limits defined by the intertemporal consumption decisions of individuals, the available resources, and the schedule of the productivity of capital. Growth must, therefore, be stimulated by special conditions placed upon the nature of capital. Such special conditions are of two kinds: first, it is assumed that the labor supply is expanding at a given rate. If this is the case, then, simply in order to preserve the capital endowment per man of the original stationary state, it is necessary to expand capital. Capital is always running after the expanding supply of labor in an effort to maintain the optimal capital–labor ratio. The result is economic growth. However, the simple expansion of the labor supply is insufficient to sustain the growth process. It is further required that the recipients of income in each period be encouraged to save a portion of it appropriate to the preservation of a rate of expansion sufficient to maintain the capital–labor ratio in the face of the increasing supply of labor.

It is important in this connection to draw clearly the distinction between the expansion of the labor supply and the growth of population. The total population is the sum of individuals capable of holding factors and of defining a system of consumption preferences. Labor, on the other hand, is a factor endowment which individuals may or may not possess and which they may possess in varying amounts and in varying forms. The simple expansion of population can have no effect either on the capital stock or on the growth of the economy. It is only the expansion of the supply of the factor labor which can stimulate and make possible growth. Thus, sustained growth depends on the expansion of factor endowment. Factor endowment depends in the case of labor on the supply of labor and in the case of capital on the intertemporal consumption preferences of individual holders of factors. Growth can take place in the form of capital deepening even in the absence of a growing labor supply so long as individuals are willing to increase without limit their stock of capital, to put off further and further into the future the realization in consumption of their investment. This notion of capital deepening was typical of the original theories of capital within the neo-classical tradition which focus consistently upon that aspect of expansion which is the object of individual decision. Such a focus was not, however, capable of explaining sustained growth. For the latter the additional assumption was needed that the supply of a particular factor – labor – was expanding independently. This assumption is not only wholly arbitrary but inconsistent with the construction of the exchange economy. The process of capital formation may be subsumed within the exchange economy as the product of choice. The supply of capital, therefore the endowment of the factor capital, is itself produced, given the conditions of scarcity of time and of the productivity of round-about methods of production. The determination of the labor endowment, on the other hand, is simply given outside altogether of subjective consumption decisions expressed within the exchange system. For a consistent conception of labor as a factor it is necessary to make the supply of labor also the product of individual decision, to recognize explicitly that individuals make consumption decisions and that labor is a factor about whose consumption individuals decide. It has, however, generally been considered simpler and less problematic to derive sustained growth upon the basis that the supply of labor and its rate of increase are simply given. This assumption is the essential foundation for the idea of economic growth within the theory of the exchange economy. Clearly if such an assumption were disallowed on general methodological grounds and the growth of the labor factor made the product of individual decision making it would be difficult to account for sustained growth. In fact, the process of economic growth itself would fall outside of the theory of exchange and production unless special and hardly justifiable assumptions were introduced to the effect that the supply of labor does undergo a given rate of expansion.

The essential core of the neo-classical theory of growth is set out utilizing the concept of a production function as described in the previous section. Its contents can be sketched as follows.

Let there be given quantities of corn-as-capital-good K_0 and of labor L_0 available for employment. At any moment the available supply of factors is thrown inelastically upon the market. Factor markets can clear if factor prices settle at a level such that firms are willing to choose, in accordance with the profit-maximizing criterion expressed in equations (4) and (5), the particular combination of factors consistent with the available supply (K_0, L_0). In this sense there can always be full employment of available labor and 'capital' provided that wage and rental rates in real terms (that is, in terms of corn as numeraire) are free to settle at the appropriate level. Unemployment can occur only if, for some unexplained reason, the wage rate (or rental rate) is too high. In formal terms, what this means is that the procedure described in the previous section for obtaining the profit-maximizing choice of technique is now reversed. Instead of finding the corn–labor ratio appropriate to given wage and profit rates, it is necessary to find the wage and profit rates appropriate to given quantities of the factors. The assumed properties of the production function ensure the existence of a unique solution at positive levels of w and r for any arbitrary quantities K_0, L_0.

On the side of demand it is required for equilibrium that saving equals investment. Of course, in the parable world, whatever is not consumed (saved) from the total output of corn must be invested. This is because corn is the only form in which wealth can be accumulated and its investment in production always yields the going rate of profit. Thus there can never be any discrepancy between saving and investment decisions. The Keynesian problem of unemployment due to shortage of 'effective demand' is thereby ruled out.

With only one commodity produced the system of production made up of distinct and interrelated producing units each producing inputs of others through the use of products of the others gives way completely to the self-sufficient individual unit of production which is not dependent upon other units. The production of corn is directly and without any mediation the consumption of corn by productive workers. Production and consumption are the same. With one good produced the necessity of realizing its value in money disappears and the necessity of a distinction between money and real wages is eliminated. The 'circulation of capital' takes the simple form of the purchase of labor with corn. The possibility of disturbance of equilibrium, of uncertainty, of dynamic processes, is left wholly out of the account. Since labor is not itself the product of a production process there is only one true unit of production so that there can be no process of circulation of commodities among individual units of production.

The Keynesian theory of the 'monetary economy' can have no relevance to a world in which there is only one exchange possible, labor for corn, so that the idea of a distinct mechanism for the expression of general purchasing power (money) is redundant. This characteristic of the one-good model results not from the absence of money *per se*. Rather, it is the assumption of a one-good economy that excludes any real monetary relation. To introduce a monetary commodity into the one-good model is only to compound the confusion without making any real change in the basic process. The meaningful introduction of money requires the introduction of a system of commodity production in place of the one-good model.

The economy is assumed to undergo a process of accumulation involving a continuous increase (decrease) in the stock of corn per man while the rate of profit falls (rises) and the technique of production is continually adjusted to each successive level of the profit rate. Accumulation consists of adding part of the output of corn to the stock of corn already in existence. A change in production technique for the entire stock of pre-existing and 'new' corn can be implemented instantaneously and without cost in response to a change in 'factor prices' simply by varying the quantity of corn per man employed. In this sense, there is direct substitution of 'capital' for labor. Because of the assumptions concerning the production function, such substitution can be carried out indefinitely while continuing to yield positive wage and profit rates. Therefore, full employment of available labor and 'capital' is always guaranteed whatever might be the size of the labor force and stock of 'capital.' Furthermore such substitution can always go on until the steady state is reached.

This makes explicit the reason for the neo-classical conception of 'growth' only as full employment growth. Both the rate of expansion of capital and the rate of change of the capital–labor ratio are products of individual decisions on the part of consumers taken together with the given rate of increase of the labor supply. The entire underlying rationale for growth is either the approach to the desired capital stock, or, with continuous labor-force expansion, the maintenance of a desired capital–labor ratio. Growth is the manner in which the economy adjusts to the supply of labor and to the intertemporal consumption decisions of individuals, the manner of adjustment to changed (or to changing) factor supply.

From the point of view of the problem of factor returns, it can be seen that the basic idea is that of a one-to-one correspondence between the relative size of factor endowments (the corn–labor ratio) and the price of those factors. Once the factor endowment k is known and the technology corresponding to the production function $f(k)$, it is possible to derive from the frontier the corresponding configuration of factor returns. When this notion is embedded in a treatment of capital formation a further explanation is provided, in the case of capital, for the determination of the factor endowment and on the assumption of a given expansion in the endowment of the labor factor, of the capital–labor ratio. Corresponding to a given saving proportion and growth rate of labor there is a unique corn–labor ratio consistent with steady growth. A higher saving rate is associated with a higher corn–labor ratio; a higher growth rate of labor with a lower corn–labor ratio. The rates of return on the two factors differ according to the level of the corn–labor ratio. It follows that these rates of return depend upon factor endowment and technology. The factor endowments are themselves the result of intertemporal consumption preferences of individuals represented by the uniform saving propensity s and the forces underlying expansion of the labor force at the given rate n.

It would seem the logical next step to conclude that this analysis succeeds in fixing the distribution of income between capital and labor in terms of relative scarcity of the factors and the given state of technical know-how. So long, however, as the framework is interpreted strictly, no special statement is being made with regard either to the distribution of income between 'classes' or between individuals. There is no problem of the 'distribution of the net product' between capital and labor or between owners of the means of production and the owners of 'labor-power.' Rather, the problem is one of the determination of that price of the factors which is consistent with their scarcity, therefore of the 'rate of return' on 'capital' and 'labor' consistent with (1) technical conditions, (2) saving decisions, and (3) the given rate of expansion of the labor supply. These rates of return on factors then determine the net income received by individuals according to their particular factor endowment, the amount of capital and labor which they own.

It is evident also that what sustains the growth of the economy in this scheme is the expansion of the labor force, the rate of which is presupposed as an unexplained datum. Given this growth rate and the savings habits represented by s, the rate of accumulation adjusts so as to provide the 'capital' required to maintain full employment of the available labor force at the corn–labor ratio appropriate to a steady state. Steady growth at full employment is guaranteed by the assumption of (1) producers who are willing to carry out investment corresponding to whatever saving is going on, (2) a technology which always allows for choice of the appropriate technique of production, and (3) factor markets for 'labor' and 'capital' which ensure the wage and profit rates consistent with that technique. Thus what is specific to the neo-classical theory of economic growth is the conception of growth as a form of adjustment to individual consumption decisions and factor supplies. What is specific to the neo-classical theory of production and distribution is the conception of production as a purely material interchange involving technically specified factors of production and of wage and profit rates as factor prices uniquely determined by technology and factor endowments.

In general terms, the conceptual structure of neo-classical theory is one which conceives of the distribution of income as emerging from the pricing of goods and factors of production in a general equilibrium of competitive markets, the outcome being determined by the quantity of available factor endowments, the technology of production, and the preferences of individuals. Using Euler's theorem it can be shown that the value of the output produced with those factors and estimated at the prevailing market prices is exhausted by distribution back to the factors in accordance with their marginal productivities. The owners of the factors receive an amount of income corresponding to the specified amounts of the factors which each owns times their productivities. This set of relations emerges in a particularly simple and straightforward way in the 'one-commodity' model with two factors.

5 The specificity of the simple model

The necessity of formulating the neo-classical theory of capital and distribution in terms of the simple parable has come to the fore in the debate over the various attempts to formulate a consistent relation of capital to its rate of return along the neo-classical lines where production is allowed to take place within an advanced division of labor, as production of many distinct, productively interrelated commodities. The central element of the parable is the idea of an inverse monotonic relation between the quantity of 'capital' per man and the rate of profit. On this relation rests the conception that profits are the return to a factor of production, the rate of profit varying according to the scarcity of that factor relative to labor. On this relation rests also the notion that technical substitution between 'capital' and labor as factor prices change can be relied upon to bring about a state of steady growth with full employment. For this relation to hold in a world of heterogeneous means of production the parable strictly requires that there exist some measure of the quantity of 'capital,' representing all of the different capital goods, which, when it is put into a production function of the form

(2) $y = f(k); f'(k) > 0, f''(k) < 0,$

would satisfy the marginal product condition

(4) $r = f'(k)$

and satisfy, in addition, the product-exhaustion condition

(6) $y = w + rk.$

The relation (4) provides the linch-pin of this whole approach. It posits a single-valued relation between the quantity of 'capital' per man and the rate of profit such that

$$r = \psi(k), \psi' < 0$$

and

$$k = k(r) = \psi^{-1}(k).$$

If such a relation existed, it is argued, the parable would provide a 'good' representation of the world of heterogeneous capital goods. With the production function, it would be possible to 'predict' the unique value of r corresponding to any given value of k. In this sense it could be argued that technical conditions and relative factor endowments 'explain' the rate of profit.

Outside of the conditions under which the parable itself is constructed, however, there is no justification for assuming in general that the overall quantity of 'capital' per man should be inversely related to the profit rate, let alone that it should go from zero to infinity (with output per man increasing accordingly) through technical substitution of 'capital' for labor and that the relation should be continuously differentiable. In general, the means of production consist of heterogeneous commodities. They can be expressed as a single quantity by valuing them at their respective prices, or exchange values, in terms of a chosen numeraire. There is a different set of prices for each level of the profit rate, the exact pattern of differences depending on the technical conditions of production of the different commodities. The reason for this is clear. In competitive equilibrium, prices equal money costs of production consisting of wages plus profits calculated at the ruling rate on the exchange value of the stock of capital goods employed. At a higher (lower) rate of profit the wage rate is lower (higher). The difference in total costs and price depends on the exact pattern of employment of labor and means of production throughout the whole interdependent production system. The physical quantity of the capital goods and the methods by which they are produced may also be different from one equilibrium profit rate to another. Conceived in this way, the ratio of capital to labor cannot be regarded as necessarily an inverse function of the profit rate.

The quantity of capital in this sense, that is, as a sum of exchange value obtained by valuing the different capital goods at the ruling prices, depends on the rate of profit. Therefore, one cannot argue that the quantity of this capital (or its 'marginal product,' whatever that might be supposed to mean in this context) determines the rate of profit without reasoning in a circle. For there is in general no one-way connection going from the quantity of capital in this sense to the rate of profit. To express the different capital goods in terms of a single number one could have recourse instead to a number such as their physical weight. But then there would be, in general, no unique relation between that number and the rate of profit. And, whether unique or not, it would be of no special interest from the point of view of the economic problems under consideration. By contrast, the number representing the price of the stock of means of production does have economic interest, though from a different standpoint. Namely, it represents the basis for the calculation of the distribution of profit among particular capitals and is, therefore, essential both to the conception of the competition of capitals and to the treatment of the expansion of capital as a whole.

In moving from the parable world of one good to a more complex world of production with heterogeneous commodities we find also that the neo-classical argument runs up against another difficulty which is related to, but analytically distinct from, the previous one. This takes the form of the reswitching of techniques of production, that is, the recurrence of the same technique at different levels of the profit rate even though that technique is dominated by others at intermediate levels of the profit rate.[15] It follows from this result that, in general, techniques cannot be uniquely ordered according to the rate of profit. The neo-classical production function is based on the assumption that such a unique ordering exists. It is on this basis, as we have seen, that an attempt is made to draw a direct and unique connection between technology and distribution. But this assumption is contradicted as soon as allowance is made for such a small complication as that the method of production of the capital good differs from one technique to another.[16] The presumed connection between technology and 'distribution' is thereby effectively destroyed.

As a formal matter, the essential point is that the neo-classical parable assumes that 'capital' is a homogeneous substance measurable independently of the pricing system and of the determination of profits and wages, the quantity of which can therefore be made to 'explain' the rate of profit. In this form capital is a scarce factor of production formally no different from 'labor' and 'land.' It has been shown that in order for this equation to be sustained formally it is necessary that there be assumed to be a given price system for measuring the various commodity inputs and that this price system is invariant with respect to the rate of profit. This in turn implies that only one commodity is produced or that different commodities are perfect technical substitutes in production so that the price ratio between them is fixed. This is the special construction on which the neo-classical parable is based.

The impossibility of conceiving of capital as a scarce factor once it is clearly situated within an economic process involving an average rate of profit and the production of commodities by means of commodities also extends to the interpretation of capital as 'productive,' where productive is taken to imply that investment in more mechanized or more round-about methods of production yields greater consumption per man (up to a maximum). The increment in consumption is regarded as the return to the 'sacrifice' of current consumption involved in investing in the more mechanized technique. The profit (interest) rate is supposed to reflect, on the one hand, the trade-off between the return of future consumption and the sacrifice of current consumption consistent with the prevailing preferences of the system of individual consumers. On the other it is supposed to reflect the 'net productivity of capital' viewed as a technical characteristic of the round-about methods.

Whatever might be thought of the presumption concerning time preference it can be seen that the logic of the argument requires, first, that the profit rate falls as the degree of capital intensity or round-aboutness increases in consequence of the sacrifice of present consumption. Here reliance is placed on the presumption of an inverse relation between the rate of profit and the capital intensity of production as measured, for instance, by the quantity of capital per man. Now, however, it is required in addition that consumption per man rises as the profit rate falls and capital per man increases. On this basis, it is necessary to discover that there exists in any production system an inverse relation between consumption per man and the profit rate (up to a maximum of consumption) within the range of available techniques. This is a relation which is required to hold at the level of the production process conceived as a purely technical process.

It turns out, however, that in the examination of a given production system, the very opposite relation may be found. In particular, as between different steady states, a lower rate of profit may be associated with either the same or a lower level of consumption per man.[17] This possibility is clearly demonstrated by the existence of reswitching of techniques of production. Specifically, reswitching means that the same technique is adopted at both a high and a low rate of profit though not at profit rates in between. With the same growth rate prevailing in the two situations, consumption per man would be the same. Thus it is possible for the profit rate to be lower without any alteration in technical conditions and in the associated stocks of capital goods and without any difference in consumption per man. It would seem, in this case, that the profit rate is divorced from any conception of the 'net productivity of capital' and from anything to do with the 'sacrifice' of consumption for future return.

The possibility of reswitching of techniques of production cannot be ruled out in general. Moreover, even in production systems where reswitching does not occur, it could happen that consumption per man is lower when the profit rate is lower.[18] All of this makes for the untenability of the neo-classical conception in so far as this particular element is concerned.

6 Value and capital

The difficulty involved in the argument that round-about methods are necessarily 'more productive,' far from being the result of mathematical perversity or a mere 'curiosum,' originates in the problematic conception of production with which the neo-classical theory attempts to constitute the theory of exchange as the basis for a treatment of capital. This goes back to the original introduction of production into the exchange economy. Production of commodities, first, becomes the object of rational choice due to the presumed existence of positive time preference on the part of commodity owners. This, together with the given net productivity of capital invested in production, allows for a comparison between the prevailing rate of time preference expressed in the rate of interest and the net productivity of round-about methods. When those methods are more productive than the prevailing rate of preference for present goods it becomes rational to enter into production. In this sense it is argued that the extent of productive activity and the average period chosen (the degree of capital deepening or of mechanization) are determined by the time preference of the 'community' as revealed in the market for credit. The subsequent analysis pursued on this basis contains an explanation not only for the rate of profit but equally for the very fact of production. There is, here, an explanation, at least in part, for the entire process of 'industrialization' which is deemed to typify the modern world.

At the center of the neo-classical theory of capital, then, there is a special conception of production. The specificity of this conception is connected to the particular conception of capital upon which it is based and, ultimately to the theory of value which underlies the neo-classical concept of capital. The logical connection between value, capital, and production is the conception of the 'productivity' of 'round-about methods of production' as an attribute intrinsic to their physical specification, therefore as a net productivity 'physically defined.' It is precisely this condition which underlies the contradictions attendant upon attempts to extend the neo-classical parable to a system of many commodities. In the latter, prices must be employed so that the net product is not composed of a material physically defined but of value. As a result the substance – capital – under investigation is qualitatively distinct from the substance dealt with within the confines of the simple parable. This makes it impossible to claim that the productivity of capital has a material determination.

The contradictions which have served to undermine this claim from very early on place clearly into focus the intrinsic impossibility of conceptualizing the production process at the level of particular commodities as 'productive,' i.e. capable of producing a surplus. In so far as the neo-classical conception requires that productivity of capital have a purely material substance, that it be measurable as 'surplus product,' the possibility of relating this 'surplus' to a difference in value between inputs and outputs of the production process cannot be invoked. It is essential, rather, that surplus production be conceived independently of the 'value form' as a property of the 'technology' itself. What is required is a concept of 'surplus product' in a material sense which is independent of the system of price formation. Since the production process must be productive in this material sense there must be a measure of the quantitative relation of inputs, physically specified, to outputs, also physically specified, which is different from the value measure. Given this requirement the development of the 'one-commodity model' appears not as a simple parable but as the necessary manner of exposition of the neo-classical conception of surplus production. It is clear that the conditions of the neo-classical theory of capital and production can be met, in principle, only by equating the material character of the inputs with the material character of the product, therefore by eliminating all differences in useful form of commodities. Paradoxically, this reduction must leave aside all specification of the production process, all conception of the peculiarly technical features of that process. The equation of the useful forms of commodities is also the elimination of all specificity of those forms and, further, of the conditions which give rise to that specificity. The distinctions between use-values involve distinctions of their production processes, and in the specification of productive inputs.

Means of production, viewed technically, have certain determinate characteristics which can be described in mathematical, chemical, and mechanical terms. From the point of view of their technical aspect it is their specification in such terms which is central and which makes possible the physical production of objects. It is the fixing of labor into particular, technically distinguishable, useful forms which allows for the increased productivity of round-about methods involving the activity of living labor upon past labor.

In other words, production viewed as a technical process must be conceived in terms of the technical properties which distinguish it into the production of useful objects. Production as a technical process is intrinsically production of specific use-values distinguishable in form one from the other. For such a process, homogeneity of inputs is not only extraneous but impossible in principle. Production of use-values is specific to the use-values produced. Only production as also production of *value* (the labor process) can transcend this specification and equate inputs and outputs as values.

The specification of production in a technical sense as involving distinct and physically diverse objects is a condition for the idea of productivity of capital and for the associated idea of a 'production function.' The production function, even as conceived within neo-classical thought, requires both diversity of inputs and outputs and the application of capitalistic methods. It must be a function in labor and capital, in past and current labor. Different intensities of the cultivation of land, for example, require different means of production (intermediate products) and it is precisely the difference in technical specification of means of production which makes possible a difference in method of production. The underlying rationale for an association between productivity and capital intensity – the production function in corn and labor – is that the piling up of capital increases output per worker through the division of labor and therefore through the introduction of diverse equipment and means of production. The idea of a production function not only presupposes a division of labor but it equally presupposes a differentiation of labor taken in its physical specification.

Once this condition for the conception of the production function and the 'productivity of capital' is recognized it becomes clear that productivity has no meaning, for neo-classical theory, with respect to the individual unit of production to the extent that the latter produces as one element in a system of interdependent reproduction. The inputs and outputs are no longer quantitatively comparable in their material existence. A physical surplus only has meaning for the production system as a whole since only for the latter are the inputs and outputs materially comparable as vectors of particular commodities. Even in this case the possibility of calculating a net rate of return as a pure number presupposes certain very restrictive conditions on the proportions in which particular commodities enter into the net product and are employed in its production.* More importantly, even assuming that the system as a whole is productive and that that productivity is calculable in terms of a single measure, it is invalid to assume that any individual unit of production is capable of making production decisions in terms of that net rate of pro-

---

* As in J. von Neumann, 'A Model of General Economic Equilibrium,' *Review of Economic Studies*, 1945. It would also be possible to employ a construct such as Sraffa's 'standard commodity' and the related 'standard ratio' but while these have the property of physical measures they bear no necessary relation to the rate of profit which could be argued to fix the latter except in so far as they may be conceived to fix its upper limit.

ductivity. Some rule is still required for the distribution of the total surplus product among the particular production processes and, given that the surplus product is only meaningful as the product of the system as a whole, there is no purely material condition which is able unambiguously to effect such a redistribution in terms of the particular physical productivity of the individual producing unit. The surplus product of the system *in toto* is not visible or relevant to the particular production process except to the extent that it takes the form of the receipt of a surplus-value in the form of money. But this receipt, for example when calculated in terms of the value of capital invested, can be presumed to bear no special relation to the physical productivity of the individual unit since that unit is not conceivable as *physically* productive. The individual unit of production cannot be conceived to be productive in the Austrian sense and, therefore, production cannot be taken to arise out of the rational calculation of individual consumers or producers. The production of a surplus product cannot be taken to be the rationale for the investment of capital in production since the surplus product has a purely social existence.

It only becomes possible to constitute production as directly rational to the individual by severing production from the system of reproduction, of inter-dependent production of commodities by means of commodities. In this case the production of commodities collapses back into the conception of the individual producer-consumer and the conditions of aggregate production are equated with the conditions of individual production. The one-commodity model constitutes the production system *in toto* as a particular production process. With one commodity produced, all rationale for the division of production among many competing producing units disappears. As such, the one-commodity model is not so much a rigorous conception of a production system as it is a conception of the individual producer-consumer made directly consistent with the system of aggregate production. In this equation the aggregate production system loses its determination into many particular production units and the particular units lose their specificity in opposition one to the other. The production units all produce a single commodity using that same product as input. They are, therefore, independent of any need to exchange among themselves and need only purchase labor in the market in order to engage in continued production. To the extent that the producer himself possesses an endowment of labor it is unnecessary for him to have any recourse whatsoever to the market and production is severed entirely from dependence upon exchange. With the explicit introduction of production and capital the original rationale for exchange among individual producer-consumers disappears along with the elimination of differences among commodities and with the elimination of any scarcity of products.

The one-commodity model of production and distribution is the logical result of the attempt to conceive of the individual production process as immediately the origin of a material surplus product. The necessity of the latter conception is the result of the neo-classical treatment of the capital relation. The introduction of intertemporal preference together with the assumed material productivity of round-about methods allowed for the incorporation of a concept of production into the theory of exchange. Since the givenness of objects was the basis of exchange the notion of the object as 'product' could only be introduced in the most limited sense. The production of commodities could not serve to deny to commodities the characteristic of scarcity relative to desire. But with the production of commodities it is clear that the commodities are not themselves scarce since they are not quantitatively given. More correctly, while the commodity may still be scarce that scarcity is no longer directly connected to the givenness of its supply. Since objects are now products and not given their scarcity must emerge as an element of their production. The entire burden of the conception of exchange as involving the allocation of scarce resources falls not on the givenness of objects of desire but upon capital as a scarce factor, ultimately upon the fact that the production of utilities takes time and proportionally more time the greater the amount of produced utilities desired. With the commodity constituted as a product it ceases to be the immediate object of rational decision making within the conditions of resource constraint. All particular objects of need can be considered scarce only as embodiments of scarce factors, and particularly of capital. To the extent that production is itself the result of capital formation, of the preference for present consumption tied to the productivity of round-about methods, the effect of other scarce factors of production (i.e. 'land' and 'labor') is logically subordinate to the capital relation which accounts for all employment of other factors in production. The scarcity of commodity products is, then, in the first instance, an expression of the scarcity of capital.

As a result, capital must itself be conceived to be a *substance* which is scarce. This substance is no particular utility since it underlies, and is therefore common to, the production of all utilities. As products of capital all particular objects of need are distinguished only quantitatively – by the amount of capital embodied in them in their production. Capital, then, is that substance which remains once the equality of products is made explicit in their constitution as forms, or embodiments, of the factor capital. Since all commodities are now produced, they are equated by the indifference of the substance of their production to particular form, therefore by the ability of that substance to appear in different forms and to shift from one manifest form to another.[19] But what is this substance which is material and yet appears as indifferent to particular useful form?

Within classical and Marxian economics the substance of the commodity which is indifferent to the useful form of that commodity is its value. This value is 'intrinsic and not arbitrary,' it is the abstract, universal, social substance of the commodity. This conception is meaningful, however, only to the extent that there is retained in the theory a distinction between value – this universal social substance – and use-value, the particular relation to a given need. For the neo-classical conception, however, there is no substantive distinction between 'value' and 'use-value.' On the contrary, it is precisely the original underlying principle of that theory that value be equated with use-value so that both are suppressed and reappear as 'utility.' The value of the commodity is the relation of the commodity to individual preference. Value as relation to desire is an equation of value and use-value within which both lose their social character and appear as relations to individual preference. Since the neo-classical theory equates value and use-value it is incapable of conceiving of value as independent of use, of relation to need, therefore independent of *particularity* of the object of need.

In this case value is the immediate and irreducible relation of the isolated 'individual' to the object of his desire. Since this relation of individual to object is an immediate confrontation it is also a singular relation. It is *the* relation of individual desire to utility defined only in the immediacy and therefore in the irreducible particularity of *this* individual and *this* object. The complex social determination of the individual as a needy individual and as a commodity owner to the object as a value and a use-value gives way to the direct opposition of an autonomous, isolated individual and a utility.

This constitution of the relation of individual to object as irreducibly particular leads any attempt to abstract from that particularity in a conception of the relation into a dead end. Abstraction from the particular use-value does not lead to constitution of the value substance but, rather, to the constitution of a universal *material* substance, universal use-value. When the notion of capital expresses its requirement for a specification of the universal substance of the commodity this can only be met, within the confines of neo-classical economics, by that universal substance which is also particular, a simple universalization of particular useful form. Where value is use-value the universality of value can only appear as the universal use-value. And this universal use-value is capital; capital as corn, as 'leets,' as 'Meccano sets,' as 'putty,' etc. The fundamental significance of the one-commodity model for the theory of capital is precisely in the equation of value and use-value and therefore the constitution of value as the universal, the single, use-value. On this basis, and only on this basis, is it possible to conceptualize capital and the production of a surplus product solely as determinations of individual need.*

The idea that production can be conceptualized only by, first, leaving aside all specificity of useful form of the product in order to conceive of its capitalistic character in general is endemic to the history of economic analysis. This general treatment of production has, however, taken two opposing forms. Both of these forms appear at the origin of economic science in the works of Smith and Ricardo. First, production in general is conceived as a purely

* 'Hence, we see that behind all attempts to represent the circulation of commodities as a source of surplus-value, there lurks a *quid pro quo*, a mixing up of use-value and exchange-value,' K. Marx, *Capital* (New York: International Publishers, 1967), vol. I, p. 159.

material process, in the case of the Ricardian 'corn model' as production of corn by means of corn and labor. This is also the basis of the neo-classical parable. Second, production in general has been conceived as a 'labor-process' in which the production process once abstracted from particular material object and use form appears as the process of the production of value and surplus-value. This is the basis of the classical labor theory of value. In both cases production is conceived as surplus production, therefore as production based on capital. In the first case the surplus considered is a material surplus product. Such surplus production is given its definitive expression in neo-classical capital theory which focuses from the outset, and of necessity, upon the production of a physical surplus as the real nature of the capitalistic process.

In both cases it is the initial abstraction from particularity of useful form which makes possible the conception of productivity and it is the latter which sets the foundation for the analysis of profit and of price based upon profit-making calculation. But, so long as capital is deferred consumption, the productivity considered on this basis must be that of a material surplus product and the measure of capital, independent of price, must be a measure based upon the elimination of all possibility of distinction in useful form among the products of capital. This is no longer an initial abstraction since in the absence of the specific assumptions employed in the construction of the simple model none of the essential conclusions derived on that basis can be presumed to remain valid. The neo-classical theory, which is articulated on the basis of the absence of production, therefore of the givenness of the objects of need, once extended to the treatment of production becomes the neo-classical parable of production and capital formation in the absence of all exchange of commodities. The concept of capital, rather than providing the link between exchange and production provides an impenetrable barrier required by a conception of exchange-value which cannot be reconciled with production and a conception of production which is equally irreconcilable with any conception of exchange including that upon which it is itself founded.

Chapter 7
Problems in the theory of production

I The laws of returns and the theory of price

The effect of an increase in the demand for a given commodity on its price has been a central problem of economic analysis since the original formulation of the neo-classical conception at the end of the nineteenth century. The issue is specific to the neo-classical mode of analysis of economic relations and, indeed, constitutes its defining feature both with respect to the treatment of the pure exchange system and with respect to the treatment of commodity production. With regard to the latter it is the determination of the shape of the supply curve for the particular commodity which is central. The conditions within which this problem is originally formulated involve the association between an increase in demand for a given commodity and a rise in its price brought about by increasing costs of production; therefore the conditions of 'rising supply price.' This increase in the supply price is brought about by the increasing cost of scarce factors the price of which rises with the intensity of demand for their employment in production. This connection is the central theme of the neo-classical treatment of capital and production and it is in connection with this contention that the deficiences of the neo-classical conception of value, capital, and distribution are revealed to be fundamental. The absence of an inverse relation between the quantity of capital and the rate of return undermines the conception of the economic process as a mechanism of 'resource allocation,' the same conception which is embedded in the idea of rising supply price. In particular, it is not possible to sustain the idea of scarcity of capital where the quantity of capital is not taken to be a given datum fixed with respect to the price system but is constituted, instead, as both pre-condition and result of the totality of the economic process. With the constitution of the quantity of capital as a function of the system of economic relations as a whole both as regards its intrinsic measure and as regards its formation, capital can no longer be conceived to be a 'scarce factor of production.'

The treatment of price and production within the neo-classical conception differs fundamentally, in precisely this respect, from that of the self-reproducing economy characterized, for example, in Piero Sraffa's *Production of Commodities by Means of Commodities*. For Sraffa production is a self-sustaining process and is, by that fact, independent of any externally determined 'factors of production.' This formulation bears this quality in common with the Marxian conception of simple and expanded reproduction. In the case of the latter the equilibrium conditions of intersectoral demand are explicitly introduced so that the sense in which production creates the pre-conditions for continued production is made explicit. Not only does produc-tion of means of production preclude the idea of capital as a scarce factor but in so far as relative prices are determined within such a conception they can only arise as products of the process of reproduction itself. What is funda-mentally problematic about the neo-classical analysis of production emerges through the consideration of the relation of price to production within a context for which the primary requisite of production is not the existence of factors of production but production itself.

If the problem of price is considered in terms of the functioning of an economy operating under given conditions of technology and at a given level of production then this may be seen to imply not a given set of choices between different methods of production but the production of commodities at a given level of development of the productivity of labor. There is, in this case, neither a 'book of blue-prints' nor a 'continuous production function' but the product of the achievement of a given level of know-how. The differ-ence in conception is critical. Even in the application of the so-called 'non-substitution theorem'[1] the predominant notion is that of justifying the elimination of the choice of technique on the basis that under certain con-ditions the choice actually arrived at through the economic process will not be affected by the scale of production. Changes in demand and in the dis-tribution of income affect prices through the connection between scale and costs of production. This latter connection is based on a link between changes in scale and switches in technique. To eliminate such switching is to pro-foundly alter the conception of the economic process as a whole. But within the conditions of the non-substitution theorem it appears that the elimination of switches in technique and, therefore, the emancipation of price from the determination of the distribution of output is only possible under very special assumptions (e.g. of 'constant returns to scale'). The theorem on substitution does not so much remove the choice of technique from the theory of price as it serves to clearly express the dominant role of the choice of technique by emphasizing the special assumptions required in order to remove the effects of switches in technique on price.

The problem of the scale of production within the neo-classical theory (or, more correctly, the problem of the distribution of output) is posed in the framework of given and fixed factors of production which are allocated to different spheres of production in accordance with the distribution of output. The problem of the scale of production of a given commodity, therefore, enters into the determination of the price of that commodity in so far as changes in scale affect the cost of the inputs of factors of production necessary to the production of that commodity. Scale of production becomes important for the individual firm because of the existence of diminishing returns to scarce factors. Indeed, the idea of a 'factor of production' is synonymous with that of diminishing returns.

The importance of this result can be seen in another way. For the neo-classical theory of production the problem of the level of production for the individual firm is a problem of the existing scarce factors of production and of the demand for the product of the industry within which the firm operates. By contrast, where price is embedded within a system of reproduction, the problem of the scale of production is a problem of the theory of accumulation and of the growth and development of the economy. But the problem of scale when posed in terms of the growth of the economy as a whole has nothing to do with 'factors of production.' It is not possible to think of the accumulation and growth of the economy where there exist essential requirements of reproduction in limited supply. The idea of accumulation grasps a process which creates its own conditions of existence, reproduces and thereby determines itself over time. Expanded reproduction based on externally limited conditions, as of the supply of necessary inputs, contradicts directly its own conception. The only possible long-run rate of accumulation under such circumstances would be zero and the economy would reach the 'stationary state' when it had reached the limit naturally defined by the given supply of factors of production.

On the other hand, if the determination of the level of production is a part of the analysis of capital accumulation then the concept of a scarce factor of production is necessarily excluded. One of the most striking results of this approach to the problem is that not only does the concept of factors of production disappear but simultaneously the whole idea of a choice of technique disappears with it. Where accumulation is going on so also is technical change as a necessary part of the accumulation process, which latter could not be considered as a whole in the absence of changes in technical knowledge. There is, in this case, no choice of technique at all but the development of new techniques which are technically more advanced and which necessarily drive out the older methods of production.

Taking into account shifts in the level of production does not, under these conditions, imply the notion of marginal cost pricing. On the contrary, the notion of the marginal producer comes to be linked into the process of obsolescence and depreciation which is inseparable from technical innovation and the diffusion of new technique. Price is determined not by the demand-created need to maintain marginal units in operation but by this process of diffusion of innovation. Price is driven *down to* (and not up to) the minimum costs of operation of the marginal firms and eventually the competitive pressures will drive the price below that minimum level. The dynamic relation of marginal producers and of marginal costs to price has nothing to do with scarce resources but is, rather, tied to the expansion of the economy as a whole, to the accumulation of capital, and to the introduction of technologica innovations.

Under these conditions it is wholly incongruous to assume the existence of constant, increasing, or diminishing returns to scale. Nor is it sensible to consider the number and productivity of fixed factors. Theorems on substitution become altogether irrelevant to the determination price. It is precisely the introduction of the conditions of expansion that makes possible the treatment of the scale of production both for the firm and for the system as a whole. In this case the treatment of the scale of production is severed from any notion of scarce factors of production and is, indeed, antithetical to the implied conception of production. There need exist no 'primary factors' nor any presupposition concerning the possibility of increasing the scale of production with the given technique.

As a result of this, the problem of equilibrium price determination under conditions of resource constraint drops away. For the neo-classical theory it is essential that equilibrium involve a mechanism which directly limits the scale of production of the individual firm. Since price is a function of scale it is necessary to determine price and scale jointly so that there must exist an equilibrium scale of production of the firm which is limited and determined by the conditions of production themselves. The price system is seen to allocate fixed factors only in so far as the limit on the supply of those factors is expressed in the determination of price. The fixed factors govern price by limiting the scale of production, determining the optimal scale of production and along with it the equilibrium price and level of production.

Price determination within the system of reproduction requires no such mechanism. The conditions of competition are expressed through the relation of prices to prime costs (the 'gross margin'). The size of the firm is determined by the extent of its growth in the past. The number of firms in existence is given by the historical conditions and in particular by the level of development of technology, the market, and barriers to entry. The determination of all of these latter processes can only be considered along with the treatment of accumulation. What has arisen as a problem of the firm in neo-classical analysis and is considered there as a problem of the theory of value appears in this connection as a problem of the theory of accumulation and technical change.

In so far as the conditions of competition between firms involve directly the process of accumulation, the determination of competitive conditions (the gross margin, the size of firms, barriers to entry, etc.) is not even possible at the level of analysis of simple reproduction and of the Marxian 'prices of production.' The forms taken by competition within the accumulation process must be clearly distinguished from the elementary determination of competition which underlies the formation of price in the context of the Sraffa system. The simple distinguishing of firms according to their technical conditions of production and the derivation of price on that basis leaves out of account the various bases of competition between firms which arise once the further distinctions which relate to the requirements of accumulation are introduced.

II The factors of production

1

Once the process of production is treated within the context of a self-reproducing system, the concept of factors of production drops out. But it is possible to go one step farther and consider the meaningfulness, in a general sense, of the idea of fixed factors and therefore the rationale for eliminating them altogether from economic analysis. It is instructive, in so doing, to start with a treatment of the idea of labor as a factor of production since, even in the light of the weaknesses of the treatment of capital within the neo-classical theory of production, the idea of a factor of production is retained without question in the case of labor and land. It has even been argued that the idea of a labor theory of value is ultimately based on the idea of labor as the sole primary factor of production. From the point of view of economic analysis it is equally pertinent to question the status and meaning of labor as it is to question that of capital, the issues are, in fact, intimately connected.

Does the impossibility of determining the quantity of capital independently of its value also extend to the determination of a quantity of labor? The answer to this question is that in one sense it does raise important questions concerning the concept of labor. It must be emphasized from the outset, however, that it does not do so with respect to the possibility of measuring or aggregating labor *in general*, but only in terms of the method of measurement which implicitly underlies the idea of labor as a factor of production. The point, to anticipate the results of this discussion, is that the problem is not one of uncovering 'native' or 'natural' measures for economic variables. In so far as the attempt is made to find a natural measure of the inputs into production the analysis must remain within the confines of the 'factor of production' viewpoint. It is only by considering specifically economic measures relevant to productive inputs considered in their economic relations that it becomes possible to distinguish classes of inputs and to discover the appropriate measure for those classes.

The immediate issue, as posed within the literature on capital and distribution, is that of the origin of a principle for the equation of labors which are assumed, *a priori*, to differ, in other words of a measure for 'labor.' It is, first of all, clear that it is not necessary that 'labor' be assumed to be homogeneous. If 'labor' is considered as a purely physical entity then it is no doubt true that laborers differ in terms of skills, aptitude, strength, dexterity, attitude, and so on. Moreover, the definition of labor in terms of its technical form (as specific 'useful labor')[2] implies that the meaning to be attached to labor depends upon the particular task for which that labor has been employed. In this sense there exist as many different kinds of labor as there exist different kinds of production. The labor of the baker is one kind of labor involving one set of specific activities which differ, for example, from those of the truck driver. By what justification are these different forms of work to be reduced to the common dimension of labor time, a labor time within which wholly different activities take place?

It is obvious that this is precisely the same question which is posed in the literature on the possibility of measuring capital. If we consider a lathe, for example, there is no question but that it possesses a specifically technical definition. From the point of view of the science of technology the meaning of a 'lathe' is bound up with certain principles, with the interrelation of its parts, with particular forms of motion and power, with mathematical and geometric concepts in terms of which it is technically described. The idea of the labor which goes along with the lathe is also defined and specified in these same terms.

But, alongside its technical description, the lathe may also have an economic existence which requires a description in economic terms. This duality is expressed directly in the problem of measuring capital. This problem does not arise for technically defined means of production. These latter have no internal need to be 'added together' or 'aggregated.' They are, as technical objects, wholly indifferent to their status as elements of an aggregate of value (capital which is homogeneous as to dimension). The same is true of labor. Labor as a specific, technically defined, set of tasks is not homogeneous as to dimension. If labor is defined technically then it not only is not necessarily homogeneous but it cannot logically be homogeneous.

Yet, the idea of a factor of production is precisely that of a technically defined input. It is from this point of view that the idea of a factor of production takes on its power as a basic principle of the theory of value and distribution and in terms of which it differentiates the neo-classical approach to the conception of the economic process. It has already been shown that means of production as an element, or moment, of capital are grasped in their economic and social rather than purely material existence. Once it is understood that capital is not 'means of production physically defined' but a specific economic relationship it becomes possible to measure capital in terms of that measure which grows directly out of that economic relationship. Capital, understood as a social relationship, is 'self-expanding value,' a fund of value invested in the interest of the creation of increased value (profit). Capital is value in process and may be measured as value. The fact that at a certain level of analysis the value measure is not independent of other economic relations (such as the distribution of income between capital and labor) in no way compromises it as the valid measure of capital.

How is labor measured in its economic existence? It would be hardly reasonable to argue that such a measure is indifferent to the peculiar characteristics which labor brings to the process of production as a technical process. What must be emphasized is that the special characteristics of labor engaged in production which allow for the formation of an aggregate of 'average' or 'abstract' human labor have both a 'technical' and social origin; technical in that they evolve directly out of labor as an element of the production process, and social in that that process is itself conceived as an eminently social one. It is only with regard to the social character of labor that the notion of a sum of different kinds of labor can take on meaning.

This opposition between the 'technical' and the 'social' existence of commodities should more properly be an opposition between two aspects of the social existence of the products of labor – their 'use-value' and their 'value.' The use-value of the product is by no means a property of a purely natural or individual character having to do either with the direct relation of the object to a particular individual's need (the object's 'utility') or with the purely material properties of the object. The use-value has to do, rather, with the situation of the product within the ongoing process of social production and with the isolation of the general role which it plays in that pre-eminently social process. This point is quite clear in relation to the Sraffa system within which the useful properties of the products (or commodities) are wholly defined within the system of productively interrelated roles which they play so that the use-value of any given commodity can only be defined in connection with its interrelation with the entire system of commodities. When we speak, therefore, of the technical properties of commodities we refer to their useful character and not to any purely material, natural or individual character which they are supposed to possess.

Once this is taken into account the manner in which a homogeneous measure of labor arises becomes straightforward. Labor as an input into the economic process exists in the form of the potential to do different kinds of labor. Labor, as potential labor, 'labor-power,' may be adapted to all the various forms of work and therefore may be abstracted from the specifics of those different types of work in order to arrive at abstract general labor, which labor has lost all of its specific attributes and appears in its simple form of pure labor time. So long as differences in this abstract labor are considered they are differences of training and skill or of strength and dexterity. The former of these are specifically social differences which have nothing to do with the innate technical or physical character of the laborer and which may, therefore, legitimately be reduced according to some economic principle to a common measure. The latter differences in labor are innate to the individual but may be eliminated from the point of view of the economy as a whole for which a general average can be arrived at. This average (which only exists for labor considered in its social existence) in its turn determines the quantity of 'labor' (in an economic sense) expended by laborers of differing capacity.

This principle need not be tied directly to the remuneration of the laborer. There is nothing unreasonable about considering skilled labor to itself embody more labor than simple labor and, therefore, to be the application within a given period of time of more simple labor. The fact that practically it would be difficult, or even impossible, to accomplish this empirically in no way eliminates its relevance to the specifically theoretical problem involved. It is, perhaps, pertinent in this connection to question altogether the relevance of raising the issue of the reduction of skilled to unskilled labor at this level of analysis. The pre-conditions necessary for the emergence of skilled labor within the process of capitalist production are quite complex so that an account for skills and especially for their development can hardly be assumed at the level of analysis of the value of commodities. Here again it is the analysis of value and capital, of commodity exchange in general which sets the foundation for the consideration of the concrete problems of capitalist production which appear in the first instance to conflict with the treatment of value. This appearance can only be dispelled when the propensity of modern social science to present the entire complex of relations of modern society in its immediate existence, at once and without regard to the specific logical order implicit in those relations, is itself dispelled. The 'skilled labor reduction problem' is just such a false issue having its origin in the failure to make explicit the concrete pre-conditions for the treatment of specific relations. Here, 'skilled labor' appears as an empirical presupposition of the entire analysis so that to speak of abstract, general labor it is *first* necessary to reduce skilled to unskilled labor. This, of course, takes the category of skilled labor to possess intuitive self-evidence and not to itself require any systematic theoretical derivation. The problem is removed from the concept to the subsidiary question of its quantitative dimension.

Labor conceived as a purely technical or physical quantity in the narrow sense cannot be readily reduced along a common dimension while labor as an economic factor not only can be so reduced but is necessarily reducible to labor in general. What must be emphasized in this connection is that the idea of labor in general could never arise where the labor process is viewed as the domain of the individual isolated producer. Only where the labor of the individual is seen to constitute an element of the labor of society as a whole does it become possible to abstract from the individual peculiarities of individual processes of production and consider the manner in which those individual processes involve the application of a social substance.

This result also has a specific historical and technical origin. The ability to abstract a common substance from the different types of labor engaged in production is itself a product of a specific stage of economic development. Of central importance to this development is the creation of what Marx calls the social productivity of labor or the productivity of social labor. Prior to the development of capitalist production the working up of useful objects occurred within a rigidly fixed and, from the standpoint of modern technology, narrowly confined process whose essence lay in the specific skills of trained handicraft workers. Not only was labor in process non-transferable but so also was the capacity for labor since that capacity was not separable from the peculiar training (often over a protracted period) of the worker. The specific product of the resulting process was stamped with the character and personality of the specific worker or craftsman (who is not, strictly speaking, a 'worker') and was to that extent an artistic creation as much as it was an economic product. Labor was, in this respect, inseparable from its specific application, so that as far as the handicraft process is concerned we are not dealing with 'labor' at all.

With the development of capitalist production, and, in particular, with the development of modern machinery, these archaic relations are dissolved so that production ceases to be the domain of the individual craftsman but is now a process in which large numbers of laborers, hardly distinguishable in terms of training and skill, work together. The labor process as a technical process takes on a pre-eminently social character.

The technical potential for the full mobility of labor finds its economic expression in the development of the labor market. Within the latter the possibility of directly substituting one unit of labor (labor-power) for another reveals the social nature of that labor. The separation of the worker from the means of production which is originally a phenomenon of ownership becomes the direct corollary of the destruction of the individuation of labor and of the ties between specific laborers and specific aspects of the production process. Such a development may not, from the point of view of the historical experience, be absolute. It none the less gives expression to a dominant tendency in the development of labor which is given theoretical expression in the category of 'abstract' or 'average' human labor.

There is a difference of considerable importance between labor and means of production in terms of the possibility of aggregation and measurement which is seen to arise in both cases as a result of the consideration of their specifically economic dimensions. It is in the nature of means of production to be specifically designed to accomplish a particular task. Labor-power exists as the potential for labor in general. Means of production exist as the potential to serve a rigidly defined function. This result is not surprising if it is borne in mind that means of production are in the nature of *past* labor which has been congealed into a particular form. This, on one level, is precisely what distinguishes means of production from labor. Means of production considered not as simple tools but as machinery are restricted by the particularity of their product. This restriction is implied in the idea of a machine which, in contradistinction to a tool, embodies the idea of the product within itself. Machinery simultaneously deprives labor of its specification to the product by taking upon itself that specification. If means of production were to possess a measure independent of their price it could only be in abstracting those means of production from their specific characteristics as fixed or congealed labor of a particular form in order to consider them as the previous application of labor in general. It follows that means of production may be aggregated independently of price when they are measured as past human labor. But this principle of measuring capital by labor is no different from the principle of measuring specific forms of labor as labor in general and arises, ultimately out of the principle that labor-power is the abstract potential to produce different, particular use-values.

Capital, understood as particular means of production, can be reduced to so much embodied labor and the implied relation of capital to labor serves to reveal an essential element of the concept of capital. On the other side so long as capital is understood as 'self-expanding value,' and not as so many particular means of production, capital exists as a value relation which, in the first instance, is independent of any particular useful embodiment and can be transferred, without loss of character or magnitude, from one form to another. Capital, taken in this sense, cannot be considered simply an embodiment of labor, although it may be measured in labor time, but must be considered an economic process which taken as a whole is itself a condition for the existence of the labor measure. Once the notion of general abstract labor is taken out of any natural or intrinsic determination as so much purely material substance it comes to possess certain social pre-conditions which are bound up with the process of capital.

Capital, as a fund of value, may be transferred from one use to another; but this can only be done for capital as a fund of value. Capital in the form of means of production is not so transferable. It follows that capital can only be seen to be of homogeneous dimension when it is considered as value, or as congealed past labor. It is not, from the point of view of this result absurd to consider the correspondence between capital as value and capital as congealed human labor.

Labor, on the other hand, must be measured in terms which are independent of price, where price expresses costs of production. To measure labor by price where price reflects cost of production is to measure labor by cost of production where costs of production are nothing other than labor; therefore to measure labor by labor. A price measure of labor is, rigorously speaking, a contradiction in terms. The quantum of abstract human labor is the individual unit of labor, the definite period of labor time. Labor, therefore, understood as a social substance, is measured independently of price and therefore of the distribution of the product between wages and profit.

The possibility of aggregating and comparing quantitatively, qualitatively distinct types of labor is not a simple result of the fact that labor possesses its own natural measure. It is, rather, because of the specific role of labor in the economic system as a whole and in the process of production. Labor has, in its time of application, an objective measure as a result of the fact that the substance of specific types of labor is the abstract capacity of labor to apply itself to qualitatively distinct tasks. But this is the result not of the naturally (one might say biologically) given properties of human beings. It is, rather, the result of a process that is at once an historical process which creates labor in the abstract at a certain level of development of society, therefore within the confines of a determinate social form, and of a process of the reproduction of that specific social form; of capitalist production. That labor which is measurable as pure labor time is a social rather than natural product.

Labor possesses a further, purely economic, characteristic which fundamentally distinguishes it from means of production. The latter is produced in a two-fold sense. First, it is the product of a particular process of production, the transformation of specific inputs into a technically specific output. It is, second, a product of a production process of a capitalistic character. This is important from the point of view of determining the movement of the amount of capital. The latter is a function directly of the accumulation of capital and of those economic forces which determine the profitability of expanding production and the extent to which it is profitable to expand production in certain directions. Labor, on the other hand, is not the product of a capitalist process of production. Labor (or more correctly labor-power) does not have a price determined by the profitability calculus of the capitalist firm. The supply of labor cannot be readily contracted and expanded with the requirements of the reproduction of the economy as a whole in the manner of other commodities. It follows that there is a sense in which labor is given in supply to the economic system as a whole. This is not to say that the supply of labor is not a product of economic development, but, rather, that the character of dependence in this respect is different from that of other commodities.

2

Land, as the generic term for non-reproducible means of production, differs from both capital and labor in that it is fixed in supply and has no production equation. Land therefore is not only not produced within the capitalist firm but is not produced at all. Can land be considered a factor of production physically defined? It is clear that the fact that land can be measured in acres does not constitute even *prima facie* evidence that it may be considered as a factor of production on the same footing as labor. Clearly, if land is viewed technically it separates into an indeterminately great number of distinct types of land which it is not possible, or desirable, to add up quantitatively. In this sense the acre is no more and no less a common measure of land than is the kilogram a common measure of machinery.

Land enters into the determination of economic processes only in its economic dimension (which latter, of course, is not indifferent to its technical specifications) and only as a product of specific economic relationships. The fact that, at least in general, land is not considered to be reproducible in no way allows for it to be considered as a purely physical entity. This does, however, affect its economic conception. Whereas in the case of capital the measurement problem can be resolved directly in terms of the theory of value and in terms of the reduction of means of production to past labor, this is not the case for land.

It is from the standpoint of land as 'non-reproducible means of production' that the idea of 'scarcity' arises within the theory of production. From the point of view of the exchange of commodities scarcity appeared, within the neo-classical analysis, to be bound up with a relation between the needs of the individual and the limited supply of objects which could serve to meet those needs. This whole conception cannot, however, be sustained when the production of commodities is taken into account because in that case it is no longer sensible to consider the world of commodities as 'given' in relation to the needs of the individual. So long as the supply of goods is capable of increase without limit the notion of scarcity conceived in this manner must be seen to have lost its foundation. On the other hand it is clearly possible to sustain some idea of scarcity even where production is allowed if there exist limited supplies of certain inputs into production. Land, it is argued, is scarce in the sense that it is not reproducible; or, at least, that the extension of production may require the bringing into use of less efficient units of land so that the 'scarcity' of land will be expressed in an increased price which accompanies the increase in the scale of production. It is clear that where production is taken into account scarcity in this sense may only be attributed to land (or, in general, non-reproducible means of production). Both capital and labor are not given in quantity and although the conditions of production of labor are distinct from those of capital this distinction does not abolish the fact that the supply is in both cases (leaving land out of account) capable of increase without limit.

It should be immediately noted that even were land to be considered as limited in this sense analysis of the scale of production would still be wholly unnecessary to the determination of the price of output and the rent of land. So long as the scale of production is taken as fixed in the manner considered earlier and the distribution of income between wages and profits, the productivity of labor, along with the conditions of production with the different qualities of land are also fixed the rents and prices are determinate without regard to possible effects of changes in that scale.[3] The determination of the latter may then be left to the theory of accumulation, leaving no room for the operation of demand in the typical neo-classical sense as a force acting upon the economic system from outside. Furthermore the association between the return to land (rent) and the marginal productivity of land is left with nothing to bite on since the notion of the margin does not enter into the conditions of the problem.

Neither is it sensible to consider the scale of production to be limited by the existence of land. Such a limitation exists only where the level of output is considered to be independent of the rate of accumulation. If productivity were taken to be given while accumulation takes place the result would logically be the approach to the stationary state. The bringing into cultivation of units of land of lower and lower fertility would squeeze profit margins to the point where the rate of investment would fall to zero. In this case the level of production may be considered to be determined, or at least faced with an upper limit, by the available supply of land. On the other hand, if the accumulation process is considered as a whole rather than within static assumptions then there is no reason whatever to even consider the existence of non-reproducible inputs as limiting to the scale of production which must, rather, be determined by accumulation in the past and by the current rate of accumulation. Accumulation, when placed in direct association with technical change, is capable of creating new substitutes for existing limited inputs into production.

It is clear, even from these considerations, that the sense in which land may be taken to be a 'fixed factor' needs further consideration. Where land is treated as an element of the conditions of simple reproduction, reproduction on a given scale, the sense in which it is scarce is expressed in the idea of rent. Land is only scarce, within neo-classical economics, to the extent that it can command a price in the market (this is, in fact, the definition of scarcity). Since land is a productive input, a factor, it can only have value by merit of its return. The existence of a return is the condition of its possessing value in exchange and is the basis of the calculation of that value. The notion of scarcity of land depends therefore upon the manner of emergence of its return, therefore upon the interpretation of that return, upon the conception of rent.

The general idea of rent divides into two distinct cases which must be considered sequentially. These cases concern, first, the existence of 'absolute rent,' and second, the two forms of differential rent which arise from the two types of marginal or no-rent land.

Within the neo-classical theory of price the existence of limited supplies of factors of production may be expressed in two ways. First, it may be simply assumed that the factors are free goods up to the point at which the demand for them exceeds their supply. Under these conditions if all land were homogeneous and if the level of production were such as not to require the employment of all of the land the rent would be zero. Alternatively it might be assumed that land, even where it is not cultivated, is still appropriated so that the supply of land depends on the rent available. Therefore in order to bring land into use even where the entire available supply is not required will require some payment to the owners of the land. There is under these conditions a positive 'supply price' of land. Formally this is precisely what Marx has in mind when he analyzes 'absolute' ground rent.

This formal similarity, while important to the treatment of the problem of rent, should not be allowed to obscure important differences between the notion of an 'absolute ground rent' and the 'supply price of land.' For Marx the existence of rent was not bound up with appropriation in general but with a specific relation between landlords and capitalists.[4] It is clear that in the case of absolute rent the rent expresses a determinate social relation and not the pure physical qualities of the land. Marx himself points out that the existence of land appropriated by a class of landlords is given to capitalist production as a legacy of prior social formations,[5] and is therefore extraneous to the idea of capitalist production as a pure form. Marx notes that were the land to fall into the hands of the capitalists themselves absolute ground rent would disappear.[6] This is an important result in that it may be seen to imply that the assumption of a zero supply price of land is not an unreasonable one for a fully developed capitalist economy within which the class of landlords has lost any significant hold on the appropriation of land and therefore any significant independent existence. The latter is, of course, a matter of degree but represents the necessary standpoint for the theoretical treatment of the problem. Ultimately, the issue depends upon the origin of the appropriation of land and therefore on whether it is reasonable to simply assume that land is appropriated without regard to the specific economic and social setting within which the appropriation of the land takes place. The notion of the supply price of land is bound up with the idea that appropriation arises directly out of certain given psychological characteristics of the individual so that, regardless of the social milieu, it is necessary to assume that the supply of land is owned by individuals who must be paid a special fee for its use. By way of contrast, the idea of a zero supply price for factors which are abundant expresses directly the capitalist logic of the problem in its pure form. Abstracting from the existence of landlords, capital will be employed if and only if a profit is to be made and so long as that profit is at or above the normal rate there is no need for the additional incentive of payment for the use of land.

The neo-classical adaptation of the Ricardian theory of rent is more closely related to the question of differential rent than absolute rent. In general, it is logical to assume that the entire supply of land is not in use for two reasons. First, there exist alternatives to land of any given quality so that increase in demand rather than exhausting the supply merely requires the substitution of different types of land. Equally important, is the development of technical knowledge which creates additional replacements and substitutes for any specific form of land. The idea of an 'intensive margin' when tied in this way to the effects of changes in technique and the effect of such changes on the supply of substitute factors eliminates altogether the rationale for assuming that the entire supply of a factor is required for production.[7] The existence of an intensive rather than an extensive margin on land expresses the fact that the limitation which the existence of non-reproducible inputs places on production is relative to the state of technical knowledge. Furthermore, what is limited as far as production is concerned is not predominantly the supply of land but the level of productivity of the land which is not a factor intrinsic to the land itself but a joint product of the physical characteristics of the land and the application of technical knowledge to production on the land. With developing technical knowledge the margin on land may move in any direction with changes in the scale of production. In other words where changes in scale are tied to accumulation and technical change their effect on rent and on the determination of the movement of the margin of production is no longer amenable to the neo-classical interpretation. This underscores the earlier conclusion that under conditions of growth the idea of scarce factors is necessarily excluded.

Where the problem of value is treated under conditions of simple repro-duction the idea of a marginal product of land is without foundation and cannot be used to determine the rent either as absolute rent or as differential rent. Within the framework of simple reproduction it is possible to clearly illustrate the determination of rent and the role of scarcity. Consider an economy in which one sector (or department) produces means of production through the use of means of production and labor (sector I). Sector II produces means of consumption and employs labor and means of production produced in sector I. The means of consumption are produced on two distinct units of production employing land differing in quality and possibly techniques of different specifications. Let ρ stand for the gross profit rate,* w the wage rate (consumption goods per unit of labor), Y_{ij} is the output of sector i unit of production j, K_{ij} the means of production employed, L_{ij} labor, B_{ij} land, and η_{ij} rent per unit of land. Then

(I) $PK_1\rho + wL_1 = PY_1$

(IIa) $PK_{21}\rho + wL_{21} + \eta_{21}B_{21} = Y_{21}$

(IIb) $PK_{22}\rho + wL_{22} + \eta_{22}B_{22} = Y_{22}$

where P is the rate of exchange between means of production and the con-sumption good. It is assumed that the rates of profit, wages, and depreciation are uniform on the different units of production. It has also been assumed that land does not enter into the production of the means of production. Since there is no absolute rent one of the η_{ij} must be zero while the other is greater than zero:

(III) $\eta_{21} \cdot \eta_{22} = 0$

and

$\eta_{21} > 0$ or $\eta_{22} > 0$.

It is not, in general, possible to determine which unit of production is 'marginal' (or 'no-rent land') independently of the distribution of income between wages and profits. It is necessary to solve for the rents simultaneously with the remaining variables.

---

* Profit is calculated only on the means of production and not on any part of the wages bill for purposes of convenience of exposition. It might be mentioned that this approach yields, to a degree, to the interpretation of profit as an outgrowth of means of production rather than capital. Profit should, in principle, be tied to capital which may include a part of the wages bill.

Dividing through the equation for unit of production ij by L_{ij}

(I') $Pk_1\rho + w = Py_1$

(II'a) $Pk_{21}\rho + w + \eta_{21}\beta_{21} = y_{21}$

(II'b) $Pk_{22}\rho + w + \eta_{22}\beta_{22} = y_{22}$

where $k_{ij} = K_{ij}/L_{ij}$, $y_{ij} = Y_{ij}/L_{ij}$, and $\beta_{ij} = B_{ij}/L_{ij}$.

Taking the wage and gross profit rates as given and solving (I'), (II'a), (II'b), and (III) for first η_{21} and then η_{22}:

(condition 1): $\eta_{21} > 0$, $\eta_{22} = 0$ for

$$\eta_{21} = \frac{w(1-\mu) - y_{22} + \mu y_{21}}{\mu \beta_{21}} > 0$$

where $\mu = k_{22}/k_{21}$.

(condition 2): $\eta_{21} = 0$, $\eta_{22} > 0$ for

$$\eta_{22} = \frac{w(1-\mu) + y_{22} - \mu y_{21}}{\beta_{22}} > 0.$$

Condition 1 (2) holds where condition 3:

$$\mu > (<) \frac{y_{22} - w}{y_{21} - w}.$$

Only in the case of the Ricardian extensive margin is the marginal land determined independently of the wage. Where the difference between the two units of production is not associated with differences in technique so that $k_{21} = k_{22}$ condition 3 reduces to

$$y_{21} < (>) y_{22}.$$

The marginal land is that with the lower output per worker where the difference in output per worker is wholly attributable to differences in the quality of the land. Rent per unit in this case is

$$\eta_{21} = \frac{y_{21} - y_{22}}{\beta_{21}}, \text{ or } \eta_{22} = \frac{y_{22} - y_{21}}{\beta_{22}}.$$

Since it is possible to determine the no-rent land independently of prices and wages it also follows from (I) and (II) that prices and wages may be determined independently of the rents and, therefore, of the inputs of land by the conditions of production on the no-rent land (where land as an input does not enter), in the sector producing means of production and by the distribution of income between wages and profits. Ricardo was the first to systematically analyze this connection between price and rent. He arrives at the same conclusion and argues that the problem of relative price is prior to that of rent so that the rent of land is determined by the prices of commodities rather than the prices of commodities being determined by the rent of land. This result is expressed more generally by Sraffa who conceives of land in terms of the distinction between 'basic' and 'non-basic' commodities. This distinction makes possible the systematic connection of the conditions of self-renewal to the determination of price with the intervention of commodities which are not fully determined within the reproduction process. In this case the external determination of the consumption ('luxuries') or production ('land') of the non-basic is shown to be precisely that quality which deprives such commodities of any determining role in the formation of price. This is a result of the highest importance in establishing the determination of price within the self-reproduction and self-expansion of capital. Non-basic commodities are the peculiar subject-matter of the neo-classical theory. The latter is, however, incapable of accounting for the determination of their price precisely because it abstracts from the process within which their price is determined. Thus it is only through the activity of the basic commodities that the non-basics take on their economic character.

Within the conditions of simple reproduction where the neo-classical margin has been eliminated, there is nothing for the idea of land as a scarce factor to fix upon. The existence of rent presupposes and expresses the prevailing difference in the quality of the land but there is still no meaning to be attached to the idea of 'diminishing returns to a scarce factor.' Scarcity is expressed in the co-existing difference of quality rather than in the movement along a margin.

Furthermore, even under the simple conditions of this model the no-rent margin is capable (for $k_{21} \neq k_{22}$) of shifting from one unit of production to another where different rates of wages are compared so that:

$$\eta_{21} > 0 \text{ for } w > \frac{y_{21}\mu - y_{22}}{\mu - 1}$$

and

$$\eta_{22} > 0 \text{ for } w < \frac{y_{21}\mu - y_{22}}{\mu - 1}.$$

This is the effect of the differential impact of increases in the wage on the costs of production of the two units of productions where the proportion of those costs made up of wages differ. It is not even possible to determine which is the less productive piece of land independently of the wage.[8]

Where the economy is growing over time and technique is changing the determination of the marginal unit of production depends on the inter-relation of technology, distribution, and the 'innate' qualities of the land. Where different units of production employ different techniques the determination of the marginal land no longer emerges directly from the natural fertility of the soil. Since it is not even possible to determine the margin directly from the 'land itself' the latter can hardly be considered a 'scarce factor physically defined.' When the margin is 'intensive' in this sense the idea of diminishing returns to a factor of production becomes wholly incomprehensible. Under these circumstances it is more reasonable to consider the phenomenon of land in terms of differing techniques of production on differing kinds of soil rather than in terms of the productivity of a factor of production.

This is not to deny that the existence of differential rent expresses a natural limitation, or condition, on the production of commodities. On the other hand, it cannot be argued that rents express directly and solely the physical properties of the land. Those properties, except under special conditions, cannot be considered the direct determinants of rent and the idea of scarcity of an input is not expressible independently of the system of economic relations within which it occurs. Thus while the technical idea of differentials of quality of land may be expressed in terms of productivity the economic expression of this technical fact requires the full development of the economic analysis itself while the qualitative measure of the scarcity of land (rent) measures not only that 'scarcity' but equally and necessarily the specific economic system within which it is defined.

It follows that land can no more be considered a factor of production than, from the point of view of the social process, it can be considered 'non-produced.' The fact that land is not the commodity product of a particular firm and is equally not the product of a labor process makes of it a peculiar sort of commodity. Like means of production but unlike labor-power it is specific in its use to the production of particular commodities; and like labor-power but unlike means of production it is not produced within the firm. This specificity accounts for its peculiar economic characteristics but does not exclude it from determination within the ongoing process of reproduction and accumulation. Land, as a social relationship, is a *product* and not a *fixed factor*.

Chapter 8
Foundations of macroeconomics

I Competitive price: the individual producer-consumer and the firm

1

Neo-classical economics takes as its starting point the individual 'producer-consumer' who consumes directly the products of his own activity and whose activity involves him in relation only with physically defined factors and not with a world of individuals upon which he must depend. The significance of this condition is that production on the part of the autonomous individual involves no explicit social conditions. The economic system as a whole is reducible to the individual producer-consumer and the latter stands immediately for the totality of economic life. As indicated in chapter 6, this standpoint places intractable obstacles in the path of the emergence of a concept of the economic system as a whole, and, in so doing establishes what we have argued is the key problem of neo-classical analysis: the market system must be derived without independent determination, as the product of whim it must remain arbitrary and ungrounded – the surface expression of a reality which is indifferent to it.

There is always a tendency, however, for the abstractness of the construction of the economic system as external to the individual to break down. This breakdown occurs within the development of modern economics in the course of analysis of the phenomenon of competition and in the related rise of opposing notions of the economic system as a whole: that of 'macroeconomics' with an implicit if undeveloped and problematic specification of the world of capitals, and that of 'General Equilibrium' which drives toward the consistent construction of the whole as bearing an exclusively external relation to its individual parts.

Competition is the process of construction of the world of individual capitals. Competition, therefore, constructs both the individual capital as individual, that is as one among many opposing particular capitals, and at the same time constructs the world of capitals as the world of opposing individual capitals taken as a whole. In the competitive process the individual units meet and establish among themselves the basis of their relation as parts of a single economic system. The conception of competition reveals most clearly the prevailing relation between the individual units of capital and between each unit and the totality of particular capitals. The concept of competition is, therefore, a nodal point in the consummation of the neo-classical project of the construction of the economy. It concentrates the central contradiction of modern economic theory into a single problem: the precise manner of construction of the system as a whole, of a world of 'interacting' individuals.

2

The first attempt to work out systematically the contradictions and implications of the neo-classical treatment of competition (in its Marshallian form) appeared in Piero Sraffa's examination of 'The Laws of Returns under Competitive Conditions.'[1] Sraffa's primary concern was with the relation of demand to price. The necessity of such a relationship is synonymous with the idea of modern economics so that the recognition of its problematic character could not be lightly dismissed. To the extent that price is functionally related to demand it is at least possible that price may be interpreted in terms of the allocation of scarce resources according to need. The adjustment of price to demand leads directly into the conception of price as an index of the relation of demand to supply which directly reflects in its movement the changing relation of need (demand) to the available resources capable of fulfilling that need (supply). On one side, the demand for a product is expressed in a functional relation between the price and the quantity demanded and, on the other side, the supply of a commodity is expressed in an analogous functional form. In the demand relation the intensity of the desire for the product is offset by its price. This appears as the immediate corollary of the notion of demand itself and of the idea of diminishing marginal utility attached to that notion. It is the result of the fundamental postulates of the theory of consumer behavior. The supply curve, on the other hand, except in one instance, bears no similar immediate interpretation. So long as the supply revolves about the production of the commodity it is grounded not in the psychological predisposition, assumed irreducible, of the producer, but in the conditions of production. Only where the total supply of a commodity is fixed does its supply curve become the other side of the demand curve and come to be determined in precisely the same manner. In such a case each individual is endowed with a fixed quantity of resources and the amount that he supplies of each to the market involves the simple balancing of his desire for the object which he owns against his desire for the object which he intends to purchase with the resource. Thus, in the simple Walrasian framework the supply curve is the reverse of the demand curve (Figure 1).

Where there are two traders involved in the market, the most elementary of exchange phenomena, the demand curve for one commodity is the supply curve for the other from the standpoint of each individual. As a result demand and supply are both identical to each other, as the reverse functions expressing the same process, and are at the same time radically separate one from the other since they are the functions of different individuals. The demand for my product reflects the desire of the other trader while the supply of my product

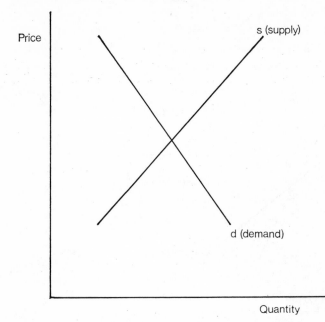

Figure 1

reflects my desire. Supply and demand are, therefore, wholly disjoint and independent so long as individual preference is itself independently, that is personally, determined. At the same time, and by that same fact, both supply and demand are determined by the same force – individual preference – and are revealed within the same process – the immediate exchange. Thus while demand and supply are wholly independent they do not differ at all in character and origin. Just as individuals are equal before the market because they are wholly opposed as self-determined without regard to any external relation, are equal therefore by merit of their absolute opposition, so also supply and demand of commodities are the same by merit of their reflecting identical processes within absolutely opposed individuals.

On the other hand, once production is considered as the foundation of supply the problem becomes more complex. The identity of supply and demand phenomena which underlies the determination of market price in the simple model breaks down. In this case it is necessary to justify the presence of supply curves which are simply the reverse functions of demand curves where supply and demand no longer have an origin which is directly equivalent. An element of indeterminacy introduces itself into the construction of the supply function which may exhibit a variety of forms (Figure 2) depending upon the determination of supply, therefore upon the conception of production which underlies that supply. Within neo-classical thought these alternatives are conceptualized in terms of the state of 'returns to scale.' The

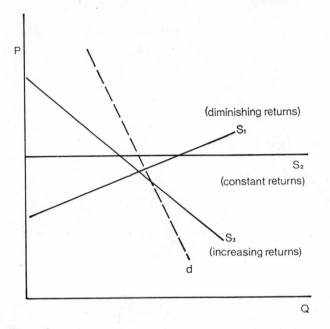

Figure 2

indeterminacy of returns to scale reflects the abstractness of the manner of conception of production itself within neo-classical thought. The determinateness of production appears three-fold: first, it appears as a state of diminishing returns where production is conceived as the allocation of scarce resources and remains dependent upon the presence of given and fixed factors of production. Second, production is expressed in constant returns to scale where scarce factors are absent and the conditions of production are products of related production processes. In this case production has nothing to do with the allocation of scarce resources but is implicitly unlimited so that price comes to be independent of demand. Third, there is the possibility of 'increasing returns' which expresses, albeit in a neo-classical form, the conditions of accumulation and technical change, the growth of the unit of capital.

The only form which is capable of sustaining the neo-classical conception is that which is identical to the simple supply curve of the exchange economy (s_1). If the state of diminishing returns is connected to the supply price of fixed factors it becomes the exact corollary within the theory of production of diminishing marginal utility in the theory of consumer behavior. Diminishing returns derived on this basis reflect the direct utility of the factor to its owner so that the supply curve of the factor comes to underly the supply curve of its product and the simple Walrasian exchange economy in which supply and demand are two sides of one phenomenon is re-established. So long as production remains the transformation of scarce factors in this manner it is consistent with, because identical to, the theory of the exchange economy. The unit of production is nothing more than an intermediary between two sets of individually generated information: the supply of scarce factors according to price offered, and the demand for the products obtainable with the use of the scarce factors according to the price of those products, therefore according to the price of the factor. The fundamental process is in no essential respect different from the original simple exchange. The only difference is in the necessity of transforming the factors into the utility or utilities demanded in the market. This transformation defines the activity of the firm.

The firm understood in this sense takes both the supply of its factors and the demand for its product as given to it since it serves a purely technical function. The unit of production serves this function to the extent that its intervention connects consumption of the utility to employment of the factors required for its production. In principle, there is no reason for a distinguishable agency to engage in this function since the individual producer-consumer can as readily gather the necessary factors required in the production of the utility demanded. This result is necessary to the extent that the 'firm' serves this limited 'technical' function. In this case the production of commodities is simply an element of their direct consumption. There is no real 'firm' or unit of capital separate from a world of independent producer-consumers. In other words there exists no systematic theoretical justification for the presence of 'firms' within this conception. In the light of this absence not only of a theory of the firm but of any possibility of such a theory modern economics is driven to deal with the problem in terms of *ad hoc* arguments relating, for example, to 'indivisibilities.' From this standpoint the specification of the firm must remain wholly arbitrary.

The constitution of the firm rests upon the development of a certain degree of interdependence of production so that the exchange system is itself dichotomized into the purchase of direct utilities and the purchase of productive inputs. The latter defines the market activity of firms in contradistinction to direct producer-consumers. The latter supply 'products' for consumption but do not produce those products with produced inputs purchased on the market. For the firm to emerge as a distinguishable entity it is, therefore, necessary that a certain interdependence of production be posited. This is conceived within the neo-classical framework as the purchase of a set of factor inputs by each producer from other producers. This condition taken by itself constitutes production as the production of commodities by means of commodities and eliminates scarcity. Case s_2 results rather than s_1. Conditions of 'constant returns to scale' are inadequate to the determination of the equilibrium of the firm and of the exchange system as a machine for the allocation of scarce resources. It is, as a result, necessary that interdependence of production be retained within a production system which also displays scarcity of products and therefore of factor inputs.

The central contradictions of the neo-classical theory of the firm all originate with the attempt to meet simultaneously two opposing conditions: interdependence of production as condition for the distinguishing of the activity of the firm from that of the producer-consumer, and scarcity of products as condition of equilibrium of the firm and of the constitution of production as consistent with the conception of exchange.

So long as all factor inputs are purchased in the market, scarcity of the products of the firm is not assured and a fixed limit to the activity of the firm does not emerge. In order for the firm to face a limit to its expansion, therefore to be able to achieve an equilibrium condition, it is necessary to assume further that there exists at least one necessary factor input which is fixed in supply. Further, for independence of the productive activity of the firm to be sustained there exists the additional requirement that the whole of the factor be employed in production of the given commodity. As Sraffa has pointed out the law of diminishing returns requires specification of factors to production processes if a determinate equilibrium of the firm is to emerge. The only basis for deriving an equilibrium of production under conditions of diminishing returns is that, in the case of at least one factor, the production process employ 'the whole of the factor of production.'[2] The conditions for the derivation of the neo-classical conception of the firm as agent of production are, therefore, the following: (1) In order that the firm not collapse back into the individual producer-consumer the former must be made dependent upon the total system of production. This dependence takes the form of the purchase of the products of other firms which serve as necessary factor inputs into its production process. (2) In order that this purchase of inputs in the market not contradict the independence of supply and demand in the determination of market equilibrium price, it is necessary that the products purchased not be scarce or fixed factors. If the inputs purchased in the market are themselves scarce, yet employed in more than one production process, then the level of production in one process would react upon costs in the other (or others) possibly affecting the demand curves for the two products (as in the case of substitute commodities). The produced factors purchased in the market cannot, therefore, be fixed but must be employed under conditions of constant cost. (3) Therefore, scarcity can be connected to production only by assuming that, in addition to the produced factors purchased at constant cost, the firm also employs a fixed factor which is not produced and is only employed in the production of a single product. Conditions (2) and (3) together assure both independence of supply and demand since all factor inputs are either purchased at constant cost or are fixed and specific to the particular production process and also interdependence of production, since each producer must go to market to acquire necessary factor inputs from other producers.

The contradiction involved in this construction is that, while it may be conceivable for any particular unit of production, it is illogical when extended to the entire system of production. If the assumed conditions held for all

particular firms then the produced inputs would appear themselves as transformations of scarce factors which could not be supplied at constant cost. To
the extent that the scarcity of the fixed input exerted a real influence on the
production costs of the particular product the employment of that product in
production of other firms cannot but affect its price. In this case independence
of supply and demand would break down since the supply of the product,
being dependent upon conditions of the production of scarce inputs would not
be independent of the demand curve for the product which latter may also be
tied into production of the scarce input.

It is possible to circumvent this difficulty only by considering a fixed factor
which limits the expansion of the firm but does not limit the expansion of the
industry as a whole within which the firm operates. The industry as a whole is
characterized, then, by constant costs while the firm is characterized by the
traditional U-shaped cost curve. The contradiction considered here is the
logical basis for the introduction of the factor 'entrepreneurship' which fixes
the conditions of cost in precisely this manner. The individual firm, since
endowed with only a limited amount of entrepreneurship (or of management
capacity) is limited in its expansion. The industry as a whole, however, and
therefore production as a whole, expands via the accretion of new firms at
constant cost (i.e. the new firms face the same conditions of cost previously
experienced by the established firms and operate at the same optimum scale
and cost). There is, it needs to be emphasized, no justification for this special
condition other than that in its absence there can be no theory of the firm
within the neo-classical conception. In particular this is in no sense a condition
which springs out of the logic of the theory of exchange and production.

The only way out of this difficulty is to establish a further condition: (4) All
essential inputs are fixed factors specific to the production of particular commodities. This condition contradicts the presumed interdependence of production and negates the essential condition for the deduction of the firm.
Where this condition prevails the effects of interdependence of production are
eliminated since interdependence of production is itself eliminated. The
specification of a commodity product to a scarce factor is complete so that the
analysis has, in effect, returned to the Walrasian exchange economy of
independent 'producer-consumers' where production is present but remains
wholly individual. Since each production process is specific to a factor (or
group of factors) the supply curve of the factor (or factors) is the supply curve
of the product. The demand curve of the product is given by the preferences of
individuals and the supply curve is the reverse of the demand curve of the
owner (or owners) of the bundle of factors. The analysis reverts to Figure 1
and the economic process is constituted as the allocation of scarce resources.
But in this instance a critical sacrifice has been made in order to achieve a
determinate equilibrium of the firm. In effect, the determinateness of the firm
as the mediating factor between the production and consumption of the
commodity produced has disappeared. The firm is now the isolated producer-

consumer who produces a surplus product which is exchanged in the market. It holds a supply of factors which can produce a particular set of utilities which are not inputs into production but only final products so that the only real market is the market for final products. The latter reverts once again to the simple exchange economy. Since each factor is specified to the production of a specific commodity the rationale for a distinguishable factor market disappears.

3

The neo-classical theory of the firm was originally constructed in order to demonstrate that production did not contradict the theory of exchange. In order to sustain this construction it is necessary, however, to add to it the special condition that production is not interdependent but the purely individual transformation of scarce factors. In effect it was necessary to collapse the firm into the immediate producer-consumer and to collapse the production of commodities by means of commodities into the exchange economy. The firm entered to mediate production and consumption in such a way as to allow for their separation as separate functions within the economy without undermining the primacy of consumption as a final and fixed goal of production. In order to accomplish this end it was necessary, however, to obliterate all sign of the social nature of the production process since it is that social determination which requires the constitution of the particular unit of production as a mediating term.

For Sraffa the condition necessary for the construction of the exchange economy with production – specification of factors to particular products – is unsatisfactory because implausible. This implausibility, however, requires a deeper consideration. What is at stake in the transition from the simple exchange economy to the system of exchange based in production is the conception of production itself, the constitution of production as a determinate process. The introduction of the firm as a necessary and separate entity within the economic process rests upon the special character of production on the part of independent firms. With an economy of firms, and production within the firm, production takes place without any direct connection to consumption. Unlike the individual producer-consumer who can consume and survive on his own product without any external relation, the firm produces not for its own consumption but for that of its customers. This separation becomes necessary to the extent and only to the extent that the independence of the producer is abrogated and he is himself required to act separately as a consumer not of his own products but of the products of other producers. It is not conceivable that each individual producer can be self-sufficient and at the same time find customers on the market who will be continually in need of his merchandise. Put more generally it is not possible to have each individual self-sufficient and yet find that his productive activity possesses a necessary social expression.

The production which is relevant to the conception of the firm is, therefore, sharply distinct from that which is relevant to treatment of the individual producer-consumer. It is this distinction in the implicit understanding of the production process which involves exchange and the formation of price on a new and more profound basis. The specific form of production which takes place within the firm bears a necessary and systematic connection to the exchange of commodities and serves ultimately to ground that exchange.

In order for production to ground exchange production cannot be conceived as the transformation of fixed factors into utilities. Such production plays no role in grounding exchange and exerts no force upon the character and magnitude of the exchange. It is, rather, the supply conditions of the scarce resources relative to the intensity of demand for their direct consumption or for the consumption of their 'products' which limits and determines the price of the product. By contrast, production which grounds exchange can only be production for exchange, production of commodities within which the quantitative and qualitative nature of production depends upon the exchange of the product and the relation of the price of the product to the costs of production (the price of commodities purchased for purposes of production). Production must also be by means of commodities which are themselves products so that exchange also depends upon production. A thoroughgoing interdependence of production is established and any conception of the direct producer-consumer becomes impossible. Once the connection between exchange and production is explicitly drawn and production is sought as the ground of exchange and not as extraneous to exchange, production comes itself to be concretized. It becomes necessary to consider production as that production which leads of necessity into exchange, which is specific in its internal requirement that it lead out of itself in order to acquire in the market the conditions for its continuation.

But such production is not production in general, or production in the abstract, a purely 'technical' process. The production of commodities by means of commodities involves production as the development of an advanced division of labor, as involving the application of fixed capital, as requiring the hiring of labor in the market, the concentration of labor and capital, and the socialization of labor. All of these concrete elements of production for exchange constitute together a production process which is intrinsically dependent upon a system of production and exchange. Furthermore, the appearance of such a system of interdependent production cannot itself be taken to be given but requires a specific development. This development involves precisely the subordination of production to exchange and of exchange to production within a general process which takes as its goal not the consumption of the individual producer-consumer but the expansion of value and the reproduction of capital.[3]

The highly developed system of reproduction which ultimately grounds the system of exchange finds no foundation within the individual producer-

consumer and can hardly be conceived to emerge upon that basis. The emergence of the system of reproduction and therefore of the system of exchange
itself presupposes that the expansion of value is the aim of the direct production process, therefore that that production process is the process of
production of commodities. The subordination of production to capital also
involves the creation of a production process adequate to the needs of capital
which grounds its expansion in the production of surplus-value via all those
processes – division of labor, mechanization, etc. – which also underly the
increasing universalization and development of the market system. Once
production takes on its distinguishable character as capitalist production the
intervention of the unit of capital as the specific form of expansion of value via
production becomes necessary. It is then that the conditions for the existence
of the firm, and hence a theory of the firm as distinguished from the simple
conception of 'production' of the neo-classical analysis, emerge.

II The foundations of the theory of the firm

1

The firm takes on a necessity of its own within economic analysis only to the
extent that a difference is posited between production and consumption. The
consumption of the product cannot be consumption on the part of its producer and consumption on the part of that producer cannot be consumption
of its own product since for production to continue the acquisition of different
products in the market is necessary. Production within the firm is consumption
of commodities not themselves produced within that firm so that the production of the commodity and its consumption become separated in time and
place. Production of commodities by means of commodities requires the
circulation of commodities as a necessity intrinsic to production as an ongoing
and continuous process. The separation of production from consumption is
no longer at the whim of the producer (the owner of the factor) but intrinsic
to the nature of the production process itself and to that extent imposed upon
both producer and consumer. While the production and the consumption of
the product are separate when viewed from the standpoint of the production
process of the firm as the production of commodities, when viewed from the
standpoint of the reproduction of the system of commodity production as a
whole, which is itself the condition for production on the part of the firm, the
two processes become, once again, moments of a single process, assert their
intrinsic unity. This unity is established through the intermediation of the
firm, the particular unit of capitalist production. For the emergence of the
firm as a distinguishable entity it is not at all adequate that the simple production of commodities be conceived or that the necessity for production to
move outside of itself into circulation be made explicit. It is, furthermore,
necessary that the conditions of capitalist production appear as themselves
the products of capitalist production; that the circulation of capital find in the

production process of capital the conditions of exchange and that that production process find through the circulation of capital the conditions for its continuation. The process of reproduction of the total social capital is a process within which capital posits through production the conditions for its circulation and through circulation the conditions of continued production. But in this case it is the production process of capital and the circulation of capital which are posited within the total reproduction process. Capital has emerged as self-sustaining, as ground of its own process which posits within itself the conditions necessary for its existence.

All the conditions of capitalist production are the products of capital and appear concretely as the products of particular capitals, of firms. Each production process finds the conditions of its existence and its expansion outside of itself in the market, yet only in the form of the products of other capitals. Therefore capital grounds itself only by taking on the form of a world of particular capitals each of which accounts for the pre-conditions of opposing capitals. It is in this sense that the conditions of production all appear as the products of production, that the conditions of capital appear as the products of capital. The production of commodities by means of commodities is only adequately grasped as the opposition of a world of particular capitals each of which reproduces itself by purchasing commodities themselves the products of capital.

This result applies no less to that condition of capitalist production which cannot be the product of the activity of the unit of capital: labor-power. Within the reproduction of the total social capital the conditions for the renewal of labor-power are also posited as conditions within the reproduction process and are, therefore, no longer taken as simply given. These conditions must now be seen to take on the form of the commodity products of particular capitals. The laborers purchase their means of consumption from capital. The buying and selling of labor-power is the condition for the maintenance of labor-power. But this must take on the concrete form of the purchase, by labor, of the conditions of its renewal from capital. The maintenance of labor-power depends essentially upon the maintenance of the system of commodity production and exchange of which labor-power is both a continuing element and a condition. Since the conditions of the existence of labor in the form of a commodity – labor-power – are the conditions of the system of commodity production those must appear as conditions posited within the process of the reproduction of the total social capital and ultimately, therefore, as commodity products of particular capitals, of firms. Labor-power is now situated concretely within the system of exchanges among particular units of capital. The general exchange of capital for labor-power is now the system of exchanges of labor-power with particular capitals and of the purchase by laborers of their means of subsistence from particular capitals.

Macroeconomics, then, must grasp two sides of the reproduction of the total capital. It must, first, constitute that level of analysis in terms of the specificity of the individual unit of capital as a commodity producer, as a firm and not as the individual producer-consumer. Second, it must constitute, in terms of the relation of particular capitals and laborers, the conditions of the expansion of the total capital.

2

The unit of capital taken in this sense exhibits certain characteristics which sharply distinguish it from the 'unit of production' as the latter appears within orthodox economic analysis. The latter is indifferent to the process of circulation just as it is indifferent to the requirements of the reproduction of the system of particular units of production taken as a whole. The absence of interdependence of production assures that the movement of the products of production into circulation and their determination as elements defined within a system of reproduction of the total capital become unnecessary. Such a locus of production is not, therefore, a unit of capital or a firm in any definite sense of the term. The unit of capital is reduced to the direct production process which is then set loose from any determination in the expansion of value and the circulation of capital. The end point of this conception is the view of production as exclusively the production of 'products,' or 'utilities' and not as the production of value. What distinguishes the unit of capital as the unity of production and circulation within the expansion of the total capital is precisely its connection to and ground in that expansion process as that process within which capital establishes wholly within itself the conditions necessary for its expansion.

Once production appears as the immediate process of the production of utilities taken without regard to its capitalistic character and, therefore, to its concrete forms (as of division of labor, etc.) it comes to relate to the world of production only in terms of its own adjustment to that world – therefore, in terms of 'optimization.' The 'firm' taken in this sense is a unit which strives to achieve a fixed point which realizes efficiency of production. By contrast the unit of capital is clearly distinguished in that it strives for no fixed state and scorns any adjustment to given conditions. The unit of capital strives to transcend all fixed and limited conditions, to create new, more universal, therefore more adequate conditions for its own activities.

The conception of the firm as holding a determinate place in the economic process as a whole involves a radical shift in the conception of the conditions within which the specific actions of the firm are determined. This problem of the determinateness of the firm appears no longer as that of the equilibrium of the firm. Production by the firm is never in equilibrium. Price response by the firm can be conceived not in terms of short- and long-run equilibrium configurations but in terms of the ability of the firm to move beyond existing conditions and in terms of the restraints which are assumed to act upon that movement. To consider a firm operating with a given stock of fixed capital is not to consider the latter as a definitive limit to firm decisions but only as a provisional limitation in order that the question can be posed of the conditions under which it will be possible for the firm to transcend the limits of the existing fixed capital, to introduce new means of production, to expand and to innovate. This perspective also reflects upon the initial investment of the firm. The neo-classical conception views this investment in terms of the optimal scale of production given the demand for the products of the firm. But such a conception is altogether antithetical to the activity of the unit of capital. The latter would not produce at all were it to expect existing demand conditions to be given and unalterable. For the firm to adjust its scale of production to an existing level of demand as an absolute barrier is for the firm to forsake its capitalistic character and settle down not to a life of continuous expansion but of production of utilities. The conditions of price determination with an unchanging stock of fixed capital are therefore not conditions of determining a fixed level of production but conditions of the growth of production within the confines of an initial investment to the point where that investment proves itself inadequate.

Formally, this contrast has a definite and clear expression in the different conditions of price determination. The unit of production viewed as an efficient optimizing mechanism establishes itself at the optimal scale of production in terms of investment of fixed capital and operates that fixed capital at its optimal rate and level. The firm produces at the minimum point of a U-shaped, long-run average cost curve which is tangent to its demand curve, and it produces at this point from here to eternity. By contrast the firm understood as the unit of capital will normally operate at less than 'full' capacity utilization. Once the firm reaches the full utilization of capacity this is not taken as a sign for it to settle down but as an indication of the necessity to pass beyond the limits of its original investment, to accumulate capital. This phenomenon is depicted in Figure 3.[4] With price P and average prime cost curve APC the

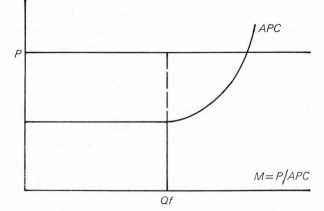

Figure 3

firm operates with the given stock of equipment so long as the demand for its products places it to the left of point Q_f. In this region the profit margin of the firm, M (or the 'degree of monopoly') is normal. With the expansion of demand the firm moves out along curve APC until demand exceeds the capacity of the given equipment and investment to increase capacity is undertaken.

The result that the firm will normally operate at less than full utilization of capacity is not tied to the imperfect operation of the competitive process or to the deviation of marginal revenue from price but to the fact that the firm is a unit of expanding value and not a unit of optimization. As a unit of value expansion, the firm will (1) normally build ahead of demand in order to take advantage of both sudden and long-run increase of its market, and (2) will normally operate under conditions of 'uncertainty' not due to imperfection of information or adjustment but due to the fact that the firm produces *commodities* and, therefore, its production involves also the mediating process of circulation.

Firms therefore normally operate on the constant portions of their average prime cost curves and such operation is not only typical but logically necessary. Fixed costs come into operation at the upper and lower reaches of production where the firm is either facing elimination from the world of capitals or is on the brink of expanding its capital investment. Since the firm normally operates with constant prime costs the price of the product will normally exceed average costs by the amount of its mark-up, its gross margin or degree of monopoly. This mark-up is a measure of the ability of the firm to set its price above its cost and still maintain its market share. It, therefore, hinges upon the competitive structure of the market and of the economy as a whole and sums up that structure. The gross margin is not an imperfection of competition but a necessary condition of competition since it is the basis for the expansion of the capital of the firm, therefore the quantitative basis of the process by which capital as a whole assures itself of the means for its own maintenance. The gross margin expresses, at the level of price, the process of extraction of surplus-value from the employment of labor. It expresses this process, not, however, directly in terms of labor time but indirectly in terms of the individual unit of capital and the competitive conditions of its expansion.

This conception of the gross margin should be clearly differentiated from that of a 'degree of monopoly.' Once the unit of production is understood as necessarily a unit of capital, the existence of a difference between average cost and price expresses an essential condition underlying all competitive processes and not a condition of the imperfection of the operation of competition. The latter is the interpretation given to the gross margin in orthodox neo-classical analysis. So long as the latter interpretation is maintained the role of demand as expressing consumer choice remains predominant in the theory of price. Rather than interpreted as a gross margin and basis of capital expansion the degree of monopoly becomes simply an alternative expression for the elasticity of demand and depends upon the relation of demand to price, the slope of the demand curve for the firm producing under conditions of 'imperfect competition.' Within the latter the degree of monopoly measures the willingness of consumers to shift between producers rather than the ability of producers to extract a surplus from production and competition in order to accumulate capital.

None the less, even in the case of the interpretation of the gross margin as a degree of monopoly determined by the elasticity of demand it becomes clear that the central process involved is that of the competition of capitals and not the formation of consumer preferences and the demand curve. The willingness of consumers to change producers hinges fundamentally not upon the irreducible psychological predispositions of individual consumers but upon the development of the conditions of competition of capital and the expansion of the market as a whole. Consumer willingness to part with current sources of their consumption needs depends upon the availability of alternative sources and this availability is fundamentally dependent upon the level of development of capital as a whole, its degree of penetration within a given regional market, the development of an infrastructure of transportation and communication, etc. It follows that the gross margin cannot be accurately understood as a phenomenon of imperfect competition but as (1) a measure of the level of development of competitive forces and therefore of the system of capitals as a whole, and (2) a measure of the ability of capital to sustain its conditions of expansion within the concrete process of price formation at the level of the individual firm and industry. The gross margin expresses the relation of gross profits to wage costs, it is the ratio of assets available for investment to the costs of labor-power. Taking depreciation costs as fixed the gross margin expresses the mark-up on labor cost which makes possible the expansion of the firm. The determination of the gross margin and, therefore, of the price of the products of the firm is a measure of (1) the extraction of profit from the production of commodities, and (2) the relative ability of different firms and different industries to appropriate that profit. Both of these elements of the gross margin are determined together within the process of competition and accumulation.

The gross margin may be taken to be determined by the competitive structure of industry, by the struggle over the wage, and by the process of expansion of capital as a whole.[5] Price, once joined to the gross margin becomes determinate in terms of the process of expansion and not in terms of the achievement of a fixed optimum. The contrast between the neo-classical 'theory of the firm' and the conception of the firm as a unit of capital could not be more acute. In the latter case the connection between the level of output and price is broken for the individual firm except when the growth of demand stimulates expansion of capital and innovation. The question of price, then, becomes a question of the relation of accumulation to innovation, to the structure of competition, and to the structure of costs within the firm and the industry. In this case the effect of demand on price is evaluated in terms of the process of the expansion of capital and of the fluctuations and cycles which characterize that expansion. The result is the absence of any 'functional relation between cost and quantity.'

The relation of the individual unit of capital to the economy as a whole is no longer conceived as that of equilibrium, whether partial or general, in which the firm relates to the totality of a world of competing capitals as an hypostatized entity outside of the determinations of its own activity, especially as fixed. The firm takes the data into hand and alters it in accordance with its own expansion. Rather than adjusting to fixed conditions it is always the aim of the firm to transcend all fixed conditions, to go beyond, both quantitatively and qualitatively, the given state of demand and production; to seek out all across the globe new sources of demand (therefore to take demand as anything but given) and to seek out new and more effective methods of production which transcend the cost limitations of the given configuration of cost and price.

So far as the firm is concerned there exist no real short-run and long-run equilibria. Given the technique, that is, given the level of development of the productivity of labor, and given the gross margin and money wage, the price and the general price level are both determinate. Utilization of capacity adjusts to changes in demand and not the price of output. Under conditions of growth and technical change there is a process of 'diffusion of innovation' which involves competition and the general process of the expansion of capital taking place through the competitive process.

Of equal importance, the conditions which make possible the expansion of the firm emerge as the effect of the expansion of capital as a whole and of the sum total of accumulation of particular capitals. Demand for the products of the firm grows, *pari passu*, with the growth of capital as a whole. The state of 'aggregate demand' expresses the conditions of expansion of capital as those conditions react back upon the particular units of that expansion, the units of capital, and determine the growth of each firm and thereby the growth of capital as a whole. The conditions of aggregate demand become relevant to the degree that the role of demand is removed from the direct determination of price and takes on its importance in terms of the movement of the system as a whole, signalling to each particular unit the state of the general conditions of its expansion. Demand appears no longer as the outward expression of individual consumption decisions but as the overall expression of accumulation of capitals. It divides not into particular demand for individual products but into demand for capital expansion, for capital maintenance, and for the consumption of labor-power. Rather than the neo-classical notion (1):

(1) $D = D(P)$

demand appears as the other side of the expansion of capital:

(2) $D = \text{Investment} + \text{Consumption} + \text{Depreciation}$, where
        $\text{Consumption} = \text{Capitalist's consumption} + \text{Worker's consumption}$.

Worker's consumption, in its turn depends, given the money wage, upon the expansion of capital itself.

It is possible to argue that equation (2) expresses the relevant notion of demand rather than equation (1) since the functional relation of quantity to price expressed in (1) has been eliminated with the elimination of the notion of production as the transformation of fixed factors. The notion of demand relevant to the unit of capital is not the functional relation of demand to price but the rate of expansion of the demand for its products over time and in the course of the expansion of the total capital. This state of demand is grasped in relation (2) which defines formally the state of the expansion of the total capital as a state of expansion of the demand for the products of capital. Not only does the supply curve lose its original status as the reverse of the demand relation but, now, the demand relation becomes, not the ground of supply, but an overall expression for the conditions of expansion of supply.

The conditions of the activity of the firm are the conditions of the expansion of capital as a whole and rest upon the determination of the particular forms of that expansion as expressed in the laws of accumulation. The theory of the firm is, therefore, only one side of the general theory of the economic system as a whole which, on the other side, involves the determination of the laws of the totality of economic relations. The theory of the firm as a unit of capital does not oppose itself to the theory of the economy as a whole as 'microeconomics' to 'macroeconomics.' The concrete analysis of the firm leads directly into the analysis of the laws of the total capital, into the treatment of 'macroeconomics.' The necessity of this transition emerges with the concrete characterization of the firm as the particular unit of capital. Macroeconomics, or, more correctly, the concept of capital as a whole and its expansion, is made at once possible and necessary by the articulation of the level of analysis of the particular unit of capital.

The concept of the total capital does not oppose itself to that of the individual firm in the manner of the opposition between micro- and macroeconomics. For the latter, the system as a whole is nothing more than the sum total of the individual parts. For the concept of the total capital, on the other hand, the economic system taken as a totality encompasses the division and reunification which constitutes simultaneously the system of capitalist production and the complex of particular units of capital. As a result the aggregate system appears as a complex phenomena which contains within it its specific character as the system of particular capitals taken as a whole. In the constitution of the total system not only are the peculiar features of individual production within particular capitals retained but it is only in relation to the total system that those features can originally emerge. The analysis of capitalist production as a whole cannot, therefore, concern itself with dead aggregates of economic magnitudes whose movement and level are only given by reference to activities of particular firms, by aggregation of microdecisions. It must, on the contrary, concern itself with the laws of the system as a whole and its movement. The analysis of the economic process as a whole cannot be defined, therefore, either as a simple aggregate of microevents or as a system of economic aggregates taken without regard to the specification of their composition. This does not require an abstract unification of micro- and macroeconomics, or the attachment of an abstract concept of a macrosystem to the individual units of production. It requires a concept of the total capital as a determinate level of analysis which is simultaneously the level of analysis of the particular firm.

III Origins of macroeconomics

1

A concept of the economic system as a whole, which is distinct from that of the general equilibrium of the exchange economy, first makes an explicit appearance in Keynes's *General Theory of Employment, Interest, and Money*. While the latter contains no explicit and systematic treatment of this connection, the critique of 'classical' theory which is at the heart of Keynes's analysis rests fundamentally upon an implicit recognition of the central connections indicated in the foregoing discussion. It is possible, in the light of our own treatment of the relation of the individual unit of production to the system of reproduction and expansion of capital as a whole, to consider Keynes's arguments against classical analysis and to determine the extent to which he has articulated a foundation for a real macroeconomics.

Keynes takes the classical theory to task, first, for its static equilibrium method. The weakness of this method, according to Keynes, is that it is inapplicable to the phenomenon of the accumulation of wealth.[6] Implicitly the problem of the *General Theory* is seen to rest upon the peculiar property of the accumulation of wealth that its object is not in immediate consumption but in (1) future consumption which differs in time and place from production, and (2) in consumption at an indefinitely distant time. The rupture between production and consumption brought about by the accumulation of capital, and especially its most advanced form – the formation of fixed capital – is, therefore, the central theme of the *General Theory*.

This rupture, we have argued, is intrinsically tied to the specification of the unit of production as a unit of capital and in that specification leads to the necessity of situating production within a system of particular capitals and of the expansion of the total capital. Keynes also articulates this condition of the accumulation of wealth when he points out that his 'difference from the traditional theory concerns its apparent conviction that there is no necessity to work out a theory of the demand and supply of output *as a whole*.'[7] The *General Theory* confronts 'classical' economics at two points: first, its static equilibrium method, and second, its lack of a concept of the economy as a whole. We will consider, first, the problems involved in the application of the equilibrium method to the accumulation of wealth.

It is Keynes's implicit and explicit rejection of the equilibrium method that has crystallized opposition to the central claims of the *General Theory*. The problem of the latter has been posed, at Keynes's own initiative, in terms of the comparison of alternative states of equilibrium rather than in terms of the equilibrium concept itself. None the less it is clear from Keynes's own statement that it is the equilibrium method which is fundamentally at issue.

Equilibrium in the neo-classical sense of the term is a state of adjustment of a group of economic agents (1) to a world of resources which are given, and (2) to the desires of the other agents within the economic system as a whole. The equilibrium state involves the prior confrontation of individuals with a world of objects and needs which must be adjusted one to the other. Equilibrium is the notion of the allocation of fixed, that is given, resources among competing ends. Algebraically the general equilibrium system involves the specification of (1) preference functions of individuals, the 'ends' which compete for (2) available resources which are given, with which each of the individuals is assumed endowed which may be, together with the products of the resources, redistributed in order to achieve (3) a consistent state of economic affairs which reconciles the competing ends with the given resources and the presupposed state of individual endowment. The state of equilibrium (3) rests simply upon the assumption that each individual acts 'rationally' in the Weberian sense. But, further, the assumption of rationality, which is the assumption of a drive towards the equilibrium state, is necessary to the conception of the problem of social and economic behavior. Action can only be understood if it is rational in this sense so that the conception of the economic system to the extent that it falls within the neo-classical idea of allocation of scarce resources, must be an equilibrium conception. That is not to say that disequilibrium cannot emerge in the actual world of economic affairs. Quite to the contrary it is intrinsic to the conception of equilibrium that the latter stand as a goal or 'utopia' towards which the actual economy strives but which it can never achieve.

Given this conception it is inconceivable that equilibrium could involve 'involuntary unemployment' since such unemployment implies that fixed and available resources, though needed, are not used. Such a result is only conceivable in terms of error and ignorance, therefore in terms of 'irrationality.' Such error and ignorance are naturally associated with any real economic system but it is inconsistent and friuolous to argue that the conception of the economic process should or can incorporate the irrational which is precisely characterized in such a way as to make it defy consistent conception. So long as both workers and employers act rationally and so long as they possess the requisite means (e.g. information) to determine a rational plan of action, involuntary unemployment is impossible. Underemployment equilibrium is a contradiction in terms. To the extent that Keynes accepted the neo-classical equilibrium notion, his claim for the possibility of underemployment equilibrium cannot be sustained.

However, to interpret the deviations of the *General Theory* from orthodox general equilibrium methodology as errors of analysis is not only to deprive Keynes of his own claim to move beyond the static equilibrium method of the 'classics' but also to make inexplicable the central insights of the Keynesian theory of employment. There exists within the *General Theory* an implicit argument for the movement of analysis away from the conception of the economy as an efficient machine for the allocation of scarce resources. In order to make sense out of certain of the essential arguments of Keynesian economics it is necessary to root them in this implicit break with general equilibrium methodology. But this necessity of eliminating altogether the neo-classical conception of adjustment to scarce resources runs up against the seemingly intractable difficulty that the latter is claimed to be not one aspect of the economic process but the *definition* of that process. Economic action is defined as the allocation of resources according to need so that the construction of a theory of employment on any other basis seems to defy not only particular laws of economic behavior but the idea of economic behavior itself. All practitioners of modern economic analysis accept explicitly its inability to account for the totality of actual economic events and states, they all agree on the presence of a myriad of economic activities (including all 'real' economic activity) which fall outside of the general equilibrium conception. For them, as much or more than for their critics, the 'actual' economy can no more be in equilibrium than feathers can fall from the leaning tower of Pisa at the same rate as rocks. Indeed the idea that the world is in a state of disequilibrium is not only consistent with this conception, it is intelligible only within it.

The ideas of equilibrium and of the price system as an allocative mechanism are, therefore, two sides of a single conception. In each case it is the notion of a reconciliation of individual preferences with given, scarce, resources which is at stake. The shift toward a conception of price determination within the unit of capital and within the system of particular capitals excludes the interpretation both of equilibrium price and of price as a 'scarcity index.'

Under the conditions of capitalist production the problem of circulation poses itself and realization of the value of commodities in money becomes necessary. Capital exists not simply as means of production but as value progressing through a circuit which begins with the investment of capital in the purchase of means of production and constitutes the consumption of those means of production (i.e. production) as the means to the reinvestment of the value realized in the sale of the product. For production based on capital production is nothing more than one phase in the total circulation process. The reason for this is that the social nature of production and especially the interdependence of production is explicitly introduced. Production as capitalist production involves the division of labor, the purchase and sale of labor-power, the separation in time and place of production and consumption, etc. With the concrete specification of the unit of production as a unit of capital the existence of a rupture between production and consumption becomes necessary and the process of circulation emerges as the determination of the unity of production and consumption.

Keynes has made this point explicitly although in a form somewhat different from that suggested here. For Keynes the reason for the necessity of an explicit treatment of expectations as regards investment is that investment involves the introduction of fixed capital and, therefore, a rupture between the time of installation of capital equipment and the time of realization of the value of its product. 'It is by reason of the existence of durable equipment that the economic future is linked to the present.'[8] The contrast with classical analysis including that of Ricardo and Smith, could not be greater. Production with fixed capital, durable equipment, cannot be self-sufficient production on the part of the individual producer-consumer but must be production within a highly advanced division of labor. It must, therefore be production as it develops within the capitalist system, production not for direct consumption but production governed by the expansion of value. This is a typical focus of Keynesian thinking – investment regarded as capital expansion rather than future consumption.

It is the conception of production and consumption as subordinate to the process of capital expansion and especially to the formation of fixed capital which requires a break between consumption and production and which at the same time expresses the central role of capital expansion in defining the general characteristics of the economic process as a whole. The key to the *General Theory* is in the treatment of capital investment since the process of accumulation creates the conditions of production within which (1) consumption and production come to be separated and consumption ceases to form the goal of production, and (2) uncertainty intervenes, therefore implicitly the process of circulation is understood to be necessary in the construction of the conception of the economic system as a whole.

2

Paradoxically it is the absence within the *General Theory* of a theory of investment that indicates most clearly the presence of a conception of capital accumulation which differs profoundly from that of neo-classical general equilibrium analysis. The absence of the theory of investment implies most importantly the elimination of the neo-classical notion of investment as capital formation and, therefore, the opening up of the possibility of a conception of accumulation as a self-determining process independent of the specification of an investment function and of the investment and consumption decisions of individuals.

The abandoning of the theory of investment by Keynes is not immediate or even explicit but occurs only gradually in the course of an exposition of the problem which begins squarely within the neo-classical domain and then works its way step by step outside of its limits. The first step in the Keynesian treatment of investment is a restatement of the neo-classical theory of capital formation. Keynes begins with the notion of a process of adjustment of the 'marginal efficiency of capital' to the rate of interest. The direct influence upon Keynes of the idea of capital formation as involving the measurement of the productivity of investment against the consumption foregone is apparent. The argument is formally reducible to the neo-classical conception. Such a reduction hinges essentially upon the interpretation of the marginal efficiency of capital and the rate of interest. If the former is conceived as synonymous with the 'marginal product of capital' or as functionally related to that marginal product, and if the rate of interest is seen as the result of balancing the inter-temporal preferences and capital productivity prevailing in society as a whole, then the determination of a project of capital formation by Keynes is in no substantial respect opposed to the predominant notion of investment as a process of approach to a desired capital stock.

The Keynesian concept of the marginal efficiency of capital is, however, only the marginal product of capital with a difference. The difference between the Keynesian interpretation of the marginal efficiency of investment and the neo-classical marginal product of capital is that for the former it is the expectation of a return, and therefore the *value* of the return which is critical while for the latter it is the 'real' return, and therefore the physical return which is relevant. This is a critical difference since it involves Keynes in the explicit acceptance of the essential implications of the treatment of the unit of production as a unit of capital. First, it accepts the process of investment as a process of expansion not of physical objects but of value. It is the realization of the value of the product in the market which is intrinsically uncertain given the dependence of that realization on the activities of a series of individual producers connected only through the market. The interpretation of the relevant return in terms of value implies that the realization of the products of the investment in money through market exchange becomes essential to the conception of investment. The emancipation of investment from future consumption is, therefore, only in the first instance the effect of uncertainty and expectations. More profoundly the latter express the character of production as capitalist production and the goal of production as the expansion of value. The specification of production to the capitalist firm involves the elimination of the equilibrium conception from the analysis of the activity of the firm. The process of value expansion of the individual firm involves, therefore, the absence of any equilibrium state as goal of its activity and at the same time requires the intervention of circulation and realization which separate the production of commodities and their continued and expanded reproduction. Once investment is separated from direct dependence upon a conception of physical productivity it comes to involve more and more the problem of expectations. Expectations depend ultimately upon 'animal spirits' so that investment is not a question of efficient allocation in the usual sense but a question of the inexplicable drive of the capitalist to expand his capital. It becomes, for Keynes, an autonomous process set loose from any determination, and especially from any determination in the calculus of individual preferences for present *versus* future consumption.

Within neo-classical economics investment is still viewed in terms of 'investment decisions,' therefore in terms of the specification of an 'investment function.' There is a definite need for such a determination of investment and of saving since all such activity is only understandable in terms of a rational subject who acts in accordance with his desires. Capital formation takes place in order to achieve a fixed goal, a particular supply of future consumption. By contrast, for Keynes and for neo-Keynesian economics, there is no real investment function, there is only an appeal to 'animal spirits and the structure of society.' The latter serves to fix the rate of investment abstractly. Investment and saving are undetermined and therefore given. They act independently upon the complex of economic relations but are not themselves acted upon. Investment is now emancipated from intertemporal preferences as expressed in the rate of interest. It is for this reason that it becomes, for Keynes, fixed. Similarly, in the implicit emancipation of saving from intertemporal consumption decisions saving is taken to be fixed and given by the average propensity of 'the community.' It is the abstract manner of fixing saving and investment which allows for their reintegration into the neo-classical theory of capital. Such a reintegration requires simply the attaching of a theory of saving or a theory of investment developed in terms of individual intertemporal consumption decisions.

None the less, at the same time that this conception of capital formation is not immune to reintegration within the neo-classical theory the fixing of investment on the part of Keynes expresses, however imperfectly, the absence of dependence of saving and investment upon individual preferences. All that can really be said about investment by Keynes is that it is fixed, by 'animal spirit.' This fixity of investment expresses the absence of determination and, while the gap which results may be filled with a neo-classical investment function, it also signals a refusal to apply the traditional method of treatment of economic activity to the problem of investment. In the case of investment Keynes notes, in particular, that the neo-classical method breaks down and, while he is unwilling or unable to go beyond that method, he is unwilling to employ it. The problem is that for modern social science determination involves reduction to the isolated individual and his decisions. Since Keynes, in the case of investment and saving, is unwilling to follow this course he is left with no determination. But the fixity and givenness of saving and investment also play a positive role. The absence of determination implicitly argues that saving and investment confront the individual as given. While for Keynes this makes them undetermined, on another level it makes them self-determining. Investment simply goes on at its own pace and in its course sweeps up the individual and his needs determining the real product of his action as the result of the movement of the whole rather than as the immediate result of individual decision.

Ultimately, Keynes takes investment as an autonomous process and fixes it not because he believes that empirically it happens that the investment function is inelastic with respect to the rate of interest, but because he considers investment to be a self-determining process. This conception of investment, implicit in the *General Theory*, becomes an essential condition of neo-Keynesian economics. To this extent it is Kalecki's formulation, rather than that of Keynes which brings out most clearly the fundamental principles of the 'General Theory of Employment.'

Kalecki first relates investment to the bifurcation of society into classes so that saving decisions are no longer determined by abstract individuals but by individuals determined by their class membership. Investment becomes a process with an explicit dependence upon the prevailing social order. Capitalists get what they spend and workers spend what they get. Both saving and consumption become comprehensible in terms of the specification of the class structure of society. In the light of this further step away from the neo-classical construction of the exchange economy it is no longer possible to 'complete' the theory of employment by attaching to the saving and investment functions a relation to individual preferences. It is no longer the division of society into individuals which is originally posited as condition of economic analysis but the division of society into classes within which the individual comes to be determined. This is a substantial break with neo-classical thinking, implicit in the *General Theory* (which reveals at numerous points an acute awareness of the importance of the specification of the structure of society in this sense) and made explicit by Kalecki and by neo-Keynesian theory.

None the less this view still gives way to that of modern economics to the extent that the social conditions of the expansion of capital appear in the abstract, especially with regard to the process of production. Production on the part of the individual firm, rather than being directly a process of capitalist production which contains within it the necessity of continuous expansion, becomes a purely technical process to which it is still necessary to attach a social specification from outside. To be sure this specification is now that of a 'class relation,' but the latter is explicitly undetermined within the analysis so that Kalecki falls back into the specification of investment as the activity of a subject, in this case the capitalist class, acting, first, upon its individual members, and second, upon the material process of production, making use of the products of that process for its class ends. It is not that this procedure leads necessarily to incorrect conclusions with regard to the conditions of capitalist production. On the contrary, it is Kalecki's great achievement to have clearly defined the connection between the determination of price at the level of the firm and industry and the expansion of capital as a whole. None the less the mode of expression of the essential connections and propositions of the analysis is wholly arbitrary and, therefore, not immune to the criticism levelled at it by neo-classical economics, that it is unnecessary and unjustifiable to restrict individual behavior in the manner suggested by Kalecki. The latter is argued, in a sense correctly, to be a special case whose importance, while undeniable, is also not definitely established.

Since class has been added on to the economic process in this abstract manner the actual implications of the specification of the class structure of society become problematic. Two alternatives within the same general orientation emerge, neither of which is clearly dominant. On one side, a class is defined by its propensity to save. Such a conception emerges directly from the fact that the only explicit role taken on by the specification of the class structure is that of determining savings behavior. Different savings propensities lead to different classes: workers tend to consume a greater proportion of their income than do capitalists. Such a specification of the class relation leads directly back into the neo-classical conception to the degree that the distinction between classes is purely quantitative. Since it is only a matter of the relative level of the 'propensity to save' there exists no foundation for the difference which establishes it as necessary. That distinction, therefore, has a tendency to dissolve.

In order to establish the difference in saving propensity as necessary it is argued to arise from a difference in relation to the means of production. Class becomes a 'property relation.' This conclusion is clearly the more profound relative to the simple differentiation of saving propensities. Yet while it attempts to ground that difference it still does so abstractly and includes no argument as to the connection between 'property' and capital accumulation. Why capitalists 'choose' to accumulate simply because they own property in the means of production is unclear. Derivative puzzles concerning the extent to which workers act like capitalists when they own such property, and whether the ownership of 'consumer durables' makes workers capitalists, also inevitably arise given the abstract conception of property employed in drawing out the essential class distinctions.

All such special assumptions become unnecessary once it is recognized that the laws of the economic system are not the product of the decisions either of 'individuals' or of 'classes' taken in the abstract (for example, as 'sociological datum') but of the process of capital as the self-sustaining process of reproduction and expansion which carries within it its own determination. What is critical in this connection is not that the owners of the firm are 'capitalists,' members of a class, but that the firm be understood concretely not as a technical unit of production which needs to be directed externally by decisions of individuals or of classes but as the particular unit of capital which is only an element of the reproduction of the system of capital as a whole and which, therefore, derives the determinateness of its own process from the determinateness of the expansion of capital as a whole. All neo-Keynesian analysis takes the production process of capital as given independently of capital and of its process so that its specifically capitalistic character needs to be attached to it by assumption. This in turn must involve the application of subjective decision, in this case in the form of the decision of a class, which is assumed arbitrarily as the determining force.

Kalecki has, however, gone further than Keynesian thinking in the specification of investment and growth as self-sustaining. At the same time that the problem appears explicitly as one of the specification of investment functions and saving decisions the actual argument focuses upon two processes intrinsically independent of any such subjective determination. Kalecki first shifts the emphasis from the propensity to save to the gross margin so that the supply of saving for investment is determined not by decisions but by the process of competition of capitals, price formation, and determination of the level of money wages. The gross margin, or degree of monopoly, is the essential source of capital expansion. Once saving is seen to be financed out of the gross margin and not out of 'revenue' its financing is no longer a subject of decision. The unit of capital is intrinsically a part of a competitive system whose development is also the development of the conditions for capital expansion. Second, when Kalecki specifies the investment function the notion of investment decisions ceases to play any independent role. The key to investment is past accumulation of capital and the rate of growth of investment. Thus Kalecki simply assumes that expansion goes on because it has gone on in the past and the question for the future is predominantly the question of the effect of past investment on the potential profitability and viability of current investment.

IV The labor theory of value

The Keynesian and neo-Keynesian theory of accumulation and price formation considered, in outline, in the preceding sections breaks definitively with the 'general equilibrium' conception of the economic system as a whole. The foundation of this rupture with traditional modes of thought is in the conception of the expansion of capital as a process which drives itself and which is not comprehensible in terms of the decisions and activities of individuals. Yet, while this alternative conception may be seen to emerge within Keynesian thinking (in however incomplete a form), the logical basis for this treatment of the economic process is nowhere explicitly subject to investigation. The real foundation of macroeconomics remains a closed book, under the title 'animal spirits and the structure of society.' In order to finally open this book it is necessary to take the foundations of the neo-Keynesian conception as an explicit subject of analysis. The key is the manner in which profit is generated in the pricing process and therefore the conception of the purchase and sale of labor-power.

First, labor-power is a commodity purchased within the circulation of capital:

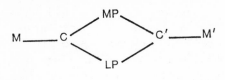

Figure 4

The capital to be invested appears, initially, as money but cannot be invested directly in that form (M) and must first be exchanged for the necessary use-values required for production (C) which take the particular forms of means of production (MP) and labor-power (LP). These are united for the purposes of the production, first, of a particular use-value or set of use-values (C') and ultimately, for the purpose of realizing the value of those objects in money (M') in order that the circuit can be begun once again, but on an expanded scale. Once labor-power comes to be absorbed in this way into capital and its circulation the entire process can establish itself as self-sustaining since the pre-conditions of its continuation appear concretely as the results of its movement which is therefore circular.

The important point, for the purposes of the present discussion, is that labor appears in this context not in a purely material form but, first, as the commodity, labor-power, which rather than being immediately available must be purchased with capital, at its price, in the market. Labor appears, therefore, as a commodity which must be purchased and which is relevant quantitatively, from the standpoint of the circulation of capital, as the relation of the wage to the money return on capital advanced. Thus labor does not simply enter production materially but enters production through a particular exchange: the exchange of capital in the form of money for labor-power. Since capital enters into a particular value relation with labor-power what is central is not the productivity of labor relative to the quantity of natural means of subsistence required for its maintenance, but the value of capital required to be expended upon wages. What is further essential is that this exchange actually occur and be taken into account not as purely formal but as a necessary element of the circulation of capital. In other words, it is necessary to take into account (1) that the relation of capital to labor is a relation of exchange and (2) that the form of that exchange is the purchase of labor-power with money. It is not, therefore, the direct confrontation of social classes in their real existence as classes which is relevant but the exchange of capital for labor-power and, therefore, the quantitative relation of the price of the products of the previous production process (M') to the price of labor-power in money, the wage. This would be directly reducible from that of capital in the money form to capital in the form of particular useful objects (the relation of *M* to *MP*) if it were not that labor-power is distinguished, fundamentally, from all other use-values on two bases. First, labor-power, although itself a commodity, is not produced within the direct production process of capital, nor is it the product of a capitalist enterprise. Second, labor-power is distinguished as the general capacity to produce all particular use-values. For the production of commodities to take place it is necessary that this abstract capacity appear in the market and be available at a price consistent with the reproduction of capital. The general ability to produce use-values must appear in the market in the form of a commodity, therefore must be separated from the objective conditions of the production of commodities. It must be both necessary and possible not only for capital to purchase labor-power on the market but equally for labor-power to purchase its means of consumption from capital. Furthermore, this necessity must be dealt with within the process of capital itself.

It is the exchange of labor-power against all other commodities that grounds the realization of profit on the part of the particular unit of capital. Logically, therefore, the analysis of accumulation rests upon this fundamental relationship and, in fact, expresses the form in which it works itself out at the level of the competition and expansion of capitals. Yet, nowhere within neo-Keynesian thinking is this particular exchange considered in its full generality, independently of the peculiarities of the exchange of labor-power with the particular unit of capital or for particular products at prices formed within the competition of capitals. Nowhere does the exchange of labor-power for capital appear as the immediate object of investigation to be considered in its true generality. Were, on the other hand, Keynesian thinking to attempt to grasp the essential foundation of its theory of accumulation and price formation it could only do so by constituting this general relation of capital to labor as the prior object of investigation since this relation has been shown, within the Keynesian theory itself, to be the logical basis of the formation of profit, price, and the firm. In order to establish this level of analysis Keynesian theory would have to abstract from the world of particular capitals within which the relations among individual units of capital are essential and consider explicitly the *general* relation of exchange between capital and labor. Such a focus would necessarily leave aside the specific useful forms in which the products of capital must appear in order to accomplish the reproduction of the total social capital. It would, therefore, leave aside the differences which characterize the production of particular commodities in order to consider the exchange of capital for labor as the ground of the production of all commodities, viewed independently of the specification of the useful form of the immediate product of labor. Such an abstraction makes possible the explicit treatment of the common character of the production of all commodities – the labor process. Having focused in directly upon the labor process and upon the general exchange between capital and labor there would no longer be any basis for considering that exchange in terms of the price system of competing individual units of capital. The basis of that competitive process in differences within the production of particular commodities (differences in concentration of capital and especially differences in organic compositions of capital) would no longer exist since it is the general exchange of capital for labor-power which is the condition for those differences. Exchange of commodities taken in general, without regard to the particular useful characteristics of those commodities, is grounded only in their general characteristics as commodities, in their existence as products of a labor process. This result appears also within modern neo-Keynesian price theory for which the basis of exchange in labor time is explicitly recognized in the case of equal organic compositions of capital. What needs to be recognized is that the special nature of this case derives not from arbitrary assumption but from the elimination of all specification of particular useful characteristics of commodities. Such elimination is the necessary condition for the analysis of the general relation of capital to labor, that relation common to the production of all commodities.

The neo-Keynesian conception of the firm rests logically upon the peculiarities of the relation entailed in the purchase and sale of labor-power. In order for this theory of the firm and of accumulation to be adequately grounded it is necessary to go beyond the simple presupposition that the mark-up on wages costs yields a general rate of profit in order to analyze explicitly the relation which underlies that mark-up. This must involve (1) the treatment of the general relation of capital to labor, and (2) the treatment of that relation as an exchange, therefore upon the basis of exchange-value. Exchange-value must itself emerge as the prior basis for the derivation of the capital–labor relation and must, therefore, be conceived independently of the individual exchanges which transpire among opposing particular units of capital. It must develop upon a general basis, independent of the differences presupposed by the competition of capitals. It is in this sense that the articulation of a real concept of the process of capitalist production as a whole – of a 'macroeconomics' – distinct from that of general equilibrium requires, as its presupposition, the analysis of the inner nature of the process of commodity production and of the production of value in the consumption of labor-power. This latter is a project the original formulation of which is to be found in the classical labor theory of value, and the original resolution of which is to be found in Marx's analysis of the immediate production process.

Chapter 9
Economy and society

I The ends of economic activity

In the original construction of the neo-classical conception of the economy, preferences of individuals were taken to form an irreducible foundation for analysis which must be taken as given and as incapable of theoretical deduction. The implication of this givenness of preferences was also that individual need could not be viewed as directly social in character. In fact, the utilitarian predilection of nineteenth-century (and even of much current) economic thought served to strongly inhibit any development of the idea that individual need was the product of a social milieu however the latter might be conceived. At the same time this idea of need as both personal datum and ultimate foundation of analysis presented economics with a real analytic impediment when it came to the deduction of the economic system as a system of inter-related economic actors taken as a whole. To the extent that economics attempted to ground itself in needs of individuals which were not of an intrinsically social character it found itself faced with the necessity of building up the economic system as the outward expression of otherwise isolated and independent units. To accomplish this, however, it was necessary to attribute to the particular units, the individual economic actors whose sum is to be the economic system, the necessary characteristics which will lead them to engage in activity appropriate to the construction of an economic world of interacting subjects and of a world of social relations as a whole, a 'social system.' This, however, implies the specification of the individual and in that contradicts the originally posited independence of the units of social life. Where the latter is maintained it is not legitimate to assume that individuals will behave in such a manner as to, through that behavior, co-operate in the construction of the economic and social system. As a result of this it is necessary at the outset to clearly specify the composition of individual preferences as possessing, for example, the characteristics of consistency and completeness. Yet, within economic theory, such a specification of individual preference must remain arbitrary. While this is necessarily the case at the same time the determinate-ness of need from the standpoint of the deduction of the market system and its requirements precludes any purely empirical derivation of preference functions. The fact that the deduction of a market requires a specific configuration of need implies that the market and those needs are connected by links of necessity which cannot be grasped by empirical arguments of a probablistic

278

character. The connection of need to a market environment reveals precisely that inner necessity of the determination of need in a particular manner which requires theoretical derivation and explanation. This necessity, in effect, connects need to the inner logic of the market system. If individual need is so determined, however, it must by that very fact, be possible to give a theoretical account for that determination.

Since there exists no basis within economic theory for the determination of need it follows that economic analysis must become dependent upon further analysis of social phenomena for the deduction of the premises of economic activity. It is necessary to find the source of the determination of need not only outside of the economy but within the sphere of social relations since only in that way is it possible to give an account for need which does not suffer the theoretical weaknesses of the abstract positing of a particular form of need through the introduction of arbitrary assumptions. Thus even to determine need in human nature is to identify the needs of the market-determined individual as natural and this is to take them as simply irreducible and given. In this regard it would seem less presumptious to take need as axiomatic thereby excluding any claim that the foundations of exchange can be grasped theoretically. It might also be mentioned that the determination of need in individual psychology poses no real alternative to the original manner of argument of neo-classical economics but only serves to shift the terms in which it is posed from the individual as such to his 'psychology.' Without doubt the market determination of the individual has also an expression at the level of personality but this expression can hardly be assumed to account for the market system.

It is worth emphasizing from the outset that the inability of the economy to account for the ends of economic activity (the given needs of its members) within economic activity itself, far from arbitrary, is a part of the neo-classical conception of economic behavior and is inseparable from the modern concept of the economic aspect of social life. For modern social science economic activity is, by definition, the adjustment of resources among alternate but given ends. This result is by no means an accident of definition or the effect of the arbitrary restriction of the subject matter of the special disciplines which make up the 'social sciences.' The peculiar division of labor which has come to characterize the social sciences since the end of the nineteenth century represents a differentiation which is necessary to the conception of social theory (and of social life) upon which all of those special sciences are based. Far from a matter of convenience, both the opposition of and unity among the social sciences expresses directly their inner character and the logic by which they attempt to conceptualize the social world. The inability of an economic analysis constrained to operate within this conception to account for the preferences of economic actors originates in this peculiar construction of the conditions of social life and of the requisites for its adequate comprehension. Were the ends of economic activity to be determined within that activity then the activity considered could no longer be correctly termed 'economic' so far as the latter is understood within modern social science. However, if it is true that the ends of economic behavior are not arbitrary but determinate then it must also be the case that science can locate that determination within itself and provide the needed rational basis for the construction of the world of exchange. Where this is the claim of sociological analysis such a sociology must derive from the conception of the economic relations its central problem and method.

The assertion that economic relations are processes of adjustment of means among competing but given ends implies that the conditions of economic life are given to it from outside. The economic sphere cannot be self-contained but must be dependent upon external relations. Since the needs to be located are in any case of an individual character there can, in principle, exist only two alternative sources of individual need. Traditionally the fact that needs are individual has lead analysis to conclude that their origin is also individual, the individual *tout court*. It is precisely this view which has lead to the contradiction introduced in the foregoing discussion. As a result of this contradiction it has seemed necessary to give up the view that individual need is also individual in origin and to consider individual need in relation to society as the world of individuals. It has thus become necessary not only to consider explicitly the social conditions of economic behavior but also to consider those conditions within the special conception of society as the world of individuals. The external relations of dependency of the economic sphere become relations of dependence upon the 'social system.'

Within this construction of the problem, the method of deduction of the social conditions of economic life cannot be arbitrary. On the contrary, the fact that the task of sociological analysis becomes, on this level, that of deducing the conditions of economic behavior restricts sharply the manner of deduction. This restriction originates in the special conception of the economy which sociological analysis attempts to appropriate. Indeed, the conceptual foundations of neo-classical economics (which defines itself as the theory of the allocation of scarce resources among competing ends) are not identical with economic science. The problem of sociological analysis is the apprehension of the 'boundary' conditions of a particular conception of economic life, a conception which is only of recent origin, establishing a real basis of development only at the end of the nineteenth century. Neo-classical economics defines in a particular manner both its own inner logic and its external relations and necessities, the location and character of its boundaries. To the degree that sociology attempts to complete the structure of economic reasoning it is necessary that sociology as a whole be consistent in its formulation not with economic theory in general but with the neo-classical economic analysis. Put somewhat more generally, it is necessary for both sociology and economics to display a unity of method and especially of conceptual foundation. That this unity does in fact exist is of the utmost importance.

On one side this unity of conception has served to lay a foundation for the emancipation of economic analysis from its utilitarian origins. With the view of economics as 'embedded' within the social system it no longer appears necessary to base the theory of exchange and production on an *a priori* conception of the nature of the economic individual. On the other side, the unity of conception between economics and sociology implies the subjection of sociological theory to the critique of economic analysis and this especially to the extent that economic concepts, and analogies for economic categories, find their way into sociological theory. This is of special relevance in connection with the central place held by the neo-classical conception of production and exchange based on production within sociological analysis. The contradictions within the neo-classical theory of production become contradictions of the whole of modern social science.

It is in the concept of 'social action' that the unity of sociology and economics is concentrated. The recognition that the general categories of the theory of action underly the entire structure of economic thought has become explicit only in the course of sociological reflection upon the foundations of economic analysis. In the following discussion the argument which underlies this result will be examined and criticized.

II The rationality of the social world

1

The notion of social action grasps society as a system of interrelating actors. Analysis begins with the individual social act. Social action first distinguishes itself from pure 'behavior' in that 'action,' as opposed to behavior, goes beyond itself. Action is behavior to which the actor *attaches* a subjective meaning. To attach a subjective meaning to an act is, *ipso facto*, to relate the behavior involved to an intention, a goal, or an end. Within the action methodology subjectivity always takes the form of intention or end since it is the nature of subjectivity to bring otherwise self-enclosed behavior out of its shell, to relate behavior outside of itself. The subjective element molds the world of behavior to its needs and thereby attaches to the behavior an end.

Behavior becomes action to the degree that it takes on such subjective meaning. Action, on the other hand, becomes social action in so far as the orientation of the act is to a socially shared meaning. Robinson Crusoe, the isolated consumer-producer, may engage in action to the extent that his behavior is adapted to his subjective intention, but, to the degree that Robinson acts as an extrasocial being he does not engage in social action. This distinction between action and social action is clearly predicated upon the possibility that subjective meaning can exist, can in fact be conceived, outside of society. This contention is a logical element of the action conception but it also raises important problems of interpretation, in particular, of the possi-

bility of the existence of meaning in a non-social context. Such problems will
not be considered explicitly here. None the less it must be borne in mind that
this opposition of action to social action is as problematic as the opposition of
action to behavior. The opposition between action and social action and the
contradictions emergent within that opposition also appear in the relation
between social action and behavior.

Since behavior becomes social action in so far as it is a means to a subjectively intended and socially defined end it is clear that the concept of social
action expresses the means–ends relationship and contains all behavior
typically considered economic to the extent that that behavior takes place
within an intersubjective context. In fact, the idea of production within
modern economics is the archetype of the general category of action and gives
to the latter its distinctive meaning. In a production relation the product
stands as the goal of activity, the resources or factors of production as the
means. To the extent that production is subordinated to a market process it
becomes social action in a definitive form: the forming of the natural world
to meet the ends defined within the market system.

As we have already seen, it is by no means necessary within modern
economic analysis that production be conceived, even where it is production
which eventuates in exchange, as production for ends of a social character.
The market may concern itself with ends of a purely individual character. On
the other hand, to the degree that needs articulated in the market are of a
social nature, production, as adjustment to those ends, becomes an element
of social action.

The means–ends relationship distinguishes among three elements: a subjective end, a means, and an actual end. This distinction implies a relation of
dependence, that of the means chosen, and therefore indirectly of the end
realized, upon the goal intended. The latter is related to the former (means
and actual end) as independent to the dependent. The positing of independent
goals is intrinsic to the idea of social action since behavior is action only to
the extent that it involves *ends* which, as such, are necessarily indeterminate.
The end is the finish or completion of a process. Within the process there can
be nothing beyond the end upon which the latter might become dependent
without sacrificing its status as end. The behavior which exists within the act
is therefore passive. Just as in the theory of exchange the objects of human
need must be *brought into* the social and human world by their owners, so in
the general theory of action it is the actor, as a locus of motives or goals,
which by attaching goals to behavior brings that behavior into the realm of
action and of social action. Thus, even human behavior, however active it may
appear, has an objective, passive, or inert, character which can only be overcome by the introduction of external and given subjective ends to which the
behavior, taken in itself, remains always indifferent. Human behavior lacking
a means–ends character drops out of the social world.

Since behavior possesses this extrahuman character as simple behavior it must by definition exist outside of consciousness. The implication of this externality is that behavior cannot be grasped within consciousness. Only to the degree that behavior is brought into the human world, the world of subjective meaning and intention, does it become possible for behavior to be apprehended. When consciousness acts upon behavior it acts upon a material explicitly defined as external to it. Behavior, therefore, defies understanding. But the 'understanding' which it defies goes beyond the empirical project of grasping within thought that which must remain outside of thought. This distinctiveness of understanding of social phenomena is for Weber, a specificity of understanding (*verstehen*) to social science. 'Understanding' seeks to engage thought upon a material which is already its own. Consciousness is only capable of grasping a material which is a part of consciousness, that behavior which has been brought into consciousness – action. In the scientific process consciousness reforms a material which is already its own, *action* as the extraction of behavior from its shell and incorporation into consciousness via the mediation of subjective intention. Understanding via social science, is understanding of social action and is, by that fact, incipiently the activity of *reason*. The connection of understanding and social action to reason and to the rationality of the social world, is critical to the action methodology. The simple fact that action is subjective in character is not sufficient to allow for the application of science to the comprehension of that action. Social theory can only concern itself with specific types of action, those which are *rational*. Rationality is that characteristic of action which allows it to be internalized into the scientific description of social life.

For sociological theory behavior follows the empirical laws of causation within the natural sphere. However, given the externality of the symbolic realm of goals and ends there exists no inner necessity that the behavior and the ends be congruent one with the other. It, therefore, becomes both possible and necessary that a distinction be drawn within the notion of social action between that action which is congruent in this sense and that action which is not. This distinction is the product of the externality of the symbolic realm, indeed of the social world, from behavior. The concept of rationality expresses this distinction. Social action possesses the characteristic of rationality to the extent that the means chosen are consistent in the foregoing sense with the ends intended.[1] An individual act is rational when it is consistent with the objective laws of the social and natural world. Within the theory of action the world of behavior is a world of objective laws, or causal relationships, which the observer must relate to cognitively on the basis of empirical science. In other words, the concrete empirical individual relates to the social and natural world as a world of laws which are external to him and which confront him in his activity as given. The individual acts irrationally when the personal determination of his action conflicts with the objective laws. The rationality–irrationality opposition dichotomizes the relation of the individual to the externally given world of laws.

The existence of natural law allows for the emergence within social action of a relation of intention to behavior which is not arbitrary but possesses the necessity of law. Rationality is the necessity of a connection between the specific intention and a specific form of behavior given the objective situation. The possibility of rational action emerges with the existence of objective law independent of and prior to the individual. The thoroughgoing isolation of the individual implied by this confrontation plays a profound role in sociological analysis. The foundation of science is nothing less than[2]

a specific 'illusionless' man who has been thrown back upon himself alone by a world become objectively meaningless and sober, and therefore, to that extent, emphatically 'realistic.' He is therefore forced to forge by himself any objective meaning and a meaningful relationship to things, and in particular the relationship to reality, as one specifically his own: in short 'to create' a meaning, practically and theoretically.

The possibility of understanding has, therefore, a two-fold basis, first, in the confrontation between the individual and the 'emphatically realistic' world outside of him, and second, in the objectivity of that world as a world of laws indifferent to the individual. Action is understood when the individual relates to the external world of laws in conformity with those laws, accepting their givenness. Since those laws are given such action which refuses to defy their workings is 'typical.' This typicality is the product of the necessity of the laws of the objective world without which all action would be arbitrary from any point of view other than that of the individual himself. Science can grasp only that which is typical (the 'ideal type') since action is typical to the extent that it is necessary:[3]

The ideal type of social action must be constructed in such a way that the actor in the living world would perform the typified act if he had a clear and distinct scientific knowledge of all the elements relevant to his choice and the constant tendency to choose the most appropriate means for the realization of the most appropriate end. Indeed, as we had anticipated in the beginning only by the introduction of the key concept of rationality can all the elements be provided for the constitution of the level called 'pure theory.'

Since the science deals with the particular event as necessary it deals with the particular to the degree that it realizes its type. All non-typical behavior can only be characterized in terms of error and ignorance. Since individual actions aspire to the realization of abstract types which stand ultimately as limiting relationships, the latter, which are the content of the theoretical system, possess a 'utopian' character which clearly sets them off above and beyond the mundane affairs and activities of everyday life. They inform life but do not constitute it. The special character of rationality is that it forms the material of the scientific treatment of social phenomena. The world, both social and natural, need not be subject to law and action need not be rational, yet both conditions are necessary for social theory since 'only action within the framework of rational categories can be scientifically discussed.'[4] Understanding within the social sciences applies only to rational action. This sets off the process of conception within the social sciences from that of the natural sciences which are indifferent to the categories of action. Understanding in this sense rests upon that concept of reason which seeks to relate the individual to a world of laws which faces him as an indifferent, external and reasonless objectivity. Such a 'subjective' reason is not the reason of laws and of inner logic but of an external logic. The conception of rationality severs social theory from the actual process which latter may only be expected to approximate more or less to its type which stands *beside*, therefore outside, the actual social world. The latter grasped as type loses its actuality.

The possibility that the empirically existing individual can behave rationally clearly depends on the existence of objective laws prior to and independent of the individual. Thus the production of corn as the aim of the activity of the individual farmer may be achieved most efficiently by the proper utilization of advanced technology and by the application of chemical fertilizer. This would amount to a case of rationalized agriculture. By contrast, to engage in a ritual with the purpose of appeasing the gods of the harvest would be irrational from the strict point of view of the end of efficient production. It needs to be emphasized that the determination of the rationality of a particular activity depends essentially upon the specification of goal involved. A rain dance as a means to increase precipitation would be irrational while the same activity taken as means to a religious or cultural end could be perfectly rational.

From the standpoint of empirical science this contrast is intuitively appealing and serves to highlight the rational character of modern society which applies to all practical problems the most advanced scientific and technological knowledge. The theory of action extends this conception of individual behavior to the totality of relations and institutions within the social world. Thus action of a purely social character, which does not involve the appropriation of the natural world, is also dichotomized into the rational and the irrational. If an individual, for example, has as his goal the achievement of a high level of income he makes a similar use of the laws of the social world to that made by the farmer of the laws of nature. Given a positive correlation in the social realm between income and education rational action might require that the individual seek education as means to enhance his income. Irrational action with this same goal of personal income (money income) might be for the same individual to join the priesthood and pray for wealth.

It is clear that the concept of rationality as it emerges within the theory of action derives from the opposition within social life between the two elements of action: the behavior on one side and the subjective, in this case also social, intention on the other. The prototype of this conception is the peculiar view adopted by the action methodology concerning the externality of the natural world. In the case of 'production' (which is of special importance in this connection) rational action appropriates the natural world, the world of causal law, and brings it, via the mediation of motivation, into the human world of intention. Since the causal world is, by definition, outside of social life it is possible to consider action which brings those laws into society as consistent or inconsistent with the previously given laws of the external, natural world, therefore as rational or irrational. It is precisely the intervention of a social goal which injects meaning and social significance into action taken towards the physical world.

The application of this conception of rationality to the economic realm appears evident given the priority of the notion of production (as appropriation of nature) within economic activity. However, the possibility of social action outside of the economic system remains problematic. Given the standard of rationality invoked by the action framework, if social action is itself to become subject to that standard then action within the social world requires a goal and a means where the latter is itself purely social in character, therefore not simply means but purposive activity. But it would seem that the possibility of rational action within the social world requires the existence of causal relations and laws within social life. This, in turn, implies the existence of pure 'behavior' within the social world which has a social character but is not intentional. The conformity of an action to such a law is the criterion of its rationality, and therefore of the possibility of its subjection to theoretical treatment, but such conformity requires natural laws of the social world whose lawful character is in contradiction with their presupposed social character. Within sociological analysis the peculiar condition of social theory, as opposed to physical science, is precisely that the objects of social theory are themselves of a social character, that is, are themselves endowed with a socially defined meaning. Society is made up of purposive activity, interaction among conscious individuals. Since the social is, by nature, intentional, it cannot also be lawful in the sense in which the physical world exists as a world of laws. The idea of such laws within the social world is a contradiction in terms.

In so far as we are dealing with laws of the natural world the setting into motion of the means (cause) automatically brings about the end (effect). In the social world, however, the causal relationship cannot take on this form. The social system is composed of social acts, which are social by merit of the intersubjective character of the intentions associated with them. Thus, within social life (taken in this sense), both the cause and effect, the means and the end, must involve subjective intention. Causal relations in the social world require that intentional behavior itself be the cause of intention. One intention is brought into being by the activity of another intention. The end of the first act is now means for the second and so on for the third, fourth, etc. Since the end of the individual act is not an end from the standpoint of the totality of the social world as the totality of social acts the means–end distinction which appears to govern the individual act within the social world disappears when the location of that act within the social system as a whole is taken into account. The intention is itself now to be viewed as *product* rather than as end, as, therefore, necessary from the point of view of the system as a whole and its ultimate goals. With the social system as a whole as frame of reference the individual social act becomes no more a goal directed activity than the law of gravity. In this case the insides of the social world – the world of natural social law – are as indifferent to the attached goals or ultimate values as is the physical world of causal law to the human values and goals which seek to make use of it.

The loss of intermediate goals which implies the loss of the intentional definition of action within the individual parts of the social system forces the action methodology to constitute the whole of social life, rather than the individual social act, as a single means–ends relationship informed by ultimate system values. Society has itself become a machine for the achievement of system values to which society, as machine, is intrinsically indifferent. This is, at first, consistent with the conception, which has become necessary, of the world of social laws as a world of simple 'behavior.' But the result is an intrinsically unstable duality of the conception of social life: on one side, society remains the sphere of 'social action,' goal-directed behavior, which is, at this stage, the social system taken as a whole; on the other side, is the world of social laws which possess the 'natural' character of laws of the physical world. The action framework has generated two opposing conceptions of social life. Society as the sphere of natural law continually drives to eliminate any external sphere of ultimate values and therefore any overall teleology. Within the social world defined as a world of lawful relations both consciousness and self-consciousness must become social products, elements internal to the social process as a whole. Consciousness, which has now, by necessity, become an element of the ongoing social process cannot take the form of goals or ends external to that process while the very conception of a goal or end implies that externality. Thus consciousness can no longer appear in the immediate form of goals while the social process as a whole cannot be conceptualized as goal-directed behavior.

This contradiction results from the peculiar form adopted by reason within the action frame of reference. Within sociological analysis there occurs a bifurcation of reason: the subjective reason of the individual and his goals, and the objective reason of a world of natural laws. The individual subject, which remains the only true source of reason, comes to stand in opposition to an objective reason devoid of subjectivity, the reasonless objectivity of an 'emphatically realistic world.' This is the empirical world which is lawful but not reasonable, within which the action of reason in the form of objective law is defined as the absence of reason. The necessity of reason is thrown out of the world into the individual subject who attempts to make his reason actual by applying it to a world indifferent to it. On one side, reason exists as subjectivity which in that form is incapable of actualizing itself. On the other side, the actual world of objective laws is considered intrinsically unreason-

able. With this division of reason neither moment retains the power to constitute itself as reason so that reason, having lost the power to actualize itself,
becomes unreason.

2

This duality of the conception of society is the foundation of the formalism
which is characteristic of sociological analysis within the action methodology.
The theory of action takes the actual systems of action as they appear
historically, to be given. It is not possible to construct them conceptually for
the reason that such activity is irreducible when taken as pure activity and can
be grasped only in relation to motives. It is the subjective element, the motivation, which renders events actions which are social and comprehensible. The
motive is the relation of object to consciousness and that relation must be
defined as one of 'goal,' 'motivation,' 'end,' or 'value' precisely because of the
pure externality of objects. It cannot, by this very fact, deny that externality of
the object, including the externality of historical events as collections of human
activities. The historical events, on one side, which are characterized by
cause–effect relations and therefore are not comprehensible, stand opposed to
the human motive or goal on the other side which due to its subjective character is capable of being grasped conceptually, by a sociological schema.
Only by fixing a motive to the string of historical events does it become
possible to understand those events and that understanding is, in effect,
synonymous with the affixing of motive to event. Theory is constituted as a
shell within which human behavior in a social context may be thought but
which is always, on another level (that of law and necessity), external to the
actual social process.[5] Sociology, and with it the very possibility of compre-
hending the process of social life, gives way in the face of the impenetrability
of history, the real process of social life which remains impervious to its conception. This externality of the actual historical process typifies the action
framework: on one side, the abstract types which are known but not real; on
the other side, the actual social relations, the 'concrete empirical institutions'
which cannot be known in themselves but only through their reduction to
general 'types.' In the reduction of historical event to ideal type the former
loses all actuality thereby becoming identical to its type.

In so far as the social world is made up of relationships which are lawful
and unintentional in nature the analysis grasps those relationships not in
themselves but in terms of their connection to motive or need. The inner logic
of the social world is grasped only as an external relation within which the
operation of social laws becomes comprehensible in terms of the goal which
consciousness attaches to them. Rather than tracing out the inner logic of the
social world the categories merely classify the intentions attached to that
logic. The social world remains opaque, closed up within itself, except to the
extent that the processes within that world become part of intentional activity.

In that case the conception identifies them with that activity, explains them in terms of it, in fact, understands them *as* that activity.

The reductionism implied by this procedure moves the analysis from lower to higher levels of formalism and in that movement drains more and more of the determinate content of the actual system of social relations from the theoretical account for those relations. In the case of the duality between ideal type and actual historical process characteristic of Weberian analysis the specificity of the categories of social life is retained even though only in the attenuated appearance of types. Social theory still concerns itself with the central categories of social life (e.g., wages, capital, etc.) and to that extent remains, at least implicitly, aware of the organic and necessary conceptual unity which is required by those categories. For Weber the choice of categories and the determination of their meaning does not involve necessary laws but 'cultural significance.' Yet, for Weber, it turns out that the 'culturally significant' is the real system of categories of bourgeois economy (wages, capital, value, etc.). The culturally significant, it appears, has itself a certain necessity. At the same time, however, that this semi-awareness is retained, the ideal-typical method abstracts from the concrete specification of the social relations in terms of the laws of an intentionless social reality in order to grasp them as goal-directed activity. Thus, the category of wages remains within the conception of the social process but only as the ideal type of the wage relation. Wage activity is understood not in terms of its determinate necessity within the social system as an ongoing and self-sustaining process but as activity directed outside of itself toward an external end. As such the wage loses its determinate location within the totality of social relations.

Functionalism takes this process of the draining of the content of concrete social relations to its logical extreme. In so doing it expunges even the concrete categories present, in however attenuated a form within the Weberian 'ideal-typical' approach, and replaces those categories with generalized functions, moving from the goal orientation of the particular act to the goal orientation of the 'social system' as a whole which latter is defined as ultimately synonymous with goal-directed behavior within the social world. The functionalist mode of explanation involves the relating of a phenomenon to a universal system need or requirement (termed by Parsons 'adaptation,' 'goal attainment,' 'pattern maintenance,' and 'integration'). Every phenomenon is classified according to the particular function which it serves. The content of the categories of social life is thus subsumed into universals which represent the needs and goals of system itself. For instance, the analysis of supply and demand takes the form of the reduction of supply and demand to the notion of performance and sanction removing in the process the specific determinations of the supply–demand relation and therefore the specific requirements and conditions of the market. The existence of market phenomena is explained in terms of the intention of the system as a whole. As a result the determinate relations of the component elements of the market fall away leaving only the general notions of sanctions and performances. Supply and demand are explained as performance and sanction and that explanation turns supply and demand into performance and sanction.

The functionalist account for the existence of the money relation is particularly revealing in this connection. The existence of money is explained by the fact that the pluralism brought about by the division of labor requires also a reconciliation of the parts, a balancing of individual activity, which is effected, at least in part, through the intermediation of money. Money serves an integrative function and comes to exist precisely in order to fulfill the system requirement of integration. It is clear, however, that the fact that money serves an integrative function in no way accounts for the specificity of the money relation, so long as the required function may equally be fulfilled through other mechanisms. If this is not the case then the 'integrative function' becomes indistinguishable from money, and, as a synonym for money can in no way give an account for it. Alternatively, where money is conceived as one among many social mechanisms capable of fulfilling an integrative function the latter term fails to distinguish the special necessity of money as opposed to the alternative relations classified into a single category according to function. In order to account for the particular integrative mechanism of money it is insufficient to simply relate money to integration. What is also required is the specification of the integrative function itself, its specification to money. Such a specification requires the derivation of the determinate world of social relations within which money becomes necessary. The various social functions to which money relates as the integrative function become the determinate social relations of the money economy within which money has become necessary only in its loss of abstractness, of that abstractness with which it is endowed by its classification as a general system function. The existence of money can only be explained via the integration of the parts of the system in so far as those parts take on their specific content. The integrative function is served by money (money *is* the integrative function) only because the system is assumed to be differentiated in a particular manner, that is, in that specific manner of differentiation which requires the mediation of money. The division of labor within a market economy is that specific differentiation which presupposes the money relation for its internal order. It is not pure difference which accounts for money but only that difference which is itself brought about by the activity of the money relation by the transformation of all relations into market relations. Money emerges not as a result of general system needs but because of the presence of a particular economic formation within which money is necessary and for which the necessity of money also accounts, on one level, for the specificity of the economic formation involving money. Money is 'functionally necessary' only for a monetary economy.

In effect, the functionalist method deduces money, shows it to be necessary to the functioning of the system as a whole only by, first, positing the preconditions of money (e.g. the division of labor), the economic forms which as a whole require money and which are inconceivable in its absence, in the absence of money, and then, deducing the necessity of money within such a system. Functionalism ultimately posits the world of social relations as a reified whole, extracts a specific relation of that whole, and then discovers that relation to be necessary to the integrity of the whole. Just as Austrian capital theory discovers the necessity of interest by, first, positing the existence of a class of workers with no means to sustain themselves through the production period other than by selling their labor in the market at a discount on the future product of that labor, so also does functionalism deduce the necessity of money by positing a monetary economy in the absence of money, and then, finding that the absence of money contradicts the conditions of the monetary economy.

The functionalist conception of society presses the dualism of the action methodology to the breaking point. The individual in the articulation of his ends (the individual as locus of goals) confronts society as the world of law which becomes the means to the end of the individual. That reason which operates within society is *end*less while that reason which characterizes the usage of society on the part of the individual is that of the teleology of the individual as end. Reason is dichotomized into the reason of the social world and the reason which informs the activity of the individual *vis-à-vis* that social world. This division of the category of reason reveals the central contradiction of modern social science.

III Reason and freedom: formal rationality and economic action

The concept of rationality as it appears within the action methodology originates in a presupposed opposition between the individual actor and the social world which confronts him as an external world of laws. Since the individual is not intrinsically social, is not posited as individual by society, and since his intention is not itself immediately a social product, there must be some process or mechanism of adjustment between the individual and society. Reason is precisely this intermediation between the individual, as goal or end, and the social as means to the achievement of that end. Since reason is the condition for the realization of the ends as defined by the individual it is the condition for the individual's self-definition. Reason is the ground of freedom.[6] The individual is free to the degree that his activity is purposive, that it is rational, and that the purpose which drives the activity is that of the actor himself and not that of another individual or group which is imposed upon the individual actor. Such freedom is synonymous with the conception of the individual of modern economics as the locus of undetermined needs. Indeterminacy, individuality, and freedom are equated within the action methodology. The individual is 'dominated' when his ends are determined for him, when he adopts as ends the goals of other individuals or groups, and is constrained by his social position to adopt such goals. It is critical to bear in mind that the notion of domination rests essentially upon a special construction of the concept of the individual and that in the light of that construction it is clear that domination presupposes the enforcement of the ends of one upon another. It must, therefore, also presuppose the presence of individuals or groups with autonomous goals which are self-determined and, thus, indeterminate with regard to society. Such individuals or groups use society to dominate the world of individuals. In this way society becomes a means of domination. The latter result, far from being applicable to the general notion of social life, emerges out of the construction of society as a means, or 'technique' for the achievement of values and ends and which therefore requires autonomous ends for its own governance.

The notion of domination is intrinsic to the derivation of the category of social action. The latter is defined as the activity of intention upon itself within which goal-directed behavior becomes the object of action. The goal-directed behavior of the individual becomes the means to the goals of other individuals or groups so that the individual is transformed into means to the goals of other individuals and groups. Since the elimination of domination involves the elimination of the social determination of the individual, of any external determination of the individual and transformation of that person into a means, the elimination of domination implicitly involves the elimination of the social order. For modern social science, society is domination.

The conception of freedom which emerges within the treatment of rationality is a predominantly economic one in the sense that it is that conception which forms the logical basis of the analysis of economic action. Such freedom originates conceptually in the market. Autonomy of the individual is explicitly recognized as the basis of the world of exchange and it is within the exchange that that autonomy is both preserved and expressed. In the world of market relations individuals relate one to the other as individual wills recognized as independent, autonomous, and free. Such recognition expresses the actual market relations themselves which are relations of freedom and equality among self-determining individuals. But even this hints at the overriding fact that that freedom, that equality, and that individuality, are the freedom, equality, and individuality of the market and are therefore implicitly concrete. Freedom is, in the first instance, determinate only in its relation to value:[7]

Out of the act of exchange itself, the individual, each one of them, is reflected in himself as its exclusive and dominant (determinant) subject. With that, then, the complete freedom of the individual is posited: voluntary transaction, no force on either side; positing of the self as means, or as serving, only as means, in order to posit the self as end in itself, as dominant and primary; finally, the self-seeking interest which brings nothing of a higher order to realization; the other is also recognized and acknowledged as one who likewise realizes his self-seeking interest, so that both know that the common interest exists only in the duality, many-sidedness, and autonomous development of the exchanges between self-seeking interests. The general interest is precisely the generality of self-seeking interests. Therefore when the economic form, exchange, posits the all-sided equality of its subjects, then the content, the individual as well as the objective material which drives towards the exchange is *freedom*. Equality and freedom are thus not only respected in exchange based on exchange-values but, also, the exchange of exchange values is the productive, real basis of all *equality* and freedom.

The freedom of the individual is his existence within the exchange relation and the system of exchanges.

The relation of exchange is not simply one, particular social act in which the individual may engage. It is that social relation within which the external relating of one person to another is the means to the realization of the freedom of each. Within bourgeois social thought exchange is defined as that social relation within which the self-determination, therefore freedom, of the individual is not only preserved but realized. The recognition of the freedom and autonomy of the individual on the part of society is realized in exchange. Thus, far from a peculiarity of the economic realm of social life, the exchange system is the specific locus of that social action which does not appear to conflict with the purely individual determination of the person and his ends. The realization of freedom and equality in exchange is, however, no longer synonymous with the implicit existence of autonomy within the isolated individual. The necessity that freedom must be recognized in order for it to be realized reveals the social positing of that freedom, that it is not the abstract freedom of the isolated individual but the freedom of the socially equated person made free by his existence within a society of equals whose recognition of him as their equal is also the basis of his freedom. Since freedom implies the equating of the individual with other individuals it involves the social determination of the individual. For the freedom of the individual to be made real it must concretize itself in a social act which involves the social recognition of that freedom. But this necessity reveals the freedom to involve determination of the individual by society and in particular the concretization of freedom within the relation of exchange and within the system of exchange.

Such freedom is not only the logical basis of abstract independence but is simultaneously the logical basis of its opposite and this to the degree that the freedom makes itself known in a social relation. The equality which forms the basis of the relation of individuals in exchange can no longer be posited by those individuals as isolated producer-consumers but is a condition imposed upon them by their social existence. Equality is sustained between opposing persons in exchange. This is their relation as persons, as commodity owners, not as property but as owners of property. The realization of freedom thus requires a social substance which makes opposing needs and disparate individuals equal. This substance is value, and its indifference to all particularity of persons and of their needs establishes their equality as a condition of their social existence. This indifference, in turn, drives the value relation to more and more universal forms of expression. The connection of freedom to value makes that freedom unlimited by particularity, makes it illimitable.

Freedom becomes the freedom to strive for the unbounded expansion of value, for unbounded universalization.

So long as bourgeois social thought holds fast to the identification of free-dom with the self-determination of the isolated producer-consumer that freedom is precluded from making itself real, from being recognized as free-dom in a social relation. On the other hand, once the social substance of that freedom is recognized it refuses to remain fixed at the abstract level of simple exchange and drives for fuller and fuller forms of expression. This is recog-nized by orthodox social science when the latter posits individual need as unbounded. And this recognition of the social character of need must take the arbitrary form of the abstract positing of a definite form of need solely in order that this determinateness of need not deny that indeterminateness of need which is required by the founding of social life upon the notion of social action. The connection between the free individual and the unbounded expansion of human need makes the dependence of individuality and freedom upon the process of capital explicit.[8]

The category of rationality as it appears within the theory of action seeks to grasp that individuality which is the peculiar product of capital as an abstract individuality, an external presupposition of social analysis. The individual relates to the external world as the infinite to the finite so far as the external world is taken as given. And this formulation of the relation of individual to society is nothing more than a reification of the relation of capital to the world of its products where capital is understood as the unending expansion of value. But since this opposition is reified into a fixed condition of the social order independent of the determinations of the capital relation it appears not as the process of capital but as that of the allocation of scarce resources among competing ends. The world becomes, in this way, a world of scarce resources which constrain the individual in the satisfaction of his wants. The individual, by acting rationally, attempts to realize the infinity of his needs within the intrinsically finite world. The adjustment of the infinite to the finite, of the subject and his needs to an external world which constrains him, is the core of not only the sociological conception of rationality but equally of the fundamental notion of social action which underlies that conception.

To be sure, within orthodox economics the need of the individual is subject to the condition of diminishing marginal utility so that need also appears to be limited. At the same time the condition of scarcity requires an implicit illimitability of need which, since always greater than available resources for its fulfillment, is in practice limited externally. This is true from the point of view of the quantitative extent of need. More to the point, the confusion within orthodox thought of value and use-value implies that the value relation is at the same time unlimited, purely quantitative, and yet fixed as a relation to need. It is simultaneously unlimited in the sense of indifferent to all particular-ity and yet limited as a relation to particularity.

The typical indentification of rationality with efficiency follows logically from this result. Efficient activity makes the optimal usage of the external world. Rationality implies optimization in this sense as a result of the scarcity of means relative to the goals of the actor. But given the limitless nature of need such scarcity follows of necessity so that adjustment must be among ends as well as means, the individual trading off ends in terms of their relative desirability. The necessity of choice among ends, given the finite nature of the conditions for the meeting of those ends, requires commensurability of ends. Rational action, therefore, implies the possibility of ordering ends along a continuum (which is in any case implicit in the condition that individual choice is founded on the value relation). Equally, allocation of qualitatively distinct means among alternate uses presupposes commensurability of means. Such commensurability implies the transcendence of the particularity of the means and ends, the draining of any individual content to ends and means and their transformation into universals. To the extent that ends themselves become universalized they lose their personal character.

The commensurability among ends and means cannot be intrinsic to those ends and means as specific, individual and personal, goals and resources, but only to the ends and means as universalized, general, social substance, as value. The close connection of rationality to the market system is by no means an accident but the expression of the necessary condition of rational action. The conception of means and ends as equally values is essential to the notion of efficient social action which must choose not only among means to given ends but also among ends in terms of the relation of the desirability of the ends and the cost of their satisfaction. Rationality requires not only, therefore, commensurability within the means and within the ends but also of the means and ends taken together which must be equated as values.

Rationality within the sphere of action comes to be synonymous with what Weber terms 'formal rationality.' Rationality of action is formal to the extent that it is indifferent, even opposed, to the personalization of ends. The universalization of the goals of action and their subsequent equation with the means of action turns action into formally rational action. The latter is, fundamentally, another expression for efficiency. Action is formally rational when it is efficient and, in particular, when the criterion for choice of alternative courses is determined wholly by consideration of the relative efficiency of the different courses of action.

Formal rationality militates against all distinctions of quality among the elements of social action. The reduction of each component of action to a universal is realized in their existence as values, as purely quantitative and shorn of any determination other than that of amount. The most exact and therefore the most efficient and rational action is possible where the relation of means to ends can be precisely estimated quantitatively. The quantitative relation of means to ends which realizes in this way the ultimate of rationality is the profit of the individual business firm which forms the basis of capital accounting.

The specificity of formal rationality to business accounting is more clearly delineated when it is opposed to 'substantive rationality' which, in the economic sphere, is defined as the[9]

degree to which the provisioning of given groups of persons (no matter how de-limited) with goods is shaped by economically oriented social action under some criterion (past, present, or potential) of ultimate values, regardless of the nature of these ends.

Substantive rationality is differentiated by the activity of ultimate values in guiding the action involved. Formal rationality is rationality without ends. By extension substantive rationality becomes the rationality of the social system taken as a whole, formal rationality the rationality of the parts, taking the social conditions as a whole to be given. It is not surprising that the latter is closely identified with the activities of business firms as the individual units of economic activity whose competitive behavior is nothing other than the adjustment of their individual requirements (of the expansion of their parti-cular capitals) to the conditions made possible and available by the economic system as a whole.

The idea of substantive rationality expresses once again the idea of society as a mechanism for the realization of ultimate values. In particular, sub-stantive rationality hypostatizes the idea of man as end into the goal or end of society itself. It is not simply the individual's goals and intentions which drive action but the *individual as goal* which drives the system as a whole, the social system of action. This abstract concept of rationality, to the extent that it reifies the explicitly conscious (or intentional) aspect of action, severing it from the actual social world, places it in conflict with the concrete determination of rationality within the ongoing social process itself. Weber is acute enough to recognize this deficiency of conception when he explicitly points out that substantive rationality conflicts with formal rationality turning formal ration-ality (the rationality of the parts) into substantive irrationality (the irration-ality of the whole). This conflict emerges with the original argument for the foundation of sociological analysis upon the motivations of individual sub-jects. That freedom which encourages social theory to conceptualize the subject as individual comes to be determined in the form of unfreedom, 'domination.' 'The fact that the maximum of *formal* rationality in capital accounting is possible only where the workers are subjected to domination by entrepreneurs, is a further specific element of *substantive* irrationality in the modern economic order.'[10] The development of the rationalization of life which is the pre-condition for freedom rests upon a foundation of domination.

The irrationality of rationalized society has its ultimate expression in bureaucracy. For Weber bureaucracy is rationalized domination. To the extent that rationalization of social life requires mechanisms of domination and the realization of reason is the realization of domination, rational social action comes to take place via bureaucratization. 'Bureaucracy is *the* means of transforming social action into rationally organized action.'[11] Bureaucracy by transforming persons into offices transforms them from persons into the means for the achievement of the goals toward which rationalized action is driven. Since bureaucracy is simply a means (*the* means for rationally organized action) it follows both that the social action within the bureaucracy is, taken in itself, undirected and therefore must be externally directed and thus that, second, office holders within the bureaucracy are dominated in their action by those individuals or groups which determine the goals of bureaucratic activity. The bureaucracy is a 'precision instrument' within which individuals are transformed into means. The individual as means loses his status as a 'person,' becomes *impersonalized*, which result is typical of bureaucratic organization of individuals. The organization of social action for the purpose of the achievement of the maximum of formal rationality of particular acts requires domination and bureaucratization so that rationality of action of the elements of the social system turns into irrationality of the whole in so far as the latter is conceived in terms of the end of freedom where freedom involves self-definition on the part of persons.

The social system as a whole becomes irrational once it is defined in terms of the values of personal freedom thrown up by its original constitution out of the individual, free and equal. The ultimate goal of freedom as individual self-definition conflicts with the real content of that freedom as the expression of the market system, the capital relation, and the organization of the whole of society according to the requirements of the expansion of value. For modern social science the abstractions of freedom and equality are immobilized in their simplest determinations and raised to the status of overarching conditions of a social process within which they are, in fact, no more than dependent moments.[12]

By posing the problem of rationality in terms of the opposition between formal and substantive rationality Weber has grasped the specificity of rationality to the bourgeois social order. At the same time the opposition of formal to substantive rationality denies that specificity and obscures the real significance of the concept of formal rationality. The concept of substantive rationality conflicts directly with the capital relationship upon which ultimately all bourgeois notions of rationality are based. The concept of formal rationality expresses that quantitative commensurability which makes efficient adjustment of means to ends conceivable. Both means and ends come to be equated as values. But once the unlimited nature of ends is realized in their conception as value rather than as fixed object their character as ends becomes immediately problematic. The end of the process is itself unlimited (without end) so that the process becomes an *end*less process. This latter is precisely the process of capital. In the conception of capital as self-expanding value the movement becomes continuous and self-sustaining so that the distinction within the process between means and ends collapses. At this point the implication of the social as the activity of intention upon intention becomes clear in the abolition of all specifically intentional, goal-directed, determination of society.

The category of formal rationality grasps the endless nature of capital. The means cease being the means to a determinate end and take on a dynamic of their own, lose their attachment to ends and thereby lose their character as means. The process of capital expansion and the process of bureaucratic organization come to express only themselves as ends. The necessity of attaching a goal or value to the bureaucratic system is transformed into the inability of any person or group of persons outside of the bureaucracy to take control of the bureaucracy which, set loose from outside control, takes on a 'life of its own.' Personal ends are anathema both to the capitalist organization of production and to the bureaucratic organization of social action. The former reduces all ends to value so that the goal of economic activity is the expansion not of 'products,' 'utilities,' or objects of need but of value – that substance of the economic process which is by nature wholly indifferent to particularity of need. This reversal is given definite expression in the transformation of the simple circulation of commodities into the circulation of capital. In the first case, money (M) serves solely as the mediating factor in the transformation of one particular commodity (C) into another, the simple circulation of commodities appears as C-M-C where the goal of exchange is consumption and through the exchange the commodity and its value drop permanently out of the circulation process. When this process of circulation appears in the more adequate and developed form of the circulation of capital, M-C-M', the goal of the process no longer appears in the consumption outside of circulation of the commodities circulated. Now the process appears as explicitly an endless process for which value and its process (capital) are set loose from any external goal of consumption.

Similarly bureaucracy is synonymous with impersonalization, the primary condition (virtually the definition) of efficiency. Reason is the loss of independence and freedom. The extension of reason becomes the domination no longer of individuals over one another – all individuals have lost 'control' of the social world within which they find themselves – but of reason itself over the individual. This result is a baffling case of domination, for the individuals within the institutions of capital are dominated not by one another (so that strictly speaking they are not dominated at all) but rather by the social process itself. Rather than the individual making use of the social world to meet ends which he defines as personal (or the system end of the 'person') the social system makes use of the individual who becomes impersonalized, reduced to an office, a 'function,' or a role over which no individual or group of individuals exerts any control. 'Instrumental rationality' drives out 'value rationality' as all individuals become instruments of society and value rationality, the end of action as man himself, is destroyed by a social system which is out of control.

For capital, the world of its activity is also the product of its activity. The reduction of all social relationships to their purely quantitative value form is the method by which capital absorbs the entire sphere of social relations into itself, in other words, creates the world market. It imposes the conditions of formal rationality upon the world of social relationships as a condition of its own existence. The social system, then, is the product of the activity of capital, and in fact is that activity taken as a whole. In this case the world of capital does not oppose itself to the individual unit simply as an external given reality but also as a product of its own activity. To be sure, each individual unit of capital faces a world of capital which is given to it and within the conditions of which its activity is defined. This is the logical basis of the notion of formal rationality. But in the competition of capitals we face a process not only in which each individual capital preys upon the objective conditions of the market which are outside of its control but also a process within which those conditions emerge themselves as nothing other than the expression of the activities of individual capitals. The world of capital is given and limited only when viewed in terms of the individual firm. This view defines and circum- scribes the conception of all orthodox social science. However, when viewed in terms of the system as a whole, the world of capital, the fixed conditions become the process of expansion of the total social capital, no longer fixed and limited but continually expanding beyond all externally given boundaries. All of the constraints which capital faces become constraints which capital has itself created.

The process by which a world of capital is created and sustained by the interaction of particular capitals is denied by the conception of substantive rationality, the rationality of the social system and its goals. The concept of substantive rationality seizes upon a category which arises within the process of capital, extracts it from the concrete process, forms it into a fixed goal, and then imposes it upon the original process to which it has now become foreign matter. Substantive rationality requires that the system as a whole have a goal, but it is only possible to uncover such a goal within the social process itself. Such a goal acts to terminate that process, to immobilize it and to hold it fixed in an abstract form. Once it takes on this form it must come into contradiction with its own determination within the process of capital.

IV Economy and society

1

The theory of social action views formal rationality as goal neutral. While such goal neutrality conflicts with the original conception of rationality as social action it is clearly implied by the necessity that formal rationality eliminate all particularity and personalization. In the course of, and as a condition of, this impersonalization the identity of ends and means as values is required. The opposition of ends to means is abolished in this identity and formal rationality comes to describe a process which has no goal. This is consistent with the conception of the process of capital as *end*less.

Within modern social science the economy is seen as a mechanism for the optimal realization of externally determined goals and as therefore consistent in organization with any set of ultimate values so long as those values are tied into the 'provisioning' of society, i.e. into the production of 'utilities.' The idea of the economy as a value-free mechanism underlies the entire modern construction of the problem of 'comparison among economic systems,' and in particular, the typical conclusion of analysis of systems of 'resource allocation' that the market mechanism is synonymous with rational allocation but is not identified with any particular 'social system' (e.g. capitalism or socialism). The same basic set of economic categories may be grafted onto a variety of fundamentally different and opposed forms of social organization structured around opposing values. This result is the foundation of the notion of 'industrial society' and 'industrialization' common to virtually all schools of modern social science. None the less the implicit equation which connects formal rationality and economic behavior throughout sociological discussion of 'economy and society' hints at the real foundation of formal rationality in the process of capital accounting and, therefore, in a concretely determined system of economic relations.

That which is really definitive about the orthodox conception of the economy, which underlies its ability to claim system neutrality for the economic process, and which allows as well for the application of the most rigorous and systematically relevant conception of rationality to the economy, is the peculiar relation which exists between social action in the economic sphere and the natural laws of the physical world. This peculiarity emerges in the definition of economic action:[13]

Action will be said to be 'economically oriented' so far as, according to its subjective meaning, it is concerned with the satisfaction of desire for 'utilities.' 'Economic action' is a peaceful use of the actors control over resources, which is rationally oriented, by deliberate planning, to economic ends.

Economic activity according to this conception appropriates the natural world (the world of finite resources) and adapts it to the human world, the world of action and of need. The economy specializes in the 'solution of the adaptive problem of the larger system.' This adaptive function[14]

implies the minimization of subjection to control by the exigencies of the external situation (e.g. floods, famines, shortages, etc.) . . . it implies the possession of a maximum of fluid disposable resources as a means to attain any goals valued by the system or its sub-units.

The means employed in economic action are nothing other than the external, physical world. The categories of economic theory grasp the inputs into the production of wealth as purely physical in character (as 'factors of production'). It is for this reason that the conception of the social (or at least human) world as the world of 'action' originates in the neo-classical conception of production and exchange. In the case of both the analysis of production and exchange the economic actors appropriate the external world of objects and laws (of factors of production and goods), incorporating that world into society. In the course of production 'land' and 'labor' as purely natural factors are transformed into 'utilities' in which form they take on a directly human (and potentially 'social') significance and meaning. The human meaning which is attached to means of consumption is via 'imputation' also indirectly attached to means of production. In the case of production the object is informed by a social, or at least human, end: the product as utility. In the case of consumption and of exchange founded on the end of consumption the appropriation of objects of potential use transforms those objects into utilities and through such appropriation overcomes their externality. It is precisely the attempt to extend this conception of adaptation from the sphere of the production of wealth that, on one level, accounts for the contradictions which undermine the action method and which were considered in the preceding section. For social as opposed to economic action the means employed are distinct in that they too must possess a directly social character. The resulting dichotomization into opposing conceptions of society reveals the inadequacy of the action framework to the conception of social life. In the face of this result the social action methodology is forced to reduce all action to implicitly economic action, action upon an external, physical reality. All truly social action within this framework, if it is to be capable of consistent formulation, must be implicitly non-social economic action: the appropriation of the extrahuman, extrasocial, world via a process of 'production' or 'consumption.'

Social action reduces, in this manner, to the set of processes described within neo-classical economic theory and especially within the neo-classical theory of production. But economic action remains indifferent to the contradictions of the category of social action for which it has set the original foundation only because economic action possesses a non-social character. This latter is precisely that property of the neo-classical conception of production which, paradoxically, allows it to absorb the whole of the 'social.' The reduction of social action to that action described within neo-classical economic theory eliminates all conception of the social from both sociological and economic science. The contradictions of modern economic theory which appear most vividly, but by no means exclusively, in the treatment of capital, center on the manner in which the theory of production grasps the means employed in production as products, therefore upon the degree to which production is conceived as a self-sustaining process rather than as a process of allocation of scarce resources introduced into production from outside. The contradictions of the attempt to establish production as the transformation of 'scarce factors' reveal directly the central contradiction of the concept of social action derived above. The contradictions of the social-action methodology rest fundamentally upon the construction of the social process as the determination of an external and given force ('end,' 'goal,' 'intention' and in this case 'preference'). Yet this construction is precisely articulated within the neo-classical conception of exchange and production, in fact within the orthodox conception of the economy. In other words, the contradictions of the neo-classical theory of production originate in precisely that property of the theory which adapts it so well to treatment in terms of the concept of action. The necessity that capital itself give an account for the world of its activities precludes it from any conception involving the application of external and fixed goals.

The identification of social action and economic behavior (in the orthodox sense) also implies the identification of social and economic action with formal rationality. This identity is instrumental in the demonstration of the contradictory nature of the formulation of social and economic action in terms of ends. So far as formal rationality expresses the process of capital, while it remains endless it cannot be indifferent to the specification of the nature of the social system taken as a whole. As Weber has himself clearly recognized, to the degree that formal rationality is the rationality of economic calculation (an identification made throughout Weber's work on the categories of economic action) it cannot be indifferent to the social conditions within which it is sustained and must imply the whole of bourgeois economy, the market system, private enterprise, separation of the worker from the means of production and his 'domination' by capital, etc. This determinateness of formal rationality is revealed, as we have seen, within sociological analysis when the attempt is made to attach to the process of formal rationality an abstract end. The necessity that the categories of social theory which seek to grasp the economic process of modern business enterprise determine the general categories of the economic system (e.g. equality and freedom) not as general, abstract, categories but as determinations of that economic process taken in itself must result in contradictions when the analysis attempts to comprehend those categories as abstract goals grafted onto an economic process presumed to be, in itself, 'value-neutral.' Thus the abstract notion of equality taken as independent of the concrete determinations of the economic system, is violated by the very conditions necessitated by and necessary to the operation of formal rationality.

This emerging contradiction points to the determinateness of the products of economic activity. The process of capital does have a real product: the world of capital. Contradictions arise when the economic sphere is closed up into itself and made dependent upon external conditions over which it exerts no force. When the economic sphere is conceived to be merely 'adaptive,' a means to the realization of values given to it, then the results of action in the economic sphere and the pre-conditions of such action together come into conflict with the goals of action in the economic realm. This conflict expresses the contradiction within the theory of action between the real product of capital and the distorted image of that product thrown out by capital. Far from the neutral intermediary of externally given values, capital is that process which posits within itself not only a world of capital but also the peculiar distortions of its concept which appear within the theory of action.

2

What is at stake in the conception of the interdependency of 'economy and society' is nothing less than the conception of the whole as the world of capital. Within the neo-classical conception the economy taken as a whole is the sum total of the self-determined activities of isolated economic agents. This conception of the whole as the simple sum of its parts hinges upon the absence of inner relations within the economy either of interdependency among the members or of dependency of the elements as products of the differentiation of a whole. The self-definition of the particular individuals within the economy is the primary and essential condition for the definition of the economy as the sum of their independently given activities so that those activities are not products of the economic process but determined by individual ends given to each individual regardless of his relations to other individuals or of his relation to the whole. Yet in the absence of such explicitly mutual dependence of conception among the units of economic life it is impossible to deduce the social and economic system as the product of the individually determined behavior of isolated individuals (producer-consumers). The deduction of the whole requires that the individual elements of that whole give up their independence both of one another and of the system of which they are the parts. Even for the deduction of the simple market system it has been shown, to be necessary that the needs of individuals as expressed in preference functions not be wholly arbitrary but possess a determinate structure. Since this is a necessity of the conception of the market and of the conception of the individual as market-directed in his activities it must also be founded within that conception. In other words it must be possible to locate theoretically the origin of individual need as well as the individuation of need.

The notion of 'economy and society' attempts to situate the needs of individuals within a conception of the whole as the 'social system.' The needs and values, the intentions and goals, the subjective meanings of action originate in society as social system. This result is the basis of the 'departure' which the action framework claims to have effected from the original self-conception of orthodox economic analysis. None the less close investigation of the results of the application of the theory of action to the foundations of neo-classical thinking reveals that the substance of the neo-classical conception of the economy remains indifferent to the reorientation presumably necessitated by the insights of the action perspective. The specific results of Marshallian economics, the conditions of equilibrium, the role of the market in the 'allocation of scarce resources,' the use of the concept of 'preference' and of the concept of 'factor of production,' the determination of prices and distribution, etc. all remain very much as they were originally within the original neo-classical construction of the economy. Just as the functionalist method provides for the real material of social theory categorical 'shells' within which that material may be located but to which that material is indifferent so also does the action method provide categories for thinking about the economic process to which that process remains indifferent and to which its neo-classical conception is equally indifferent. That the apparently profound difference between the sociological and the utilitarian approaches to the conceptualization of economic life should display a unity of results is a central paradox of the action methodology which goes to the heart of the notion of economy and society.

In practice, the action methodology resolves the contradictions within the neo-classical conception of the economy by grafting onto that framework the reified and external conception of society which alone is consistent with the inner organization of orthodox economic theory. Such a conception of society is consistent with the construction of neo-classical economic thinking for the reason that on the deepest level it is identical with that construction and is founded upon it. The theory of social action retains the notion of the individual as originating outside of society and is by that fact required to posit society as an entity which serves to bring those individuals into itself, to 'socialize' them. Just as economic theory turns individual need into market price so sociological theory turns those individuals into social beings with socially defined needs. What is critical is the analogous character of the transformation process. For sociological analysis society is an *imposition* upon the individual.

To the extent, for example, that the individual is motivated by what Weber refers to as the 'spirit of capitalism' specific utilities do not exist as satisfaction of particular need nor does satisfaction of purely individual desire, defined outside of society, account for economic activity. It is, rather, implicitly, the reverse condition in which 'the idea of a man's duty to his possessions, to which he subordinates himself as an obedient steward, or even as an acquisitive machine, bears with chilling weight on his life.' So far as the individual is concerned 'the capitalist economy of the present day is an immense cosmos' into which he is born 'and which presents itself to him, at least as an individual, as an unalterable order of things in which he must live.' This conception is in stark opposition to the conception of 'economic man' as deriving his acquisitive instinct from the human nature with which he is born and as presenting that nature to the world of individuals as a *personal* and private matter independent of an incommensurable with the similarly given needs of other individuals. For Weber birth is into a 'cosmos' which determines and defines the individual needs and desires, even instincts, of its members. The spirit of capitalism accounts for both the emergence of the individual, alone and without illusions, within the modern world and for the necessity of domination – the negation of the individual. The spirit of capitalism finds its ultimate realization in the capitalist process and in the associated bureaucratization of social life. On one side, this is the realization of freedom through the rationalization of all spheres of life. On the other, it is the realization of the domination of reason, and therefore of society itself over personal action. The permeation of society by the spirit of capitalism brings with it the subordination of all action to the end of capital which is the end without an end. The product of rationalization is therefore the elimination of all true social action. The condition of reason upon which understanding is based becomes the condition of unreason. The modern world is judged to be irrational. Acceptance of the concept of reason implicit in modern social science is tantamount to the rejection of the possibility of social theory.

The view of economic behavior associated with the spirit of captalism is antithetical to that of modern economics for which market behavior is intrinsically founded upon individual preference which must, by definition, see consumption of utilities as its goal. The conception of allocation of scarce resources among alternate ends implies the consumption act as the completion of the economic process. Yet, in the face of this opposition, both apparent and real, between the Weberian conception and that of modern economic theory there remains a real basis for unity of conception which reveals the need within the Weberian conception of society for explicit articulation of its consistency with and dependence upon the neo-classical conception of the economic process. Within the economic conception the spirit of capitalism can only exist as a goal or value and not as the expression of a real process made necessary by the determinateness of economic life as the process of the self-realization of capital. The spirit of capital becomes the goal of economic activity even in the face of the inner inconsistency of the idea of the spirit of capitalism with the idea of goal. Rather than defining the role of the individual unit of capital and of consumption within the ongoing process of capital, so that the individual becomes a moment of the social, Weber conceives of society as a cosmos which 'forces the individual . . . to conform to rules of action.'[15] The relation of the cosmos to the individual is one of the enforcement of rules and of the maintenance of conformity. The cosmos socializes the individual which must, by that fact, possess an extrasocial nature and origin next to or in addition to his social determination.

The necessity for the conception of the individual as ultimately an autonomous unit of sociological analysis derives from the conception of social action as involving subjective meaning. Meaning is attached by the individual to a world which confronts him as 'emphatically realistic.' Within the action methodology consciousness is individual consciousness since the world is outside of the individual. As a result 'action in the sense of a subjectively understandable orientation of behavior exists only as the behavior of one or more *individual* human beings.' Behavior of collectivities 'is not subjectively understandable.' While it may be convenient (in fact necessary) to speak of 'social collectivities' such as the 'state' in terms of social action, therefore to speak of them as 'if they were individual persons' none the less[16]

for the subjective interpretation of action in sociological work these collectivities must be treated as *solely* the resultants and modes of organization of particular acts of individual persons, since these alone can be treated as agents in a course of sub-jectively understandable action.

Within the functionalist conception of the action methodology society does in fact become the reified origin of the subjective element within individual action, separate from and determinate of the individual act. At the same time that the society as a whole is seen to possess an autonomous teleology which is imposed upon its individual elements the concrete character of that teleo-logy remains dependent upon the autonomous differentiation of the whole which is posited as different, that is, individualized, not as a functional necessity of its goals but as a pre-condition of its existence. Without the differentiation of society, its individuation, the social order would itself dis-appear. Yet, this differentiation is not posited by society but only as prior to and independent of society. Society is assumed to be differentiated and the teleology of the social system becomes the maintenance of the whole as a coherent and integrated system. Since society comes to be synonymous with integration, individuation becomes an irreducible premise.

The social system is constructed out of the action of separate units, indivi-dual social acts. Society becomes a functional necessity only to the degree that the individual units lose that 'independence' with which the conception of economic man seeks to endow them. The aggressive independence of such individuals leaves them indifferent to the construction so that it can only be in the breakdown of that original independence (and of the individuation founded upon it) that the possibility and necessity of society can emerge. It is the differentiation of the whole which calls forth society as a functional necessity of the whole. Society is the integration on a higher level of those individuals whose opposition, on another level, makes up that society. But this abstract opposition within a differentiated whole only requires 'integra-tion' on a higher level, e.g. via shared values, to the degree that those differ-ences have lost their individuality; that is, have become individual parts of a *self-differentiated* whole. In the light of this result the individual parts lose their conceptual priority. The functions of society, the social as goal, is the social system to the extent that the latter stands in opposition to disintegration rather than as a unity of differences themselves posited by society. The original differentiation cannot itself be posited by society so that the latter must, ultimately, stand in external opposition to the individual parts, as an imposi-tion upon them or socialization of them which takes the differentiation of the whole, its specific form and level of development, to be given. So long as modern social science takes this differentiation as an irreducible premise it must remain unable to consummate a true conception of social life.

Notes

Chapter 1 The science of wealth

1 Cf. Adam Smith, *The Wealth of Nations* (New York: Modern Library, 1937), pp. lviii, 47.
2 See, for example, the Marquis de Mirabeau, 'The Tableau Economique and its Explanation,' in R. Meek (ed.), *Precursors of Adam Smith* (London: J. M. Dent, 1973), p. 121.
3 Compare G. W. F. Hegel, *Philosophy of Right*, tr. T. M. Knox (London: Oxford University Press, 1952), pp. 126–9.
4 Karl Marx, *Capital* (New York: International Publishers, 1967), vol. I, p. 35.
5 Cf. Hegel, *op. cit.*, pp. 105–10, 122–6.
6 See Sir James Steuart, *An Inquiry into the Principles of Political Economy* (Edinburgh: Oliver & Boyd, 1966), pp. 89–92.
7 F. Quesnay, 'Dialogue on the Work of Artisans,' in R. Meek (ed.), *The Economics of Physiocracy* (Cambridge, Mass.: Harvard University Press, 1963), p. 207.
8 F. Quesnay, 'General Maxims,' in Meek, *The Economics of Physiocracy*, pp. 242–3.
9 A. R. J. Turgot, 'Reflections on the Formation and the Distribution of Wealth,' in R. Meek (ed.), *Turgot on Progress, Sociology and Economics* (Cambridge University Press, 1973), p. 159.
10 *Ibid.*, p. 158.

Chapter 2 Adam Smith: Division of labor, capital, and exchange

1 *The Wealth of Nations* (New York: Modern Library, 1937), p. lvii. All subsequent references are to this edition and will be given immediately following the quotation.
2 Cf. Karl Marx, *Capital* (New York: International Publishers, 1967), vol. I, pp. 350–9.
3 Cf. K. Marx, *Grundrisse*, tr. Martin Nicolaus (Harmondsworth: Penguin Books, 1973), pp. 167–72.
4 P. Sraffa (ed.), *The Works and Correspondence of David Ricardo* (Cambridge University Press, 1951), vol. VIII, p. 278; emphasis added. All references are to the Sraffa edition and the volume number followed by the page number will be given in parentheses subsequent to the quotation.

Chapter 3 David Ricardo: Value and capital

1 That Ricardo had not considered the problem of value at this time is suggested

307

by Sraffa in his 'Introduction' to the *Works and Correspondence of David Ricardo* (Cambridge University Press, 1951), vol. I, p. xiv.

2 This is the interpretation of Ricardo's position on value in the 'Essay on Profits' first put forward by Sraffa, *Works*, vol. I, p. xxxi.

3 A. R. J. Turgot, 'Reflections on the Formation and the Distribution of Wealth,' in R. Meek (ed.), *Turgot on Progress, Sociology and Economics* (Cambridge University Press, 1973).

4 The formal aspect of the problem is given systematic treatment in P. Sraffa, *Production of Commodities by Means of Commodities* (Cambridge University Press, 1960).

5 Cf. K. Marx, *Grundrisse*, tr. M. Nicolaus (Harmondsworth, Penguin Books, 1973), p. 485.

Chapter 4 The world of capital

1 Cf. Karl Marx, *Theories of Surplus-Value* (Moscow: Progress Publishers, 1968), vol. II, pp. 494–5.

2 Cf. K. Marx, *Grundrisse*, tr. M. Nicolaus (Harmondsworth: Penguin Books, 1973), p. 407 *et seq.*

3 Marx, *Theories of Surplus-Value*, vol. II, p. 470.

4 Marx, *Grundrisse*, p. 650; see also pp. 649–58.

5 Cf. G. W. F. Hegel, *Philosophy of Right*, tr. M. Knox (London: Oxford University Press, 1952), pp. 134–45.

6 As in *ibid.*, pp. 129–34.

Chapter 5 The specificity of classical political economy

1 Karl Marx, *Capital* (New York: International Publishers, 1967), vol. I, p. 80.

2 *Ibid.*, pp. 80–1n and 80.

3 *Ibid.*, p. 81.

4 Marx, *Theories of Surplus-Value* (Moscow: Progress Publishers, 1968), vol. I, pp. 164, 172.

5 Marx, *Letters to Dr. Kugelmann* (New York: International Publishers, 1934), p. 73, letter of July 11, 1868.

6 Marx, *Capital*, vol. I, p. 81n.

7 Marx, *Letters to Dr. Kugelmann*, p. 74.

8 Cf. Edward Wolff, 'Models of Production and Exchange in the Thought of Adam Smith and David Ricardo' (Ph.D. thesis, Yale University, 1974), chapter 5.

9 P. Sraffa, *Production of Commodities by Means of Commodities* (Cambridge University Press, 1960).

10 K. R. Bharadwaj, 'Value through Exogeneous Distribution,' *Economic Weekly* (Bombay), 24 (August 1963), reprinted in G. C. Harcourt and N. F. Laing (eds), *Capital and Growth* (Harmondsworth: Penguin Books, 1971).

Chapter 6 The allocation of resources

1 P. Sraffa, *Production of Commodities by Means of Commodities* (Cambridge University Press, 1960).

2 L. Walras, *Elements of Pure Economics*, tr. W. Jaffe (London: Allen & Unwin, 1954), p. 65.
3 *Ibid.*, p. 66.
4 K. Menger, *Principles of Economics*, tr. J. Dingwell and B. F. Hoselitz (Chicago: Free Press, 1950), p. 101.
5 Walras, *op. cit.*, pp. 66–7.
6 Cf. T. C. Koopmans, *Three Essays on the State of Economic Science* (New York: McGraw-Hill, 1957), part II.
7 *Ibid.*, p. 137.
8 *Ibid.*, p. 21.
9 Walras, *op. cit.*, p. 143.
10 Menger, *op. cit.*, p. 177.
11 Koopmans, *op. cit.*, p. 59.
12 *Ibid.*, p. 20.
13 See K. Inada, 'On Neo-classical Models of Economic Growth,' *Review of Economic Studies* (April 1965).
14 Cf. Sraffa, *op. cit.*
15 On this, see *ibid.*, chapter 12.
16 See, for instance, M. Bruno, E. Burmeister, and E. Sheshinski, 'Nature and Implications of the Reswitching of Techniques,' *Quarterly Journal of Economics* (November 1966).
17 This was pointed out by Morishima, *Equilibrium, Stability and Growth* (Oxford: Clarendon Press, 1964), p. 126.
18 On this see Bruno *et al.*, *op. cit.*, pp. 548–50.
19 Cf. J. B. Clark, *The Distribution of Wealth* (New York: Kelley, 1965).

Chapter 7 *Problems in the theory of production*

1 See *Activity Analysis of Production and Allocation*, ed. T. C. Koopmans *et al.*, Cowles Commission for Research in Economics Monograph No. 13 (New York, 1951).
2 Karl Marx, *Capital* (New York: International Publishers, 1967), vol. I, especially section 2 of chapter 1.
3 Cf. P. Sraffa, *Production of Commodities by Means of Commodities* (Cambridge University Press, 1960), chapter XI.
4 Marx, *Capital*, vol. III, chapter XXXVII.
5 Marx, *Theories of Surplus-Value* (Moscow: Progress Publishers, 1968), vol. II, p. 243.
6 Marx, *Capital*, vol. III, p. 751.
7 Compare Sraffa, *op. cit.*, p. 76.
8 *Ibid.*, p. 74n.

Chapter 8 *Foundations of macroeconomics*

1 P. Sraffa, 'The Laws of Returns under Competitive Conditions,' *The Economic Journal* (1926).
2 *Ibid.*

3 The connection between production for exchange, production which grounds exchange, and the production of capital, cannot be drawn out in detail here. These connections are, however, clearly established in Marx, *Capital* (New York: International Publishers, 1967), parts I–IV of vol. I, and will be considered in vol. I of *Economic Theory*.

4 This analysis is adapted from M. Kalecki, 'Money and Real Wages,' in *Studies in the Theory of Business Cycles, 1933–1939* (New York: Kelley, 1969).

5 The determination of the margin in the course of the accumulation process as a whole is considered in J. Steindl, *Maturity and Stagnation in American Capitalism* (Oxford: Blackwell, 1952); see also D. Levine, 'The Theory of the Growth of the Capitalist Economy,' *Economic Development and Cultural Change*, vol. 24 (October 1975).

6 J. M. Keynes, 'The General Theory of Employment,' *Quarterly Journal of Economics*, vol. 51 (1937).

7 *Ibid.*

8 J. M. Keynes, *The General Theory of Employment, Interest, and Money* (New York: Harcourt, 1936), p. 146.

Chapter 9   Economy and society

1 T. Parsons, *The Structure of Social Action* (Chicago: Free Press, 1949), p. 58.

2 K. Loewith, 'Weber's Interpretation of the Bourgeois-Capitalistic World in Terms of the Guiding Principle of "Rationalization",' in D. Wrong (ed.), *Makers of Modern Social Science* (New Jersey: Prentice-Hall, 1970), p. 107.

3 A. Schutz, *Collected Papers* (The Hague: Martin Nijhoff, 1971), vol. II, p. 86.

4 *Ibid.*, p. 87.

5 M. Weber, *Economy and Society* (New York: Bedminster Press, 1968), p. 116, also pp. 19–22.

6 Cf. Loewith, *op. cit.*

7 K. Marx, *Grundrisse*, tr. by M. Nicolaus (Harmondsworth: Penguin Books, 1973), pp. 244–5.

8 The systematic derivation of this connection is the object of the analysis of the first parts of *Capital* and the opening sections of the chapter on capital in the *Grundrisse* (pp. 239–75); compare Marx, *Capital* (New York: International Publishers, 1967), vol. I, parts I and II.

9 Weber, *Economy and Society*, p. 85.

10 *Ibid.*, p. 138.

11 *Ibid.*, p. 987.

12 See Marx, *Grundrisse*, pp. 247–8.

13 Weber, *Economy and Society*, p. 63.

14 T. Parsons and N. J. Smelser, *Economy and Society* (Chicago: Free Press, 1957), p. 21.

15 M. Weber, *The Protestant Ethic and the Spirit of Capitalism* (New York: Charles Scribner's Sons, 1958), p. 54.

6 Weber, *Economy and Society*, p. 13.

Index

Accumulation of capital, *see* Capital accumulation, capital formation
Action: rational and irrational, 283–6; typical, 282–3; *see also* Social action
Adaptive function: of economy, 300
Aggregate production function, 211–12
Agriculture: and wealth, 7–8, 39
Allocation of resources: as adjustment of individual to external condition, 294; concept of, 175; concept of undermined by absence of inverse relation of capital and its return, 231; economy as mechanism for, 187, 199, 279–80, 299–300; and notion of equilibrium, 267–8; *see also* Scarcity; Factors of production
Animal spirits, 271
Appropriation: as condition which makes objects scarce, 184–5; divorced from social life, 182–3; grounded in scarcity, 181–3; as social condition, 183–4
Arrow, K. and Debreu, G., 195–6
Assumptions of neo-classical economics, 187–9

Behavior: distinguished from social action, 281–3
Behaviorist conception of economic activity, 189–90
Bharadwaj, K. R., 309
Böhm-Bawerk, E. von: reasons for positive interest rate, 204
Bortkiewicz, L. von, 206
Bruno, M. *et al.*, 310
Bureaucracy: Weberian conception of, 296–7

Capacity utilization: and the theory of the firm, 261–2
Capital: and abstract labor, 240; and allocation of resources over time, 203; calculation of amount and return in pure exchange economy, 203; circuit of, 275, 298; concept of denies notion of purposive activity, 211; conditions of also produced by, 259; as consumption forgone, 203, 210, 212–13; as durable product, 111; as endless process, 297–8; and growth, 216f.; as material substance indifferent to particular form, 228–9;

measurable independent of price, 223; measurement of, 203, 221–2, 236; mobility of, 239; and multiplication of needs, 7; as need for world of commodities, 125; neo-classical concept of, 203; in one-good production system, 212–13, 223; particular or individual, 119; particularization of, 119, 225; price of, 222; as produced means of production, 203, 209–10; productivity of in neo-classical economics, 223f.; productivity as physical attribute of, 224–30; quantity of and rate of profit, 214–22; as scarce factor of production, 172, 223, 228–9, 231; as self-expanding value, 118–19, 210–11, 213, 236; as self-generating wealth, 28–9, 211; as self-moving value, 14; self-sustaining process of, 258–9; and stock, 44, 52, 111; supply of produced in neo-classical economics, 216–17; as unity of production and exchange, 118–19; as universal use-value, 229
Capital accounting: realizes the ultimate of rationality, 295–6
Capital accumulation: as act of capital formation, 216; as consumption of productive labor, 213; excluded in neo-classical economics, 216; importance of to development of Ricardo's theory, 77–80; inconceivable in context of scarce factors, 233; limits to in Ricardo, 121–5, 139; as means to acquisition of future consumption, 123–4, 208–9; neo-classical conception of, 219
Capital circuit: simple circulation of commodities extended over time, 207–11
Capital deepening, 216–17
Capital goods: heterogeneity of and theory of distribution, 221f.; model of production with many, 214
Capital intensity: related to savings, 216
Capital-labor relation: and classical theory of value, 49–51; as ground of exchange, 14; and labor-commanded theory, 62–3; and reproduction of total capital, 117; and theory of distribution, 105
Capital stock: desired, 219